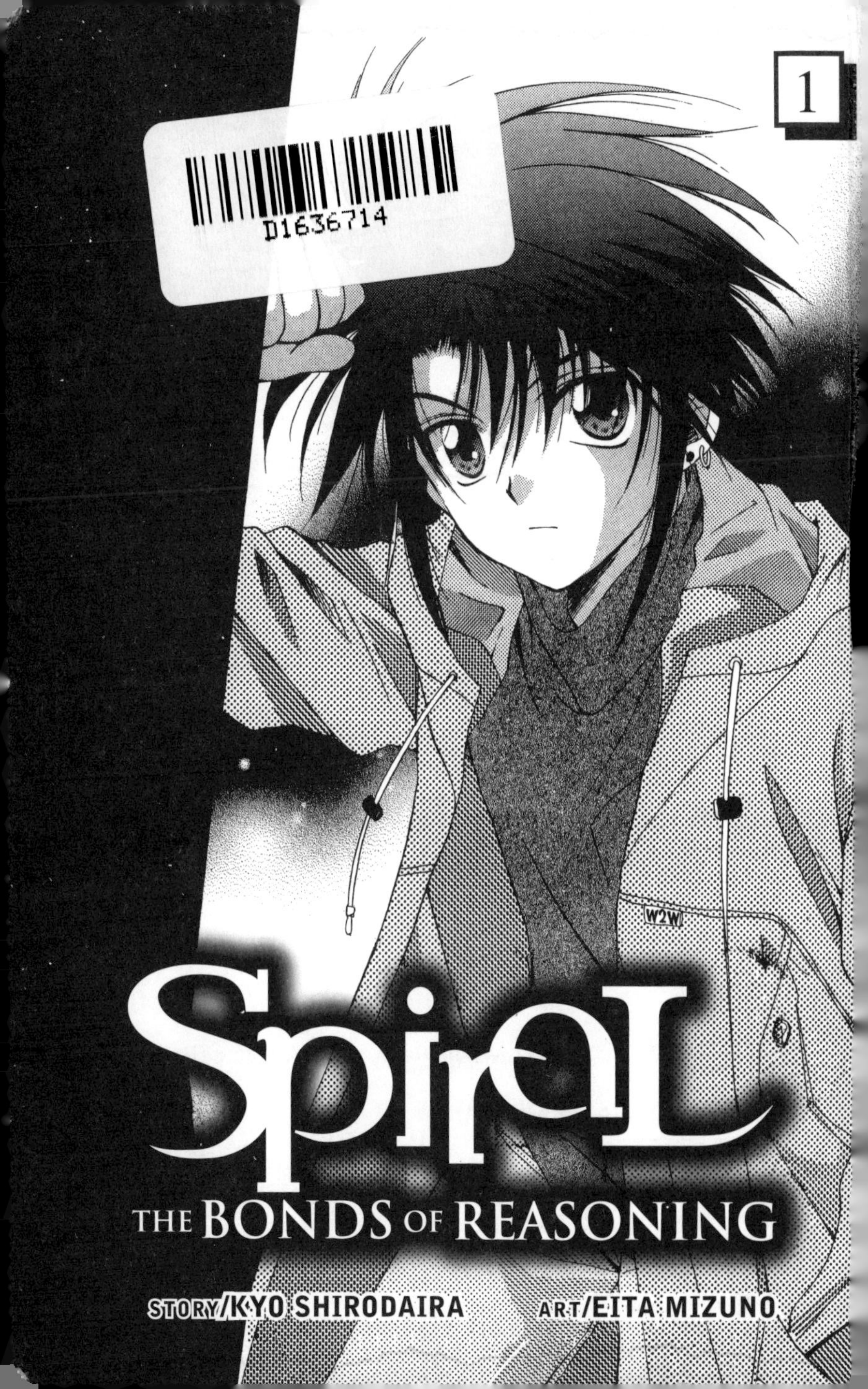
1
Spiral
THE BONDS OF REASONING
STORY/KYO SHIRODAIRA
ART/EITA MIZUNO
W2W

CONTENTS

CHAPTER ONE	The Invisible Hand on the Landing (Part I)	5
CHAPTER TWO	The Invisible Hand on the Landing (Part II)	59
CHAPTER THREE	Apollo's Arrow	85
CHAPTER FOUR	Room Behind the Ward Lock (Part I)	129
CHAPTER FIVE	Room Behind the Ward Lock (Part II)	167

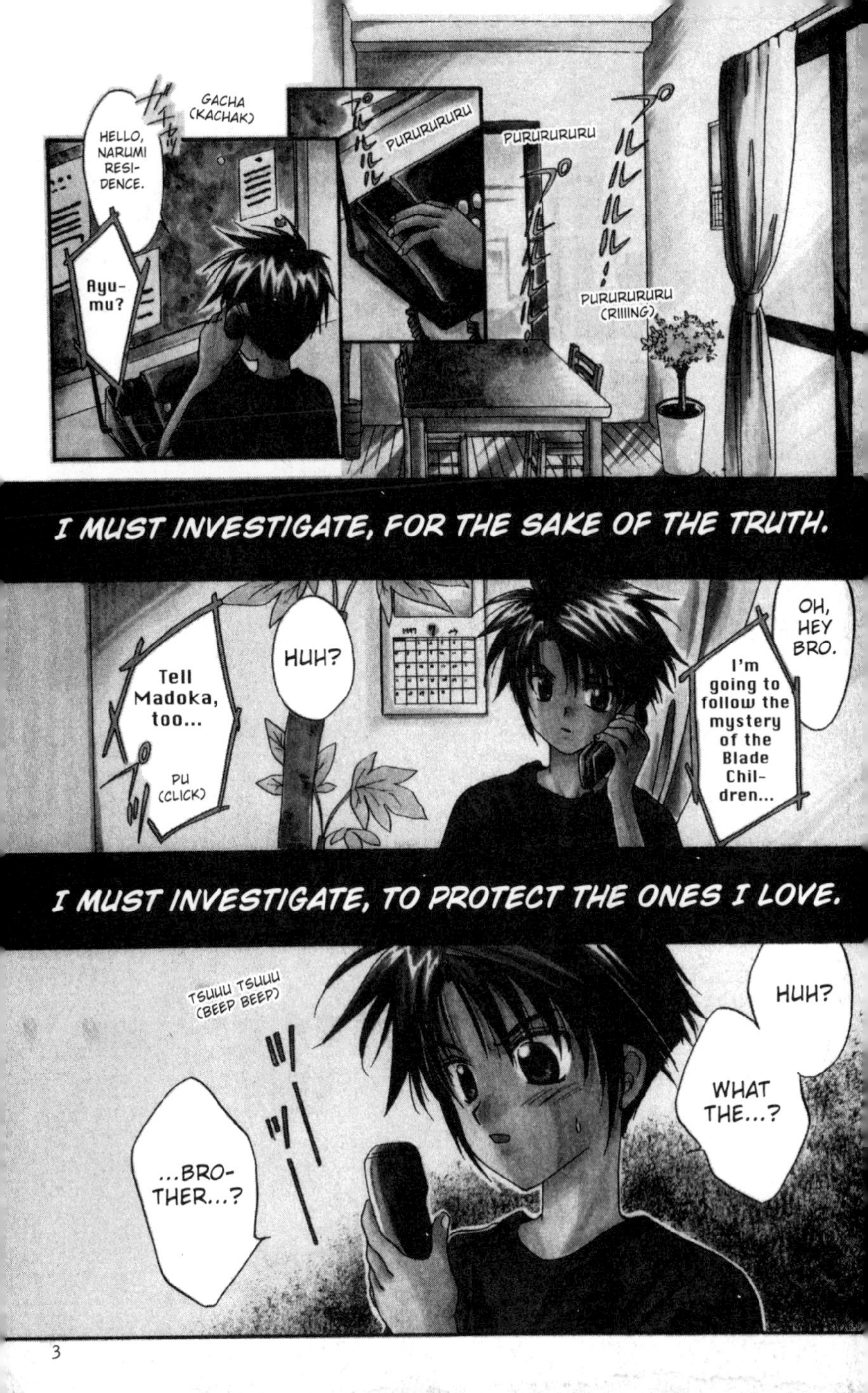

PURURURURU (RIIIING)
PURURURURU
PURURURURU
GACHA (KACHAK)
HELLO, NARUMI RESI-DENCE.
Ayu-mu?
I MUST INVESTIGATE, FOR THE SAKE OF THE TRUTH.
OH, HEY BRO.
I'm going to follow the mystery of the Blade Chil-dren...
HUH?
Tell Madoka, too...
PU (CLICK)
I MUST INVESTIGATE, TO PROTECT THE ONES I LOVE.
HUH?
WHAT THE...?
TSUUU TSUUU (BEEP BEEP)
...BRO-THER...?

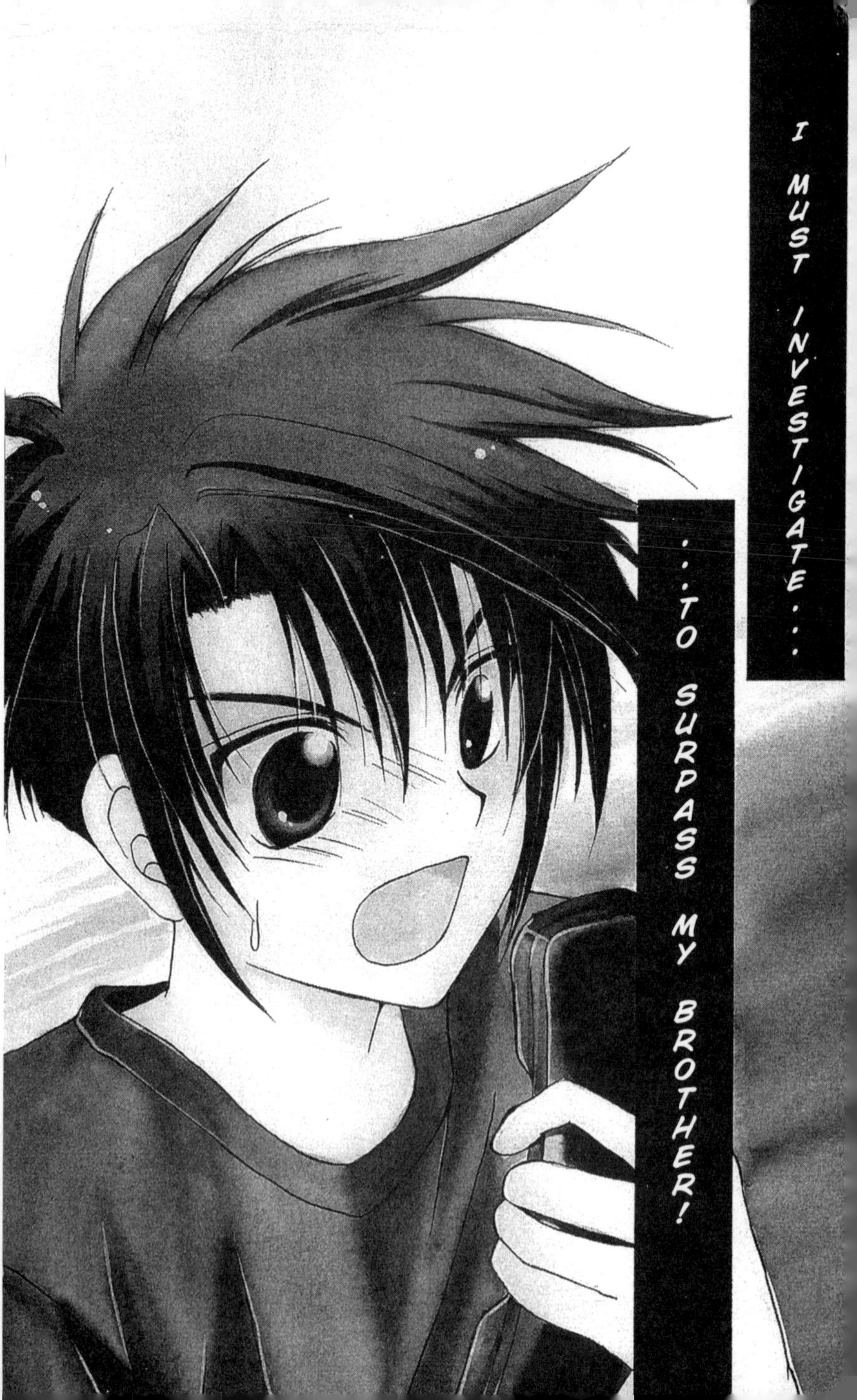
I MUST INVESTIGATE...
...TO SURPASS MY BROTHER!

CHAPTER ONE

The Invisible Hand on the Landing (Part I)

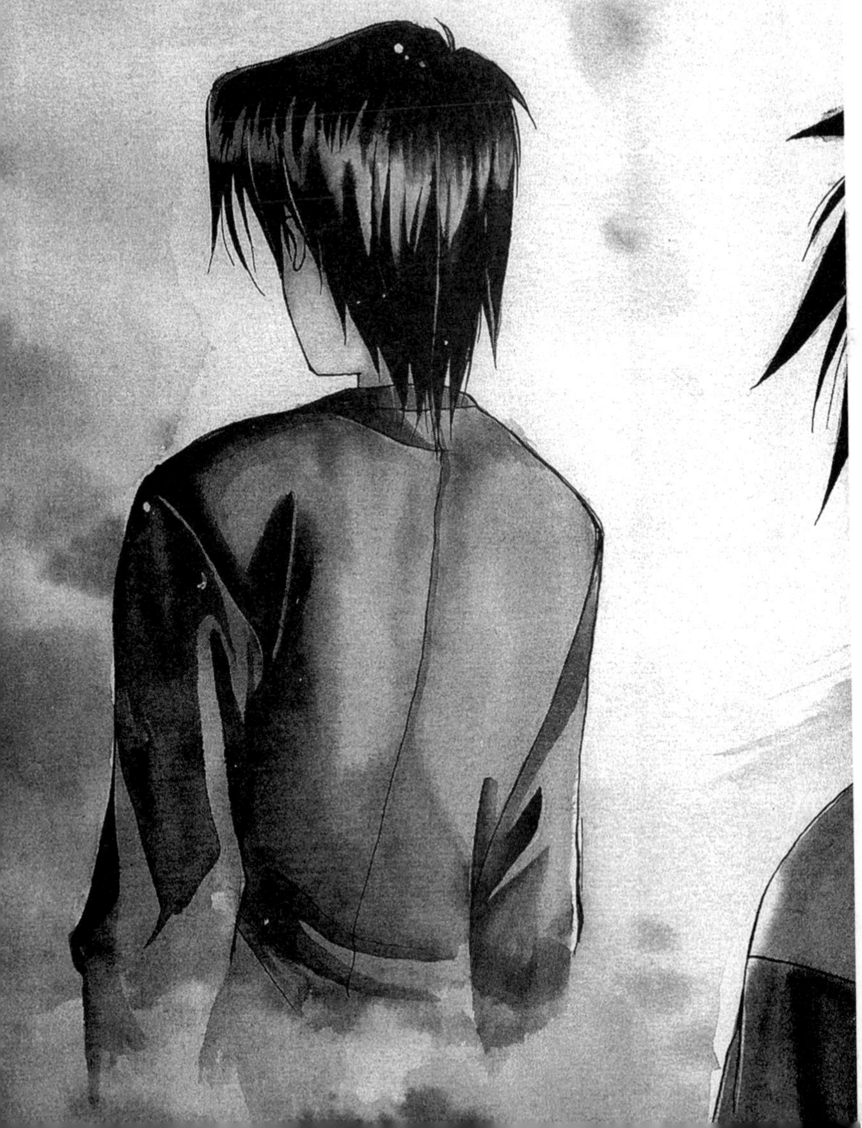

Spiral

THE BONDS OF REASONING

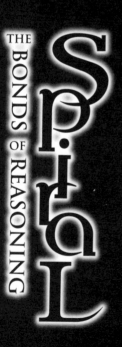

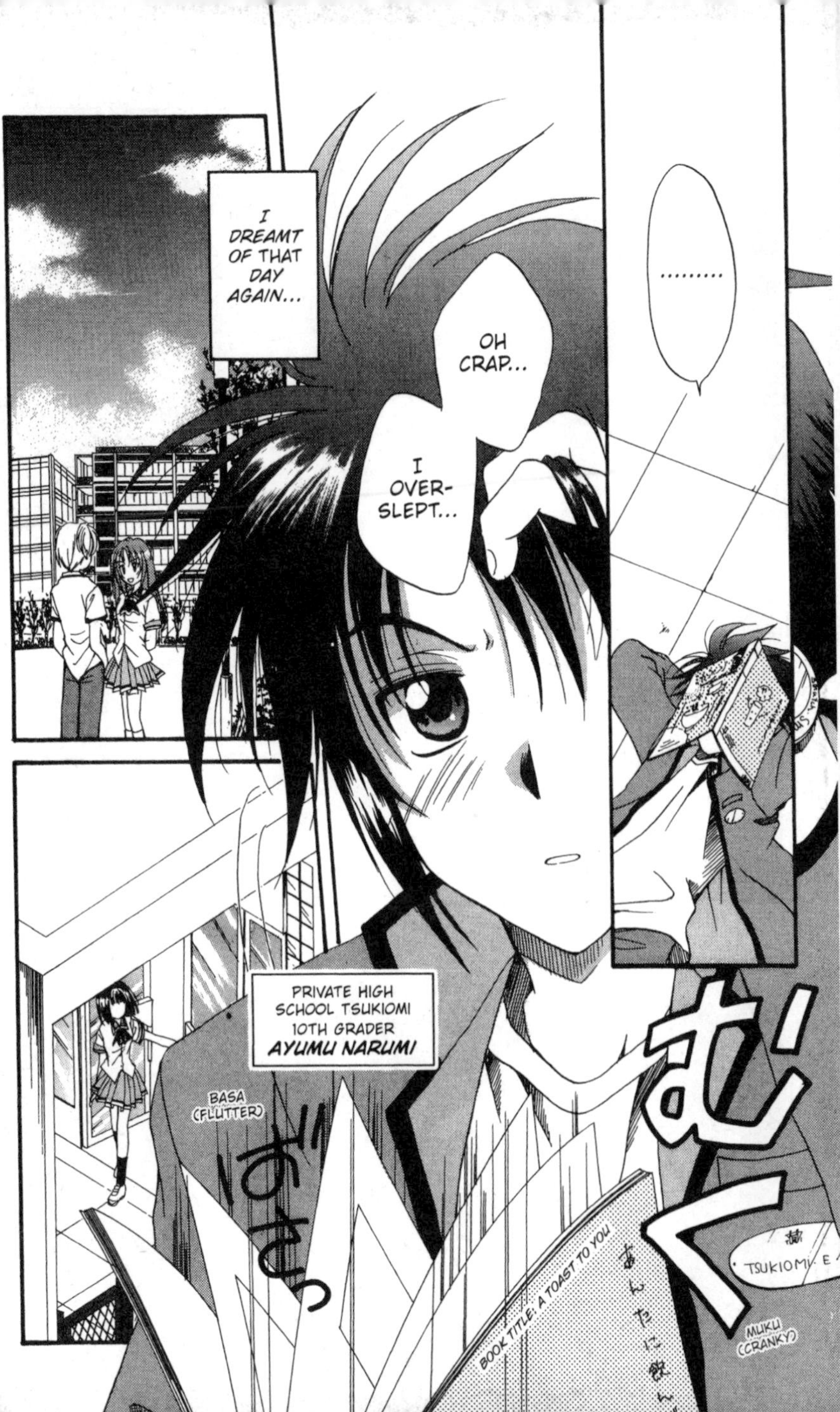
....
TSUKIOMI-E
I DREAMT OF THAT DAY AGAIN...
OH CRAP...
I OVER-SLEPT...
PRIVATE HIGH SCHOOL TSUKIOMI 10TH GRADER AYUMU NARUMI
MUKU (CRANKY)
BOOK TITLE: A TOAST TO YOU
BASA (FLUTTER)

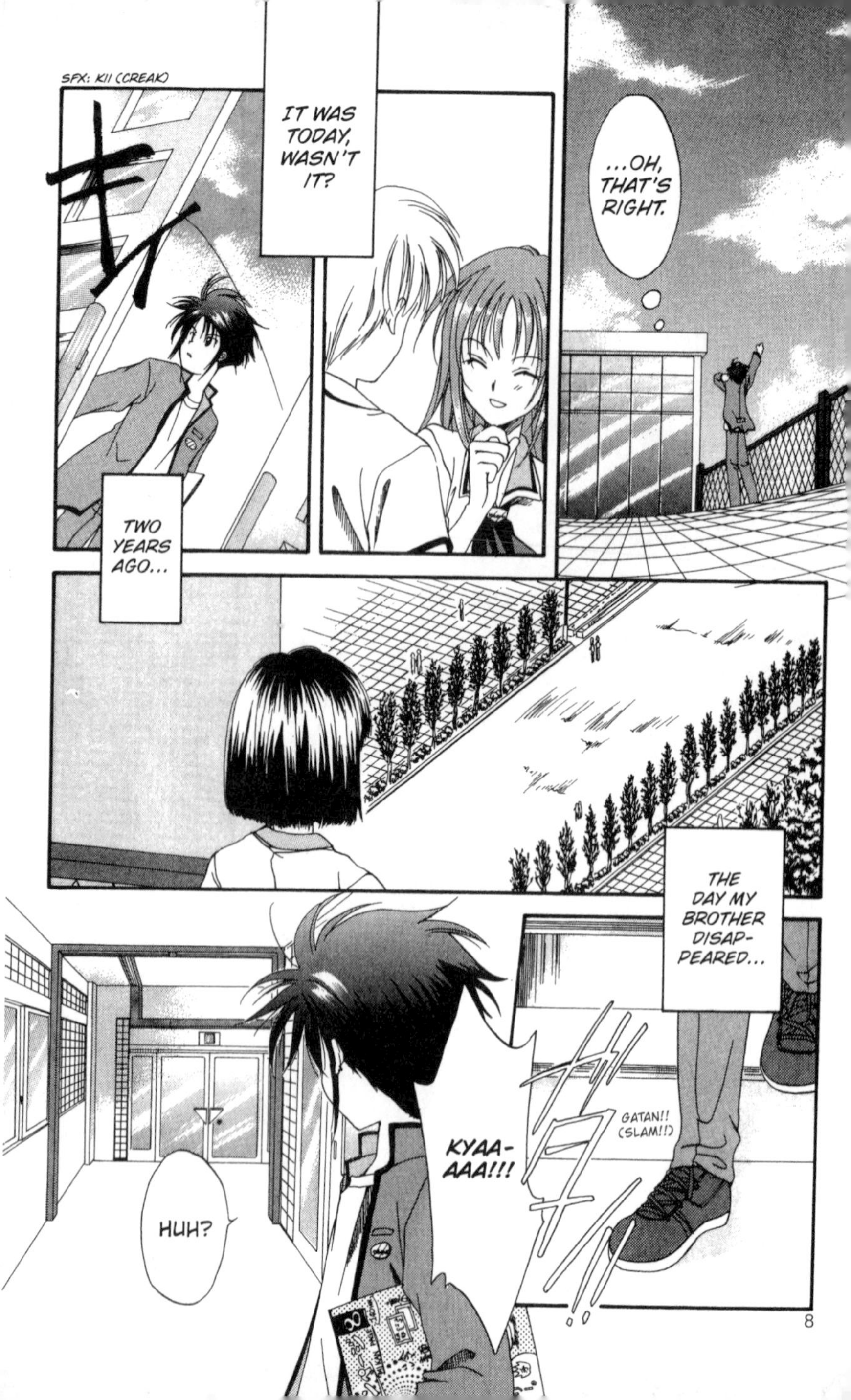
...OH, THAT'S RIGHT.
IT WAS TODAY, WASN'T IT?
SFX: KII (CREAK)
TWO YEARS AGO...
THE DAY MY BROTHER DISAP-PEARED...
GATAN!! (SLAM!!)
KYAA-AAA!!!
HUH?

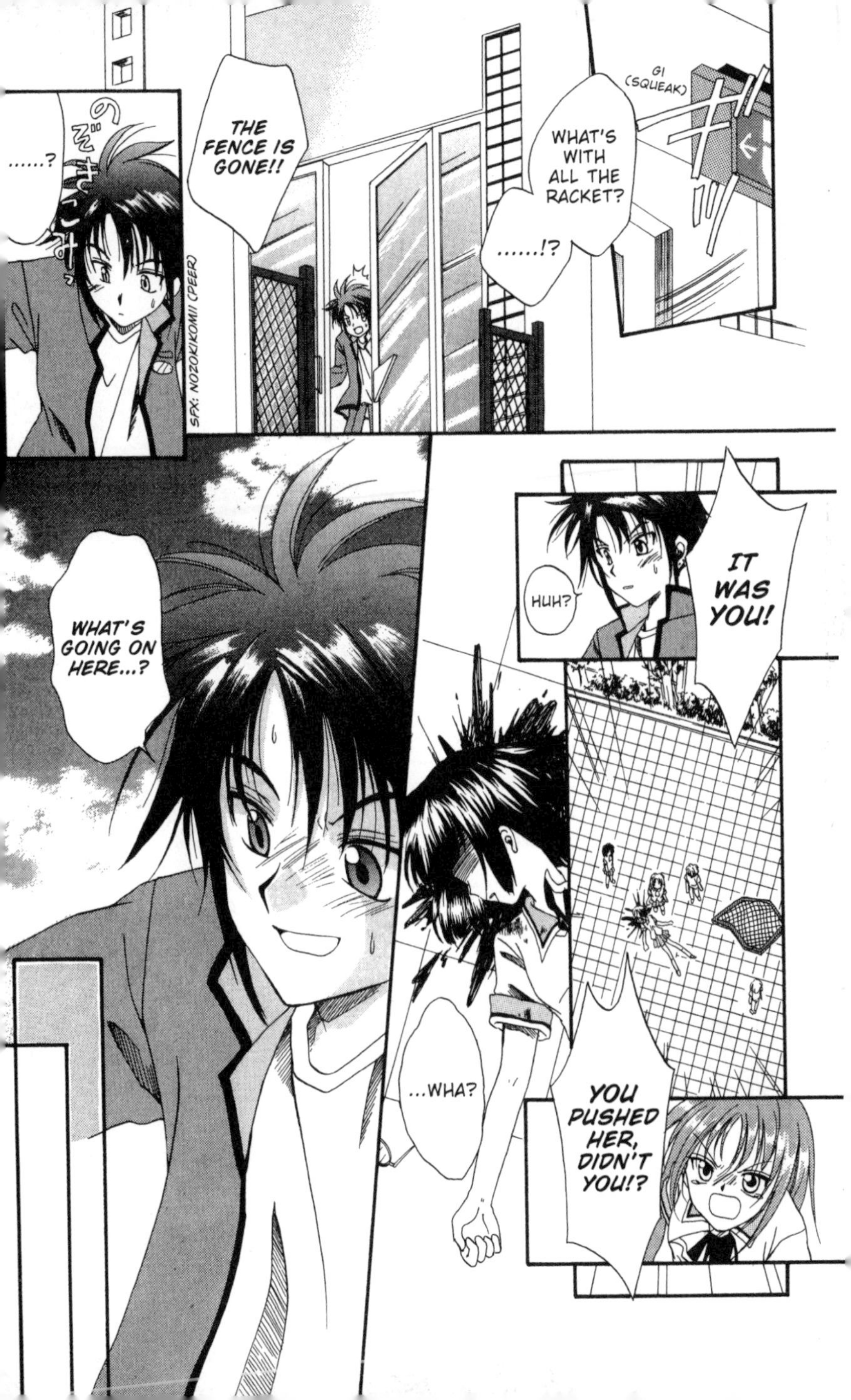
GI (SQUEAK)
WHAT'S WITH ALL THE RACKET?
......!?
THE FENCE IS GONE!!
......?
SFX: NOZOKIKOMI (PEER)
IT WAS YOU!
HUH?
YOU PUSHED HER, DIDN'T YOU!?
...WHA?
WHAT'S GOING ON HERE...?

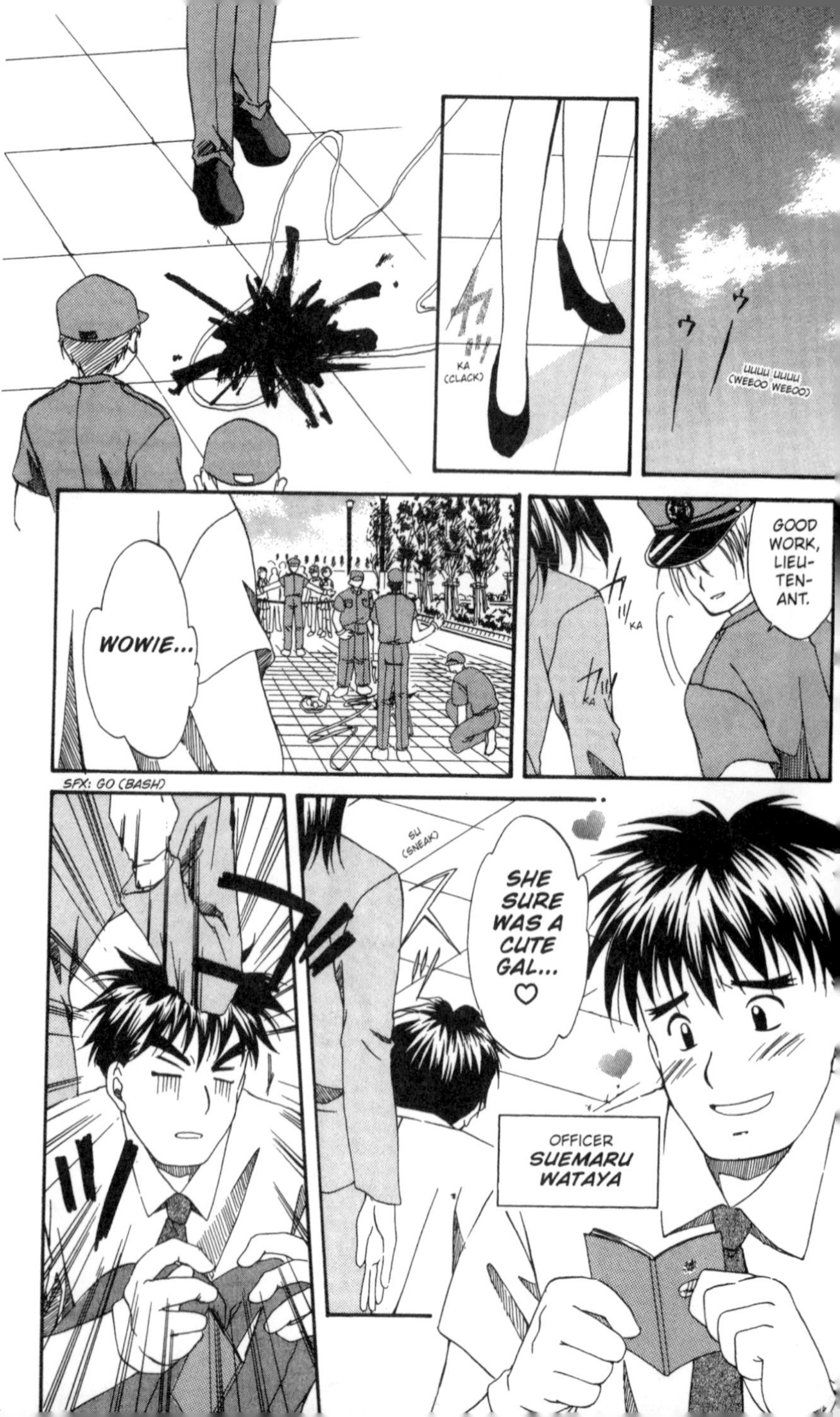
ウ ウ
UUUU UUUU (WEEOO WEEOO)
KA (CLACK)
GOOD WORK, LIEU-TEN-ANT.
KA
KA
WOWIE...
SFX: GO (BASH)
SU (SNEAK)
SHE SURE WAS A CUTE GAL... ♡
OFFICER SUEMARU WATAYA

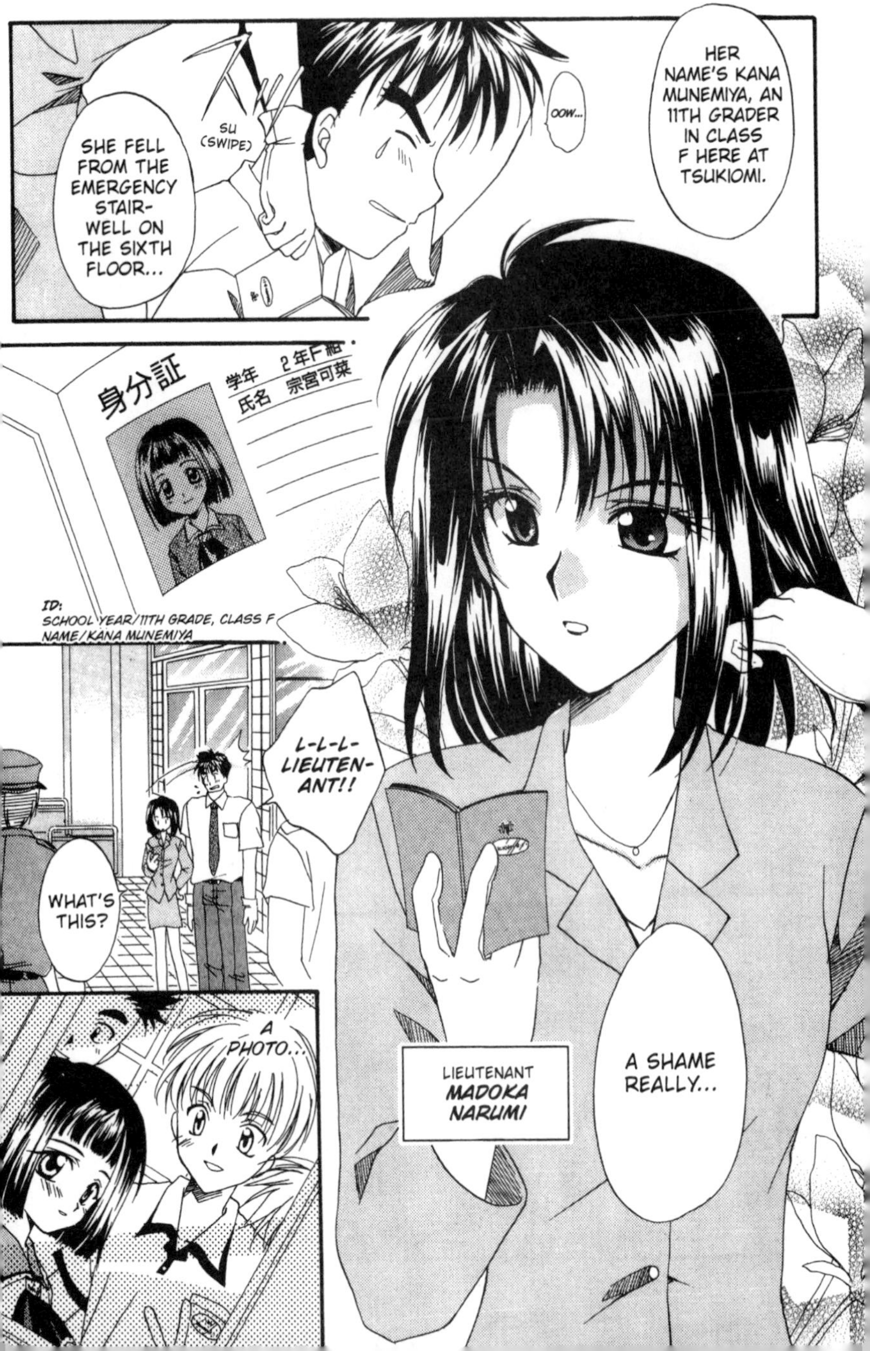
HER NAME'S KANA MUNEMIYA, AN 11TH GRADER IN CLASS F HERE AT TSUKIOMI.
OOW...
SU (SWIPE)
SHE FELL FROM THE EMERGENCY STAIR-WELL ON THE SIXTH FLOOR...
A SHAME REALLY...
LIEUTENANT MADOKA NARUMI
身分証
学年 2年F組
氏名 宗宮可菜
ID: SCHOOL YEAR/11TH GRADE, CLASS F NAME/KANA MUNEMIYA
L-L-L-LIEUTEN-ANT!!
WHAT'S THIS?
A PHOTO...

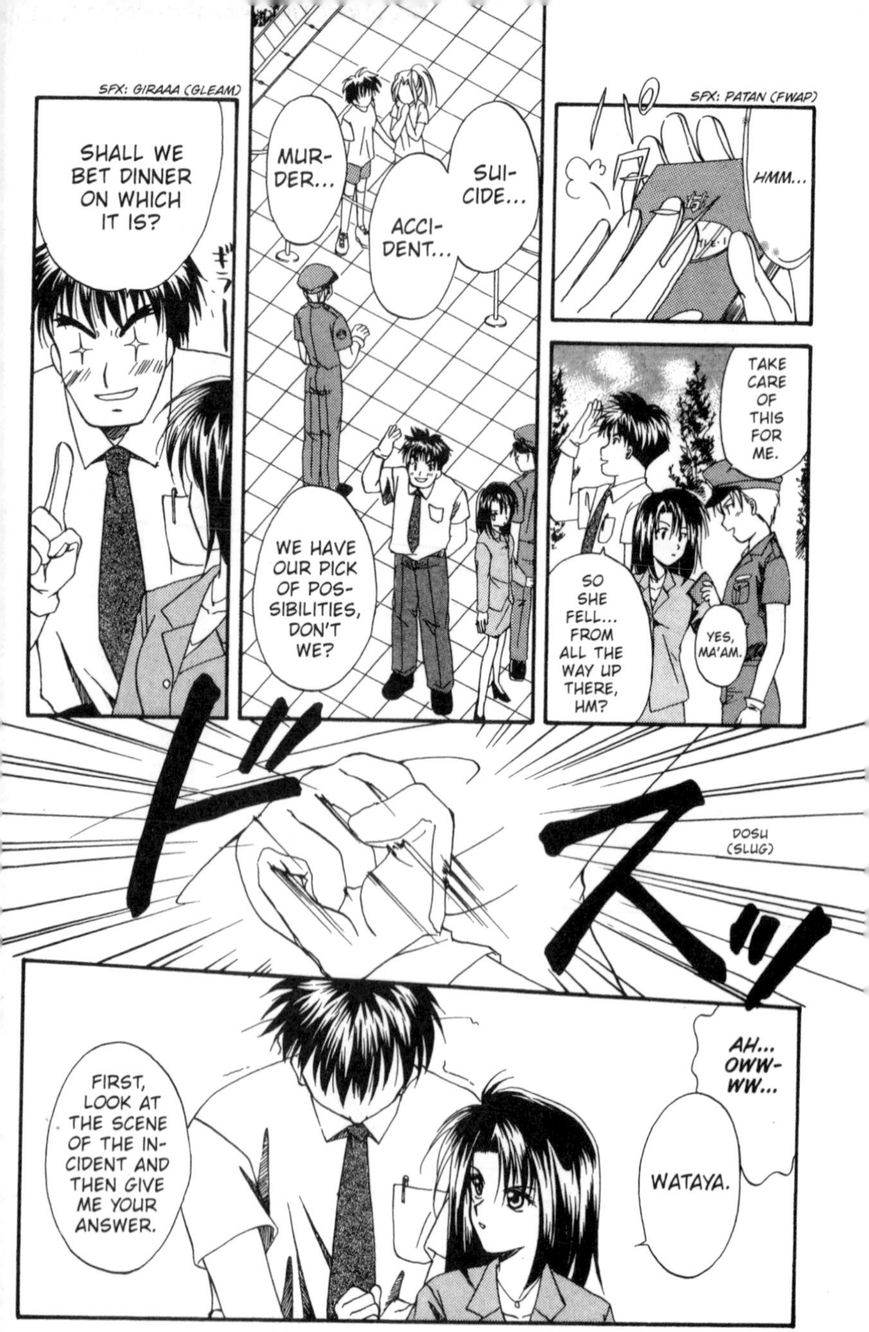
SFX: PATAN (FWAP)
HMM...
TAKE CARE OF THIS FOR ME.
SO SHE FELL... FROM ALL THE WAY UP THERE, HM?
YES, MA'AM.
SUI-CIDE...
MUR-DER...
ACCI-DENT...
WE HAVE OUR PICK OF POS-SIBILITIES, DON'T WE?
SFX: GIRAAA (GLEAM)
SHALL WE BET DINNER ON WHICH IT IS?
DOSU (SLUG)
AH... OWW-WW...
WATAYA.
FIRST, LOOK AT THE SCENE OF THE IN-CIDENT AND THEN GIVE ME YOUR ANSWER.

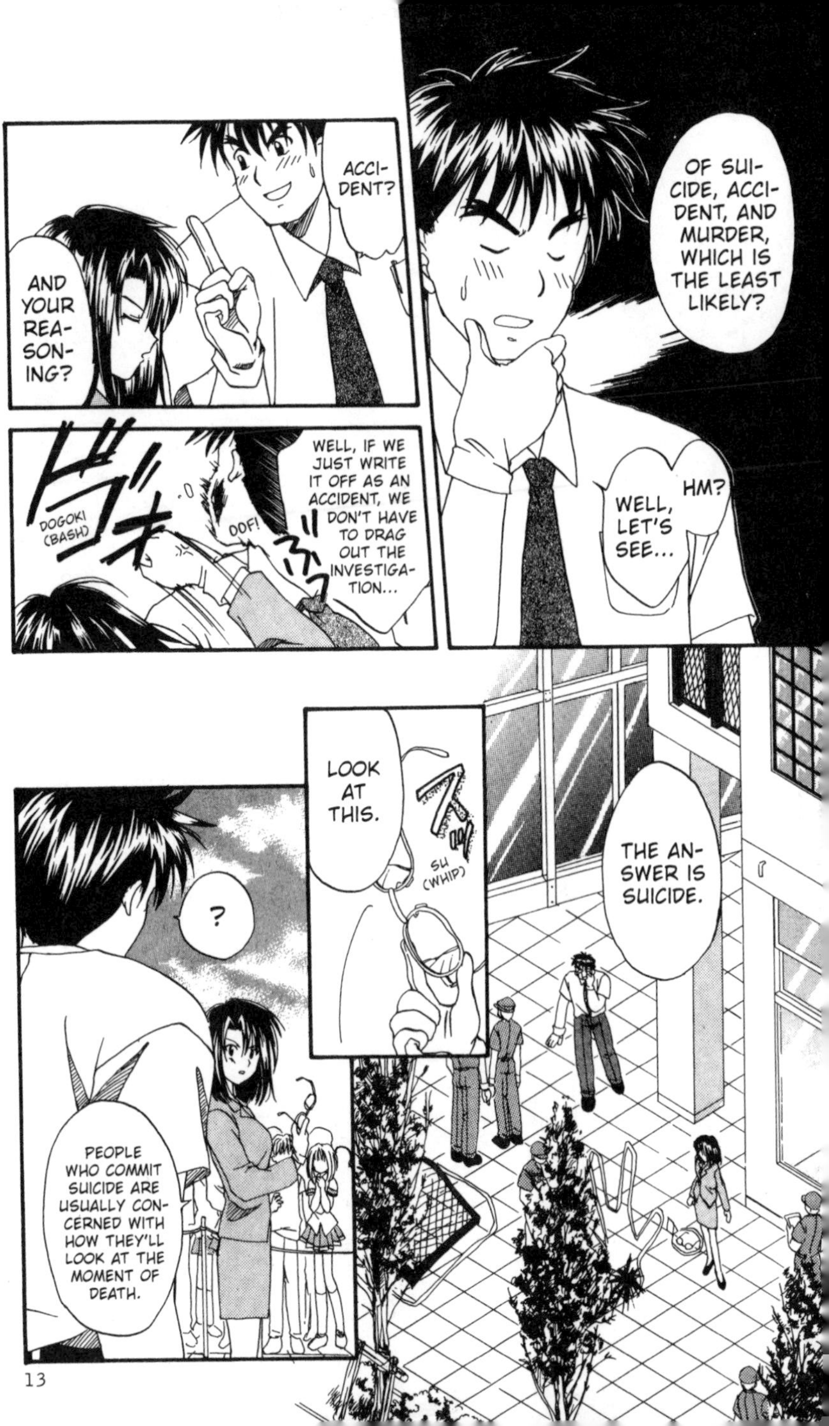
OF SUICIDE, ACCIDENT, AND MURDER, WHICH IS THE LEAST LIKELY?
HM?
WELL, LET'S SEE...
ACCIDENT?
AND YOUR REASONING?
WELL, IF WE JUST WRITE IT OFF AS AN ACCIDENT, WE DON'T HAVE TO DRAG OUT THE INVESTIGATION...
OOF!
DOGOKI (BASH)
THE ANSWER IS SUICIDE.
LOOK AT THIS.
SU (WHIP)
?
PEOPLE WHO COMMIT SUICIDE ARE USUALLY CONCERNED WITH HOW THEY'LL LOOK AT THE MOMENT OF DEATH.

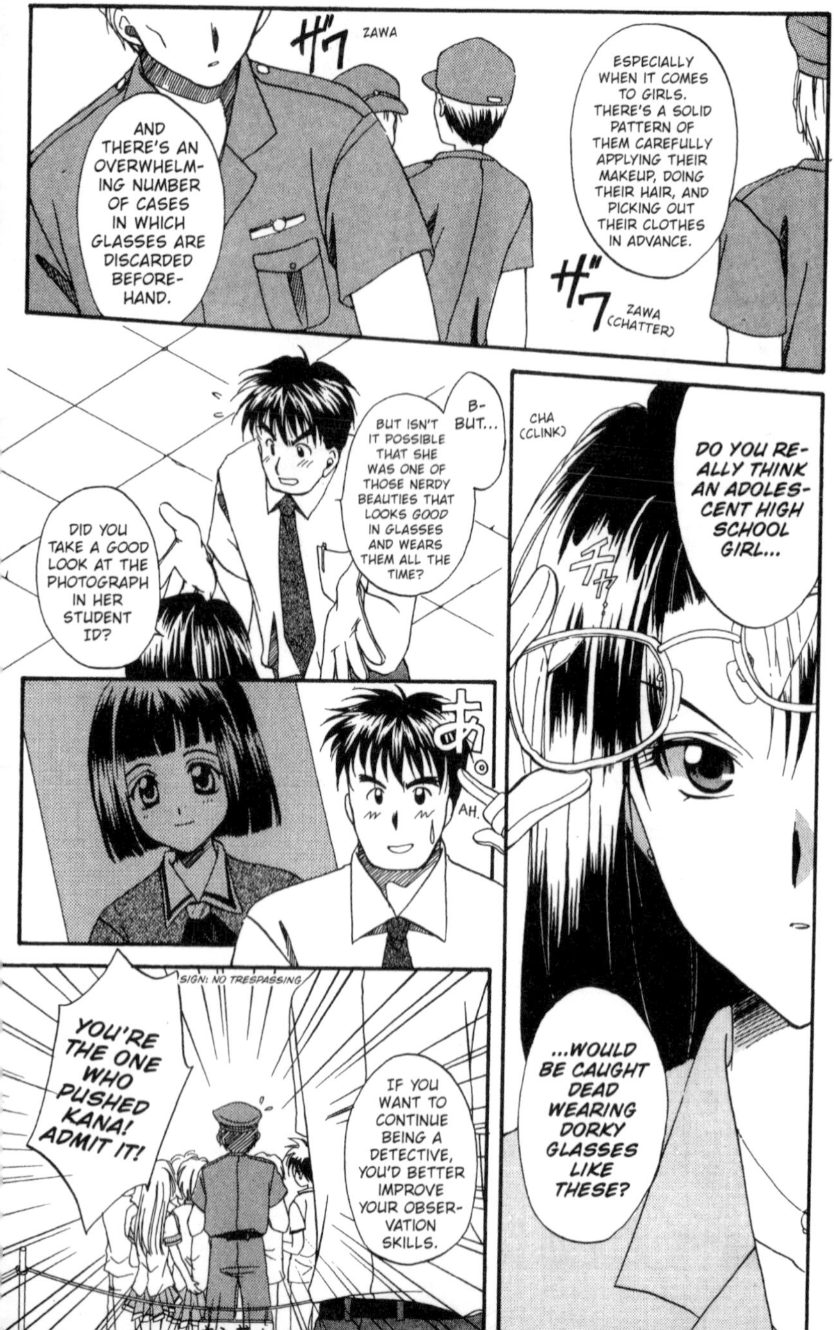
ZAWA
ESPECIALLY WHEN IT COMES TO GIRLS. THERE'S A SOLID PATTERN OF THEM CAREFULLY APPLYING THEIR MAKEUP, DOING THEIR HAIR, AND PICKING OUT THEIR CLOTHES IN ADVANCE.
AND THERE'S AN OVERWHELMING NUMBER OF CASES IN WHICH GLASSES ARE DISCARDED BEFOREHAND.
ZAWA (CHATTER)
CHA (CLINK)
DO YOU REALLY THINK AN ADOLESCENT HIGH SCHOOL GIRL...
...WOULD BE CAUGHT DEAD WEARING DORKY GLASSES LIKE THESE?
B-BUT...
BUT ISN'T IT POSSIBLE THAT SHE WAS ONE OF THOSE NERDY BEAUTIES THAT LOOKS GOOD IN GLASSES AND WEARS THEM ALL THE TIME?
DID YOU TAKE A GOOD LOOK AT THE PHOTOGRAPH IN HER STUDENT ID?
AH.
IF YOU WANT TO CONTINUE BEING A DETECTIVE, YOU'D BETTER IMPROVE YOUR OBSERVATION SKILLS.
SIGN: NO TRESPASSING
YOU'RE THE ONE WHO PUSHED KANA! ADMIT IT!

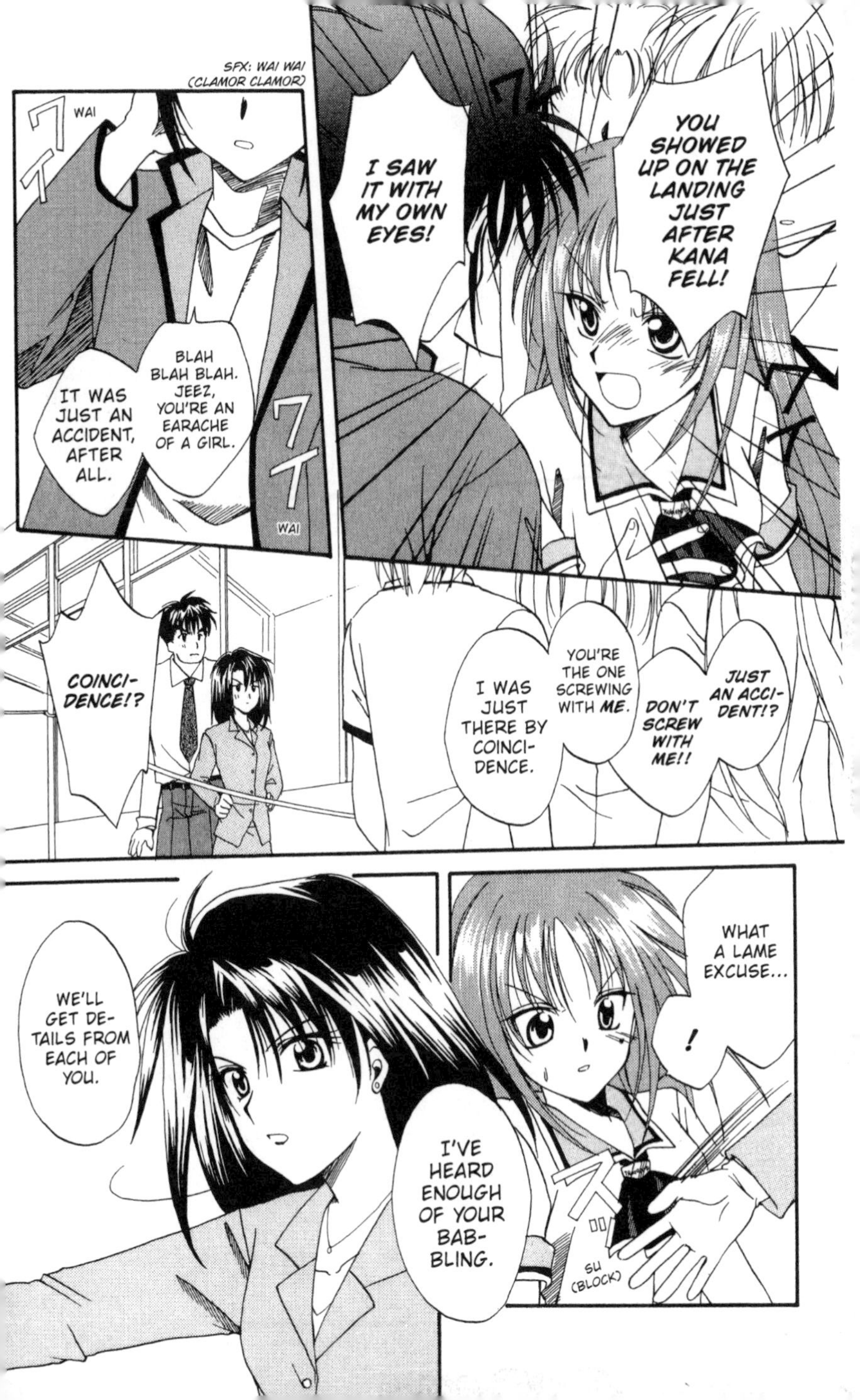
YOU SHOWED UP ON THE LANDING JUST AFTER KANA FELL!
I SAW IT WITH MY OWN EYES!
SFX: WAI WAI (CLAMOR CLAMOR)
WAI
BLAH BLAH BLAH. JEEZ, YOU'RE AN EARACHE OF A GIRL.
IT WAS JUST AN ACCIDENT, AFTER ALL.
WAI
JUST AN ACCIDENT!?
DON'T SCREW WITH ME!!
YOU'RE THE ONE SCREWING WITH ME.
I WAS JUST THERE BY COINCIDENCE.
COINCIDENCE!?
WHAT A LAME EXCUSE...
!
SU (BLOCK)
I'VE HEARD ENOUGH OF YOUR BABBLING.
WE'LL GET DETAILS FROM EACH OF YOU.

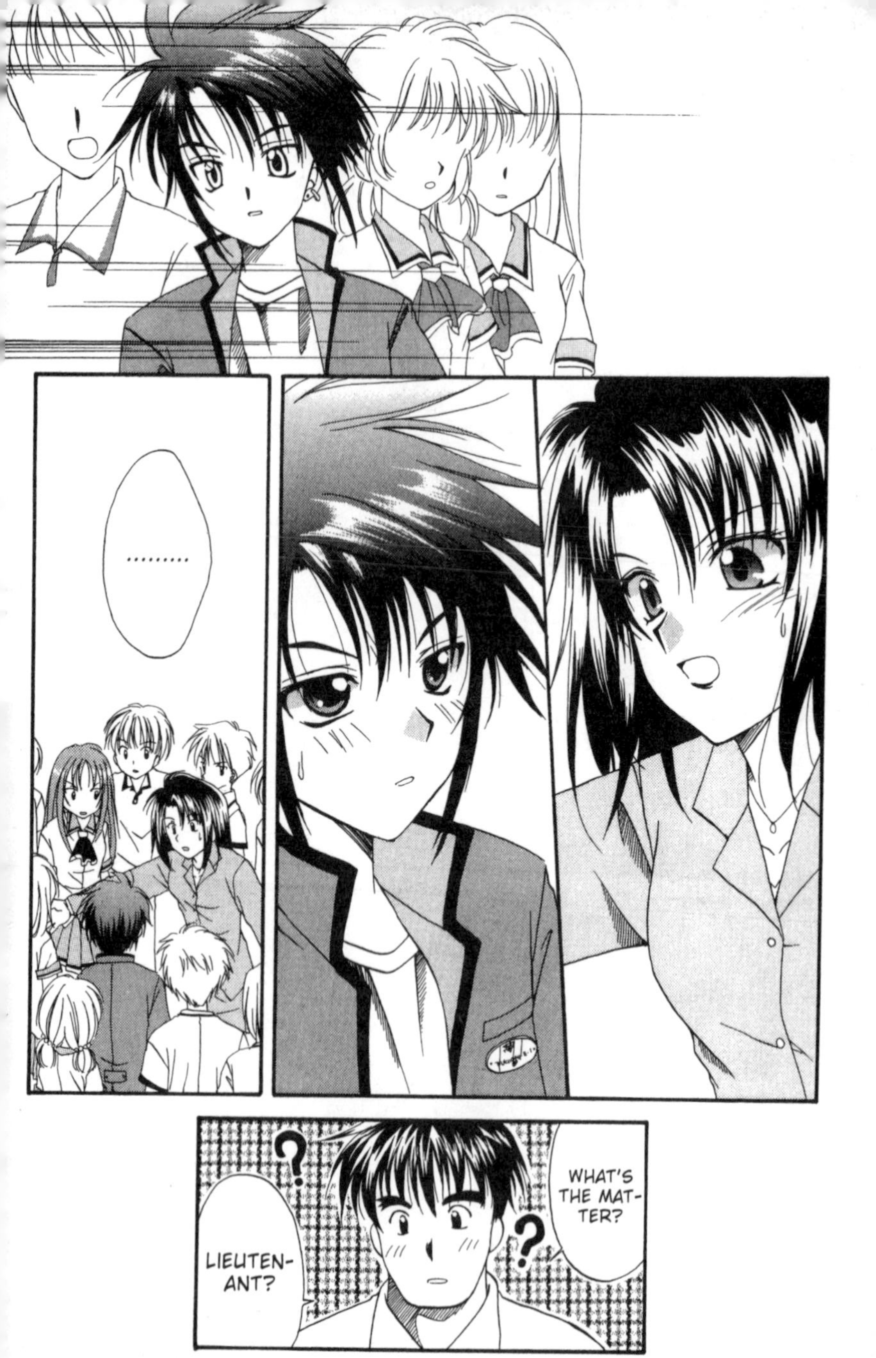
....
WHAT'S THE MAT-TER?
LIEUTEN-ANT?

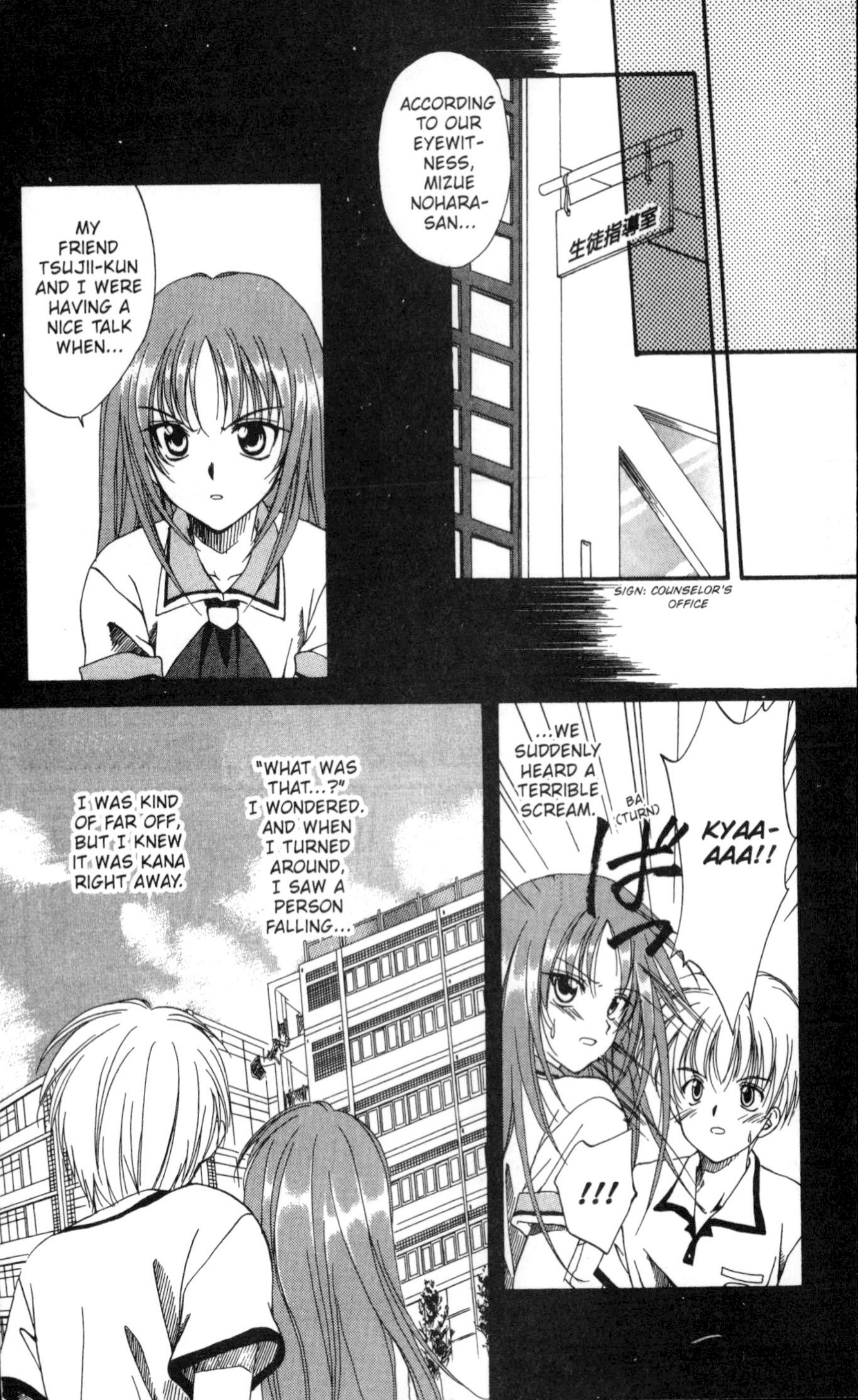
ACCORDING TO OUR EYEWIT-NESS, MIZUE NOHARA-SAN...
生徒指導室
SIGN: COUNSELOR'S OFFICE
MY FRIEND TSUJII-KUN AND I WERE HAVING A NICE TALK WHEN...
...WE SUDDENLY HEARD A TERRIBLE SCREAM.
KYAA-AAA!!
BA (TURN)
!!!
"WHAT WAS THAT...?" I WONDERED. AND WHEN I TURNED AROUND, I SAW A PERSON FALLING...
I WAS KIND OF FAR OFF, BUT I KNEW IT WAS KANA RIGHT AWAY.

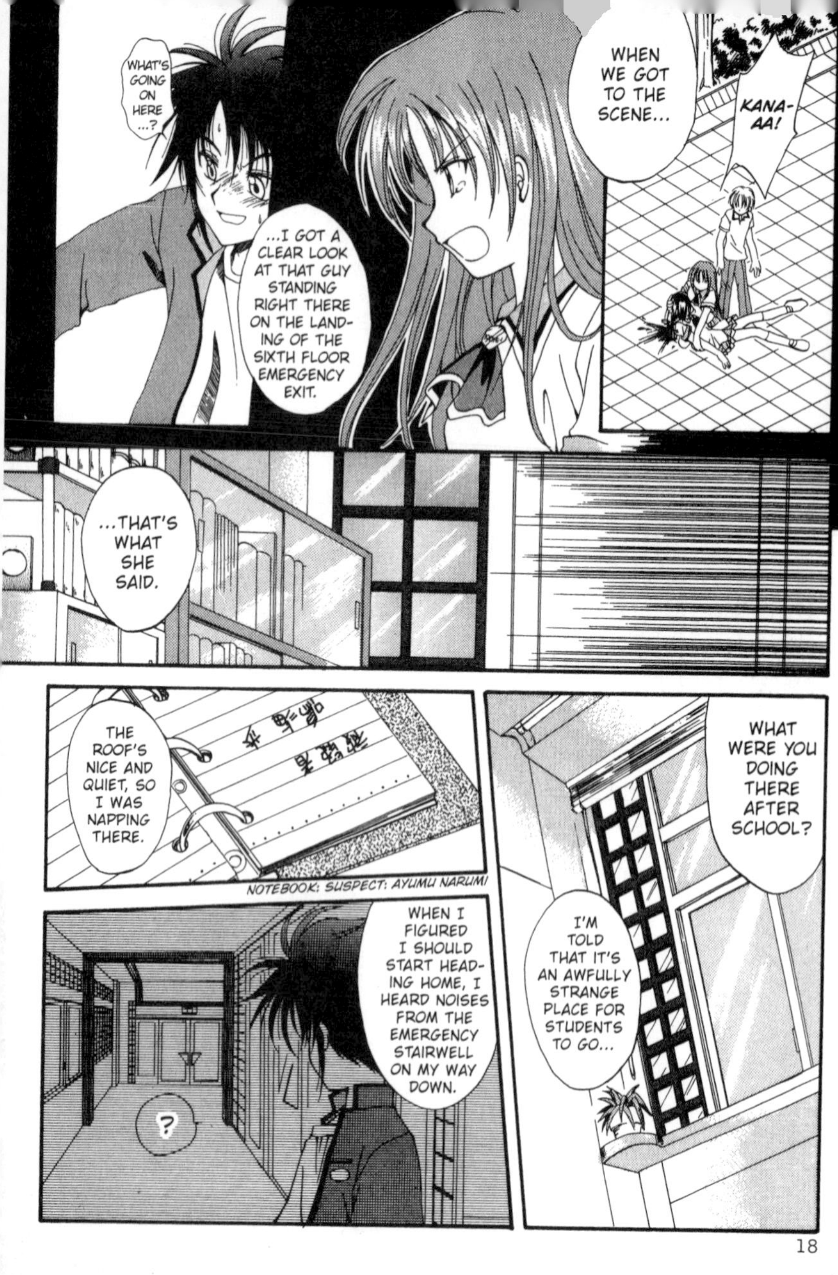
WHEN WE GOT TO THE SCENE...
KANA-AA!
...I GOT A CLEAR LOOK AT THAT GUY STANDING RIGHT THERE ON THE LANDING OF THE SIXTH FLOOR EMERGENCY EXIT.
WHAT'S GOING ON HERE ...?
...THAT'S WHAT SHE SAID.
WHAT WERE YOU DOING THERE AFTER SCHOOL?
I'M TOLD THAT IT'S AN AWFULLY STRANGE PLACE FOR STUDENTS TO GO...
THE ROOF'S NICE AND QUIET, SO I WAS NAPPING THERE.
NOTEBOOK: SUSPECT: AYUMU NARUMI
WHEN I FIGURED I SHOULD START HEADING HOME, I HEARD NOISES FROM THE EMERGENCY STAIRWELL ON MY WAY DOWN.
?

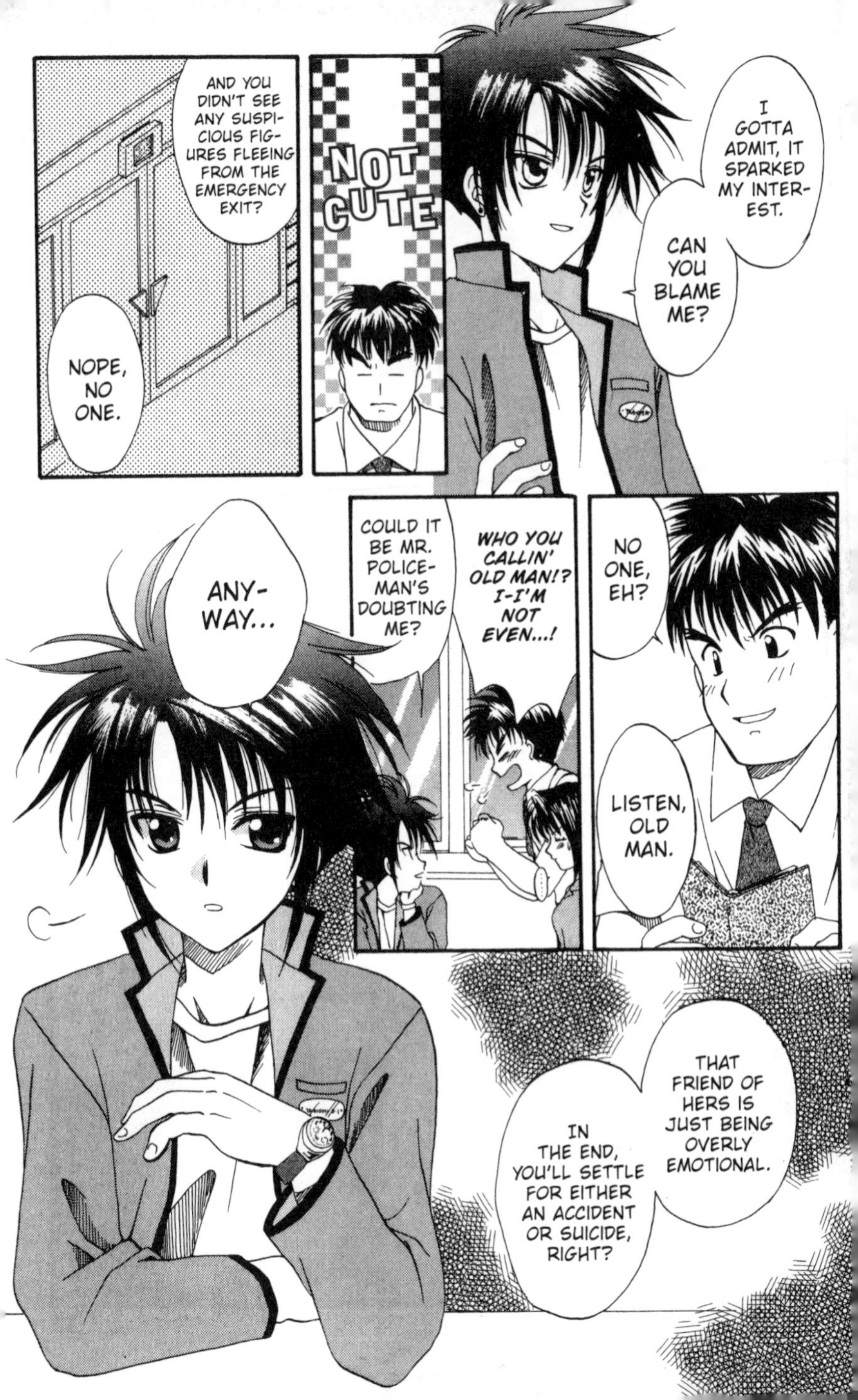
I GOTTA ADMIT, IT SPARKED MY INTEREST.
CAN YOU BLAME ME?
NOT CUTE
AND YOU DIDN'T SEE ANY SUSPICIOUS FIGURES FLEEING FROM THE EMERGENCY EXIT?
NOPE, NO ONE.
NO ONE, EH?
LISTEN, OLD MAN.
WHO YOU CALLIN' OLD MAN!? I-I'M NOT EVEN...!
COULD IT BE MR. POLICEMAN'S DOUBTING ME?
ANYWAY...
THAT FRIEND OF HERS IS JUST BEING OVERLY EMOTIONAL.
IN THE END, YOU'LL SETTLE FOR EITHER AN ACCIDENT OR SUICIDE, RIGHT?

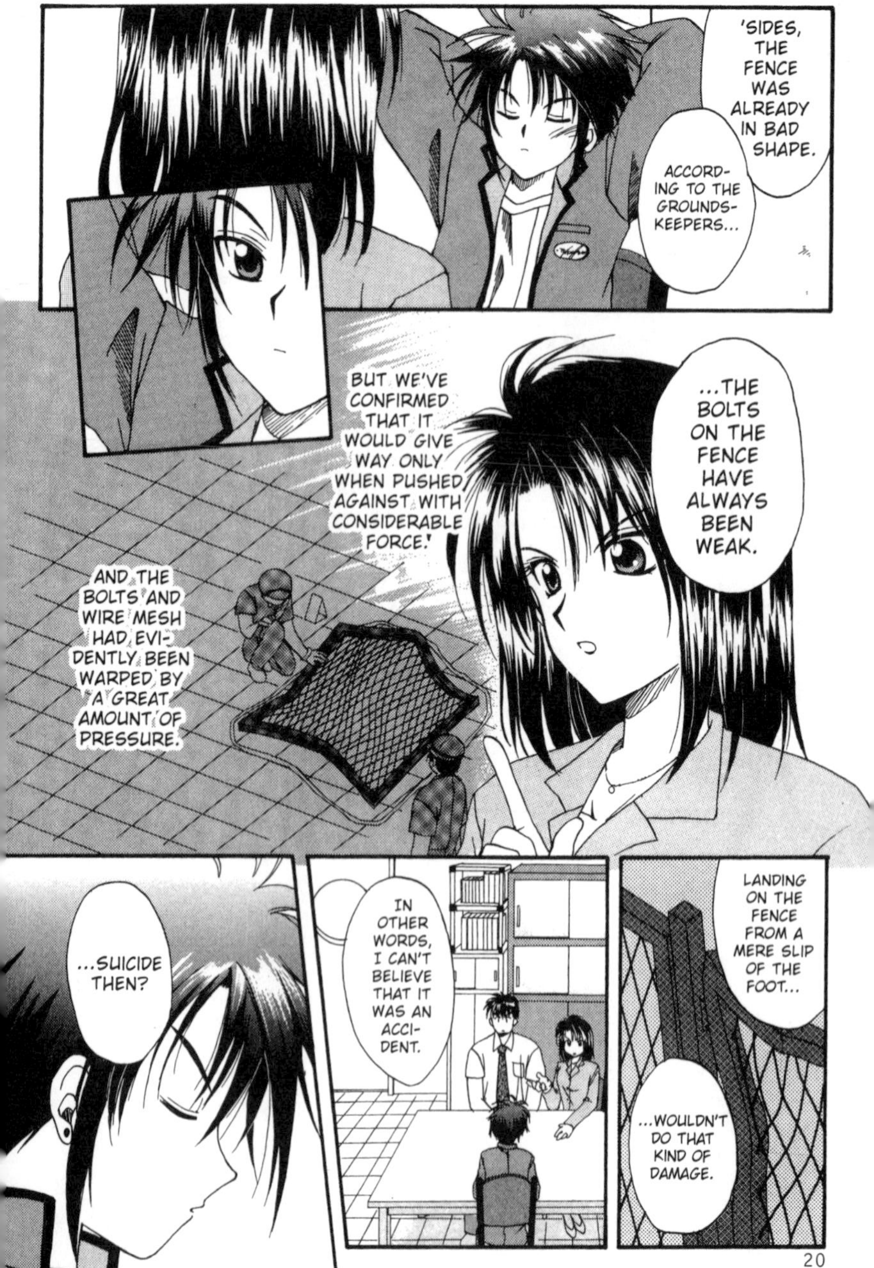
'SIDES, THE FENCE WAS ALREADY IN BAD SHAPE.
ACCORD-ING TO THE GROUNDS-KEEPERS...
...THE BOLTS ON THE FENCE HAVE ALWAYS BEEN WEAK.
BUT WE'VE CONFIRMED THAT IT WOULD GIVE WAY ONLY WHEN PUSHED AGAINST WITH CONSIDERABLE FORCE.'
AND THE BOLTS AND WIRE MESH HAD EVI-DENTLY BEEN WARPED BY A GREAT AMOUNT OF PRESSURE.
LANDING ON THE FENCE FROM A MERE SLIP OF THE FOOT...
...WOULDN'T DO THAT KIND OF DAMAGE.
IN OTHER WORDS, I CAN'T BELIEVE THAT IT WAS AN ACCI-DENT.
...SUICIDE THEN?

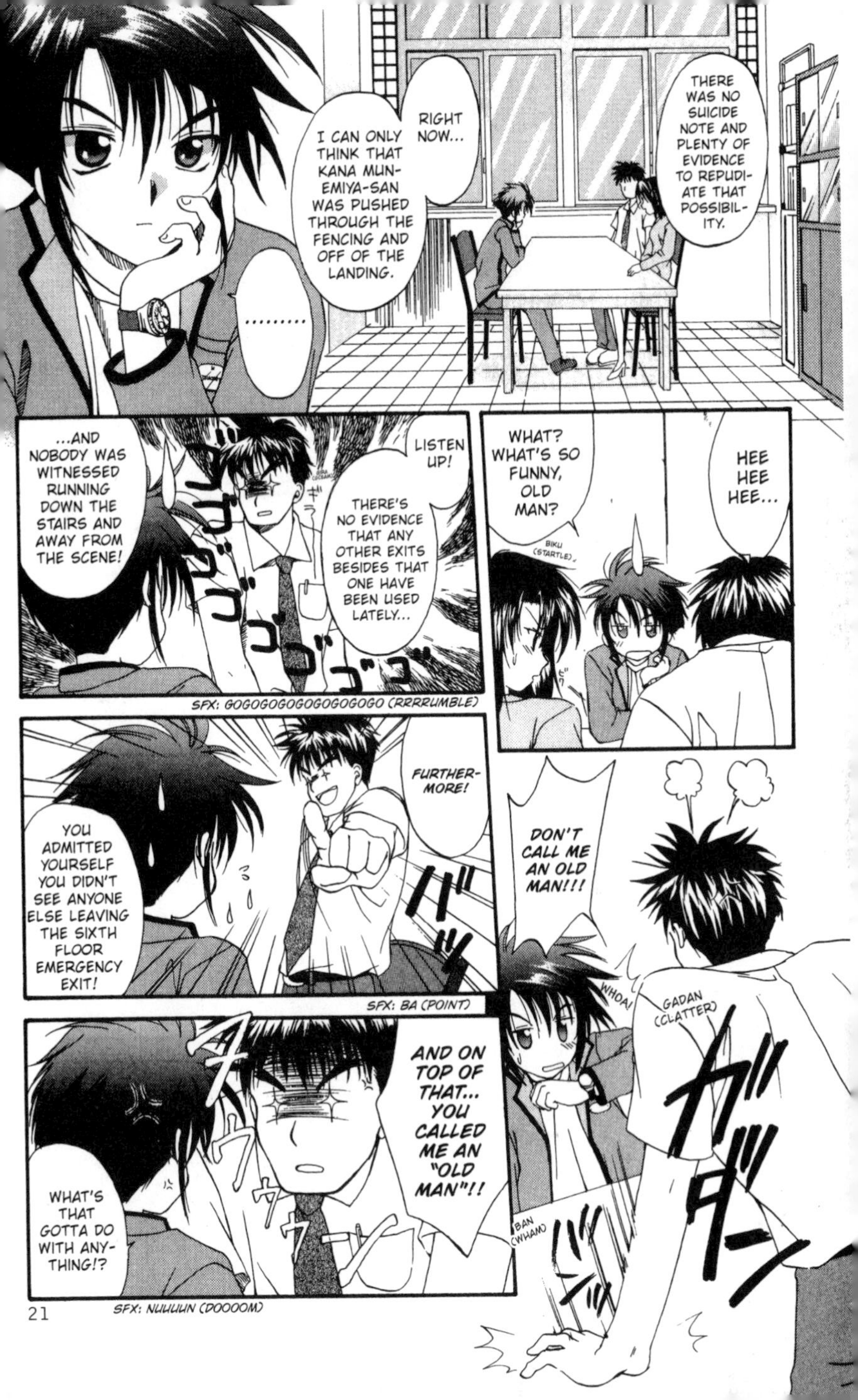
THERE WAS NO SUICIDE NOTE AND PLENTY OF EVIDENCE TO REPUDIATE THAT POSSIBILITY.
RIGHT NOW...
I CAN ONLY THINK THAT KANA MUNEMIYA-SAN WAS PUSHED THROUGH THE FENCING AND OFF OF THE LANDING.
....
HEE HEE HEE...
WHAT? WHAT'S SO FUNNY, OLD MAN?
BIKU (STARTLE)
LISTEN UP!
THERE'S NO EVIDENCE THAT ANY OTHER EXITS BESIDES THAT ONE HAVE BEEN USED LATELY...
...AND NOBODY WAS WITNESSED RUNNING DOWN THE STAIRS AND AWAY FROM THE SCENE!
SFX: GOGOGOGOGOGOGOGOGO (RRRRUMBLE)
DON'T CALL ME AN OLD MAN!!!
WHOA!
GADAN (CLATTER)
BAN (WHAM)
FURTHERMORE!
YOU ADMITTED YOURSELF YOU DIDN'T SEE ANYONE ELSE LEAVING THE SIXTH FLOOR EMERGENCY EXIT!
SFX: BA (POINT)
AND ON TOP OF THAT... YOU CALLED ME AN "OLD MAN"!!
WHAT'S THAT GOTTA DO WITH ANYTHING!?
SFX: NUUUUN (DOOOOM)

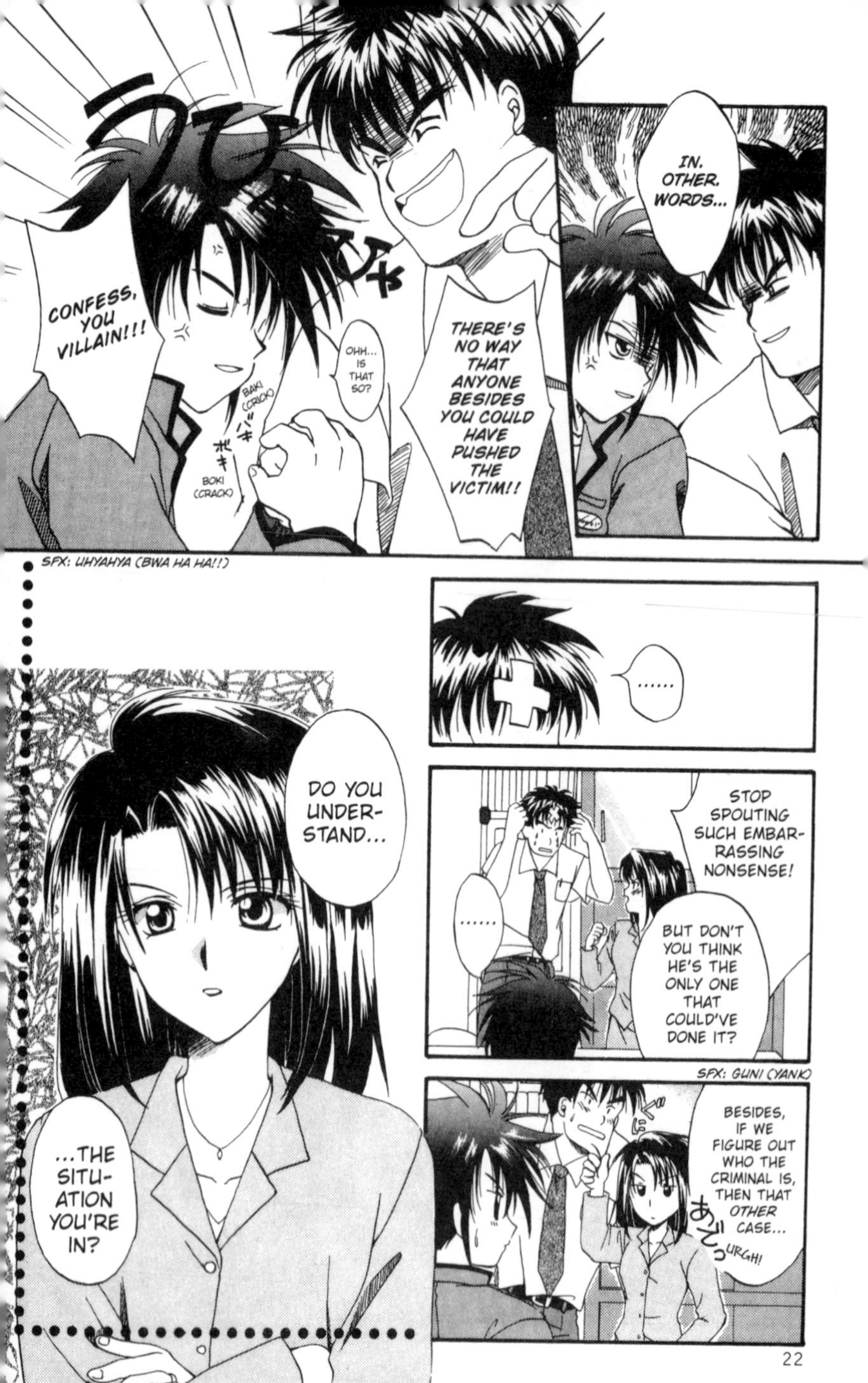
IN. OTHER. WORDS...
THERE'S NO WAY THAT ANYONE BESIDES YOU COULD HAVE PUSHED THE VICTIM!!
OHH... IS THAT SO?
BAKI (CRICK)
BOKI (CRACK)
CONFESS, YOU VILLAIN!!!
SFX: UHYAHYA (BWA HA HA!!)
......
STOP SPOUTING SUCH EMBARRASSING NONSENSE!
BUT DON'T YOU THINK HE'S THE ONLY ONE THAT COULD'VE DONE IT?
......
SFX: GUNI (YANK)
BESIDES, IF WE FIGURE OUT WHO THE CRIMINAL IS, THEN THAT OTHER CASE...
URGH!
DO YOU UNDERSTAND...
...THE SITUATION YOU'RE IN?

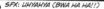

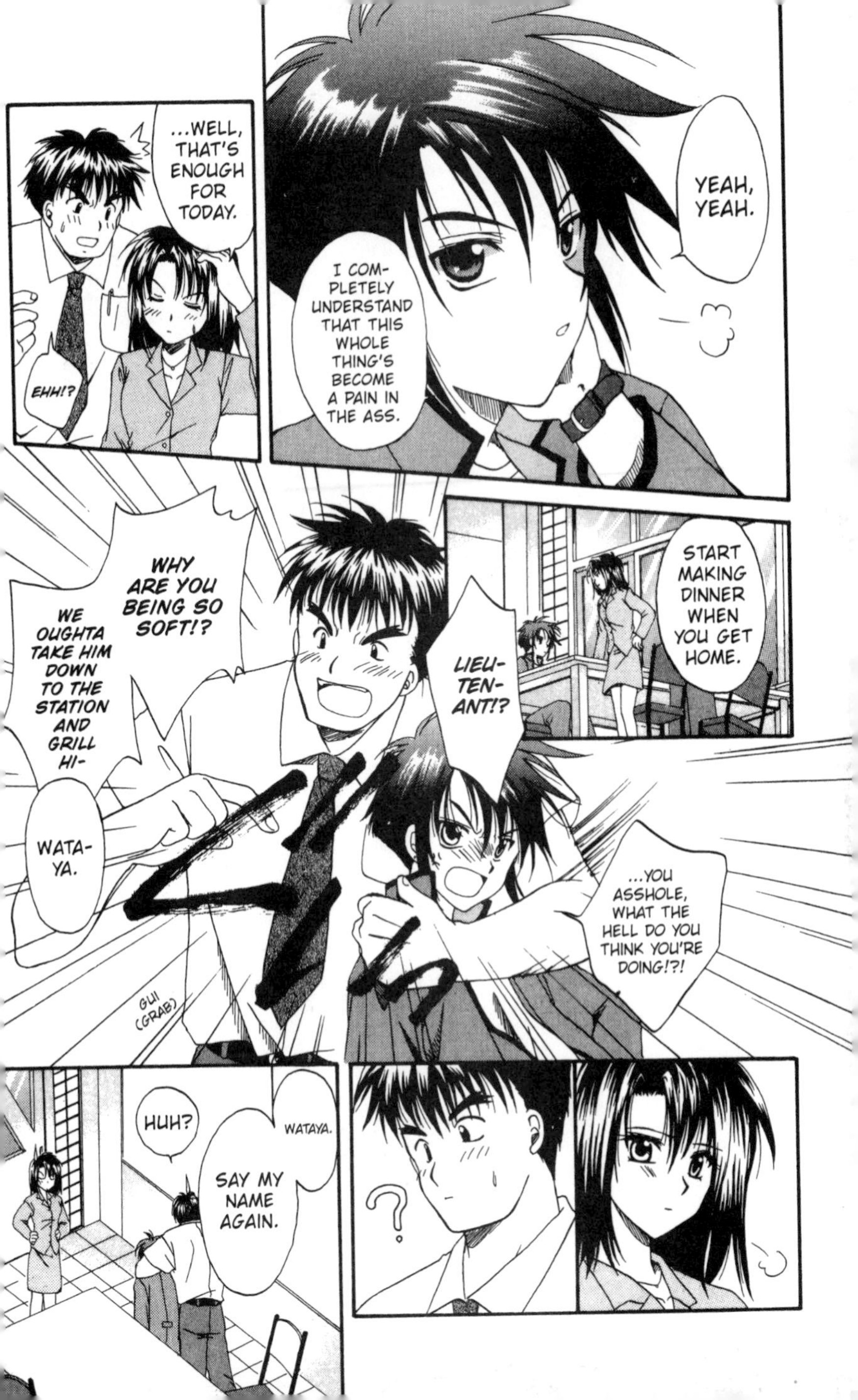
YEAH, YEAH.
I COMPLETELY UNDERSTAND THAT THIS WHOLE THING'S BECOME A PAIN IN THE ASS.
...WELL, THAT'S ENOUGH FOR TODAY.
EHH!?
START MAKING DINNER WHEN YOU GET HOME.
...YOU ASSHOLE, WHAT THE HELL DO YOU THINK YOU'RE DOING!?!
LIEUTENANT!?
WHY ARE YOU BEING SO SOFT!?
WE OUGHTA TAKE HIM DOWN TO THE STATION AND GRILL HI-
WATAYA.
GUI (GRAB)
WATAYA.
SAY MY NAME AGAIN.
HUH?

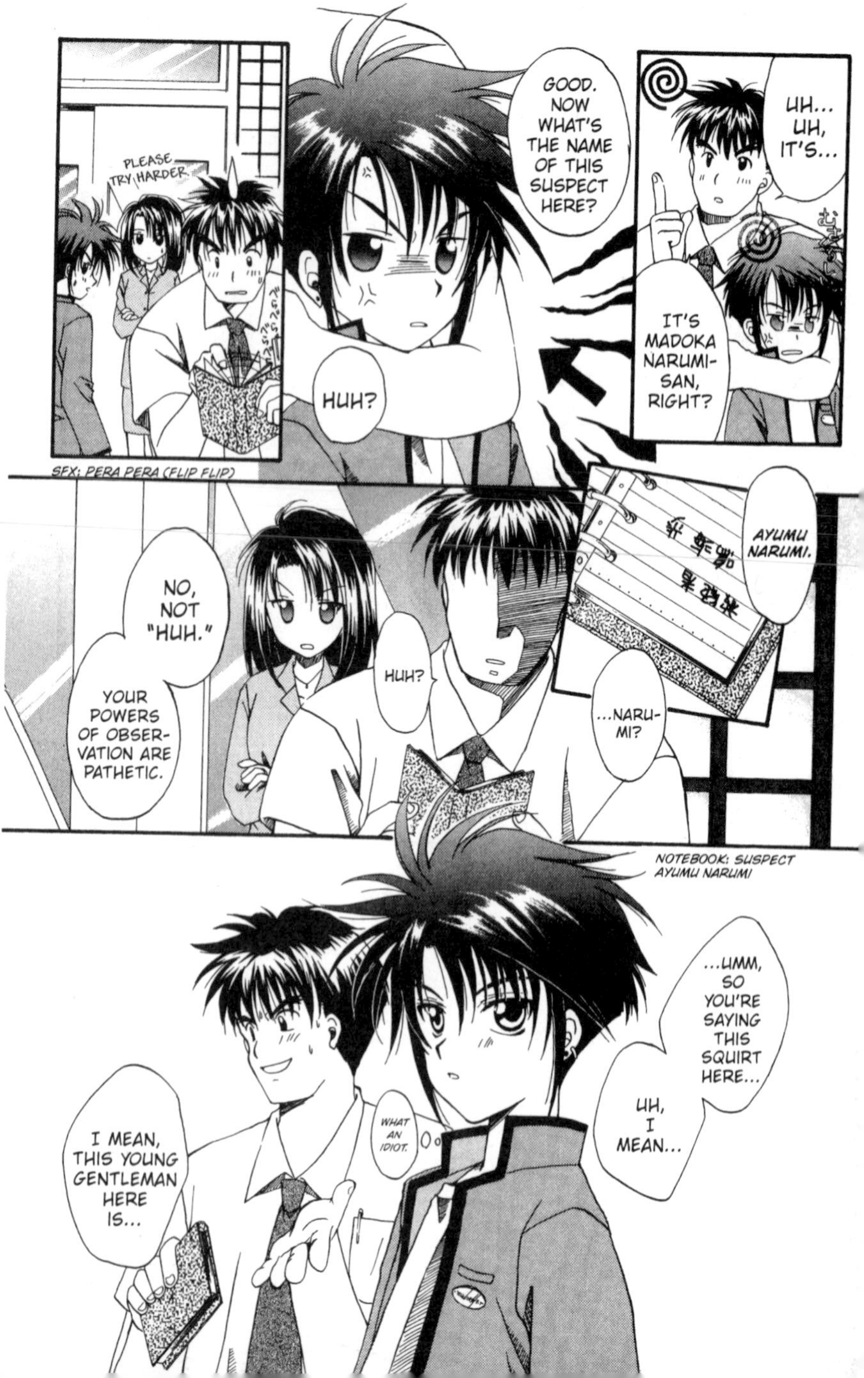
UH... UH, IT'S...
IT'S MADOKA NARUMI-SAN, RIGHT?
GOOD. NOW WHAT'S THE NAME OF THIS SUSPECT HERE?
HUH?
PLEASE TRY HARDER
SFX: PERA PERA (FLIP FLIP)
AYUMU NARUMI.
...NARUMI?
HUH?
NO, NOT "HUH."
YOUR POWERS OF OBSERVATION ARE PATHETIC.
NOTEBOOK: SUSPECT AYUMU NARUMI
...UMM, SO YOU'RE SAYING THIS SQUIRT HERE...
UH, I MEAN...
WHAT AN IDIOT.
I MEAN, THIS YOUNG GENTLEMAN HERE IS...

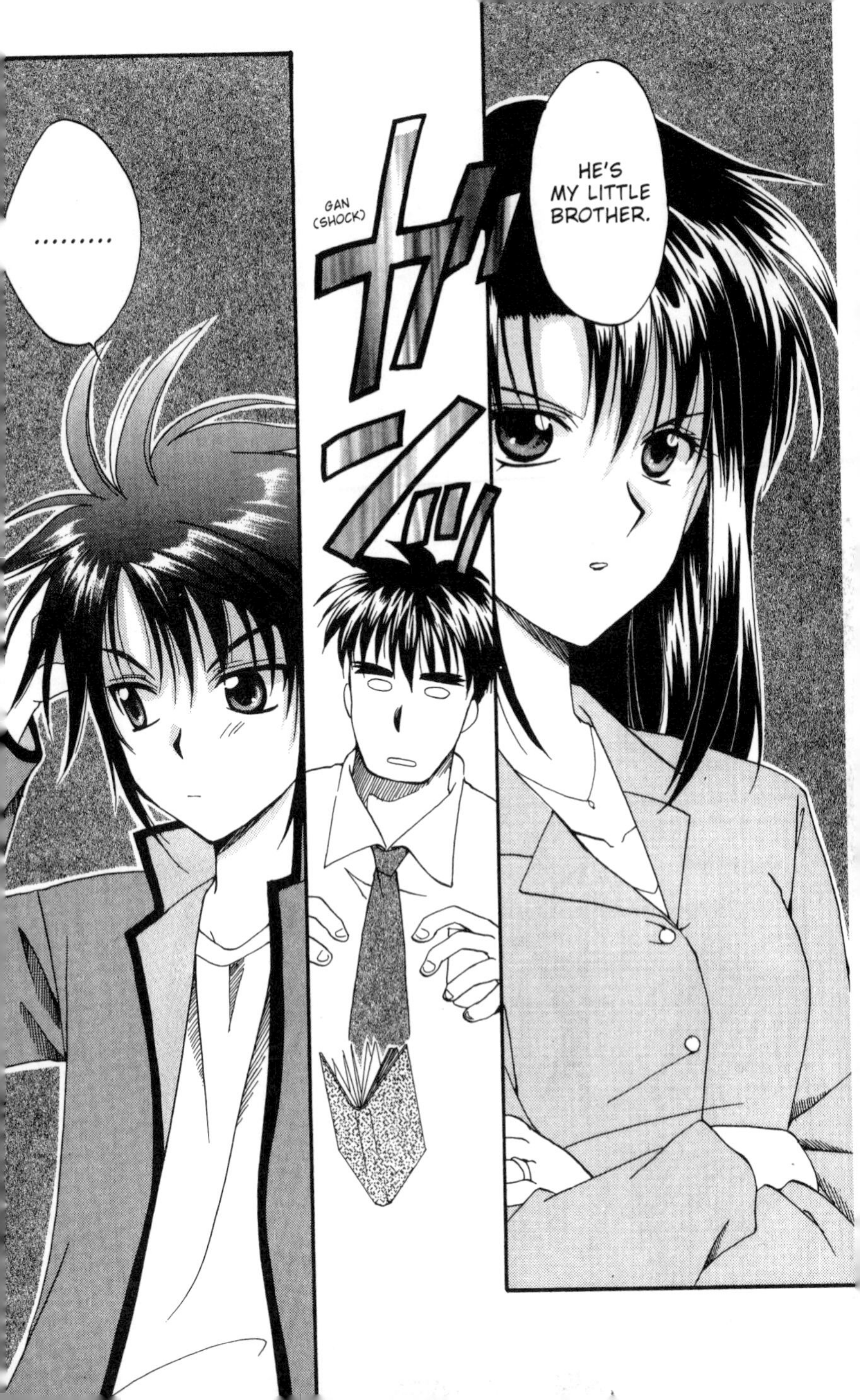
HE'S MY LITTLE BROTHER.
GAN (SHOCK)
....

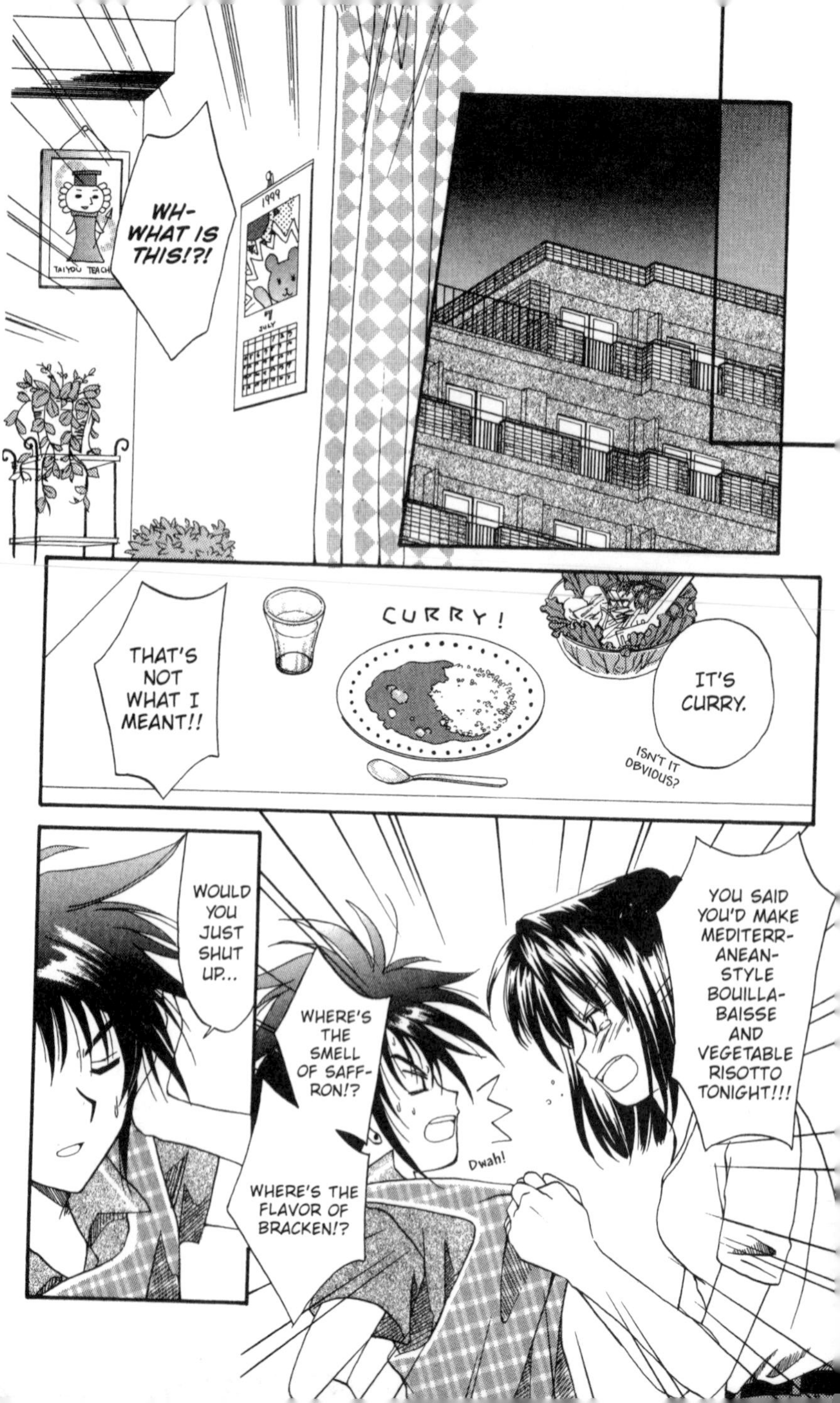
TAIYOU TEACH
1999
WH- WHAT IS THIS!?!
IT'S CURRY.
ISN'T IT OBVIOUS?
CURRY!
THAT'S NOT WHAT I MEANT!!
YOU SAID YOU'D MAKE MEDITERR-ANEAN-STYLE BOUILLA-BAISSE AND VEGETABLE RISOTTO TONIGHT!!!
Dwah!
WHERE'S THE SMELL OF SAFF-RON!?
WHERE'S THE FLAVOR OF BRACKEN!?
WOULD YOU JUST SHUT UP...

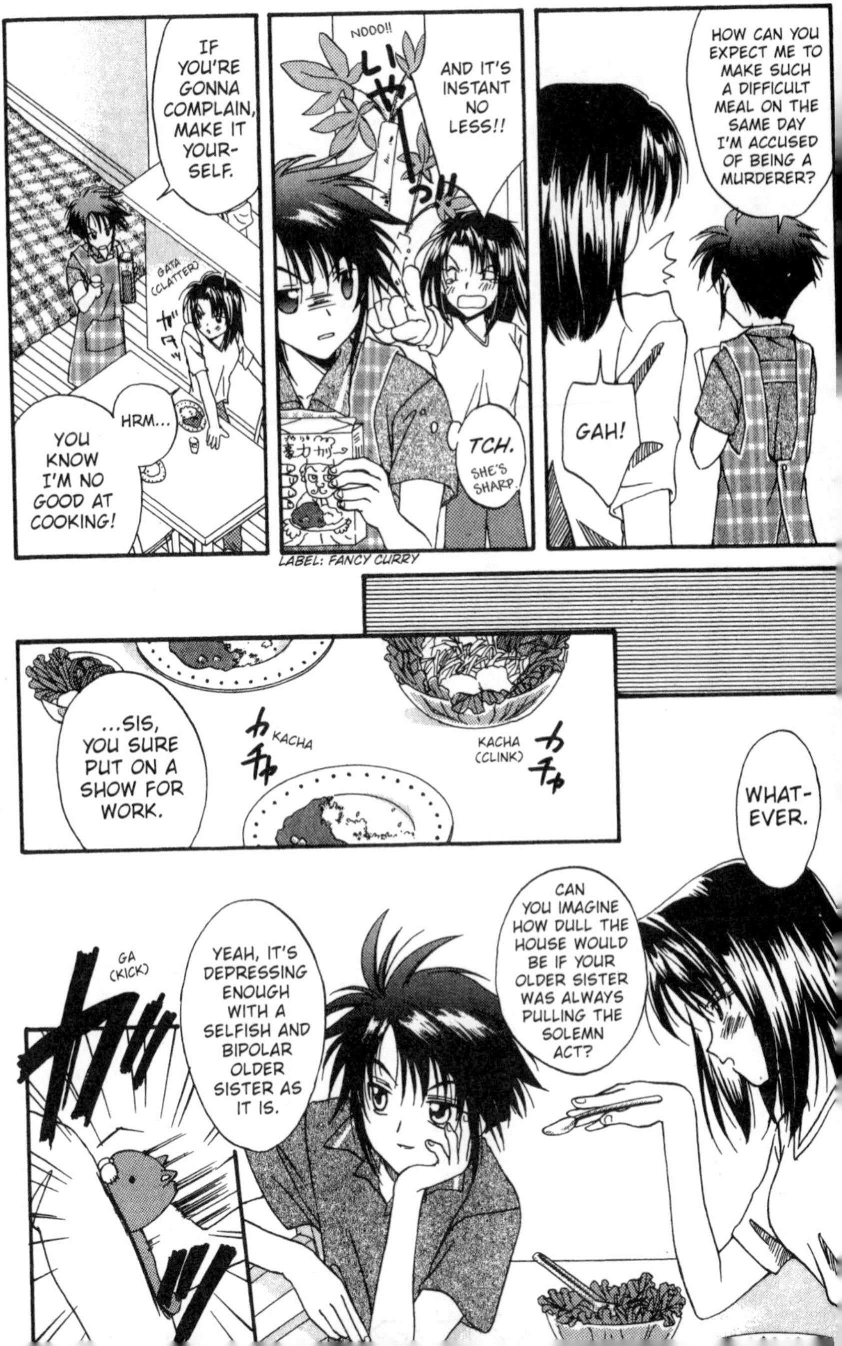
HOW CAN YOU EXPECT ME TO MAKE SUCH A DIFFICULT MEAL ON THE SAME DAY I'M ACCUSED OF BEING A MURDERER?
GAH!
NOOO!!
AND IT'S INSTANT NO LESS!!
TCH.
SHE'S SHARP.
LABEL: FANCY CURRY
IF YOU'RE GONNA COMPLAIN, MAKE IT YOUR-SELF.
GATA (CLATTER)
HRM...
YOU KNOW I'M NO GOOD AT COOKING!
KACHA (CLINK)
KACHA
...SIS, YOU SURE PUT ON A SHOW FOR WORK.
WHAT-EVER.
CAN YOU IMAGINE HOW DULL THE HOUSE WOULD BE IF YOUR OLDER SISTER WAS ALWAYS PULLING THE SOLEMN ACT?
YEAH, IT'S DEPRESSING ENOUGH WITH A SELFISH AND BIPOLAR OLDER SISTER AS IT IS.
GA (KICK)

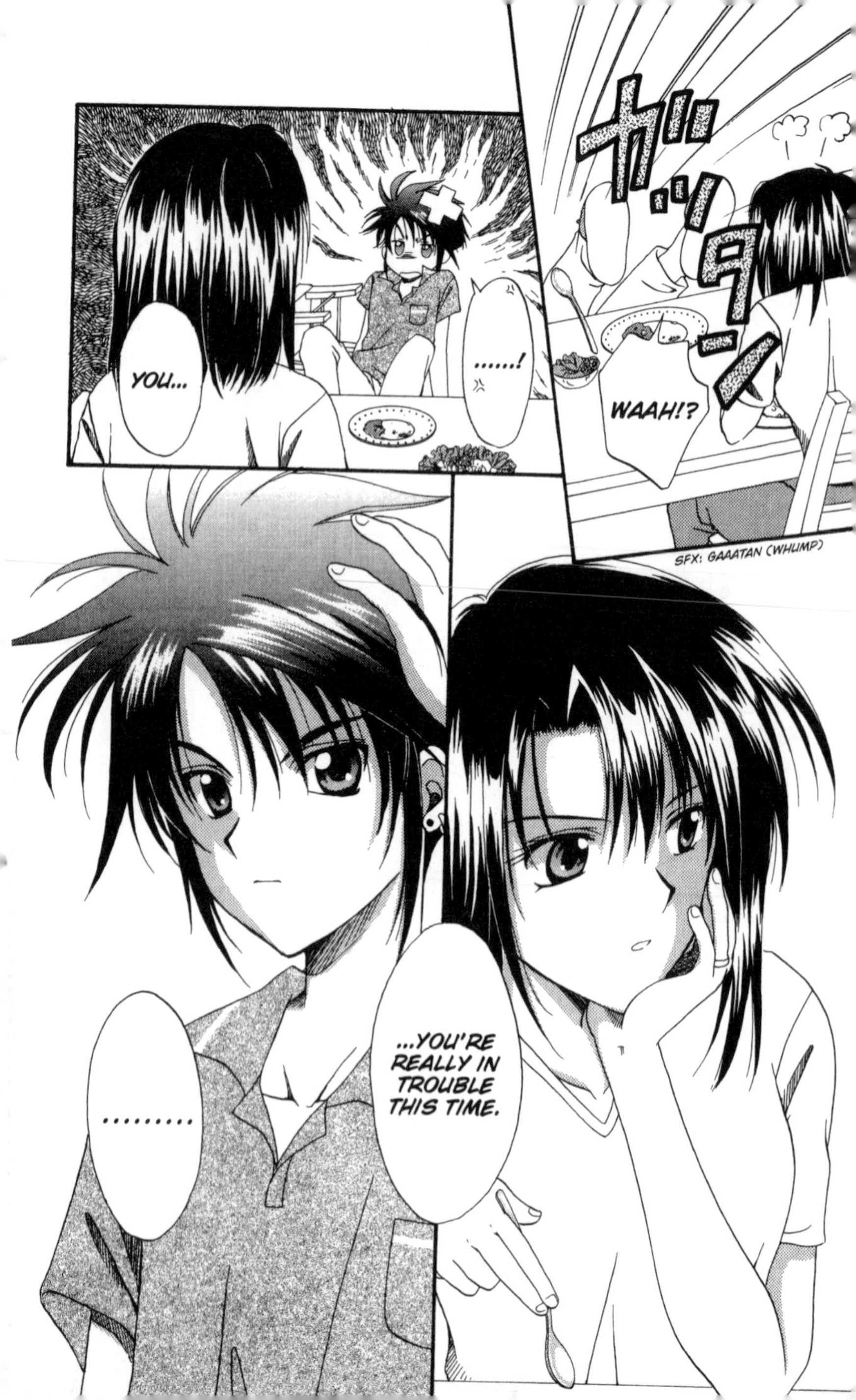
WAAH!?
SFX: GAAATAN (WHUMP)
......!
YOU...
...YOU'RE REALLY IN TROUBLE THIS TIME.
....

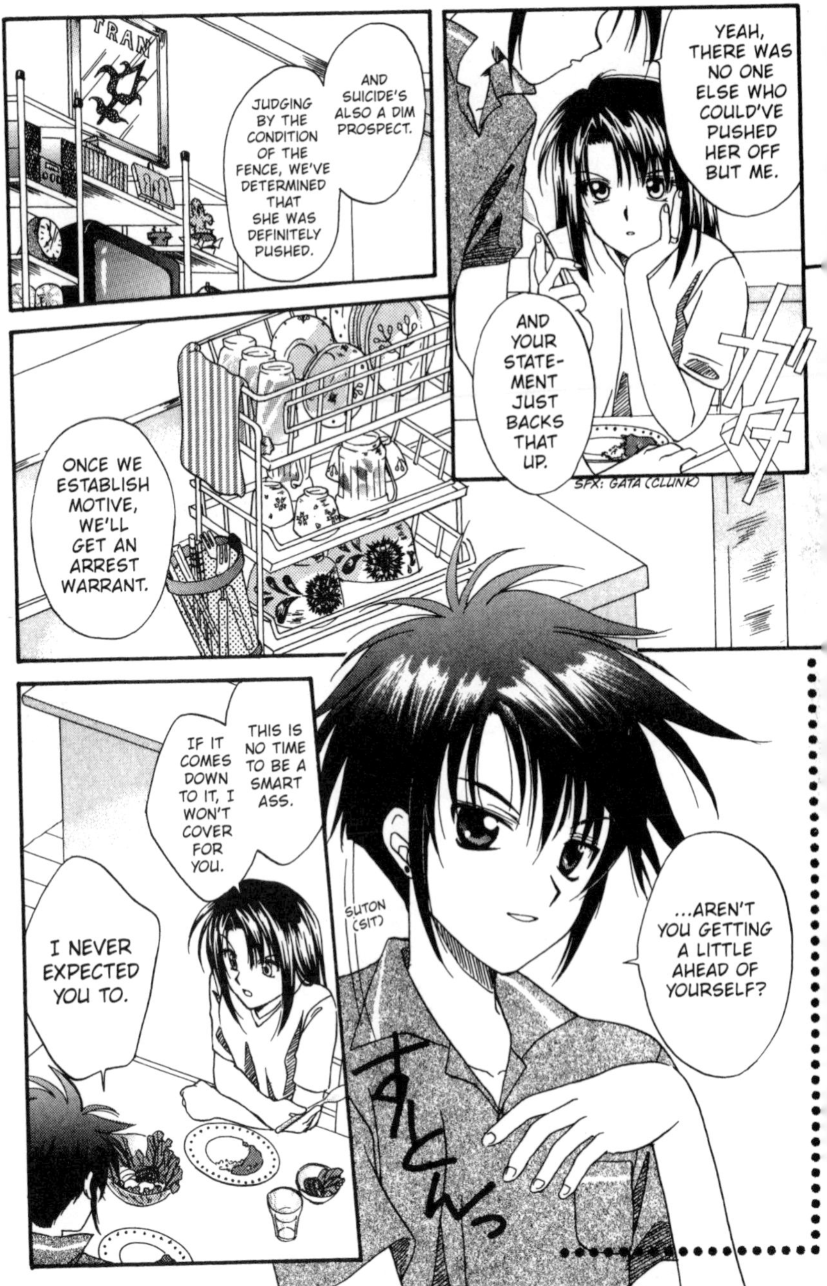

YEAH, THERE WAS NO ONE ELSE WHO COULD'VE PUSHED HER OFF BUT ME.
AND YOUR STATE-MENT JUST BACKS THAT UP.
SFX: GATA (CLUNK)
JUDGING BY THE CONDITION OF THE FENCE, WE'VE DETERMINED THAT SHE WAS DEFINITELY PUSHED.
AND SUICIDE'S ALSO A DIM PROSPECT.
TRAN
ONCE WE ESTABLISH MOTIVE, WE'LL GET AN ARREST WARRANT.
...AREN'T YOU GETTING A LITTLE AHEAD OF YOURSELF?
SUTON (SIT)
THIS IS NO TIME TO BE A SMART ASS.
IF IT COMES DOWN TO IT, I WON'T COVER FOR YOU.
I NEVER EXPECTED YOU TO.

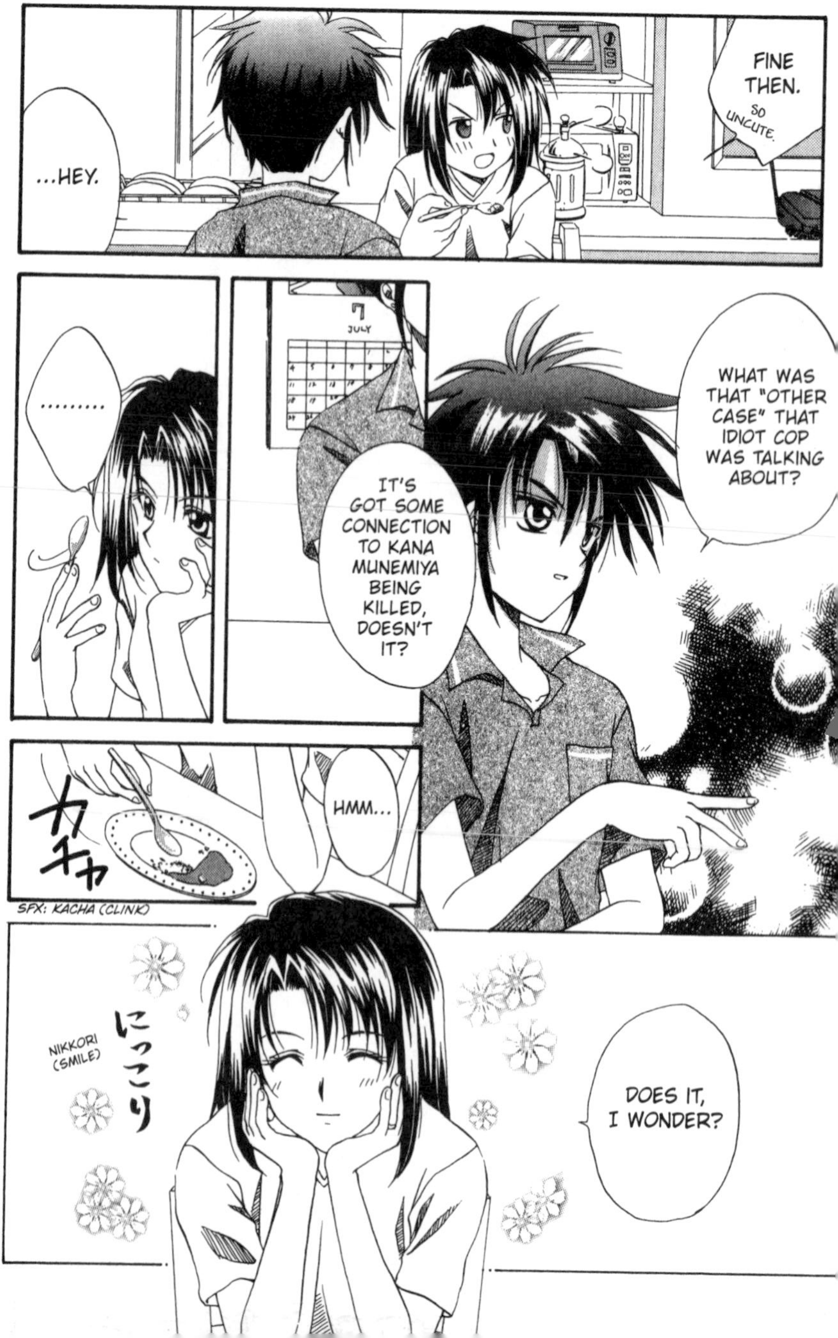
FINE THEN.
SO UNCUTE.
...HEY.
WHAT WAS THAT "OTHER CASE" THAT IDIOT COP WAS TALKING ABOUT?
IT'S GOT SOME CONNECTION TO KANA MUNEMIYA BEING KILLED, DOESN'T IT?
7
JULY
....
HMM...
カチャ
SFX: KACHA (CLINK)
にっこり
NIKKORI (SMILE)
DOES IT, I WONDER?

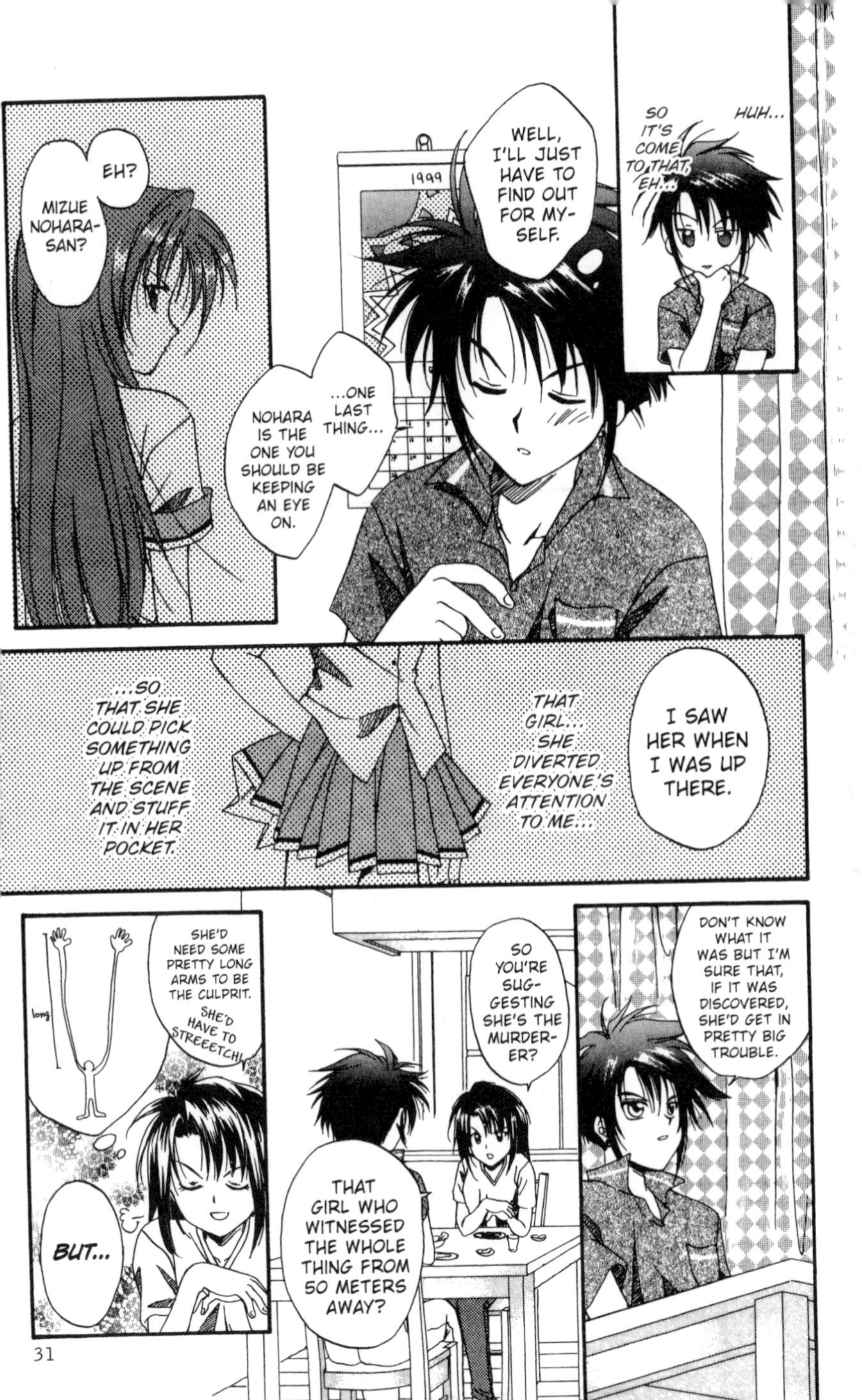
HUH...
SO IT'S COME TO THAT, EH...
WELL, I'LL JUST HAVE TO FIND OUT FOR MY-SELF.
...ONE LAST THING...
NOHARA IS THE ONE YOU SHOULD BE KEEPING AN EYE ON.
EH?
MIZUE NOHARA-SAN?
I SAW HER WHEN I WAS UP THERE.
THAT GIRL... SHE DIVERTED EVERYONE'S ATTENTION TO ME...
...SO THAT SHE COULD PICK SOMETHING UP FROM THE SCENE AND STUFF IT IN HER POCKET.
DON'T KNOW WHAT IT WAS BUT I'M SURE THAT, IF IT WAS DISCOVERED, SHE'D GET IN PRETTY BIG TROUBLE.
SO YOU'RE SUG-GESTING SHE'S THE MURDER-ER?
THAT GIRL WHO WITNESSED THE WHOLE THING FROM 50 METERS AWAY?
SHE'D NEED SOME PRETTY LONG ARMS TO BE THE CULPRIT.
SHE'D HAVE TO STREEETCH!
long
BUT...

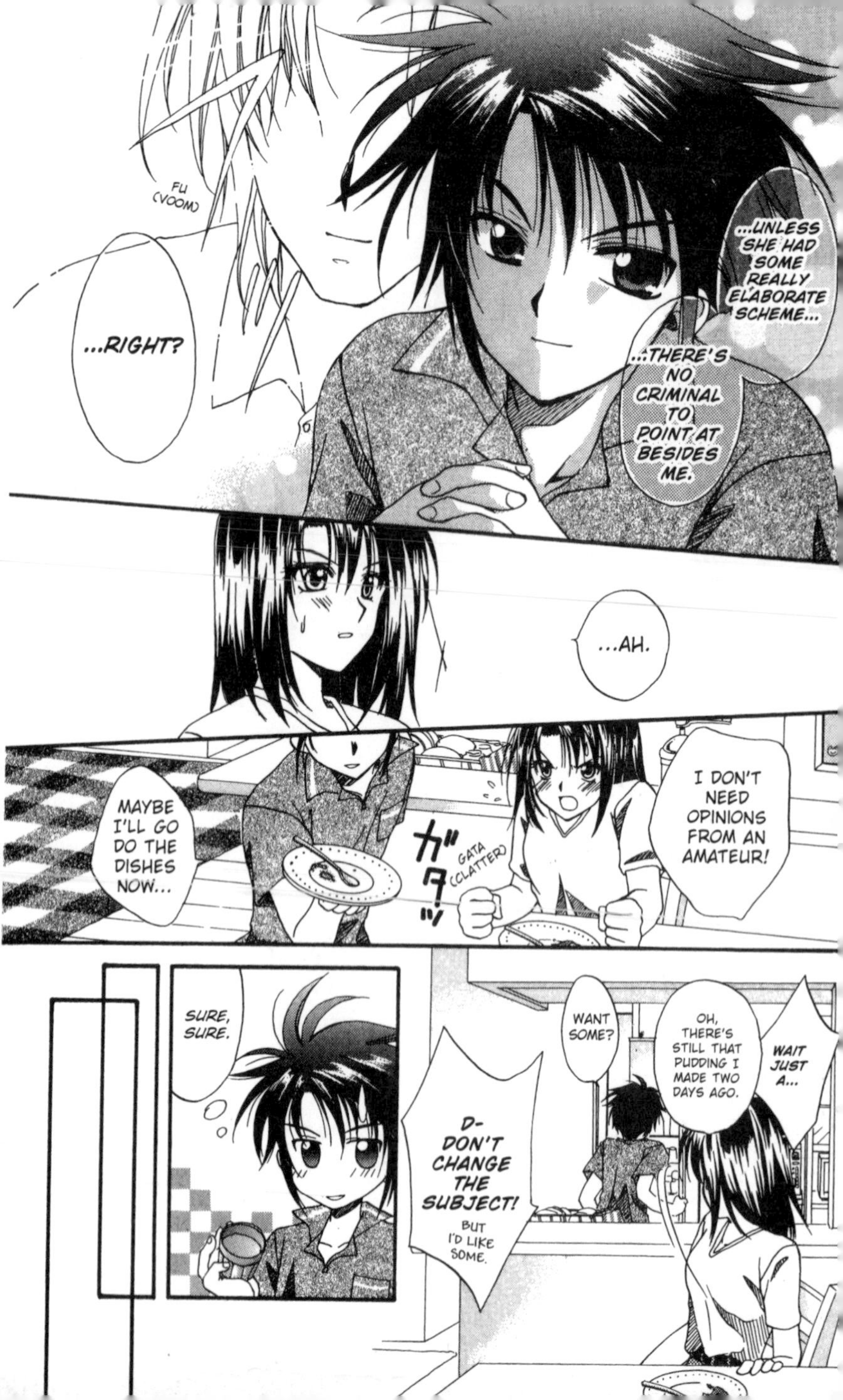
...UNLESS SHE HAD SOME REALLY ELABORATE SCHEME...
...THERE'S NO CRIMINAL TO POINT AT BESIDES ME.
FU (VOOM)
...RIGHT?
...AH.
I DON'T NEED OPINIONS FROM AN AMATEUR!
GATA (CLATTER)
MAYBE I'LL GO DO THE DISHES NOW...
WAIT JUST A...
OH, THERE'S STILL THAT PUDDING I MADE TWO DAYS AGO.
WANT SOME?
D-DON'T CHANGE THE SUBJECT!
BUT I'D LIKE SOME.
SURE, SURE.

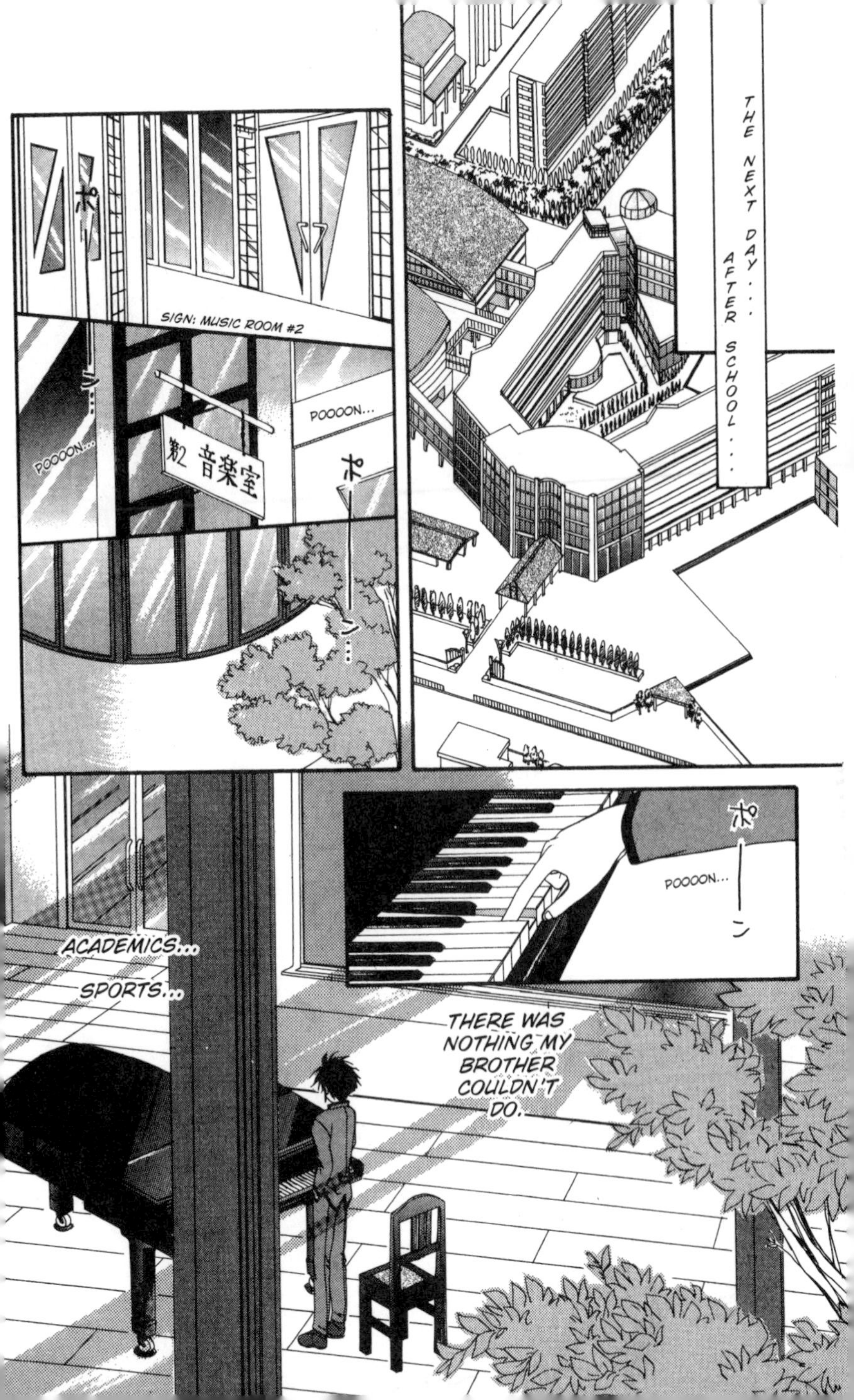
THE NEXT DAY... AFTER SCHOOL...
ポ
SIGN: MUSIC ROOM #2
第2 音楽室
POOOON...
ポ
POOOON...
ポーン
POOOON...
ACADEMICS...
SPORTS...
THERE WAS NOTHING MY BROTHER COULDN'T DO.

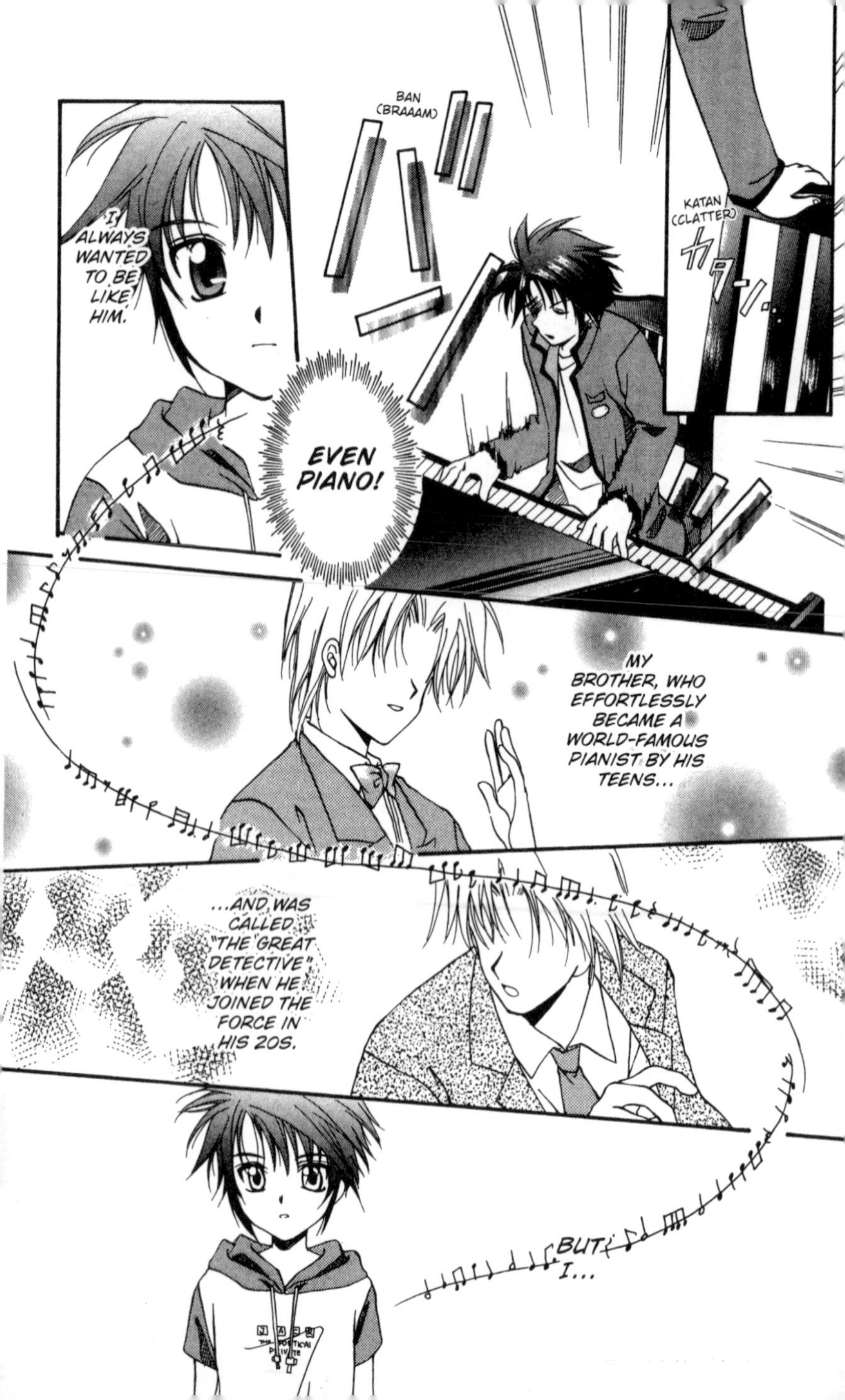
KATAN (CLATTER)
BAN (BRAAAM)
EVEN PIANO!
I ALWAYS WANTED TO BE LIKE HIM.
MY BROTHER, WHO EFFORTLESSLY BECAME A WORLD-FAMOUS PIANIST BY HIS TEENS...
...AND WAS CALLED "THE GREAT DETECTIVE" WHEN HE JOINED THE FORCE IN HIS 20S.
BUT I...

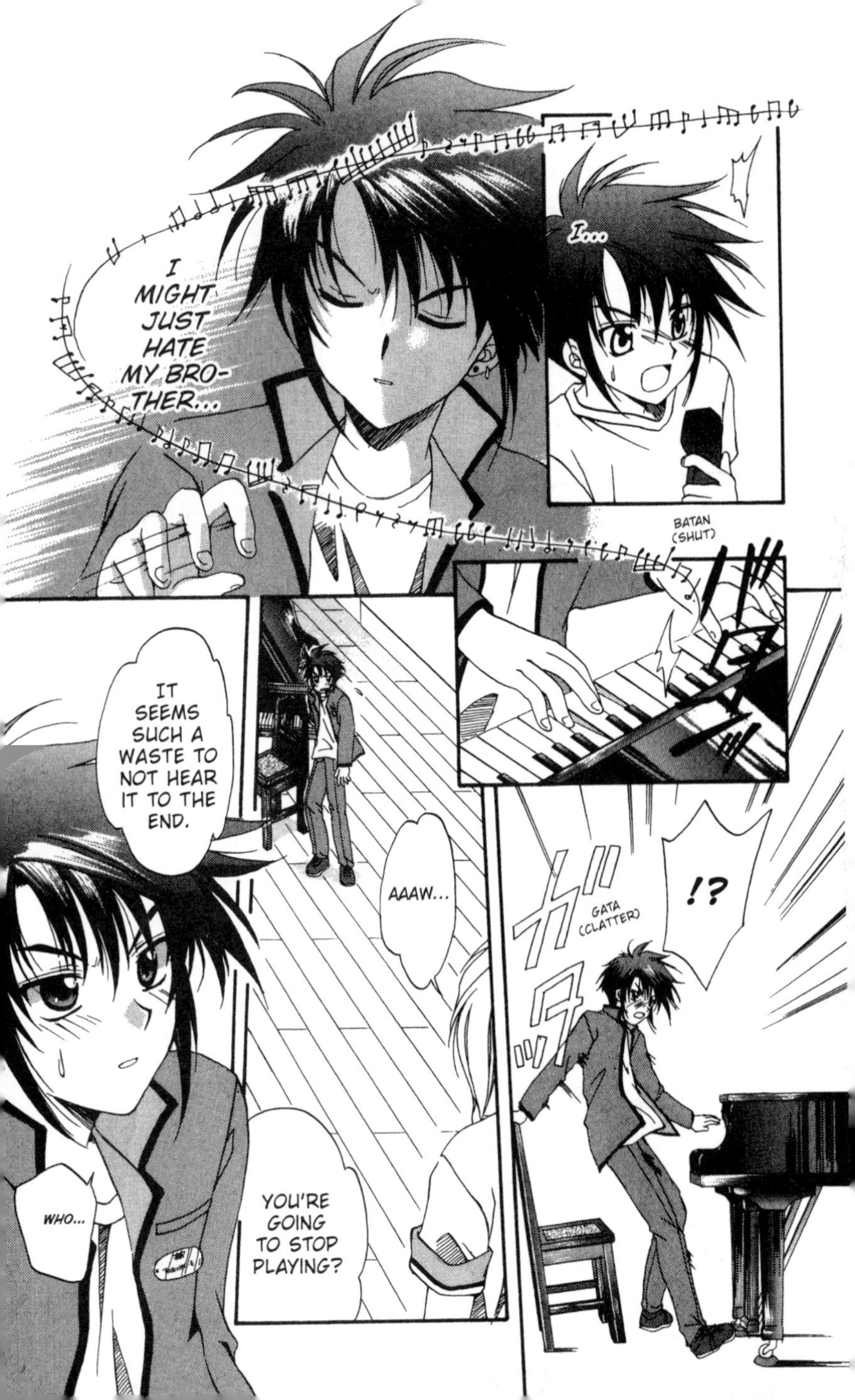
I...
I MIGHT JUST HATE MY BRO-THER...
BATAN (SHUT)
!?
GATA (CLATTER)
AAAW...
YOU'RE GOING TO STOP PLAYING?
IT SEEMS SUCH A WASTE TO NOT HEAR IT TO THE END.
WHO...

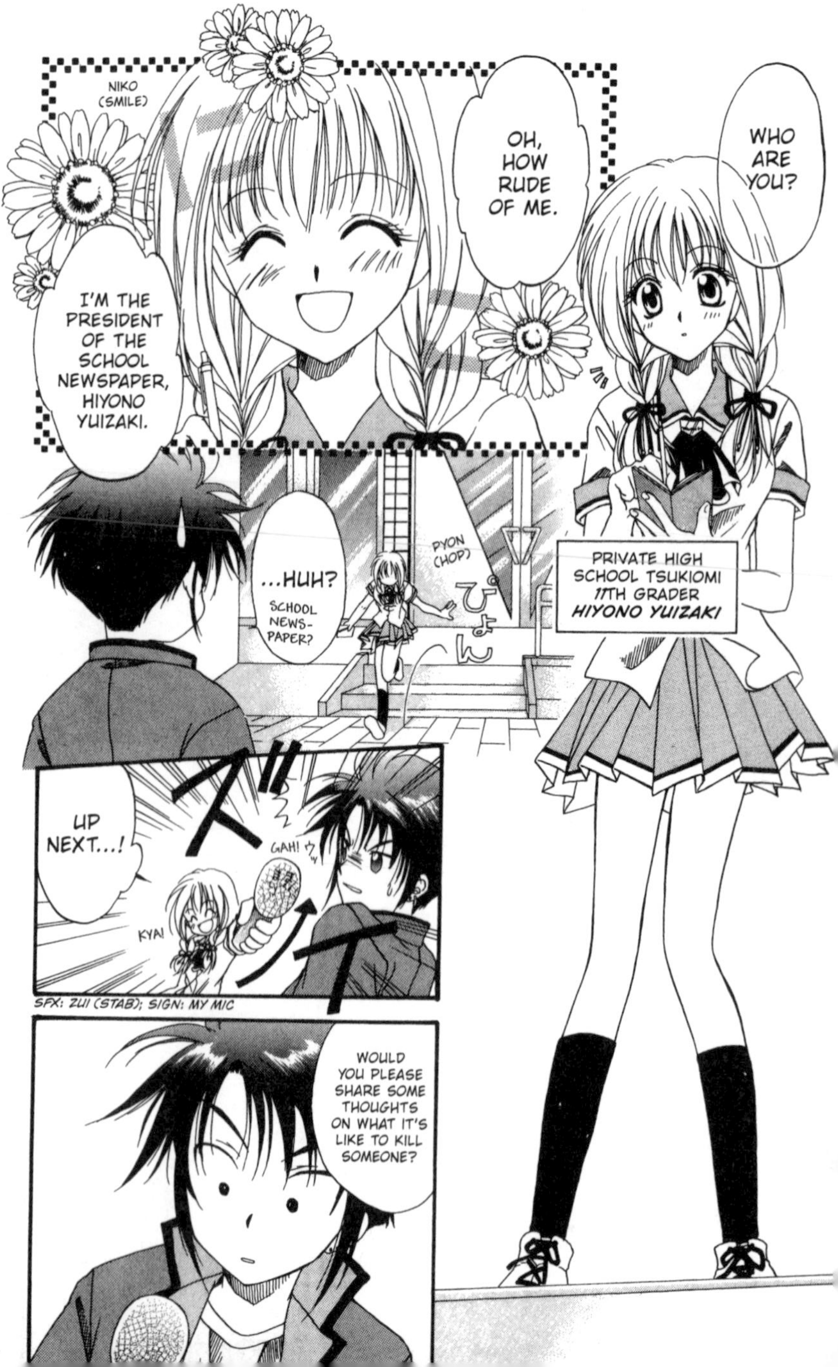
WHO ARE YOU?
PRIVATE HIGH SCHOOL TSUKIOMI 11TH GRADER *HIYONO YUIZAKI*
OH, HOW RUDE OF ME.
NIKO (SMILE)
I'M THE PRESIDENT OF THE SCHOOL NEWSPAPER, HIYONO YUIZAKI.
PYON (HOP)
...HUH?
SCHOOL NEWS-PAPER?
UP NEXT...!
GAH!
KYA!
SFX: ZUI (STAB); SIGN: MY MIC
WOULD YOU PLEASE SHARE SOME THOUGHTS ON WHAT IT'S LIKE TO KILL SOMEONE?

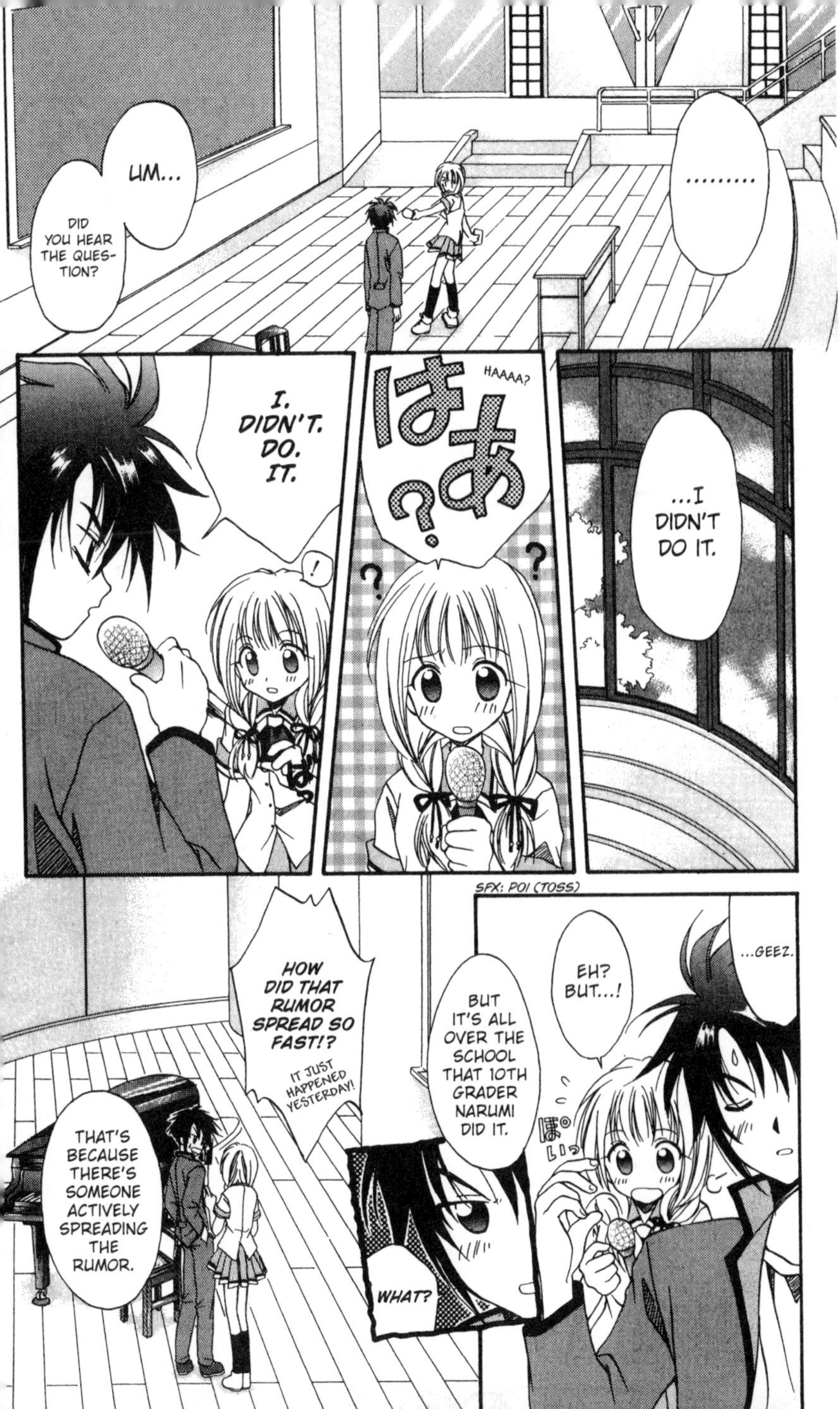
....
UM...
DID YOU HEAR THE QUESTION?
...I DIDN'T DO IT.
はあ？
HAAAA?
I. DIDN'T. DO. IT.
!
SFX: POI (TOSS)
...GEEZ.
EH? BUT...!
BUT IT'S ALL OVER THE SCHOOL THAT 10TH GRADER NARUMI DID IT.
ぽいっ
WHAT?
HOW DID THAT RUMOR SPREAD SO FAST!?
IT JUST HAPPENED YESTERDAY!
THAT'S BECAUSE THERE'S SOMEONE ACTIVELY SPREADING THE RUMOR.

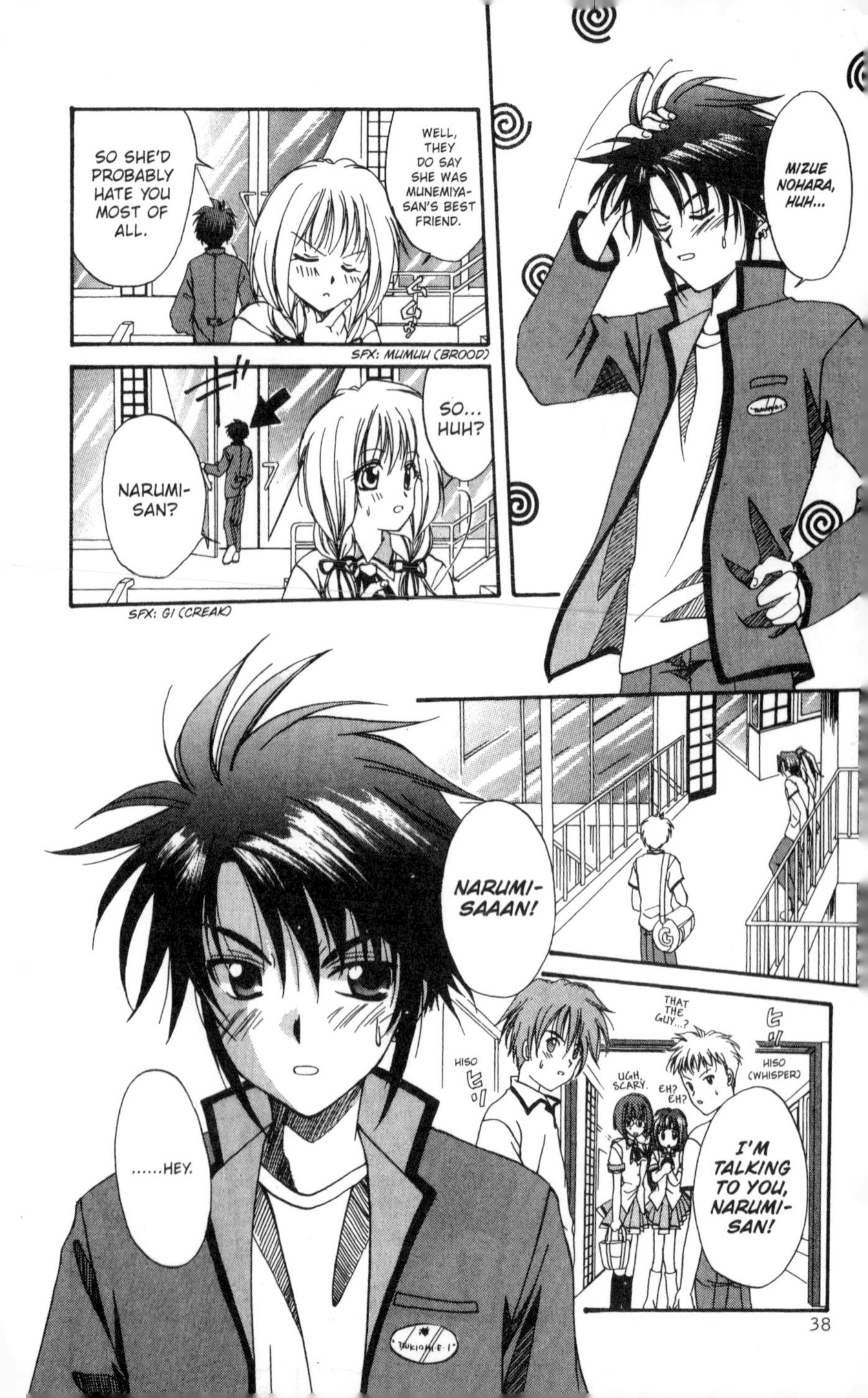
MIZUE NOHARA, HUH...
WELL, THEY DO SAY SHE WAS MUNEMIYA-SAN'S BEST FRIEND.
SO SHE'D PROBABLY HATE YOU MOST OF ALL.
SFX: MUMUU (BROOD)
SO... HUH?
NARUMI-SAN?
SFX: GI (CREAK)
NARUMI-SAAAN!
HISO (WHISPER)
THAT THE GUY...?
EH? EH?
UGH, SCARY.
HISO
I'M TALKING TO YOU, NARUMI-SAN!
......HEY.

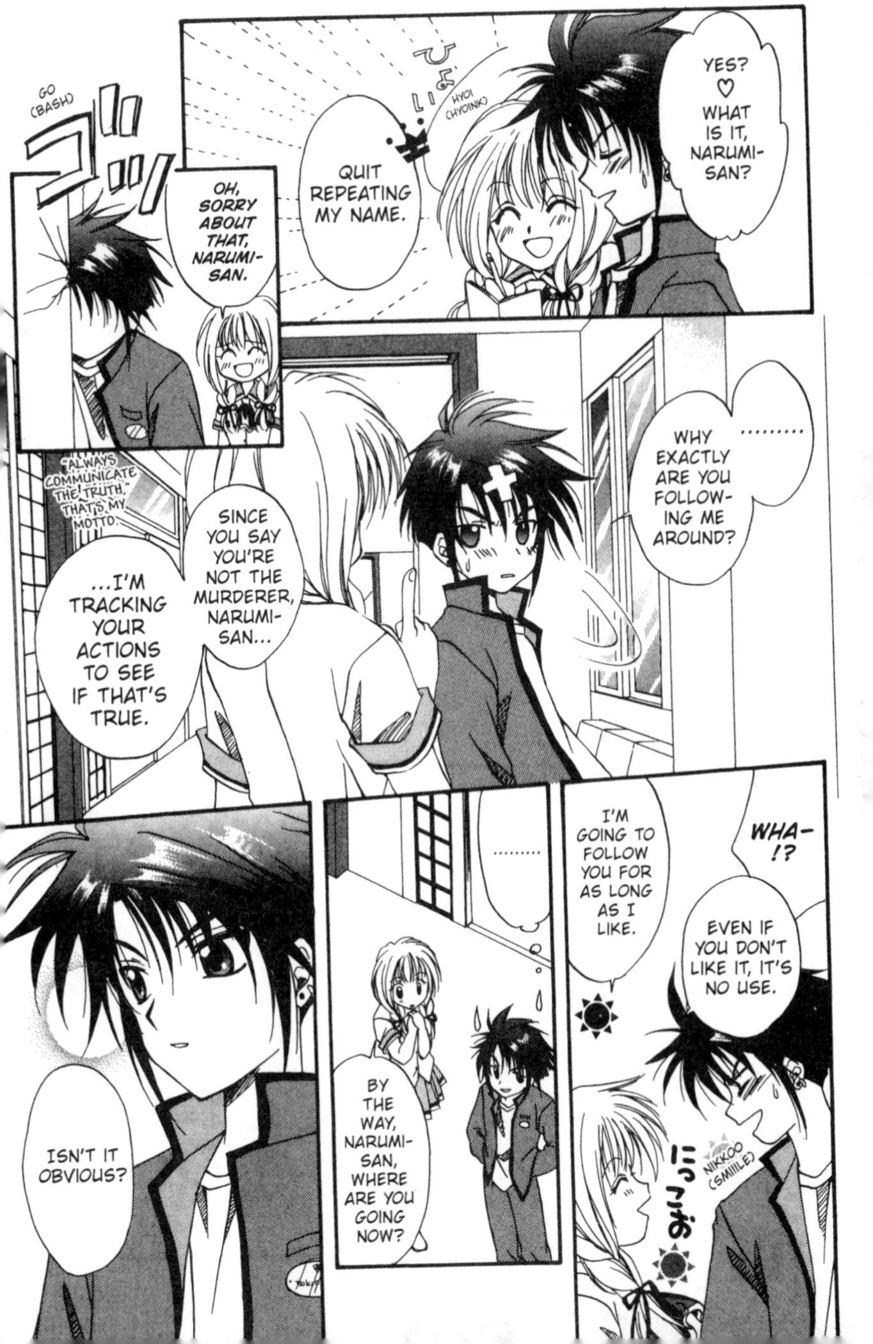

YES? ♡ WHAT IS IT, NARUMI-SAN?
HYOI (HYOINK)
QUIT REPEATING MY NAME.
GO (BASH)
OH, SORRY ABOUT THAT, NARUMI-SAN.
....
WHY EXACTLY ARE YOU FOLLOWING ME AROUND?
SINCE YOU SAY YOU'RE NOT THE MURDERER, NARUMI-SAN...
...I'M TRACKING YOUR ACTIONS TO SEE IF THAT'S TRUE.
"ALWAYS COMMUNICATE THE TRUTH." THAT'S MY MOTTO.
WHA-!?
I'M GOING TO FOLLOW YOU FOR AS LONG AS I LIKE.
EVEN IF YOU DON'T LIKE IT, IT'S NO USE.
NIKKOO (SMIIILE)
....
BY THE WAY, NARUMI-SAN, WHERE ARE YOU GOING NOW?
ISN'T IT OBVIOUS?

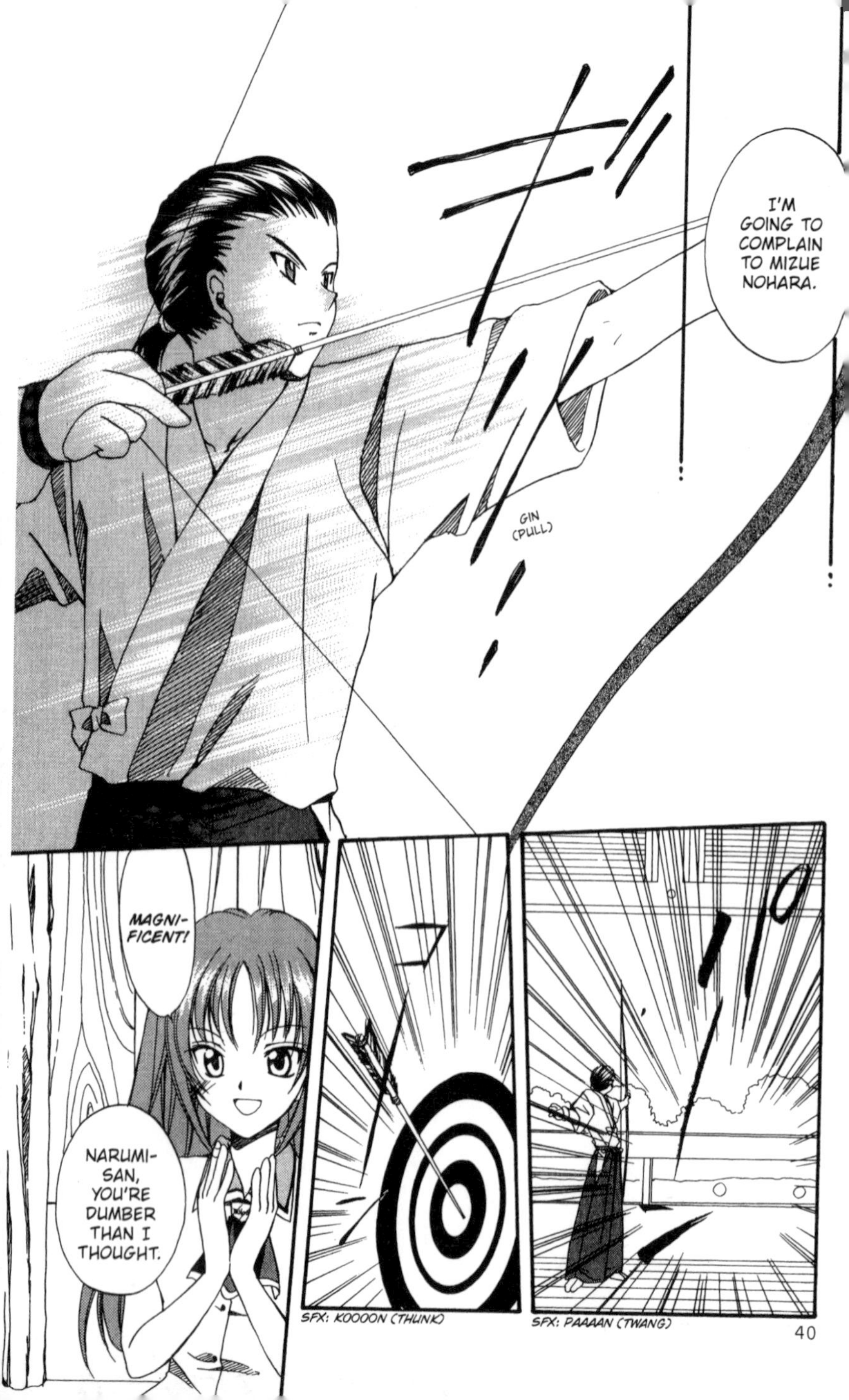
I'M GOING TO COMPLAIN TO MIZUE NOHARA.
GIN (PULL)
SFX: PAAAAN (TWANG)
SFX: KOOOON (THUNK)
MAGNI-FICENT!
NARUMI-SAN, YOU'RE DUMBER THAN I THOUGHT.

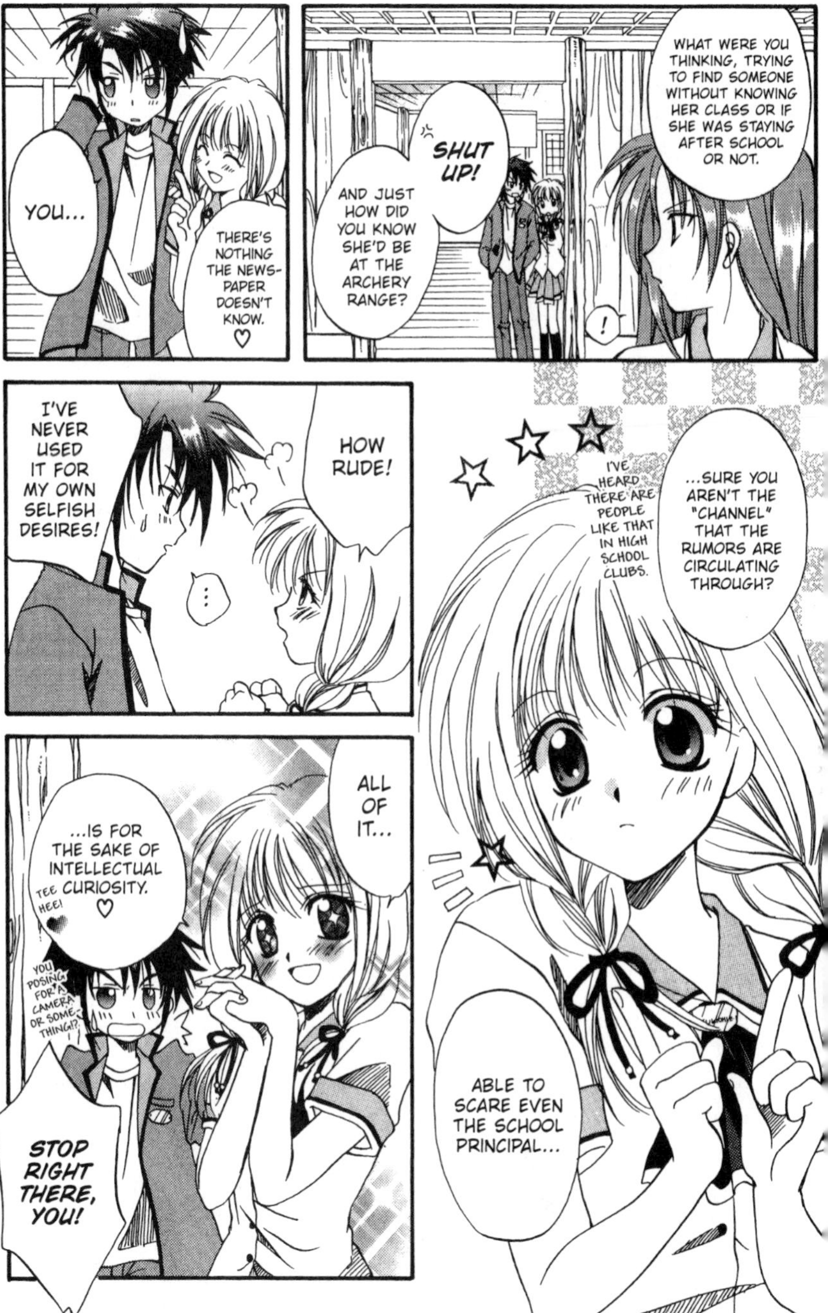
WHAT WERE YOU THINKING, TRYING TO FIND SOMEONE WITHOUT KNOWING HER CLASS OR IF SHE WAS STAYING AFTER SCHOOL OR NOT.
SHUT UP!
AND JUST HOW DID YOU KNOW SHE'D BE AT THE ARCHERY RANGE?
!
THERE'S NOTHING THE NEWS-PAPER DOESN'T KNOW. ♡
YOU...
...SURE YOU AREN'T THE "CHANNEL" THAT THE RUMORS ARE CIRCULATING THROUGH?
I'VE HEARD THERE ARE PEOPLE LIKE THAT IN HIGH SCHOOL CLUBS.
ABLE TO SCARE EVEN THE SCHOOL PRINCIPAL...
HOW RUDE!
I'VE NEVER USED IT FOR MY OWN SELFISH DESIRES!
...
ALL OF IT...
...IS FOR THE SAKE OF INTELLECTUAL CURIOSITY. ♡
TEE HEE!
YOU POSING FOR A CAMERA OR SOME-THING!?
STOP RIGHT THERE, YOU!

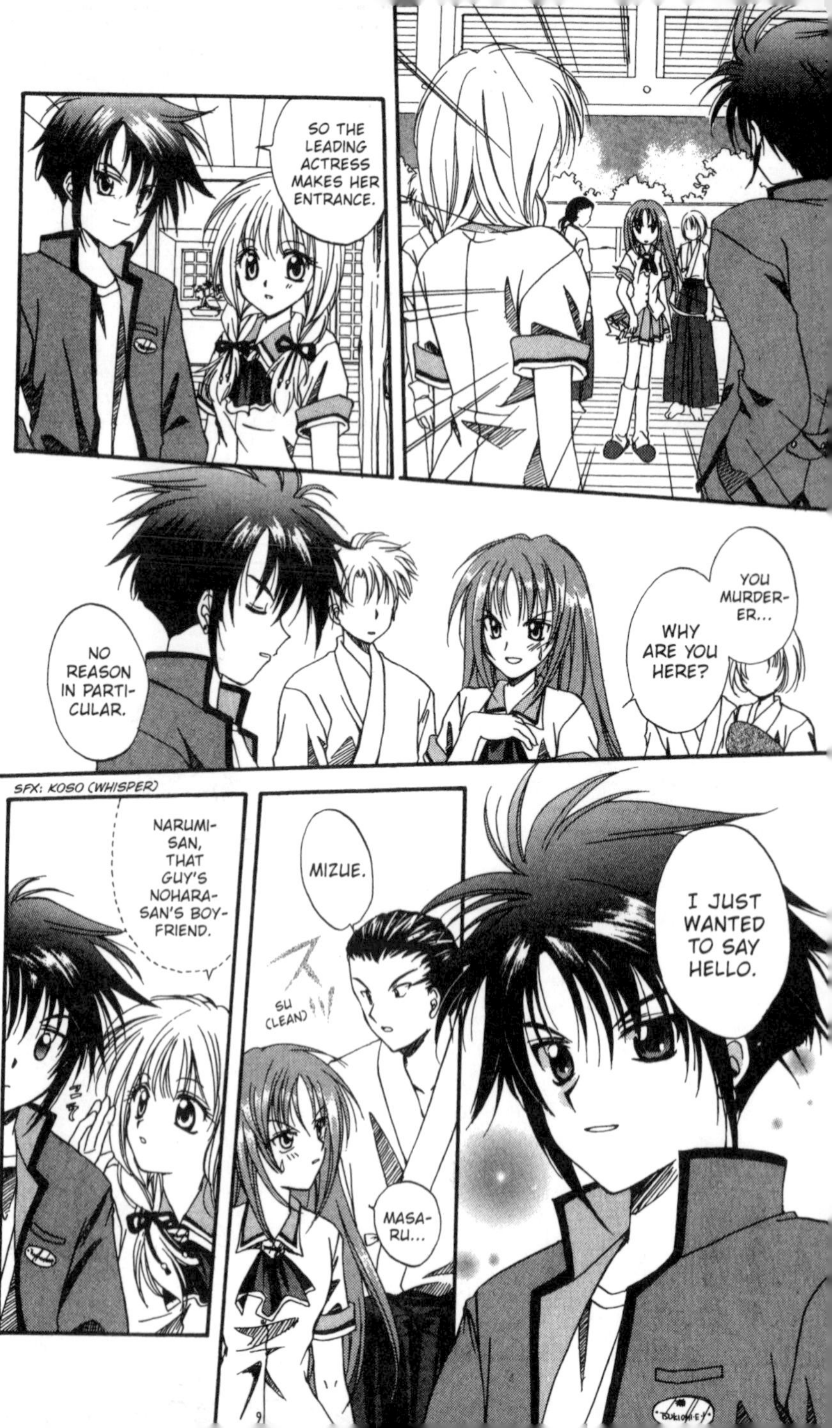
SO THE LEADING ACTRESS MAKES HER ENTRANCE.
YOU MURDERER...
WHY ARE YOU HERE?
NO REASON IN PARTICULAR.
I JUST WANTED TO SAY HELLO.
MIZUE.
SU (LEAN)
MASARU...
SFX: KOSO (WHISPER)
NARUMI-SAN, THAT GUY'S NOHARA-SAN'S BOYFRIEND.

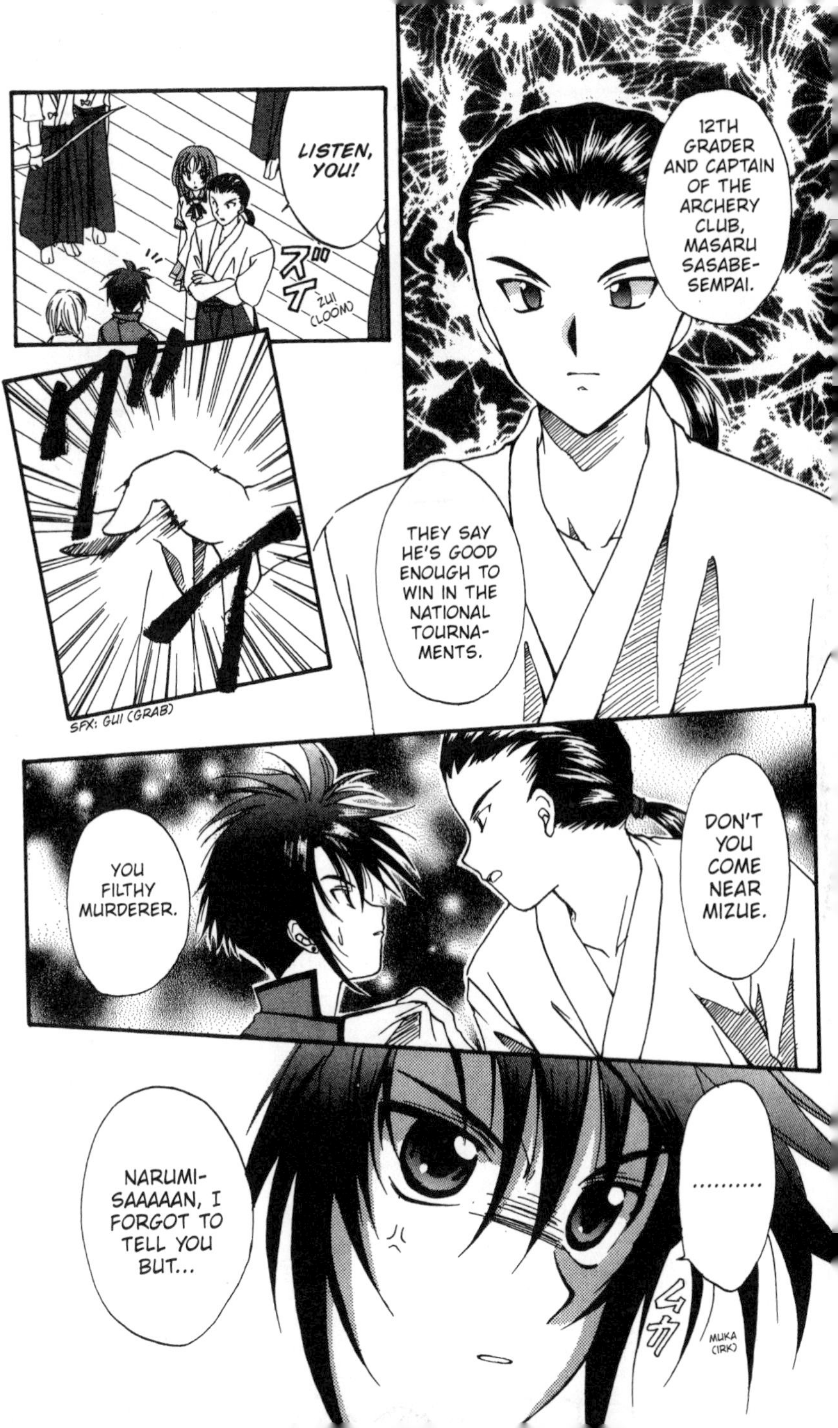
12TH GRADER AND CAPTAIN OF THE ARCHERY CLUB, MASARU SASABE-SEMPAI.
THEY SAY HE'S GOOD ENOUGH TO WIN IN THE NATIONAL TOURNAMENTS.
LISTEN, YOU!
ZUI (LOOM)
SFX: GUI (GRAB)
DON'T YOU COME NEAR MIZUE.
YOU FILTHY MURDERER.
....
MUKA (IRK)
NARUMI-SAAAAAN, I FORGOT TO TELL YOU BUT...

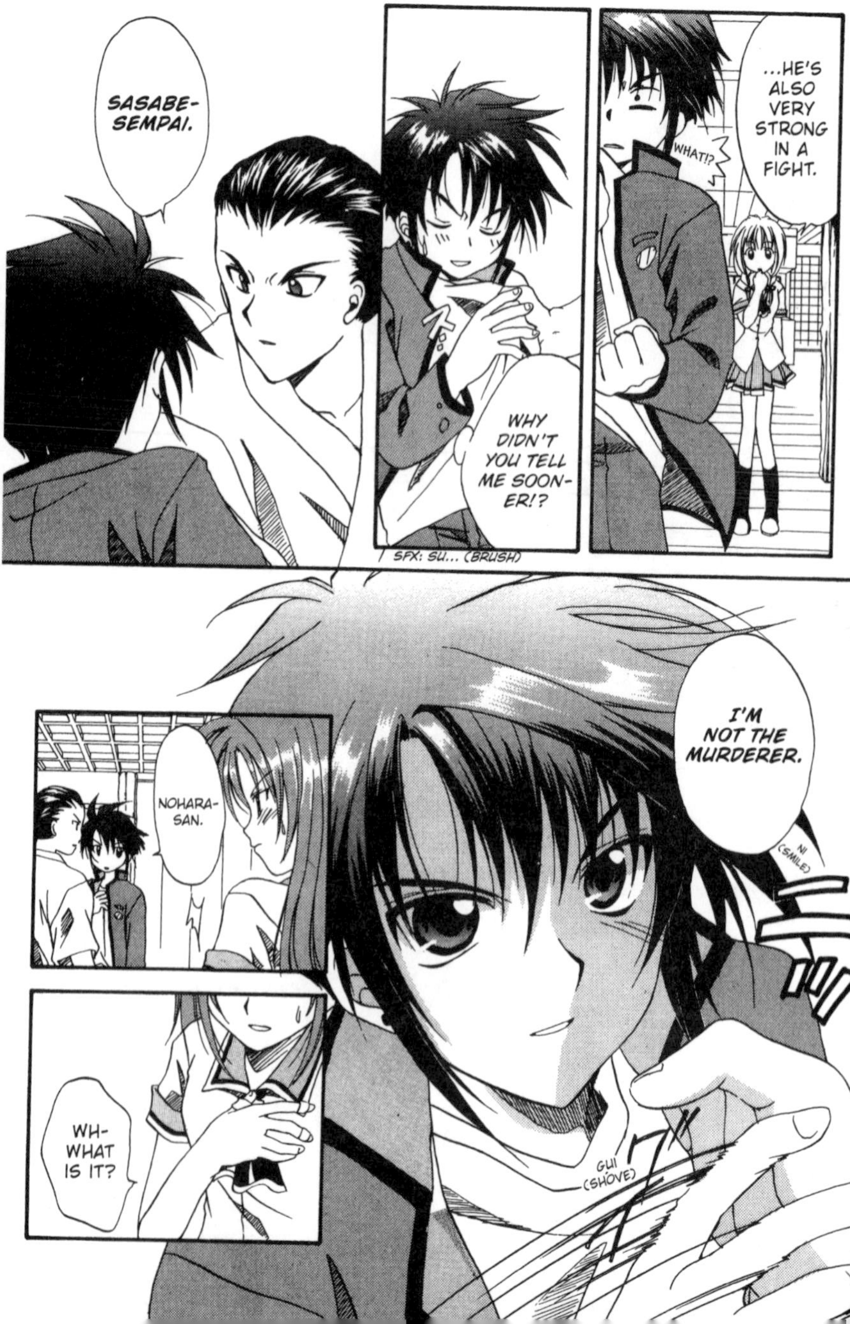
...HE'S ALSO VERY STRONG IN A FIGHT.
WHAT!?
WHY DIDN'T YOU TELL ME SOONER!?
SFX: SU... (BRUSH)
SASABE-SEMPAI.
I'M NOT THE MURDERER.
NI (SMILE)
GUI (SHOVE)
NOHARA-SAN.
WH-WHAT IS IT?

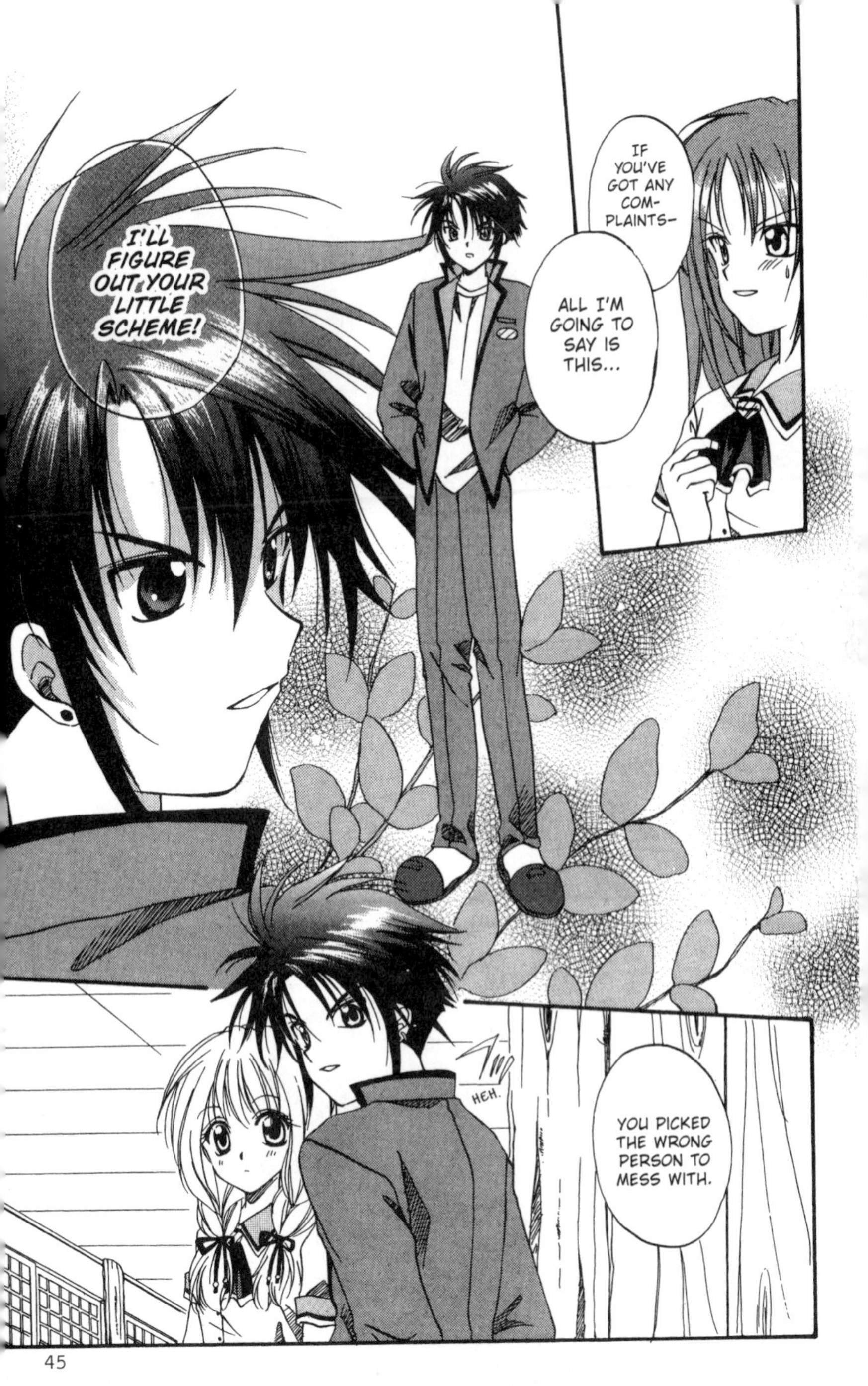
IF YOU'VE GOT ANY COMPLAINTS–
ALL I'M GOING TO SAY IS THIS...
I'LL FIGURE OUT YOUR LITTLE SCHEME!
HEH.
YOU PICKED THE WRONG PERSON TO MESS WITH.

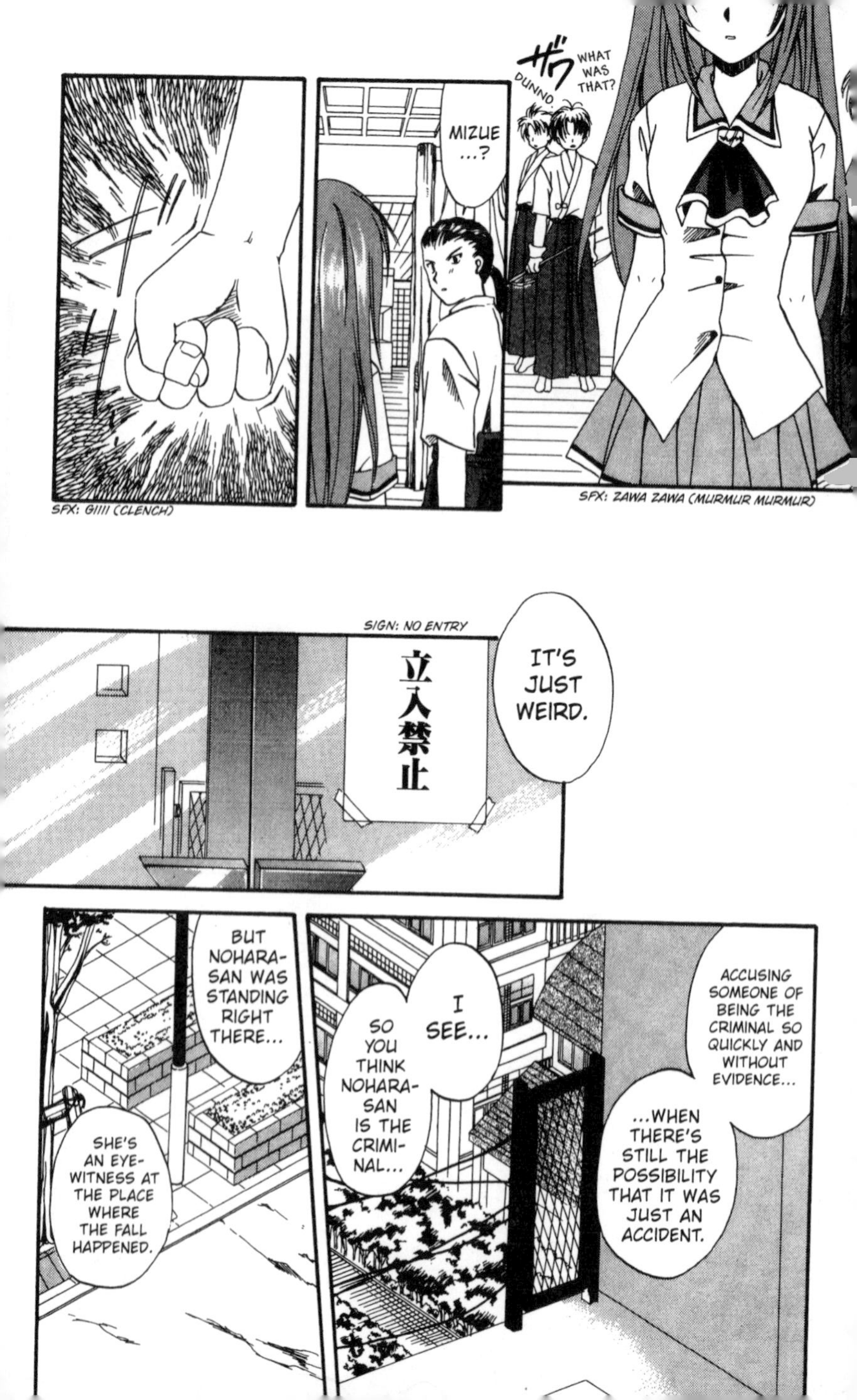
ザワ
WHAT WAS THAT?
DUNNO.
SFX: ZAWA ZAWA (MURMUR MURMUR)
MIZUE ...?
SFX: GIIII (CLENCH)
IT'S JUST WEIRD.
SIGN: NO ENTRY
立入禁止
ACCUSING SOMEONE OF BEING THE CRIMINAL SO QUICKLY AND WITHOUT EVIDENCE...
...WHEN THERE'S STILL THE POSSIBILITY THAT IT WAS JUST AN ACCIDENT.
I SEE...
SO YOU THINK NOHARA-SAN IS THE CRIMINAL...
BUT NOHARA-SAN WAS STANDING RIGHT THERE...
SHE'S AN EYE-WITNESS AT THE PLACE WHERE THE FALL HAPPENED.

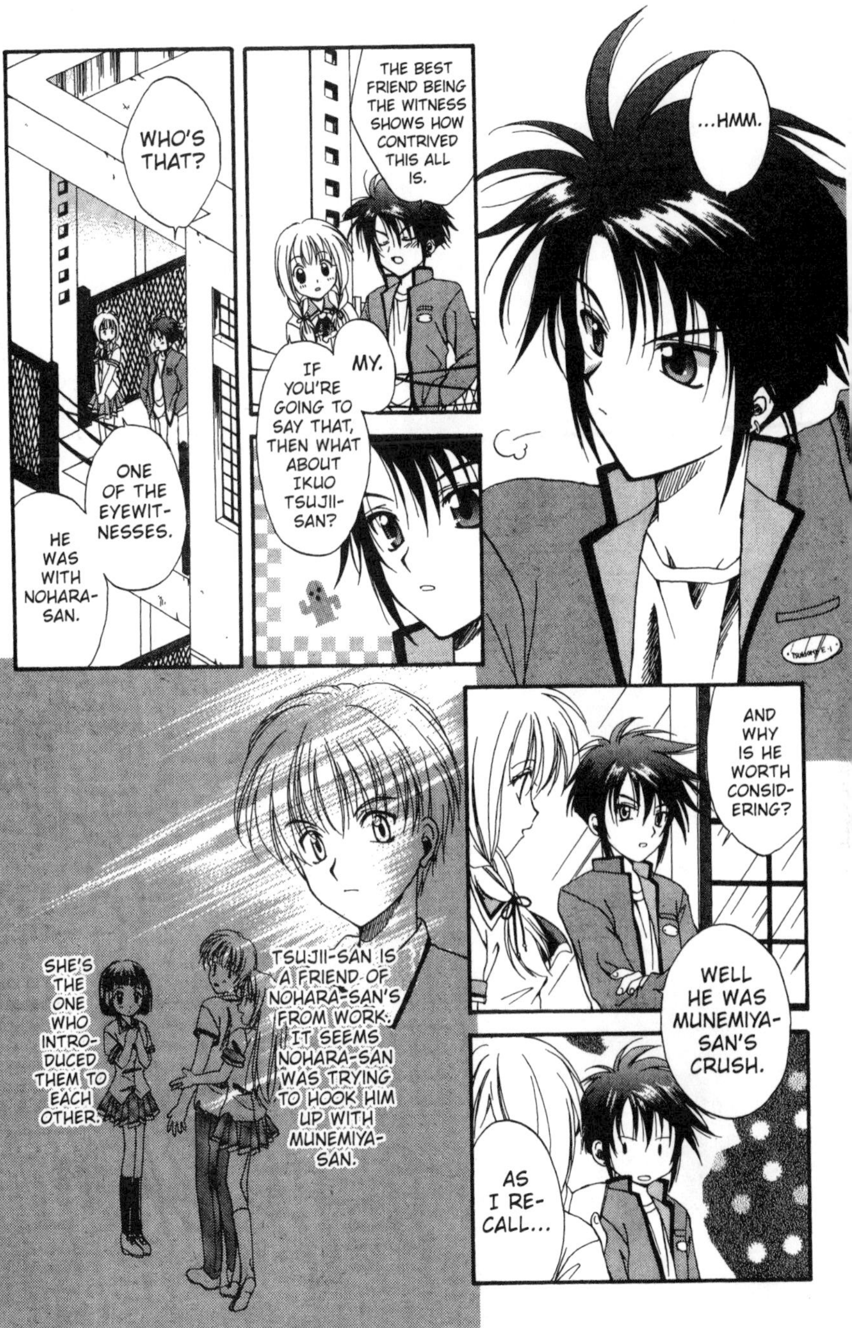
...HMM.
THE BEST FRIEND BEING THE WITNESS SHOWS HOW CONTRIVED THIS ALL IS.
MY.
IF YOU'RE GOING TO SAY THAT, THEN WHAT ABOUT IKUO TSUJII-SAN?
WHO'S THAT?
ONE OF THE EYEWIT-NESSES.
HE WAS WITH NOHARA-SAN.
AND WHY IS HE WORTH CONSID-ERING?
WELL HE WAS MUNEMIYA-SAN'S CRUSH.
AS I RE-CALL...
TSUJII-SAN IS A FRIEND OF NOHARA-SAN'S FROM WORK. IT SEEMS NOHARA-SAN WAS TRYING TO HOOK HIM UP WITH MUNEMIYA-SAN.
SHE'S THE ONE WHO INTRO-DUCED THEM TO EACH OTHER.

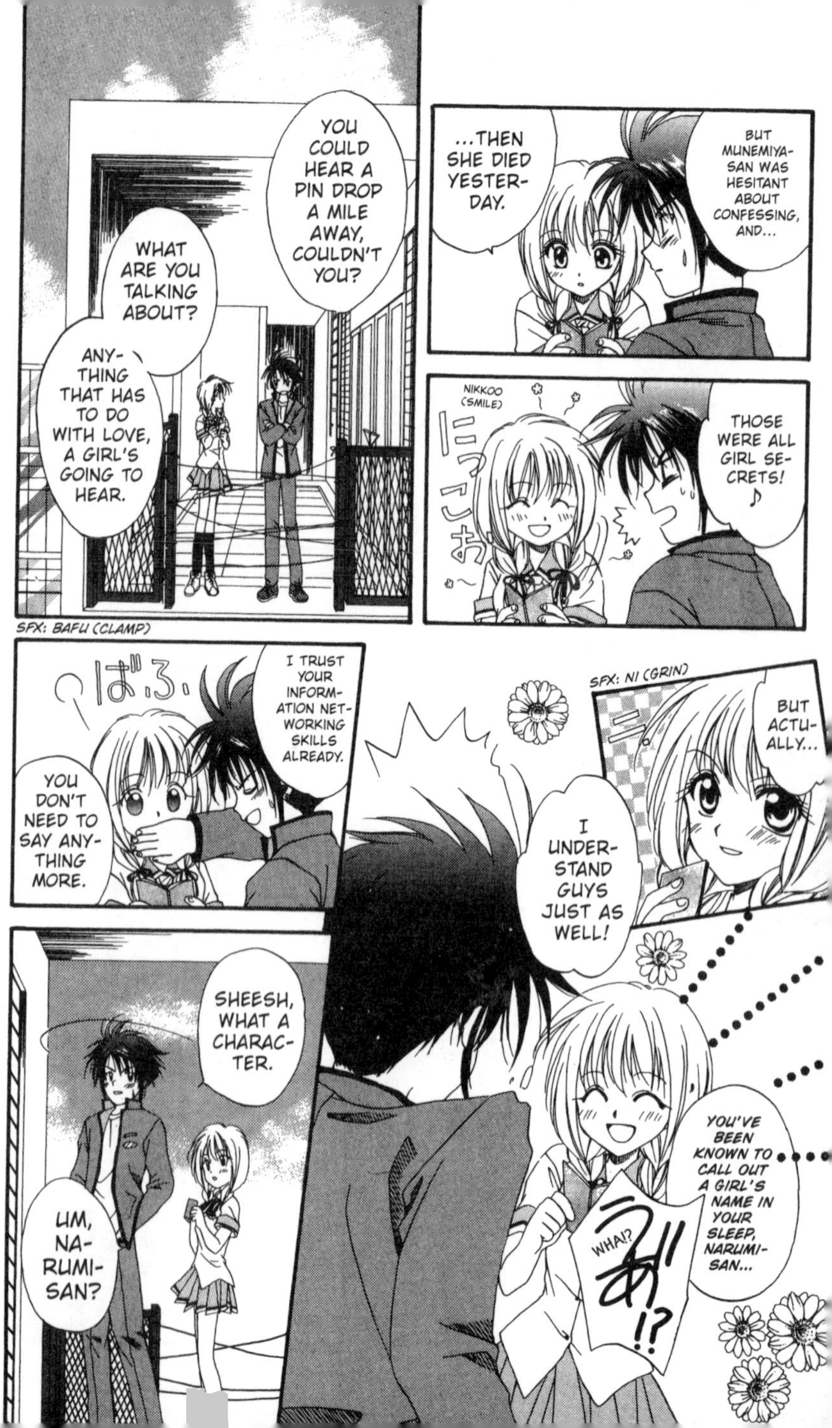
BUT MUNEMIYA-SAN WAS HESITANT ABOUT CONFESSING, AND...
...THEN SHE DIED YESTERDAY.
NIKKOO (SMILE)
THOSE WERE ALL GIRL SECRETS! ♪
YOU COULD HEAR A PIN DROP A MILE AWAY, COULDN'T YOU?
WHAT ARE YOU TALKING ABOUT?
ANYTHING THAT HAS TO DO WITH LOVE, A GIRL'S GOING TO HEAR.
SFX: BAFU (CLAMP)
SFX: NI (GRIN)
BUT ACTUALLY...
I TRUST YOUR INFORMATION NETWORKING SKILLS ALREADY.
YOU DON'T NEED TO SAY ANYTHING MORE.
I UNDERSTAND GUYS JUST AS WELL!
YOU'VE BEEN KNOWN TO CALL OUT A GIRL'S NAME IN YOUR SLEEP, NARUMI-SAN...
WHA!?
SHEESH, WHAT A CHARACTER.
UM, NARUMI-SAN?

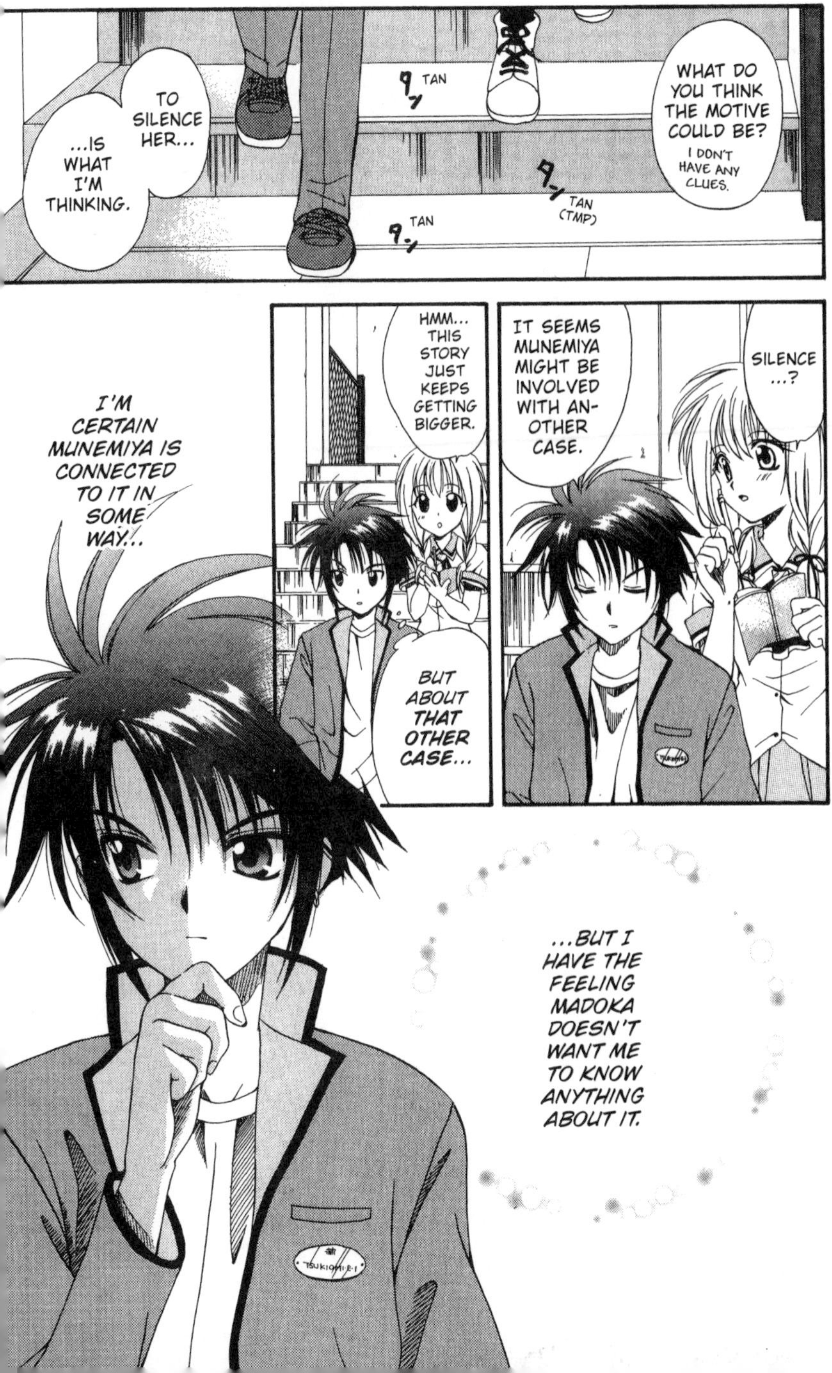
WHAT DO YOU THINK THE MOTIVE COULD BE?
I DON'T HAVE ANY CLUES.
TAN (TMP)
TAN
TAN
TO SILENCE HER...
...IS WHAT I'M THINKING.
SILENCE ...?
IT SEEMS MUNEMIYA MIGHT BE INVOLVED WITH AN-OTHER CASE.
HMM... THIS STORY JUST KEEPS GETTING BIGGER.
BUT ABOUT THAT OTHER CASE...
I'M CERTAIN MUNEMIYA IS CONNECTED TO IT IN SOME WAY...
...BUT I HAVE THE FEELING MADOKA DOESN'T WANT ME TO KNOW ANYTHING ABOUT IT.

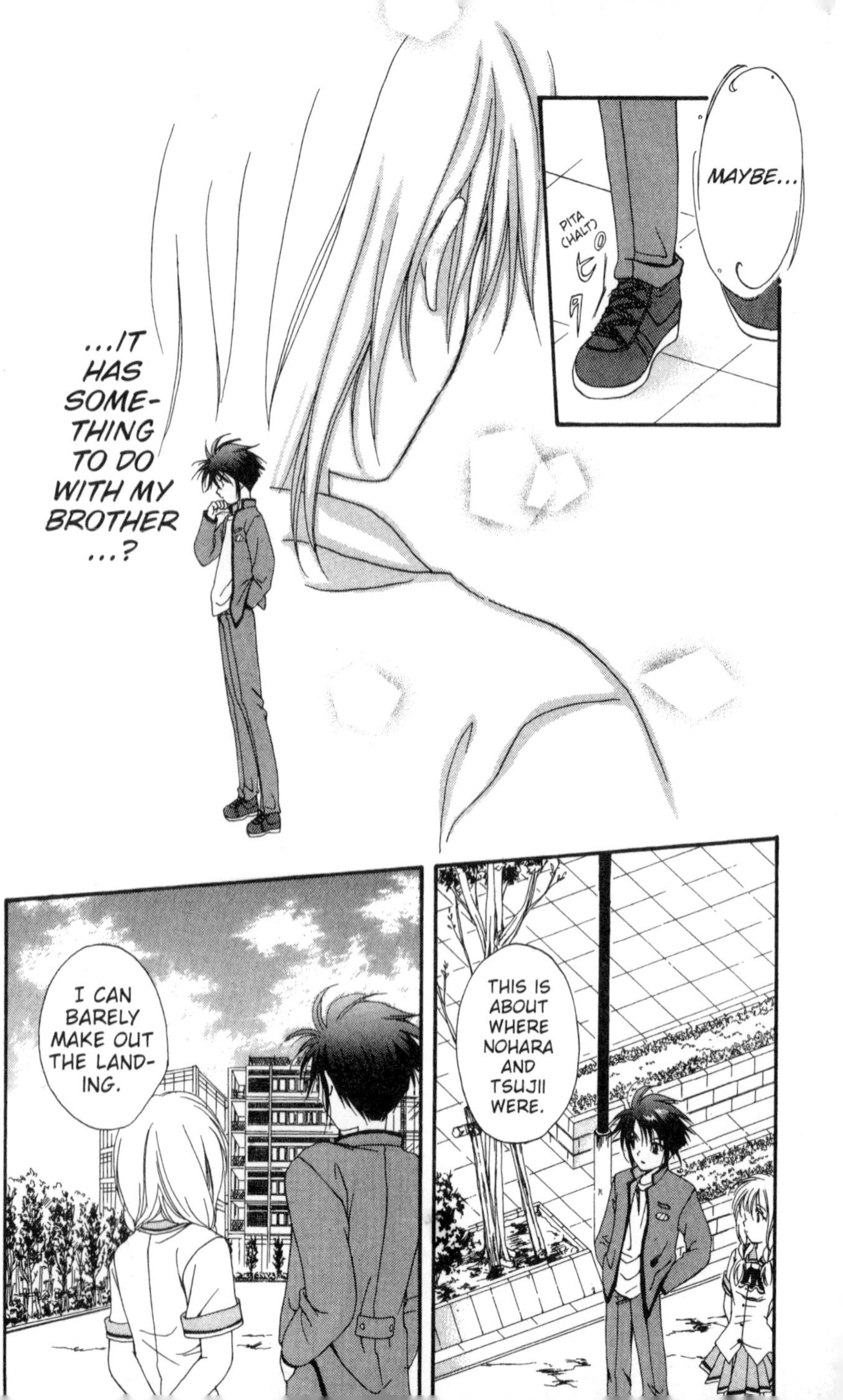
MAYBE...
PITA (HALT)
...IT HAS SOMETHING TO DO WITH MY BROTHER...?
THIS IS ABOUT WHERE NOHARA AND TSUJII WERE.
I CAN BARELY MAKE OUT THE LANDING.

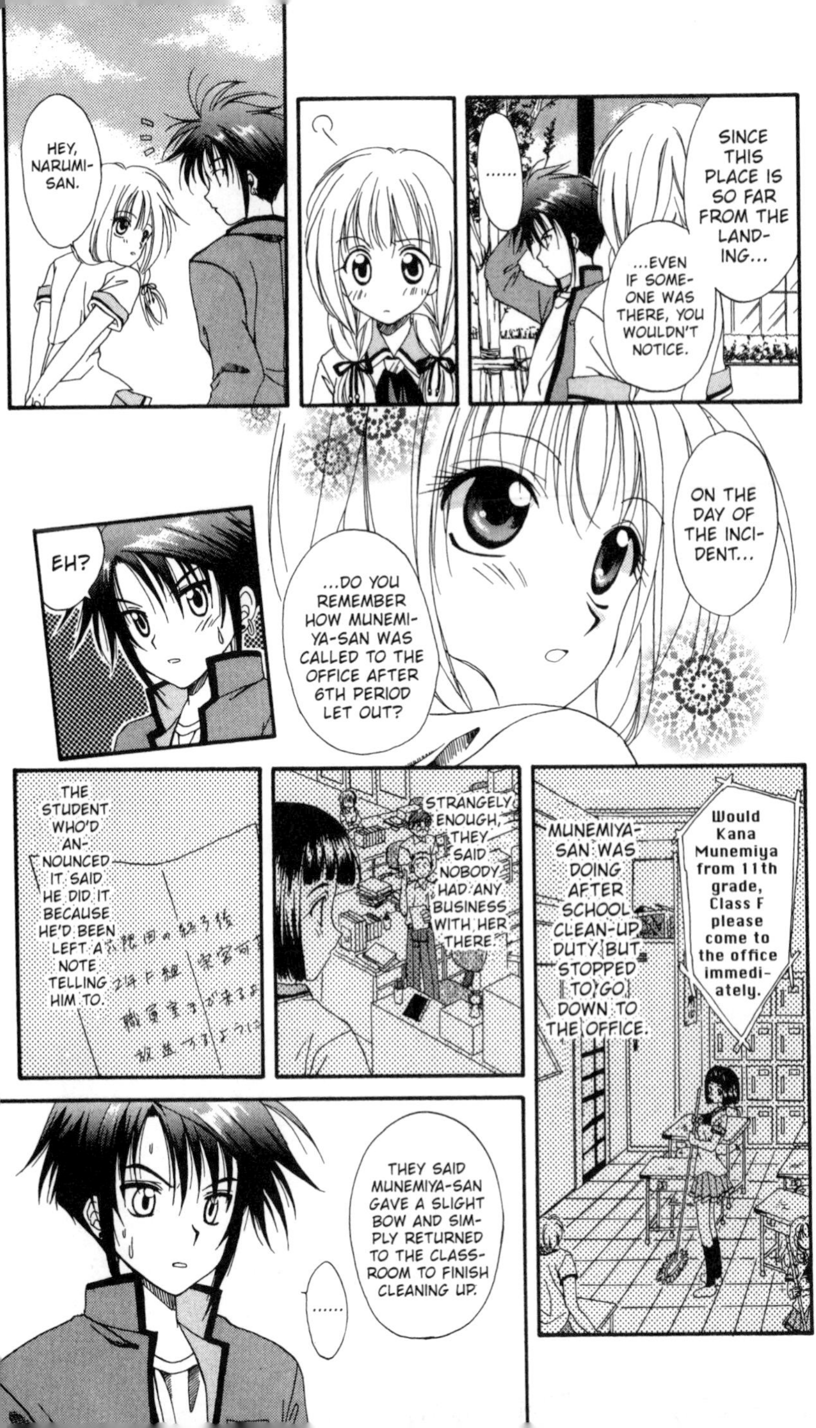
SINCE THIS PLACE IS SO FAR FROM THE LANDING...
...EVEN IF SOMEONE WAS THERE, YOU WOULDN'T NOTICE.
......
HEY, NARUMI-SAN.
ON THE DAY OF THE INCIDENT...
...DO YOU REMEMBER HOW MUNEMIYA-SAN WAS CALLED TO THE OFFICE AFTER 6TH PERIOD LET OUT?
EH?
Would Kana Munemiya from 11th grade, Class F please come to the office immediately.
MUNEMIYA-SAN WAS DOING AFTER SCHOOL CLEAN-UP DUTY BUT STOPPED TO GO DOWN TO THE OFFICE.
STRANGELY ENOUGH, THEY SAID NOBODY HAD ANY BUSINESS WITH HER THERE.
THE STUDENT WHO'D ANNOUNCED IT SAID HE DID IT BECAUSE HE'D BEEN LEFT A NOTE TELLING HIM TO.
THEY SAID MUNEMIYA-SAN GAVE A SLIGHT BOW AND SIMPLY RETURNED TO THE CLASSROOM TO FINISH CLEANING UP.
......

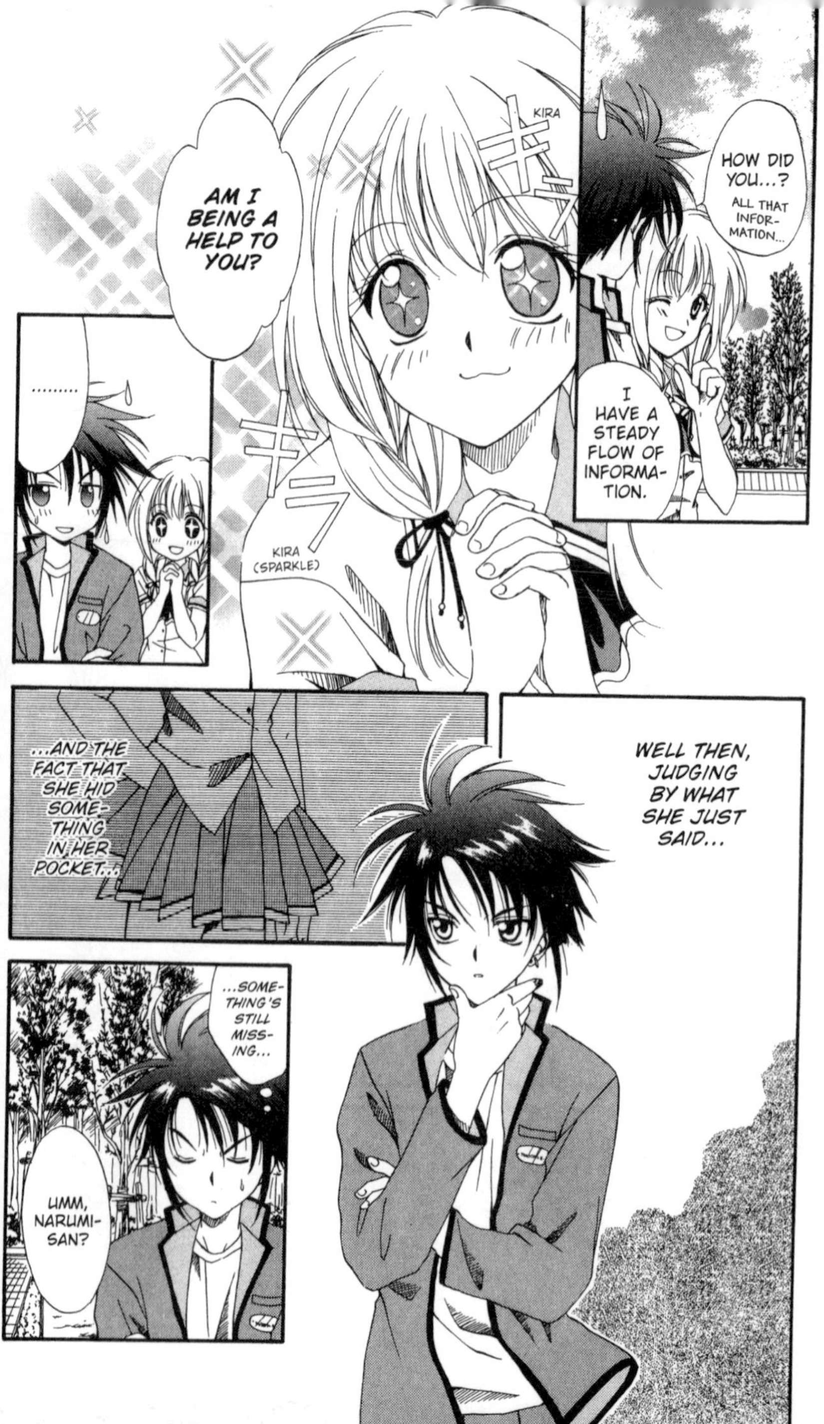
HOW DID YOU...?
ALL THAT INFORMATION...
I HAVE A STEADY FLOW OF INFORMATION.
KIRA
AM I BEING A HELP TO YOU?
KIRA (SPARKLE)
....
WELL THEN, JUDGING BY WHAT SHE JUST SAID...
...AND THE FACT THAT SHE HID SOMETHING IN HER POCKET...
...SOMETHING'S STILL MISSING...
UMM, NARUMI-SAN?

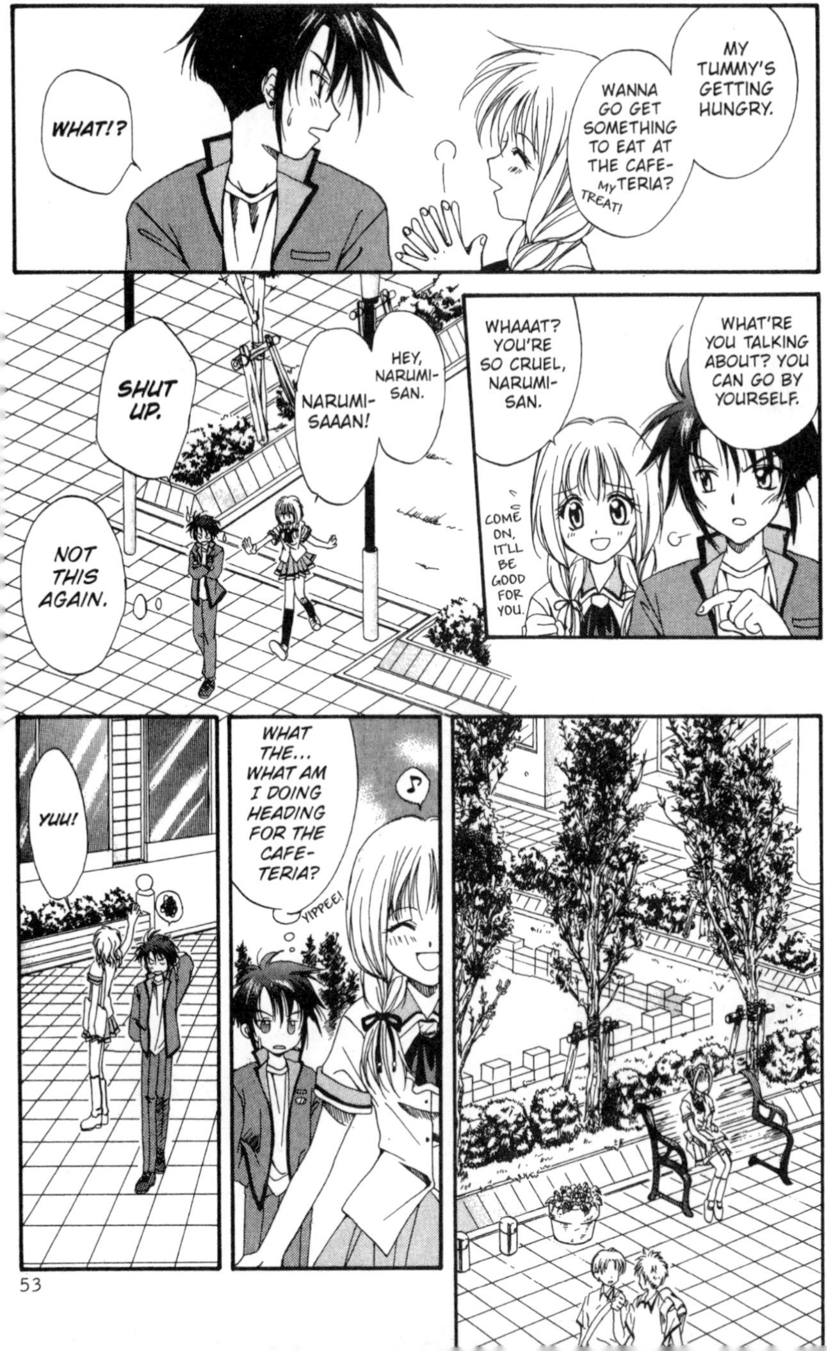
MY TUMMY'S GETTING HUNGRY.
WANNA GO GET SOMETHING TO EAT AT THE CAFE-TERIA?
MY TREAT!
WHAT!?
WHAT'RE YOU TALKING ABOUT? YOU CAN GO BY YOURSELF.
WHAAAT? YOU'RE SO CRUEL, NARUMI-SAN.
COME ON, IT'LL BE GOOD FOR YOU.
HEY, NARUMI-SAN.
NARUMI-SAAAN!
SHUT UP.
NOT THIS AGAIN.
WHAT THE... WHAT AM I DOING HEADING FOR THE CAFE-TERIA?
YIPPEE!
YUU!

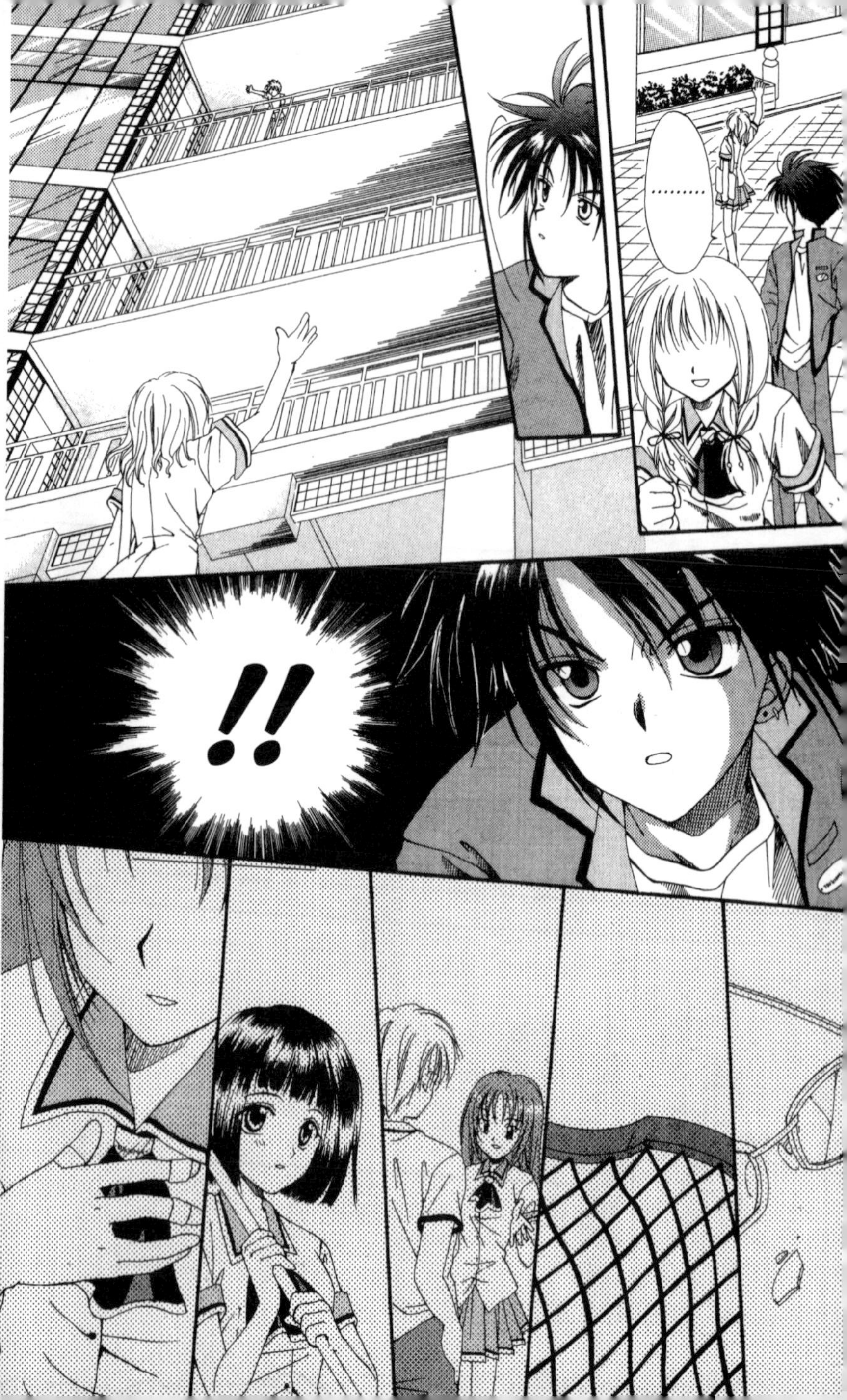
....
!!

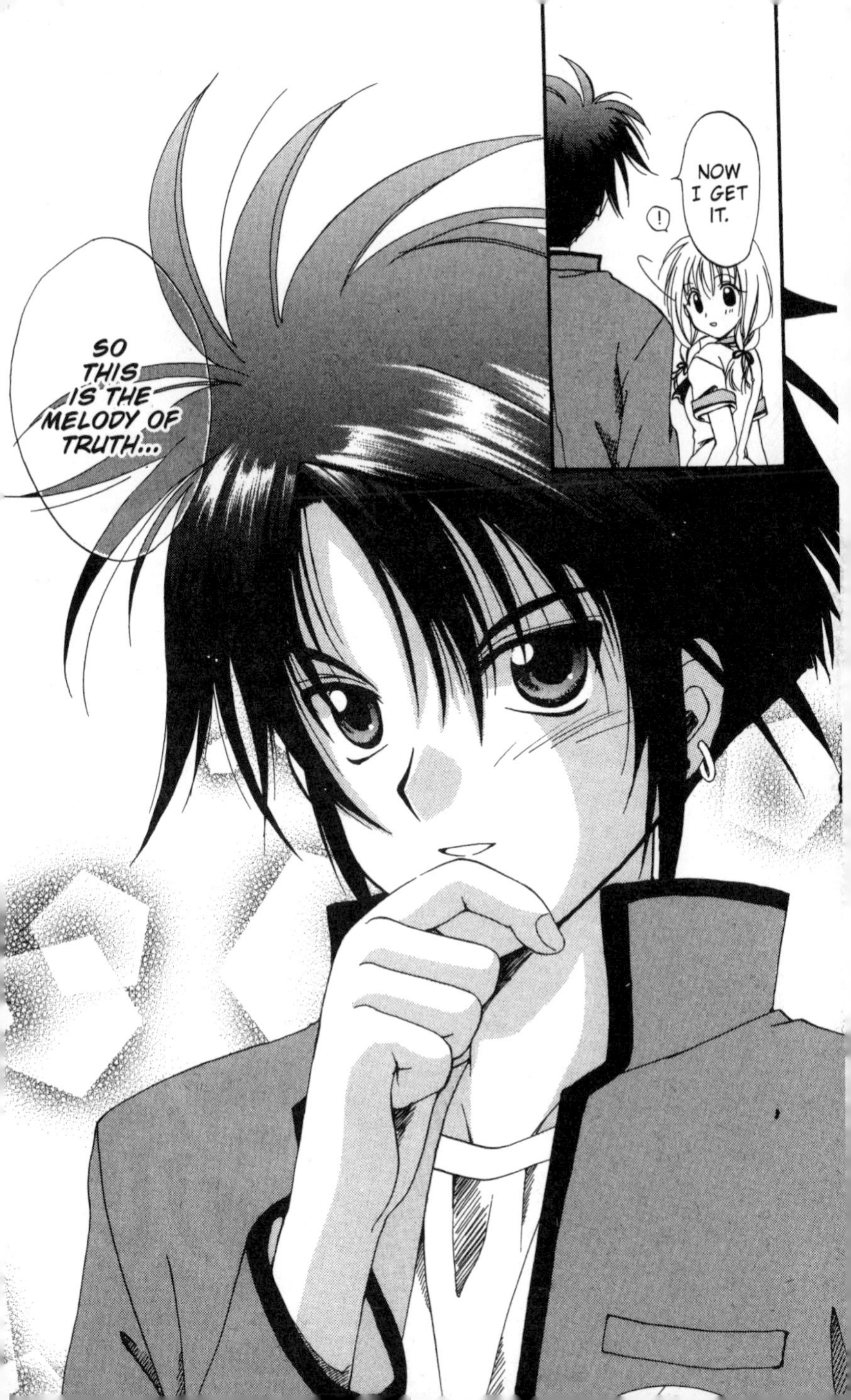
NOW I GET IT.
!
SO THIS IS THE MELODY OF TRUTH...

Spiral

The Bonds of Reasoning

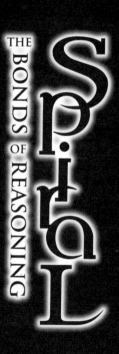

CHAPTER TWO

The Invisible Hand on the Landing (Part II)

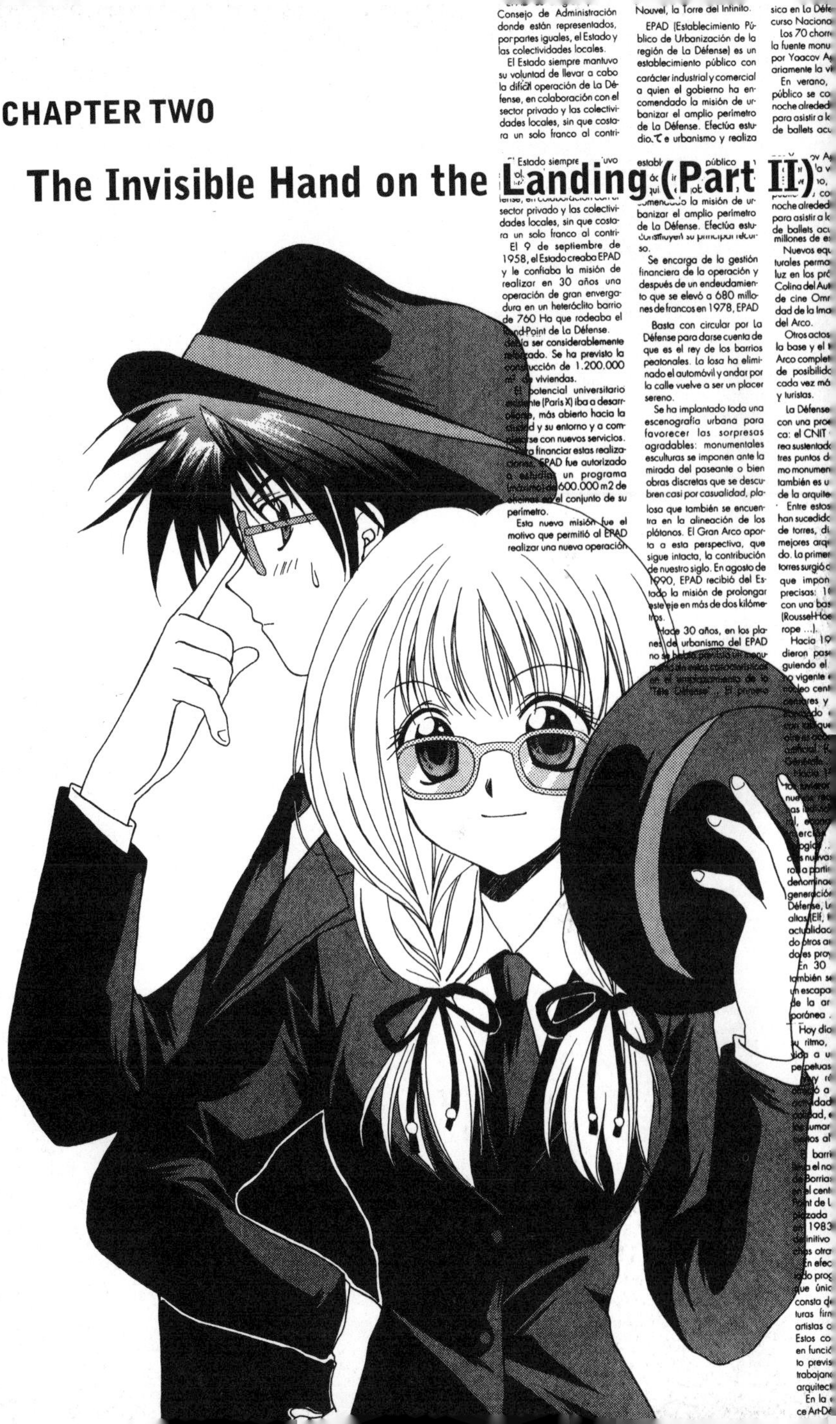
Consejo de Administración donde están representados, por partes iguales, el Estado y las colectividades locales.
El Estado siempre mantuvo su voluntad de llevar a cabo la difícil operación de La Défense, en colaboración con el sector privado y las colectividades locales, sin que costara un solo franco al contri-
sector privado y las colectividades locales, sin que costara un solo franco al contri-
El 9 de septiembre de 1958, el Estado creaba EPAD y le confiaba la misión de realizar en 30 años una operación de gran envergadura en un heteróclito barrio de 760 Ha que rodeaba el
Esta nueva misión fue el motivo que permitió al EPAD realizar una nueva operación
Nouvel, la Torre del Infinito.
EPAD (Establecimiento Público de Urbanización de la región de La Défense) es un establecimiento público con carácter industrial y comercial a quien el gobierno ha encomendado la misión de urbanizar el amplio perímetro de La Défense. Efectúa estu-
banizar el amplio perímetro de La Défense. Efectúa estu-
Se encarga de la gestión financiera de la operación y después de un endeudamiento que se elevó a 680 millones de francos en 1978, EPAD
Basta con circular por La Défense para darse cuenta de que es el rey de los barrios peatonales. La losa ha eliminado el automóvil y andar por la calle vuelve a ser un placer sereno.
Se ha implantado toda una escenografía urbana para favorecer las sorpresas agradables: monumentales esculturas se imponen ante la mirada del paseante o bien obras discretas que se descubren casi por casualidad, pla-
losa que también se encuentra en la alineación de los plátanos. El Gran Arco aporta a esta perspectiva, que sigue intacta, la contribución de nuestro siglo. En agosto de 1990, EPAD recibió del Estado la misión de prolongar este eje en más de dos kilómetros.
Hace 30 años, en los planes de urbanismo del EPAD

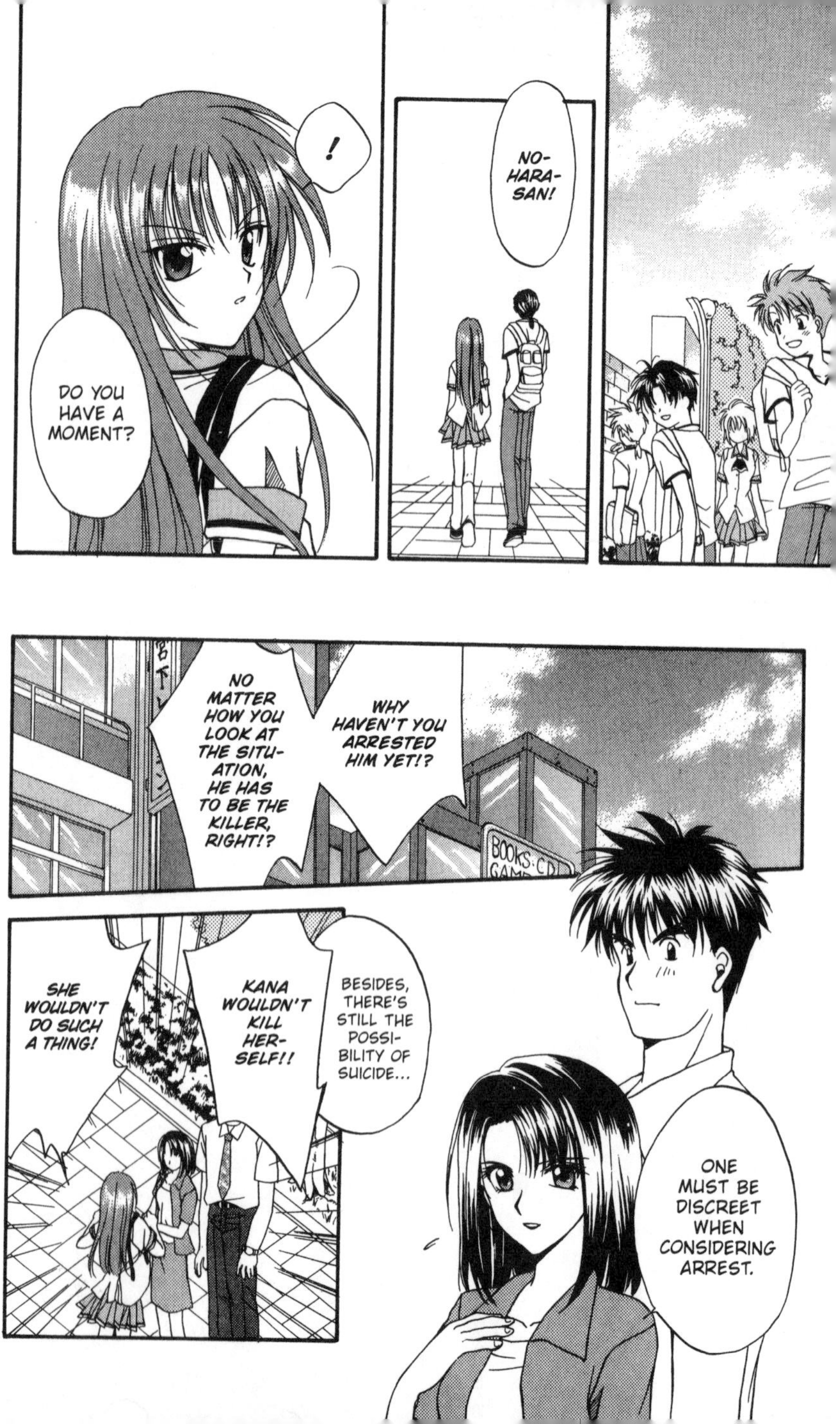
NO-HARA-SAN!
!
DO YOU HAVE A MOMENT?
WHY HAVEN'T YOU ARRESTED HIM YET!?
NO MATTER HOW YOU LOOK AT THE SITUATION, HE HAS TO BE THE KILLER, RIGHT!?
ONE MUST BE DISCREET WHEN CONSIDERING ARREST.
BESIDES, THERE'S STILL THE POSSIBILITY OF SUICIDE...
KANA WOULDN'T KILL HERSELF!!
SHE WOULDN'T DO SUCH A THING!

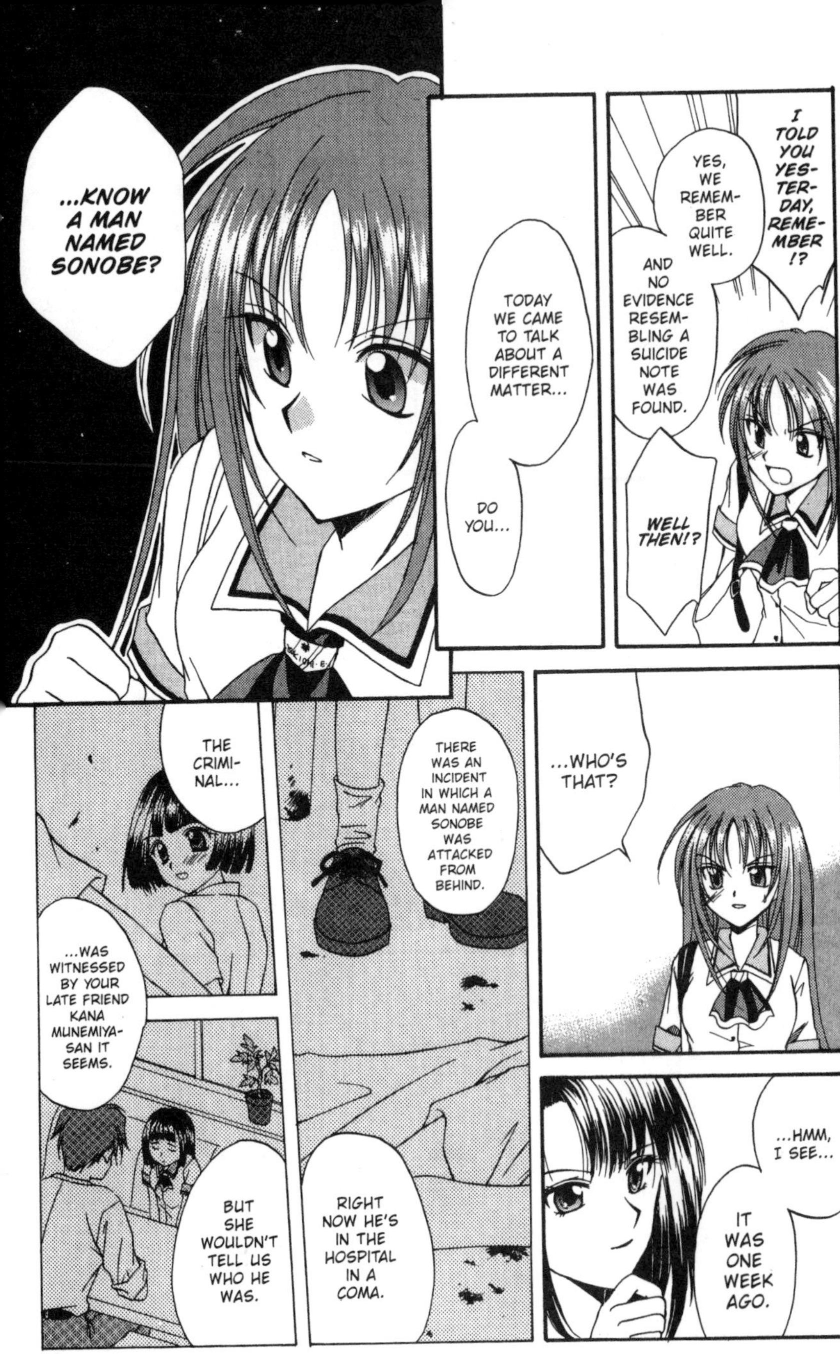
I TOLD YOU YESTERDAY, REMEMBER!?
YES, WE REMEMBER QUITE WELL.
AND NO EVIDENCE RESEMBLING A SUICIDE NOTE WAS FOUND.
WELL THEN!?
TODAY WE CAME TO TALK ABOUT A DIFFERENT MATTER...
DO YOU...
...KNOW A MAN NAMED SONOBE?
...WHO'S THAT?
...HMM, I SEE...
IT WAS ONE WEEK AGO.
THERE WAS AN INCIDENT IN WHICH A MAN NAMED SONOBE WAS ATTACKED FROM BEHIND.
RIGHT NOW HE'S IN THE HOSPITAL IN A COMA.
THE CRIMINAL...
...WAS WITNESSED BY YOUR LATE FRIEND KANA MUNEMIYA-SAN IT SEEMS.
BUT SHE WOULDN'T TELL US WHO HE WAS.

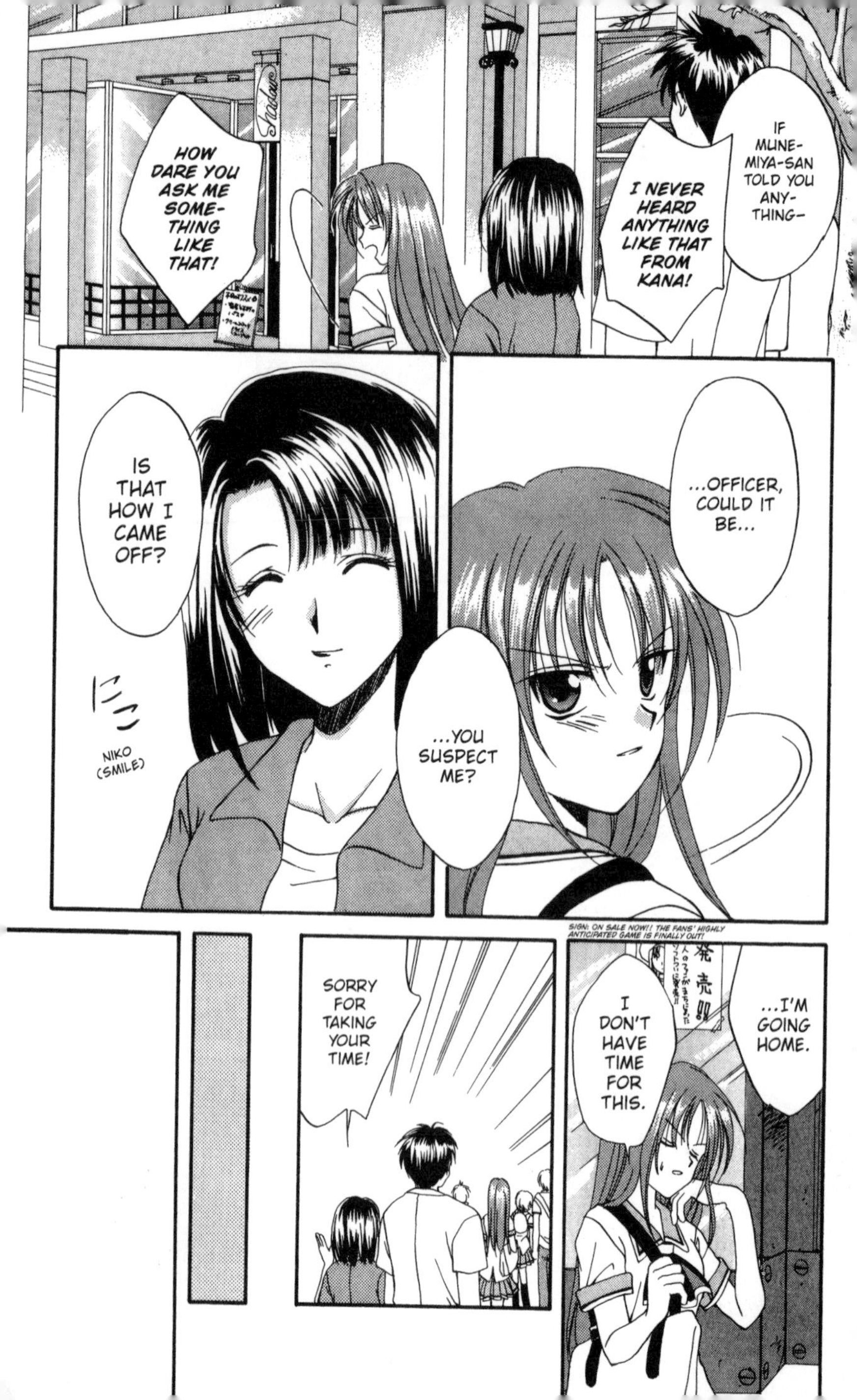
IF MUNE-MIYA-SAN TOLD YOU ANY-THING-
I NEVER HEARD ANYTHING LIKE THAT FROM KANA!
HOW DARE YOU ASK ME SOME-THING LIKE THAT!
...OFFICER, COULD IT BE...
...YOU SUSPECT ME?
IS THAT HOW I CAME OFF?
NIKO (SMILE)
SIGN: ON SALE NOW!! THE FANS' HIGHLY ANTICIPATED GAME IS FINALLY OUT!
発売!!
...I'M GOING HOME.
I DON'T HAVE TIME FOR THIS.
SORRY FOR TAKING YOUR TIME!

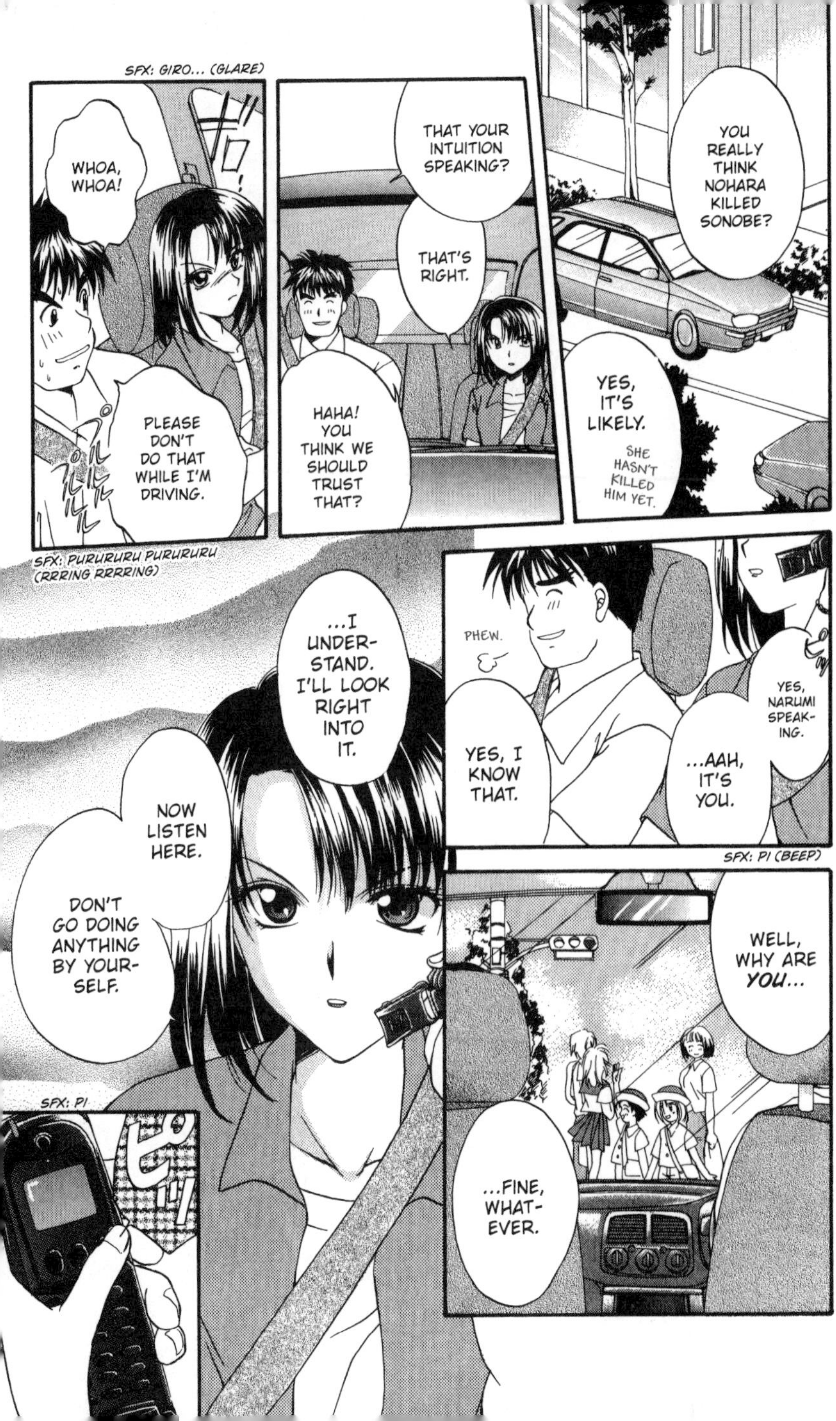
YOU REALLY THINK NOHARA KILLED SONOBE?
YES, IT'S LIKELY.
SHE HASN'T KILLED HIM YET.
THAT YOUR INTUITION SPEAKING?
THAT'S RIGHT.
HAHA! YOU THINK WE SHOULD TRUST THAT?
SFX: GIRO... (GLARE)
WHOA, WHOA!
PLEASE DON'T DO THAT WHILE I'M DRIVING.
SFX: PURURURU PURURURU (RRRING RRRRING)
YES, NARUMI SPEAKING.
...AAH, IT'S YOU.
PHEW.
YES, I KNOW THAT.
SFX: PI (BEEP)
WELL, WHY ARE YOU...
...FINE, WHATEVER.
...I UNDERSTAND. I'LL LOOK RIGHT INTO IT.
NOW LISTEN HERE.
DON'T GO DOING ANYTHING BY YOURSELF.
SFX: PI

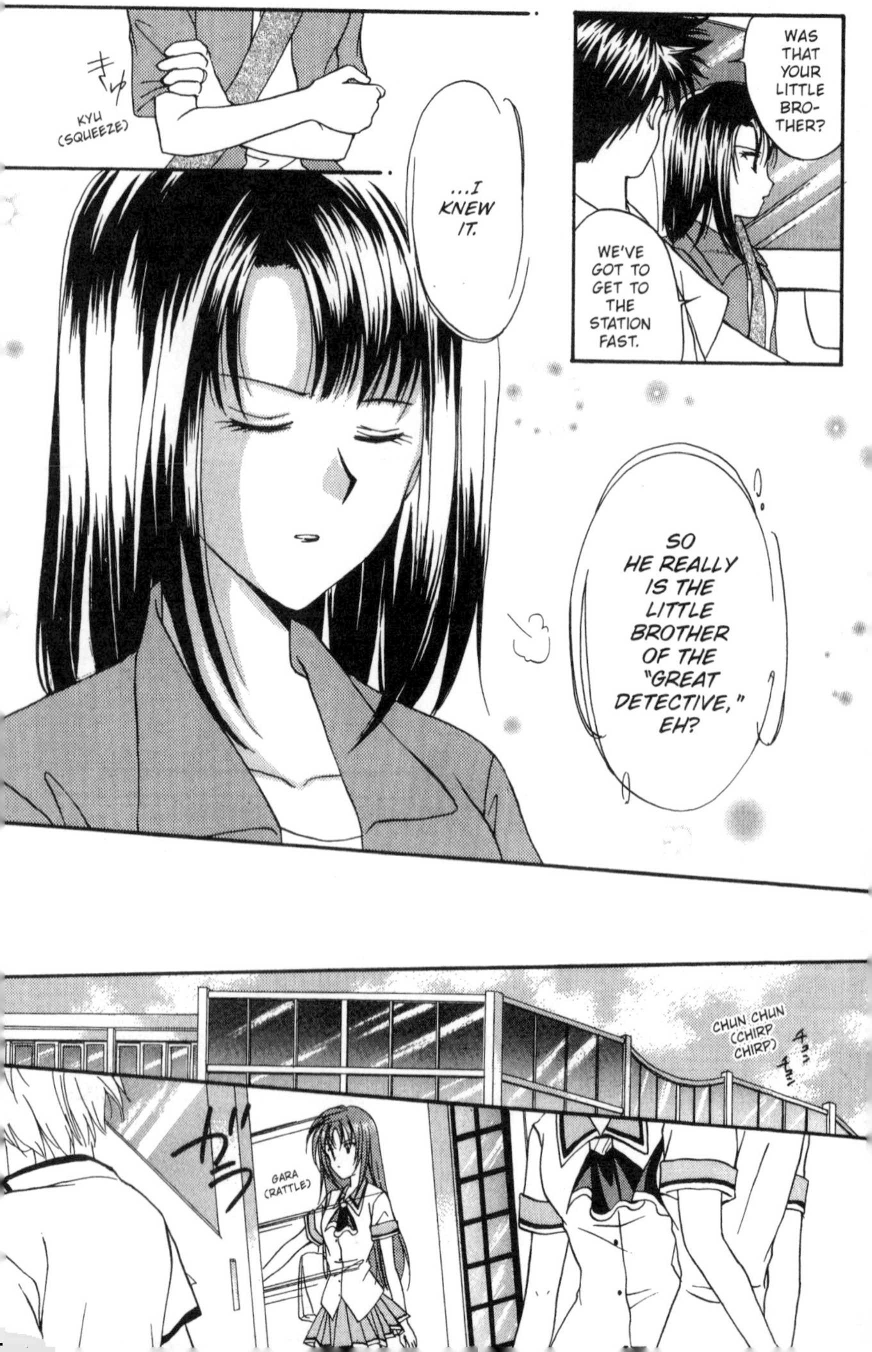
WAS THAT YOUR LITTLE BRO- THER?
WE'VE GOT TO GET TO THE STATION FAST.
きゅ
KYU (SQUEEZE)
...I KNEW IT.
SO HE REALLY IS THE LITTLE BROTHER OF THE "GREAT DETECTIVE," EH?
CHUN CHUN (CHIRP CHIRP)
GARA (RATTLE)

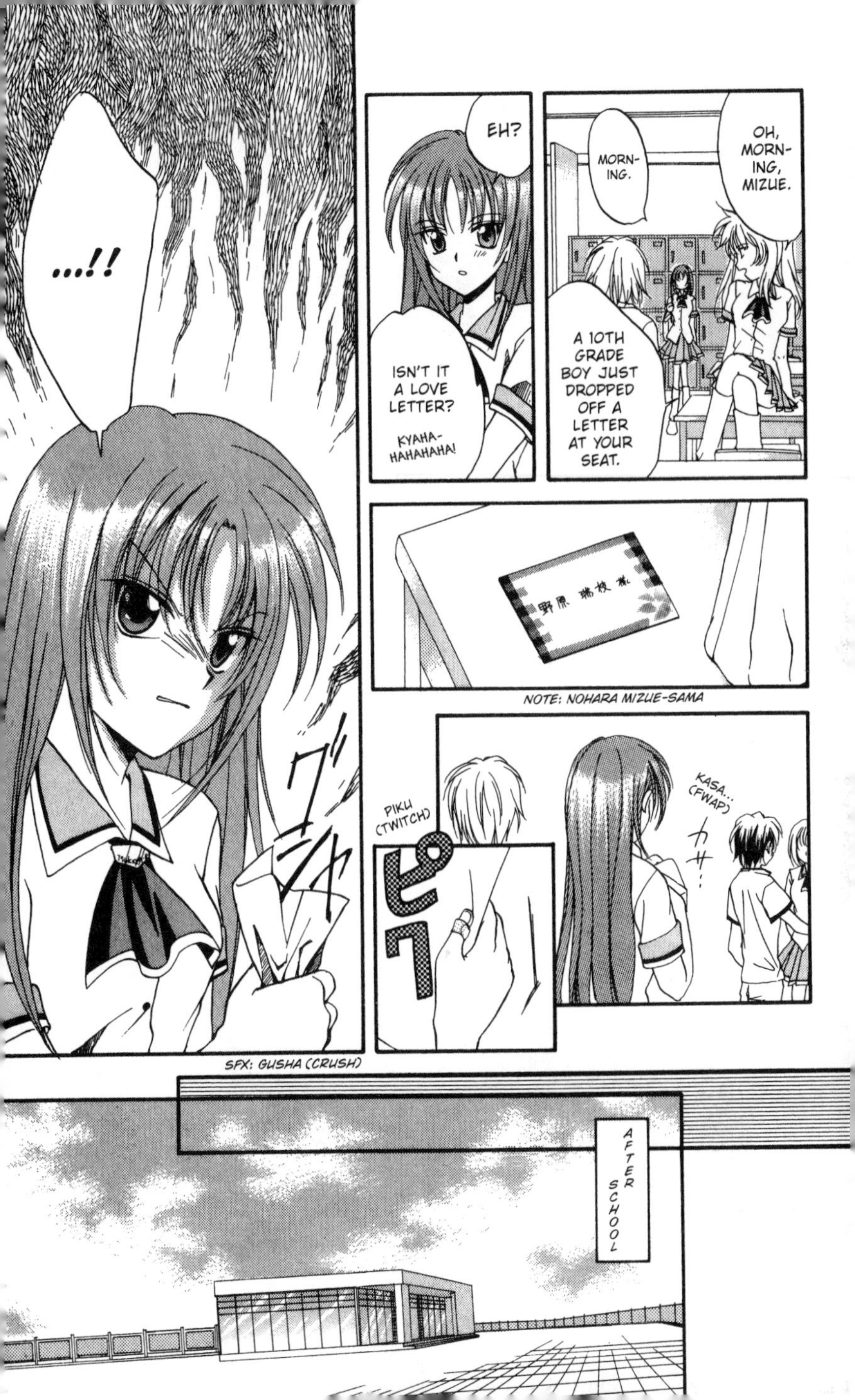
OH, MORNING, MIZUE.
MORNING.
A 10TH GRADE BOY JUST DROPPED OFF A LETTER AT YOUR SEAT.
EH?
ISN'T IT A LOVE LETTER?
KYAHA-HAHAHAHA!
野原 瑞枝 様
NOTE: NOHARA MIZUE-SAMA
KASA... (FWAP)
カサ...
PIKU (TWITCH)
ピク
...!!
グシャ
SFX: GUSHA (CRUSH)
AFTER SCHOOL

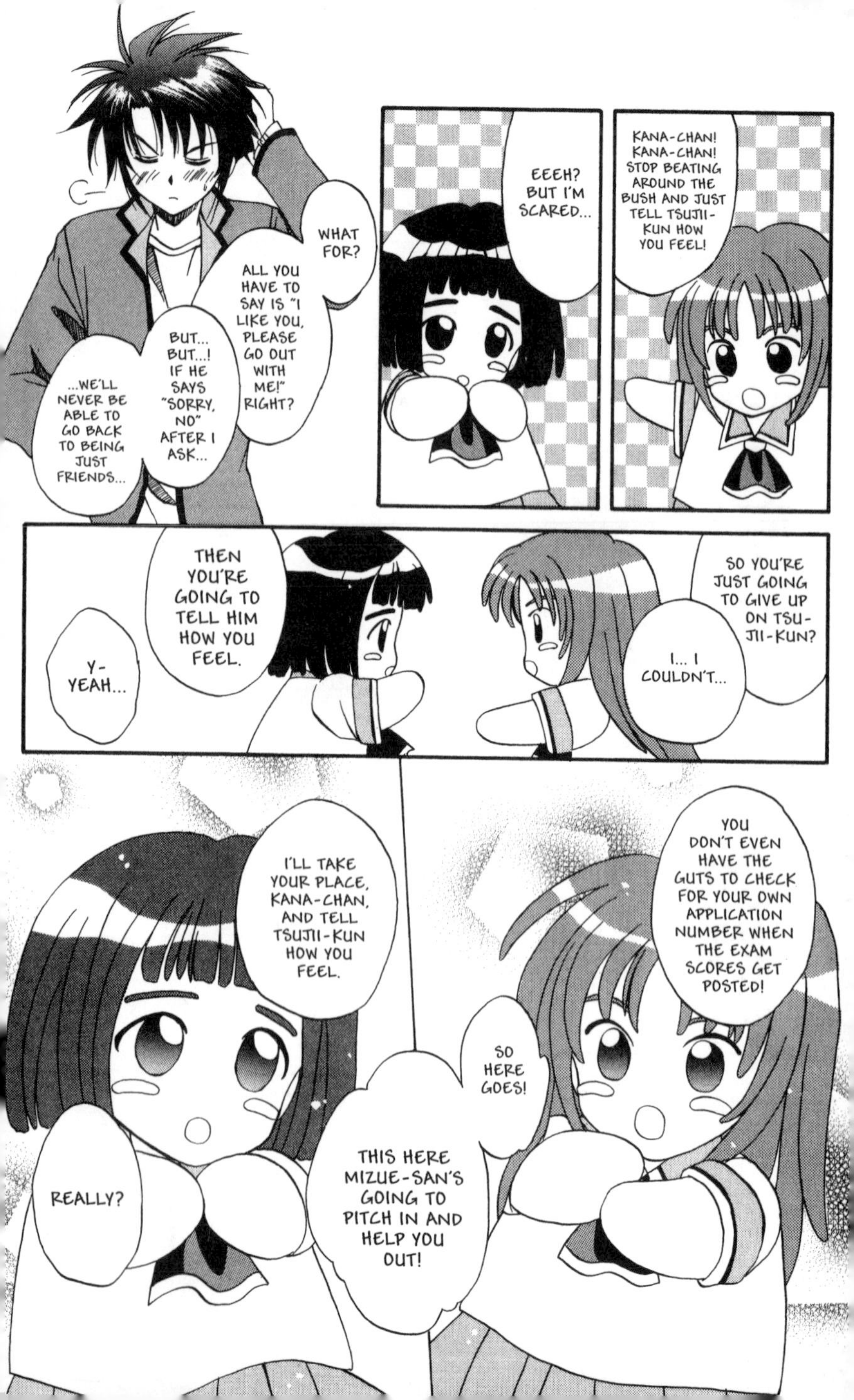
KANA-CHAN! KANA-CHAN! STOP BEATING AROUND THE BUSH AND JUST TELL TSUJII-KUN HOW YOU FEEL!
EEEH? BUT I'M SCARED...
WHAT FOR?
ALL YOU HAVE TO SAY IS "I LIKE YOU, PLEASE GO OUT WITH ME!" RIGHT?
BUT... BUT...! IF HE SAYS "SORRY, NO" AFTER I ASK...
...WE'LL NEVER BE ABLE TO GO BACK TO BEING JUST FRIENDS...
SO YOU'RE JUST GOING TO GIVE UP ON TSUJII-KUN?
I... I COULDN'T...
THEN YOU'RE GOING TO TELL HIM HOW YOU FEEL.
Y-YEAH...
YOU DON'T EVEN HAVE THE GUTS TO CHECK FOR YOUR OWN APPLICATION NUMBER WHEN THE EXAM SCORES GET POSTED!
I'LL TAKE YOUR PLACE, KANA-CHAN, AND TELL TSUJII-KUN HOW YOU FEEL.
SO HERE GOES!
THIS HERE MIZUE-SAN'S GOING TO PITCH IN AND HELP YOU OUT!
REALLY?

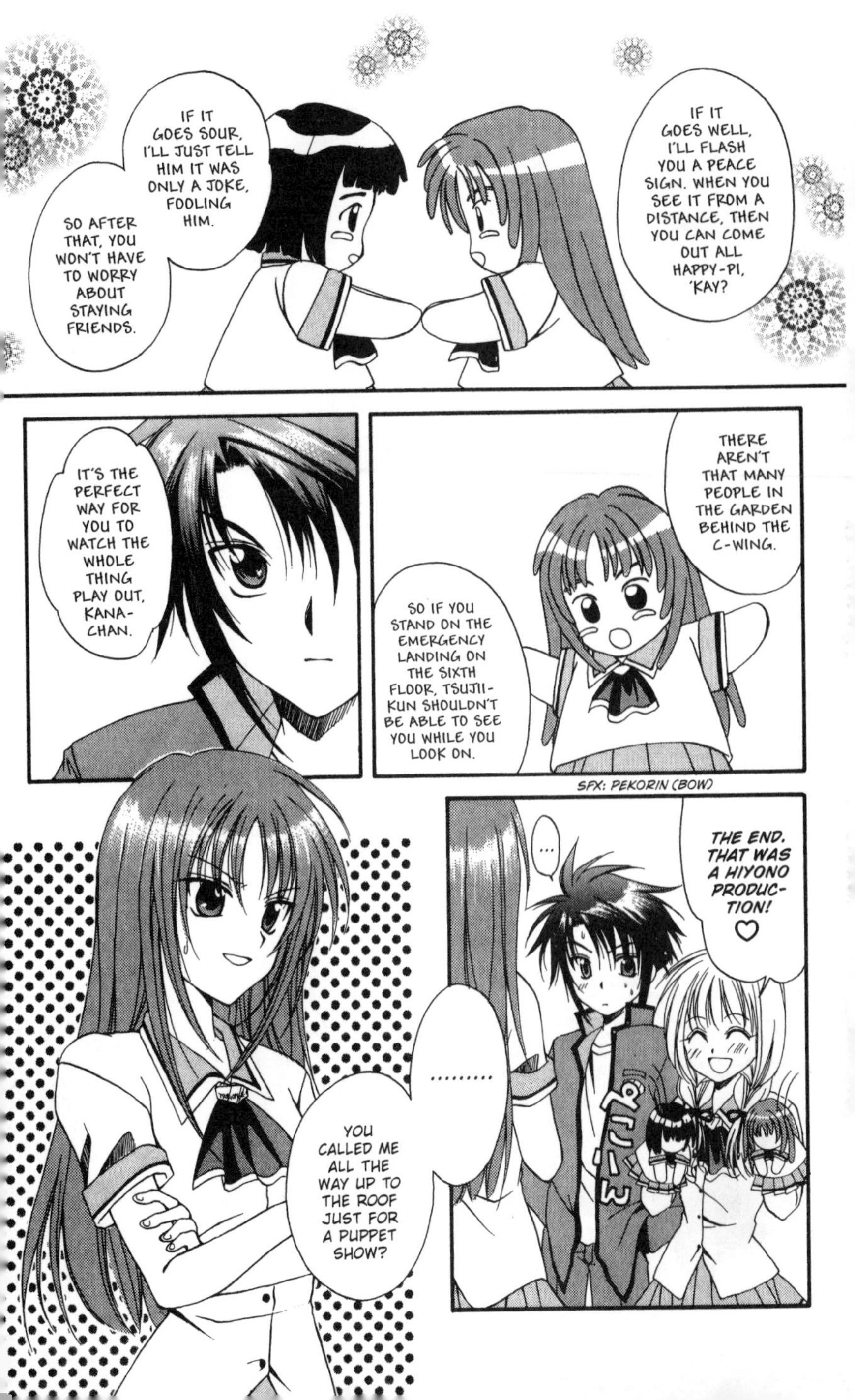
IF IT GOES WELL, I'LL FLASH YOU A PEACE SIGN. WHEN YOU SEE IT FROM A DISTANCE, THEN YOU CAN COME OUT ALL HAPPY-PI, 'KAY?
IF IT GOES SOUR, I'LL JUST TELL HIM IT WAS ONLY A JOKE, FOOLING HIM.
SO AFTER THAT, YOU WON'T HAVE TO WORRY ABOUT STAYING FRIENDS.
THERE AREN'T THAT MANY PEOPLE IN THE GARDEN BEHIND THE C-WING.
SO IF YOU STAND ON THE EMERGENCY LANDING ON THE SIXTH FLOOR, TSUJII-KUN SHOULDN'T BE ABLE TO SEE YOU WHILE YOU LOOK ON.
IT'S THE PERFECT WAY FOR YOU TO WATCH THE WHOLE THING PLAY OUT, KANA-CHAN.
SFX: PEKORIN (BOW)
THE END. THAT WAS A HIYONO PRODUCTION! ♡
...
....
YOU CALLED ME ALL THE WAY UP TO THE ROOF JUST FOR A PUPPET SHOW?

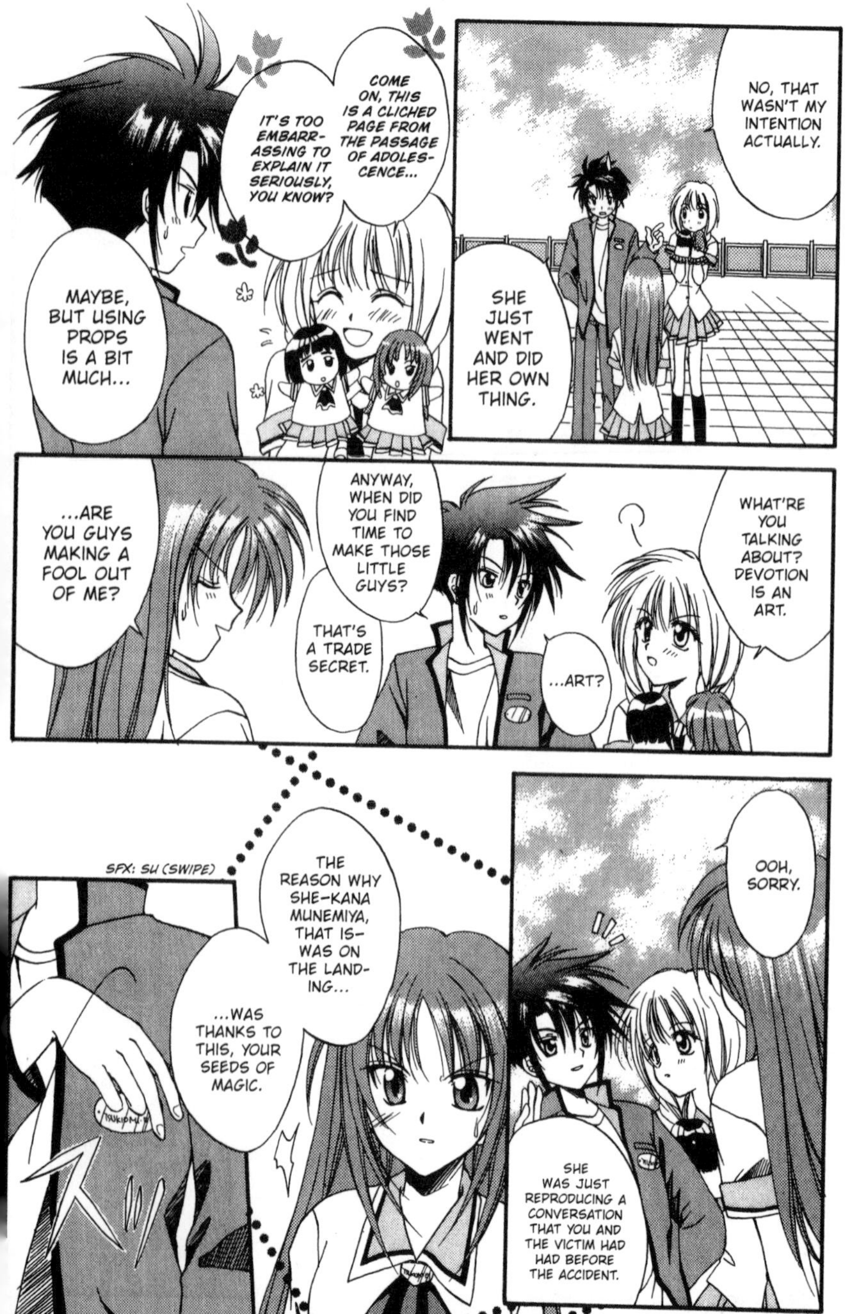
NO, THAT WASN'T MY INTENTION ACTUALLY.
SHE JUST WENT AND DID HER OWN THING.
COME ON, THIS IS A CLICHED PAGE FROM THE PASSAGE OF ADOLESCENCE...
IT'S TOO EMBARRASSING TO EXPLAIN IT SERIOUSLY, YOU KNOW?
MAYBE, BUT USING PROPS IS A BIT MUCH...
WHAT'RE YOU TALKING ABOUT? DEVOTION IS AN ART.
...ART?
ANYWAY, WHEN DID YOU FIND TIME TO MAKE THOSE LITTLE GUYS?
THAT'S A TRADE SECRET.
...ARE YOU GUYS MAKING A FOOL OUT OF ME?
OOH, SORRY.
SHE WAS JUST REPRODUCING A CONVERSATION THAT YOU AND THE VICTIM HAD HAD BEFORE THE ACCIDENT.
THE REASON WHY SHE—KANA MUNEMIYA, THAT IS—WAS ON THE LANDING...
...WAS THANKS TO THIS, YOUR SEEDS OF MAGIC.
SFX: SU (SWIPE)

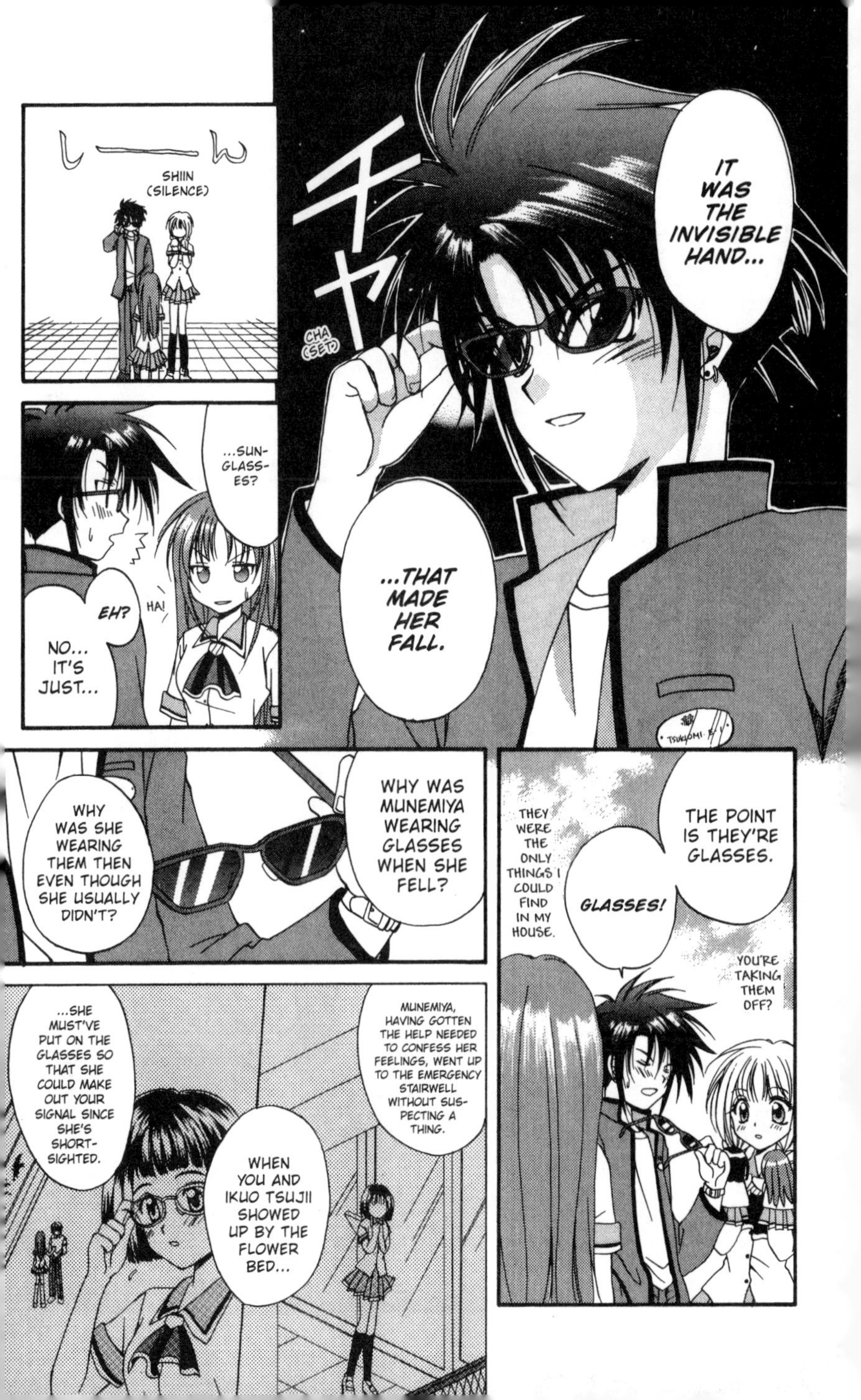
IT WAS THE INVISIBLE HAND...
チャ
CHA (SET)
...THAT MADE HER FALL.
TSUKIOMI
しーーん
SHIIN (SILENCE)
...SUN-GLASS-ES?
EH?
HA!
NO... IT'S JUST...
THE POINT IS THEY'RE GLASSES.
THEY WERE THE ONLY THINGS I COULD FIND IN MY HOUSE.
GLASSES!
YOU'RE TAKING THEM OFF?
WHY WAS MUNEMIYA WEARING GLASSES WHEN SHE FELL?
WHY WAS SHE WEARING THEM THEN EVEN THOUGH SHE USUALLY DIDN'T?
MUNEMIYA, HAVING GOTTEN THE HELP NEEDED TO CONFESS HER FEELINGS, WENT UP TO THE EMERGENCY STAIRWELL WITHOUT SUS-PECTING A THING.
WHEN YOU AND IKUO TSUJII SHOWED UP BY THE FLOWER BED...
...SHE MUST'VE PUT ON THE GLASSES SO THAT SHE COULD MAKE OUT YOUR SIGNAL SINCE SHE'S SHORT-SIGHTED.

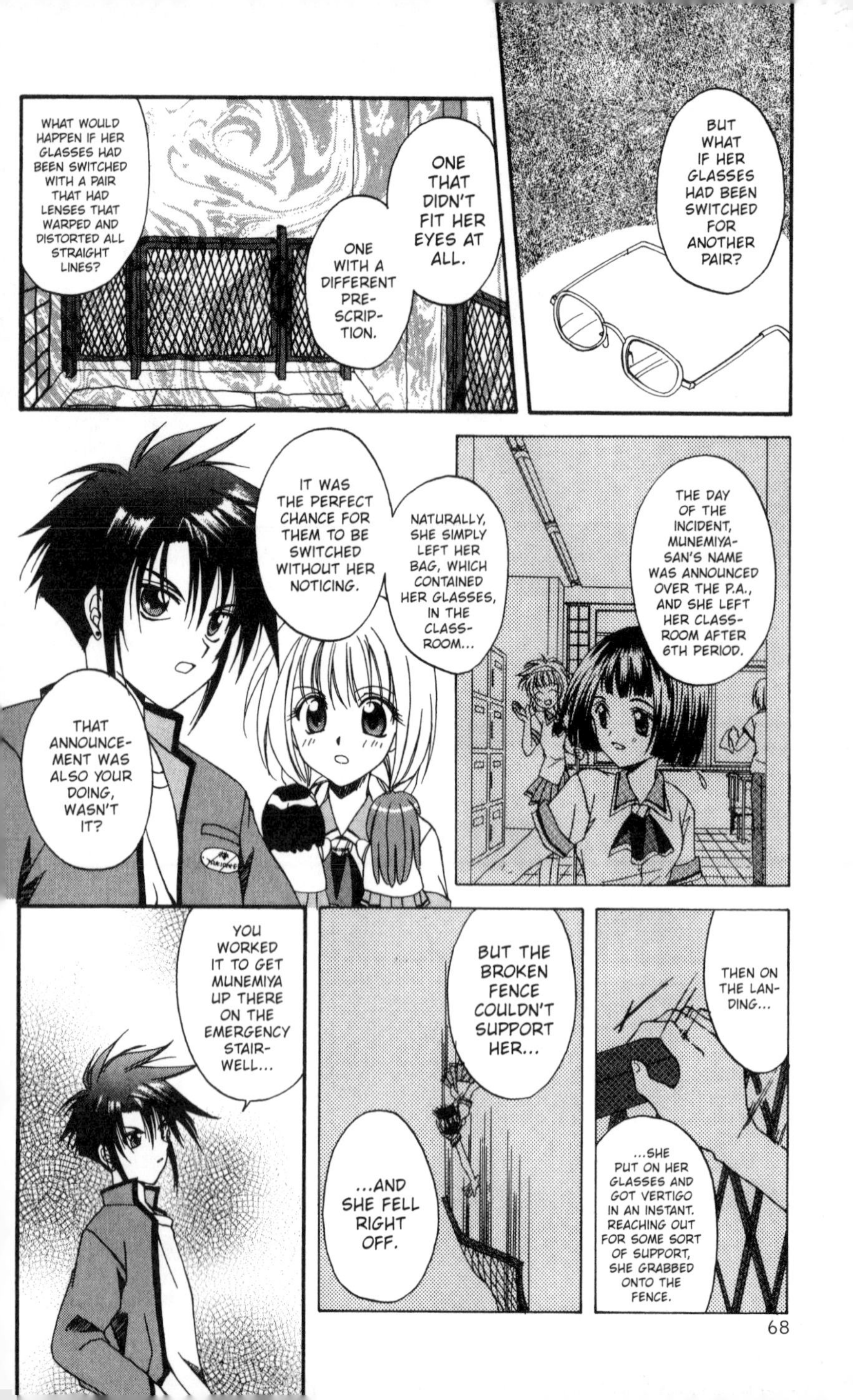
BUT WHAT IF HER GLASSES HAD BEEN SWITCHED FOR ANOTHER PAIR?
ONE THAT DIDN'T FIT HER EYES AT ALL.
ONE WITH A DIFFERENT PRE-SCRIP-TION.
WHAT WOULD HAPPEN IF HER GLASSES HAD BEEN SWITCHED WITH A PAIR THAT HAD LENSES THAT WARPED AND DISTORTED ALL STRAIGHT LINES?
THE DAY OF THE INCIDENT, MUNEMIYA-SAN'S NAME WAS ANNOUNCED OVER THE P.A., AND SHE LEFT HER CLASS-ROOM AFTER 6TH PERIOD.
NATURALLY, SHE SIMPLY LEFT HER BAG, WHICH CONTAINED HER GLASSES, IN THE CLASS-ROOM...
IT WAS THE PERFECT CHANCE FOR THEM TO BE SWITCHED WITHOUT HER NOTICING.
THAT ANNOUNCE-MENT WAS ALSO YOUR DOING, WASN'T IT?
THEN ON THE LAN-DING...
...SHE PUT ON HER GLASSES AND GOT VERTIGO IN AN INSTANT. REACHING OUT FOR SOME SORT OF SUPPORT, SHE GRABBED ONTO THE FENCE.
BUT THE BROKEN FENCE COULDN'T SUPPORT HER...
...AND SHE FELL RIGHT OFF.
YOU WORKED IT TO GET MUNEMIYA UP THERE ON THE EMERGENCY STAIR-WELL...

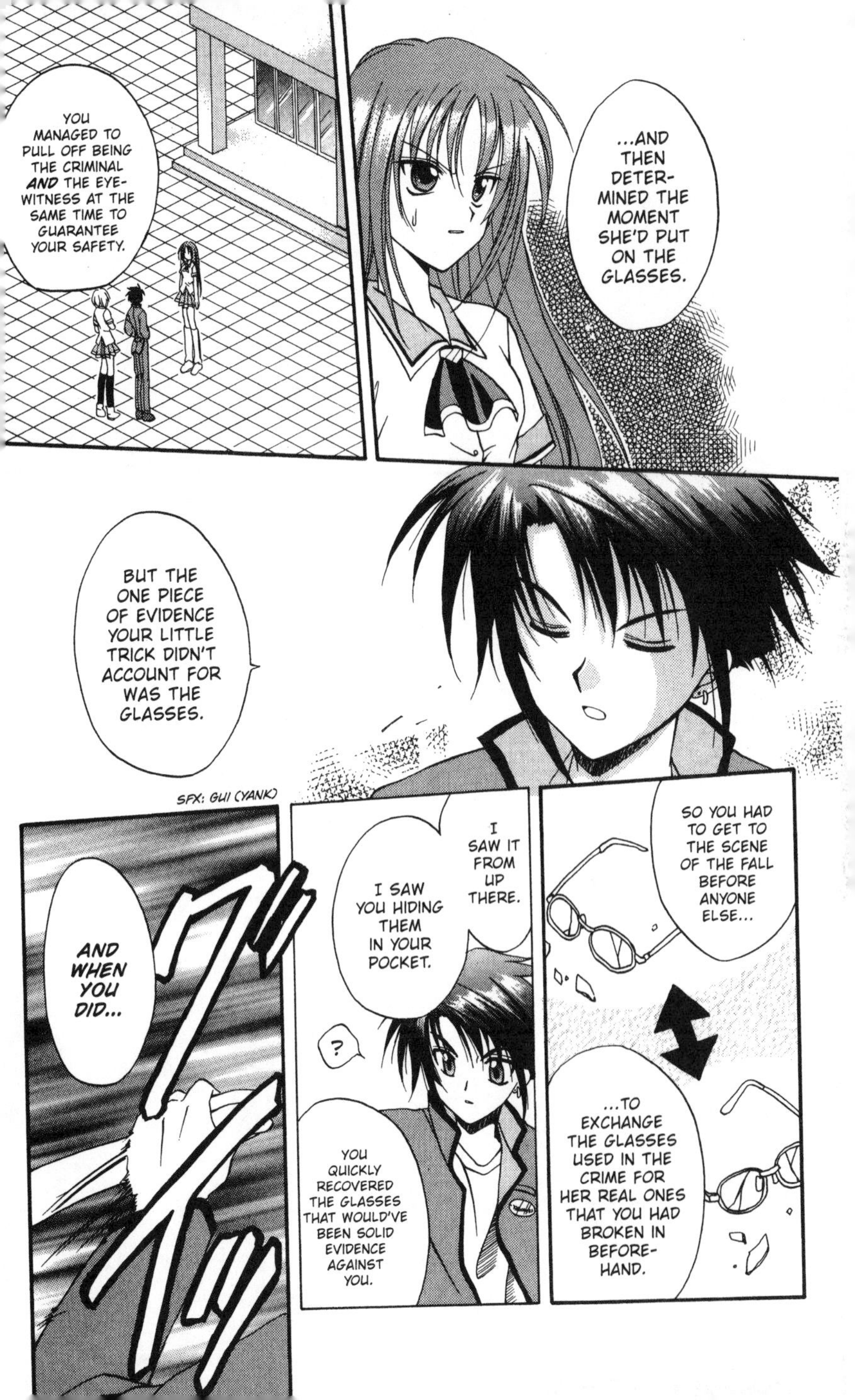
...AND THEN DETER-MINED THE MOMENT SHE'D PUT ON THE GLASSES.
YOU MANAGED TO PULL OFF BEING THE CRIMINAL AND THE EYE-WITNESS AT THE SAME TIME TO GUARANTEE YOUR SAFETY.
BUT THE ONE PIECE OF EVIDENCE YOUR LITTLE TRICK DIDN'T ACCOUNT FOR WAS THE GLASSES.
SO YOU HAD TO GET TO THE SCENE OF THE FALL BEFORE ANYONE ELSE...
...TO EXCHANGE THE GLASSES USED IN THE CRIME FOR HER REAL ONES THAT YOU HAD BROKEN IN BEFORE-HAND.
I SAW IT FROM UP THERE.
I SAW YOU HIDING THEM IN YOUR POCKET.
?
YOU QUICKLY RECOVERED THE GLASSES THAT WOULD'VE BEEN SOLID EVIDENCE AGAINST YOU.
SFX: GUI (YANK)
AND WHEN YOU DID...

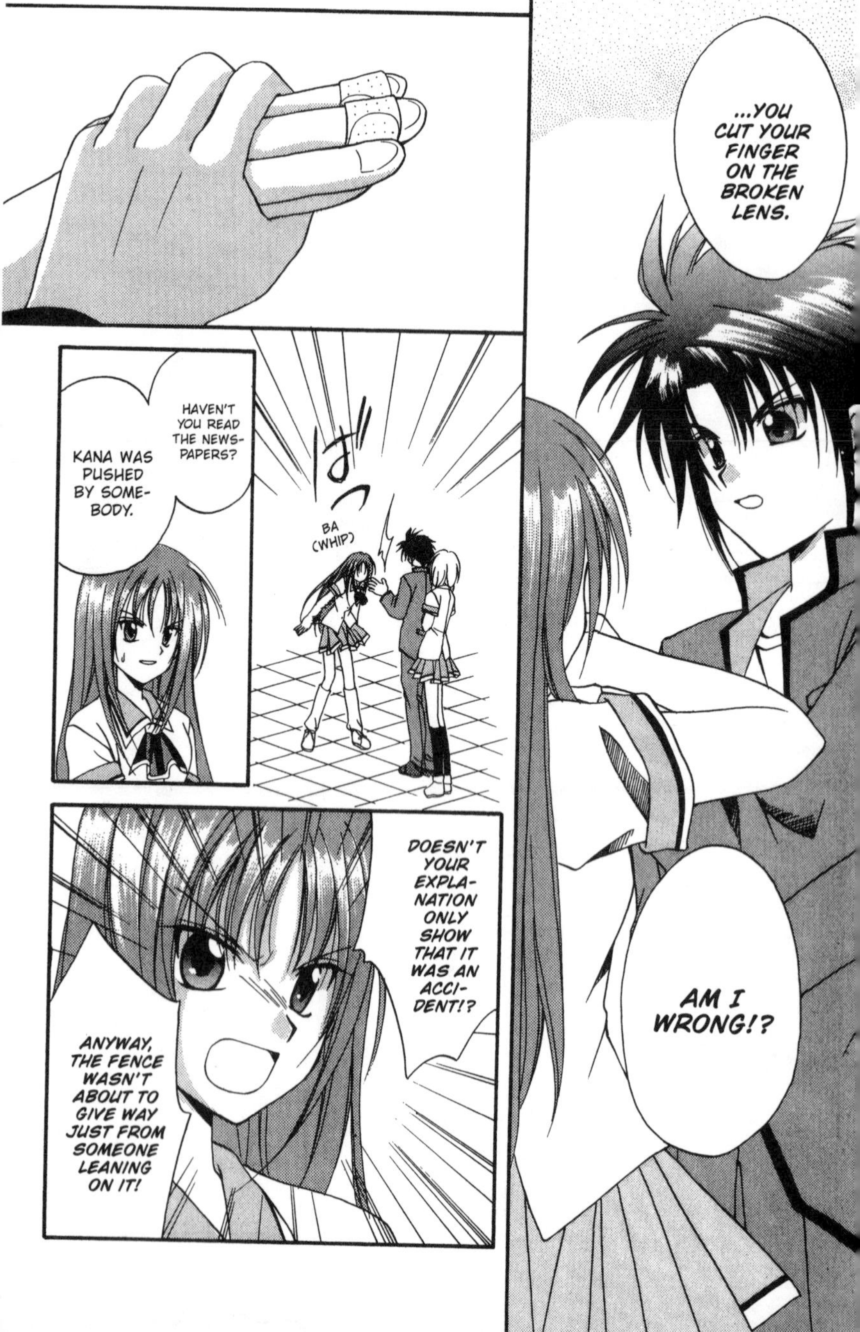
...YOU CUT YOUR FINGER ON THE BROKEN LENS.
AM I WRONG!?
ばっ
BA (WHIP)
HAVEN'T YOU READ THE NEWS-PAPERS?
KANA WAS PUSHED BY SOME-BODY.
DOESN'T YOUR EXPLA-NATION ONLY SHOW THAT IT WAS AN ACCI-DENT!?
ANYWAY, THE FENCE WASN'T ABOUT TO GIVE WAY JUST FROM SOMEONE LEANING ON IT!

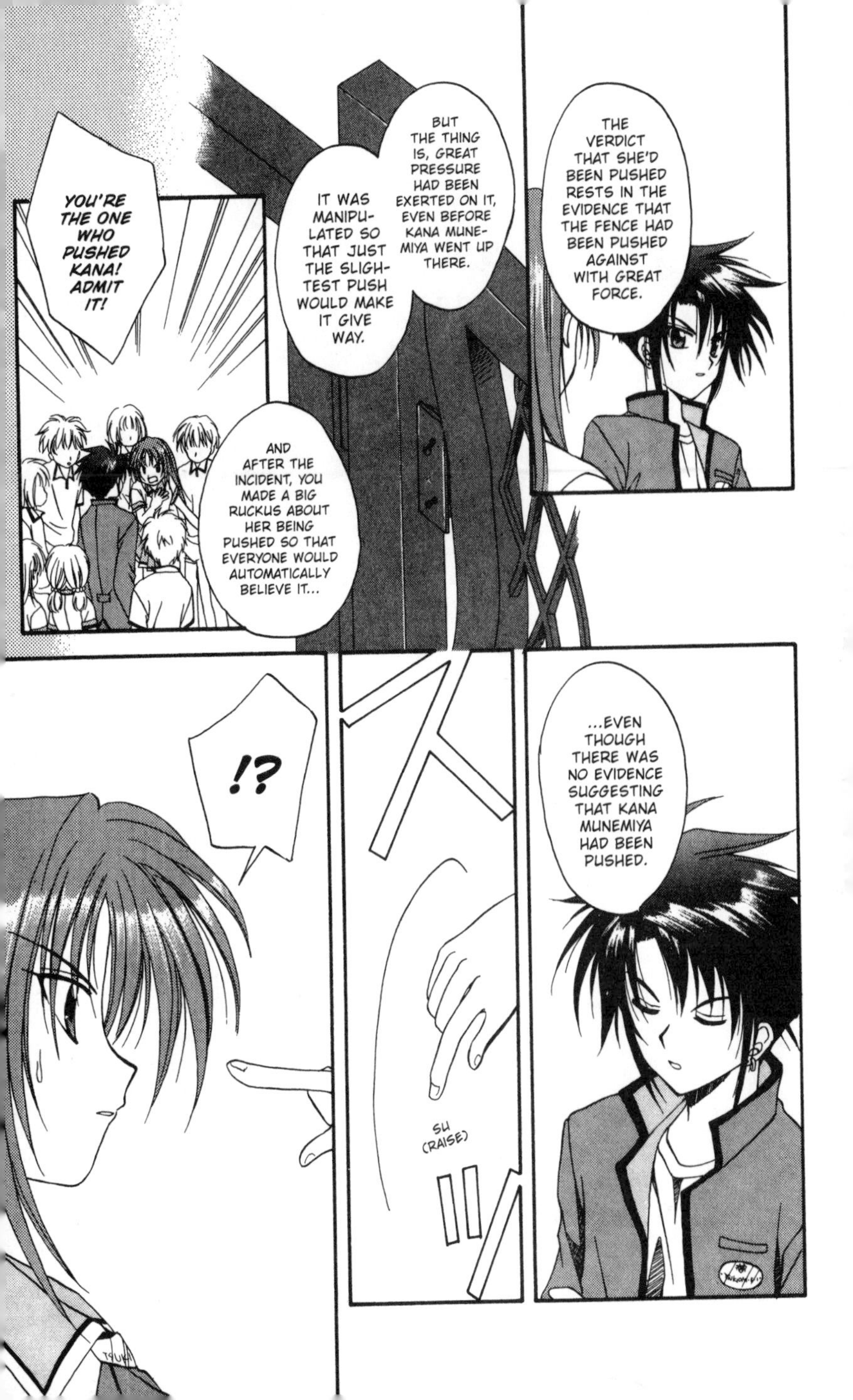
THE VERDICT THAT SHE'D BEEN PUSHED RESTS IN THE EVIDENCE THAT THE FENCE HAD BEEN PUSHED AGAINST WITH GREAT FORCE.
BUT THE THING IS, GREAT PRESSURE HAD BEEN EXERTED ON IT, EVEN BEFORE KANA MUNE-MIYA WENT UP THERE.
IT WAS MANIPU-LATED SO THAT JUST THE SLIGH-TEST PUSH WOULD MAKE IT GIVE WAY.
AND AFTER THE INCIDENT, YOU MADE A BIG RUCKUS ABOUT HER BEING PUSHED SO THAT EVERYONE WOULD AUTOMATICALLY BELIEVE IT...
YOU'RE THE ONE WHO PUSHED KANA! ADMIT IT!
...EVEN THOUGH THERE WAS NO EVIDENCE SUGGESTING THAT KANA MUNEMIYA HAD BEEN PUSHED.
SU (RAISE)
!?

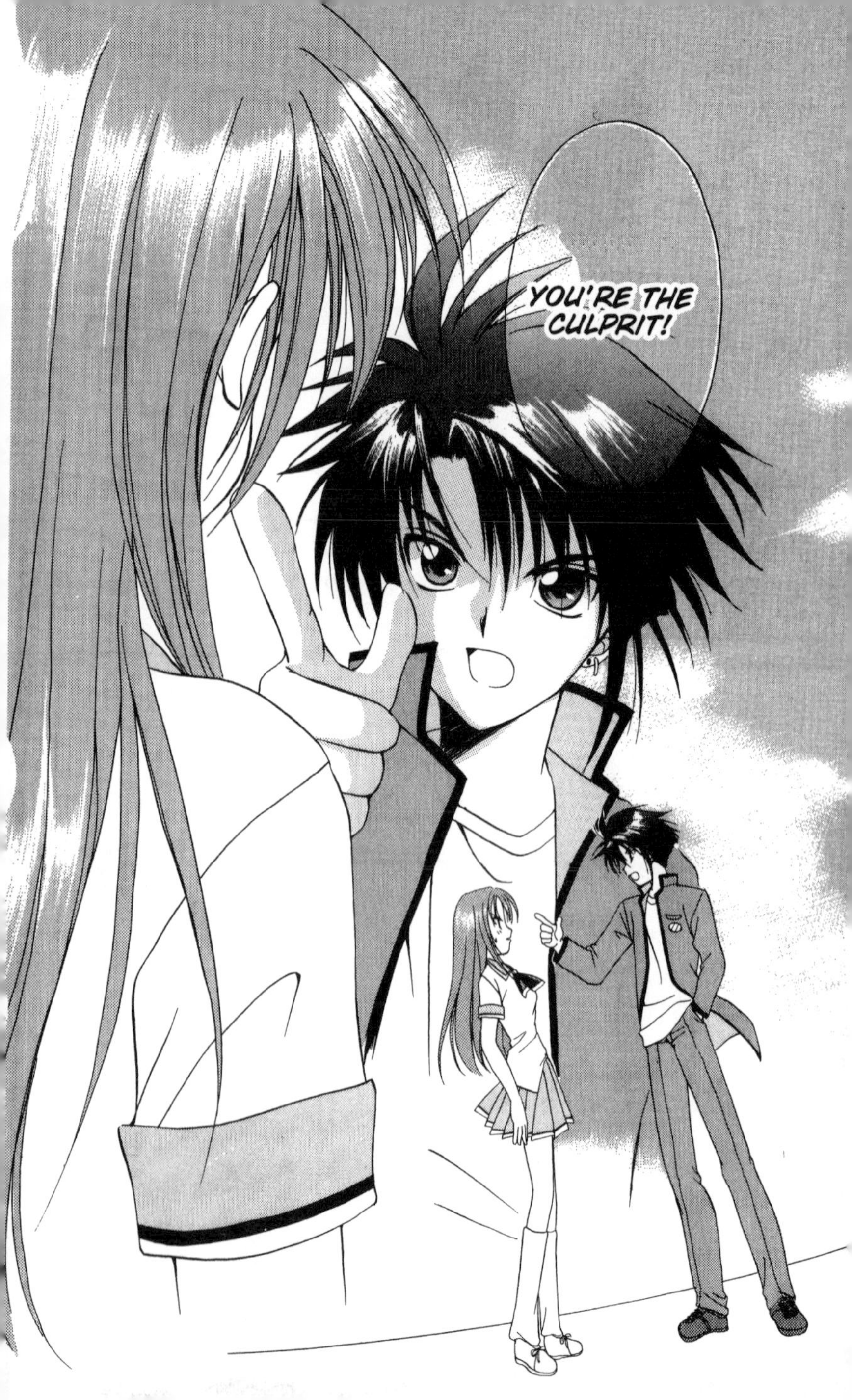
YOU'RE THE CULPRIT!

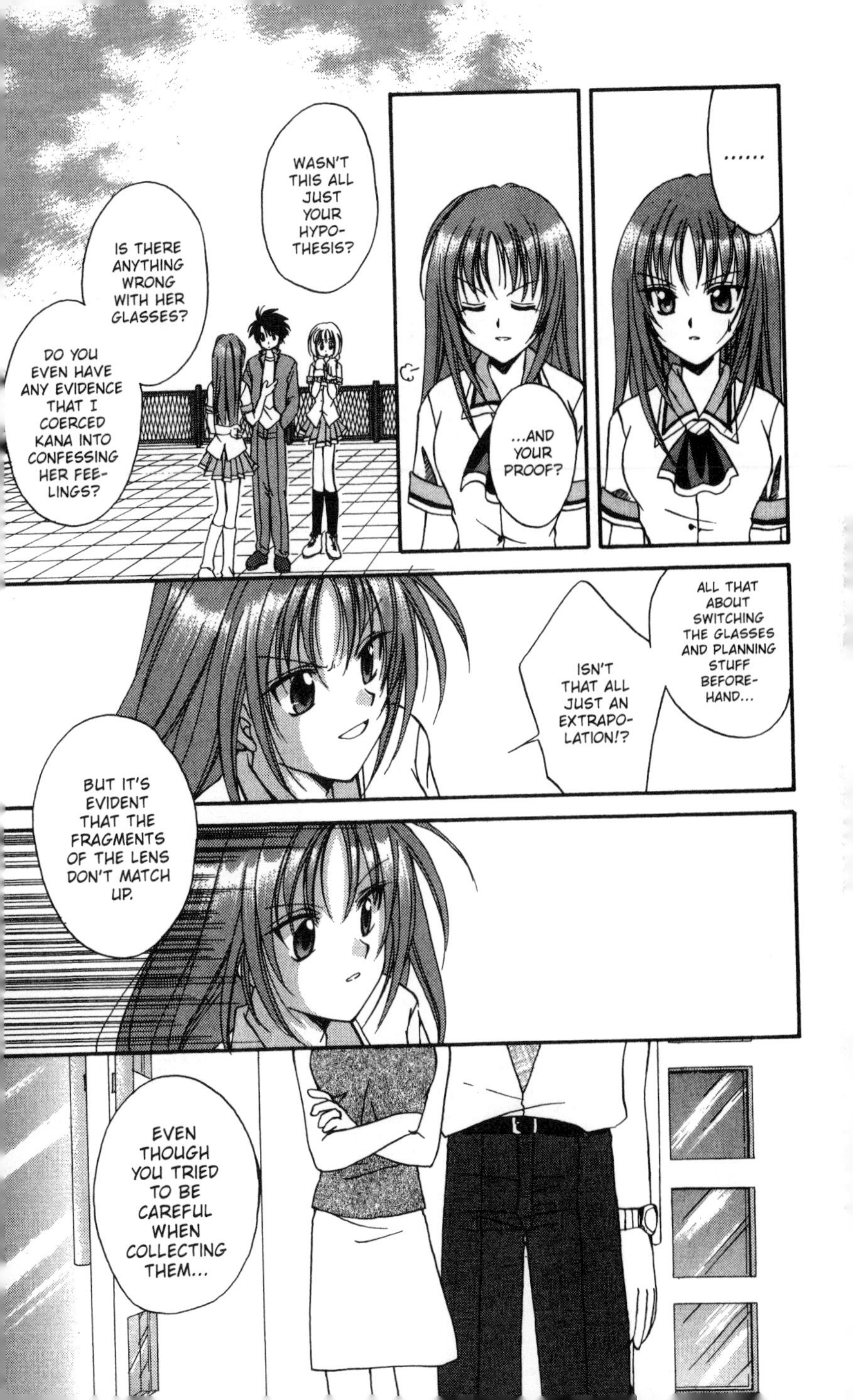
......
...AND YOUR PROOF?
WASN'T THIS ALL JUST YOUR HYPOTHESIS?
IS THERE ANYTHING WRONG WITH HER GLASSES?
DO YOU EVEN HAVE ANY EVIDENCE THAT I COERCED KANA INTO CONFESSING HER FEELINGS?
ALL THAT ABOUT SWITCHING THE GLASSES AND PLANNING STUFF BEFOREHAND...
ISN'T THAT ALL JUST AN EXTRAPOLATION!?
BUT IT'S EVIDENT THAT THE FRAGMENTS OF THE LENS DON'T MATCH UP.
EVEN THOUGH YOU TRIED TO BE CAREFUL WHEN COLLECTING THEM...

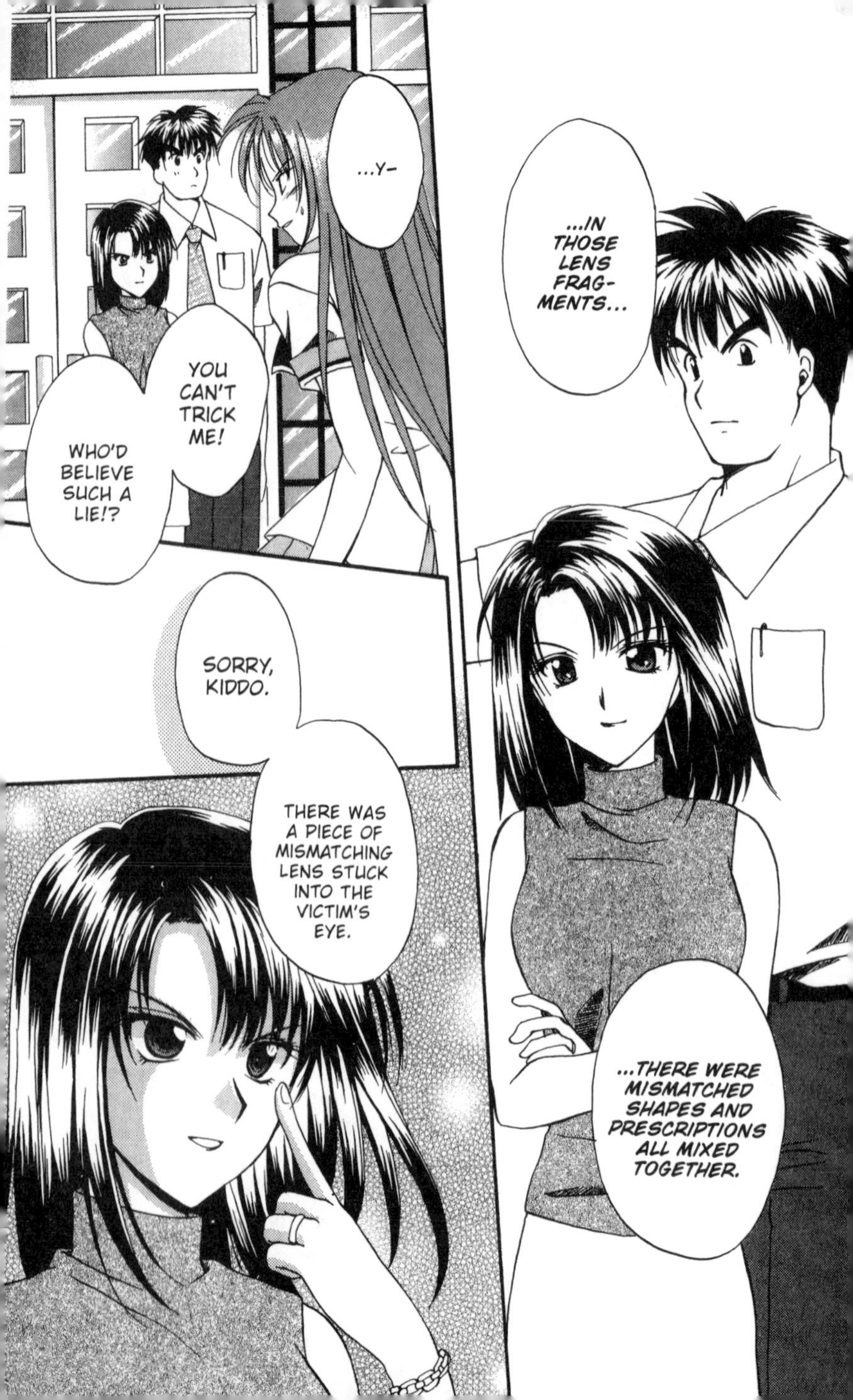
...IN THOSE LENS FRAG- MENTS...
...THERE WERE MISMATCHED SHAPES AND PRESCRIPTIONS ALL MIXED TOGETHER.
...Y-
YOU CAN'T TRICK ME!
WHO'D BELIEVE SUCH A LIE!?
SORRY, KIDDO.
THERE WAS A PIECE OF MISMATCHING LENS STUCK INTO THE VICTIM'S EYE.

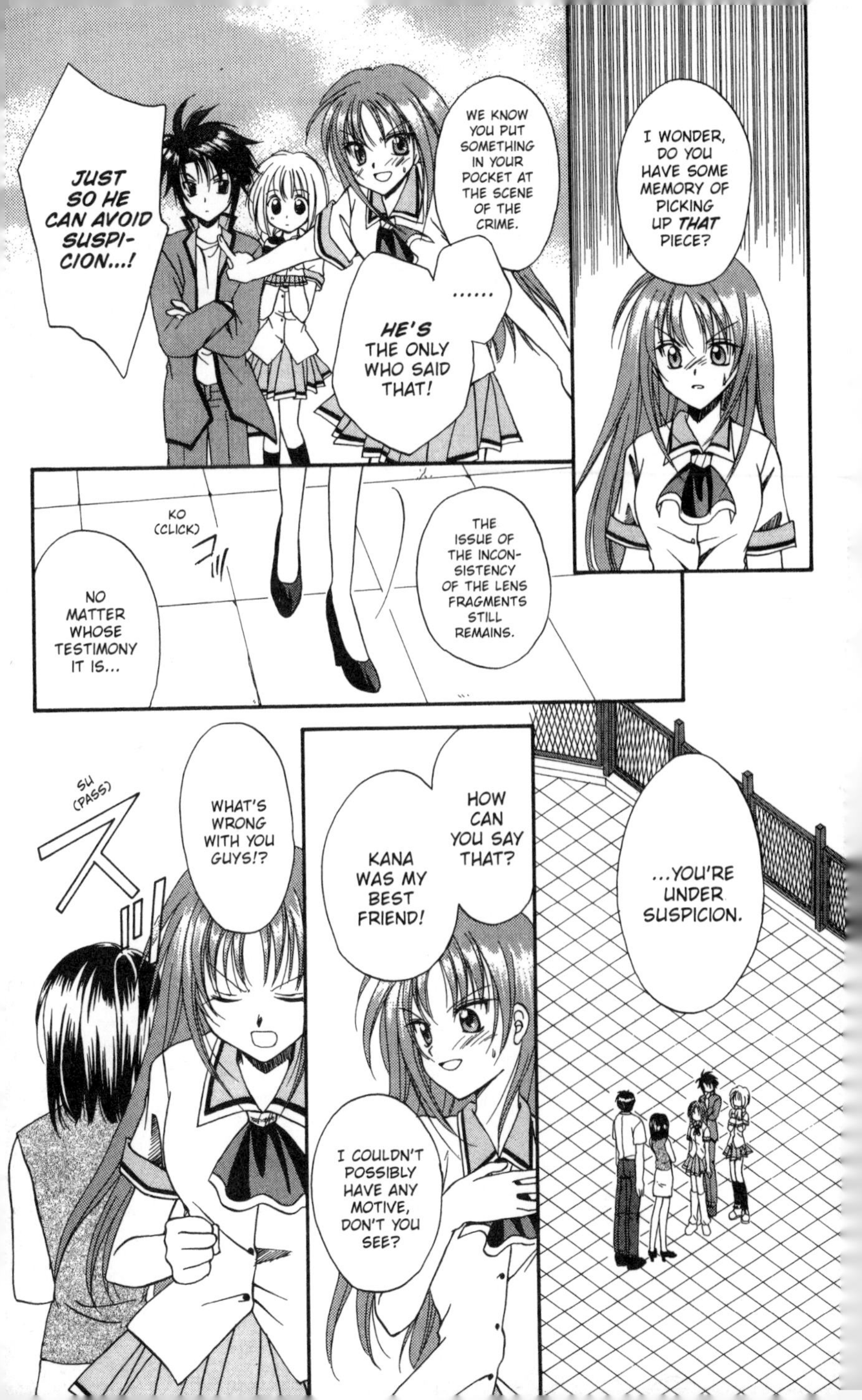
I WONDER, DO YOU HAVE SOME MEMORY OF PICKING UP *THAT* PIECE?
WE KNOW YOU PUT SOMETHING IN YOUR POCKET AT THE SCENE OF THE CRIME.
......
HE'S THE ONLY WHO SAID THAT!
JUST SO HE CAN AVOID SUSPI-CION...!
KO (CLICK)
THE ISSUE OF THE INCON-SISTENCY OF THE LENS FRAGMENTS STILL REMAINS.
NO MATTER WHOSE TESTIMONY IT IS...
...YOU'RE UNDER SUSPICION.
HOW CAN YOU SAY THAT?
KANA WAS MY BEST FRIEND!
I COULDN'T POSSIBLY HAVE ANY MOTIVE, DON'T YOU SEE?
SU (PASS)
WHAT'S WRONG WITH YOU GUYS!?

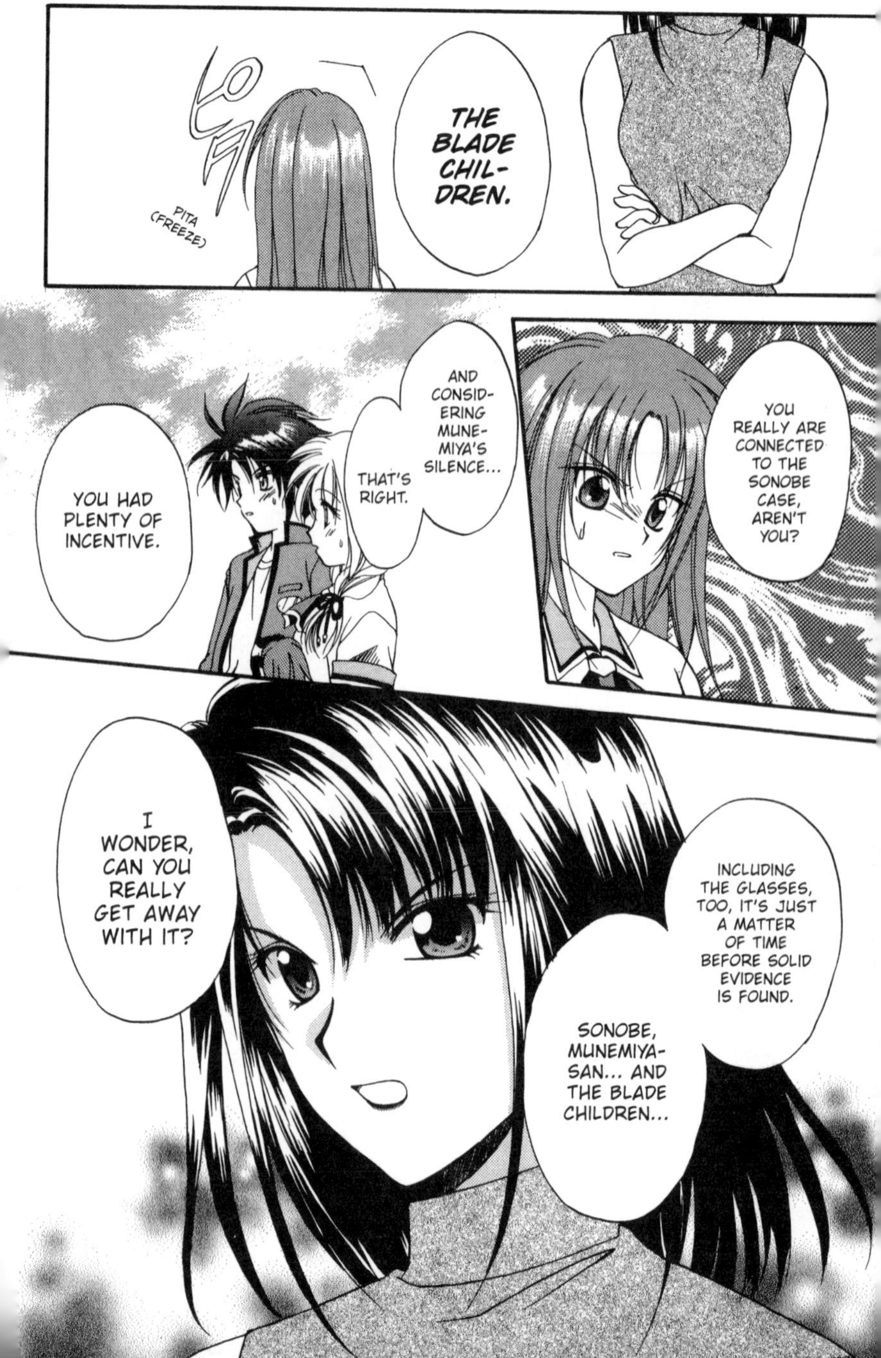
THE BLADE CHIL-DREN.
PITA (FREEZE)
YOU REALLY ARE CONNECTED TO THE SONOBE CASE, AREN'T YOU?
AND CONSID-ERING MUNE-MIYA'S SILENCE...
THAT'S RIGHT.
YOU HAD PLENTY OF INCENTIVE.
INCLUDING THE GLASSES, TOO, IT'S JUST A MATTER OF TIME BEFORE SOLID EVIDENCE IS FOUND.
SONOBE, MUNEMIYA-SAN... AND THE BLADE CHILDREN...
I WONDER, CAN YOU REALLY GET AWAY WITH IT?

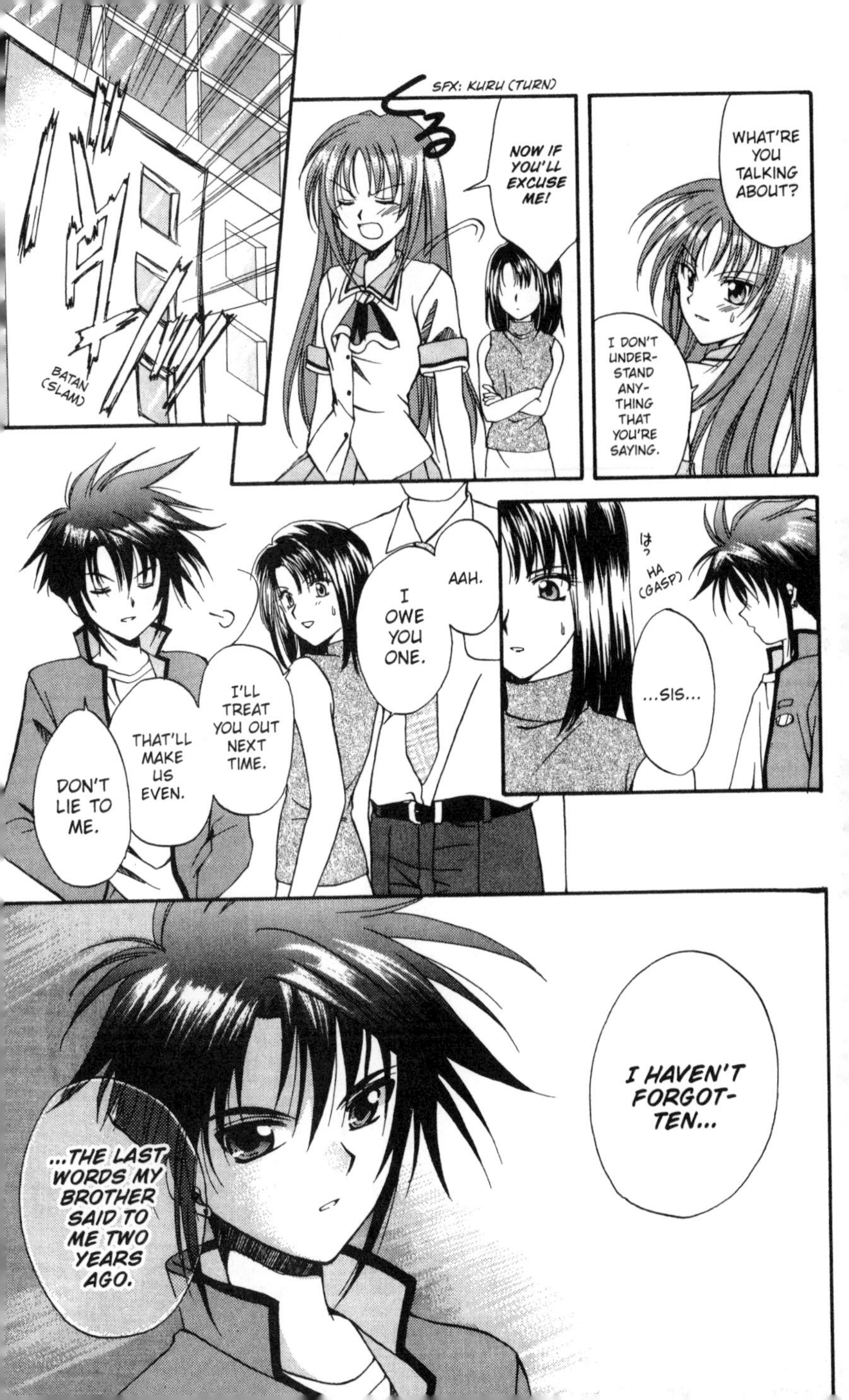
WHAT'RE YOU TALKING ABOUT?
I DON'T UNDER-STAND ANY-THING THAT YOU'RE SAYING.
SFX: KURU (TURN)
NOW IF YOU'LL EXCUSE ME!
BATAN (SLAM)
はっ
HA (GASP)
...SIS...
AAH.
I OWE YOU ONE.
I'LL TREAT YOU OUT NEXT TIME.
THAT'LL MAKE US EVEN.
DON'T LIE TO ME.
I HAVEN'T FORGOT-TEN...
...THE LAST WORDS MY BROTHER SAID TO ME TWO YEARS AGO.

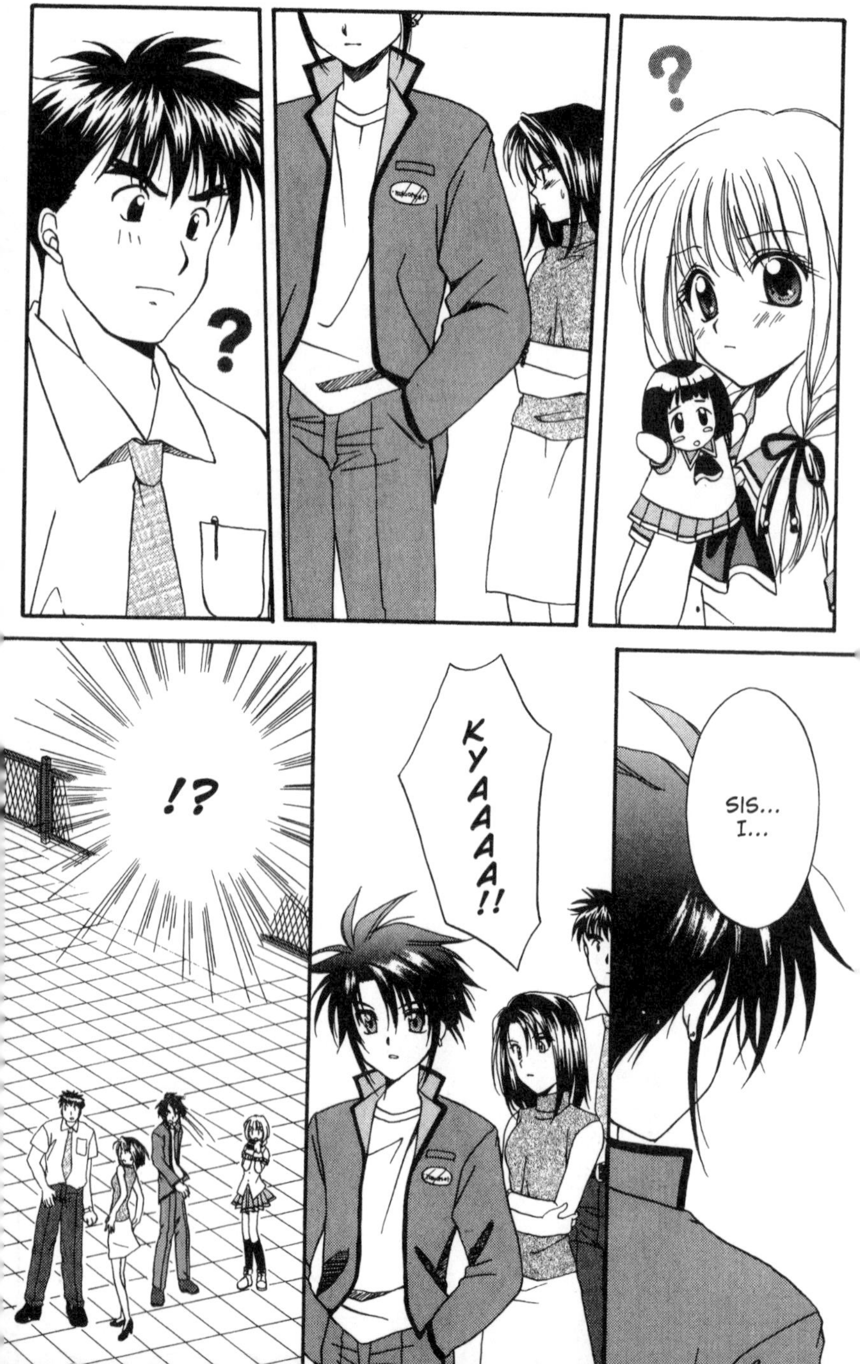
?
?
SIS... I...
KYAAAAA!!
!?

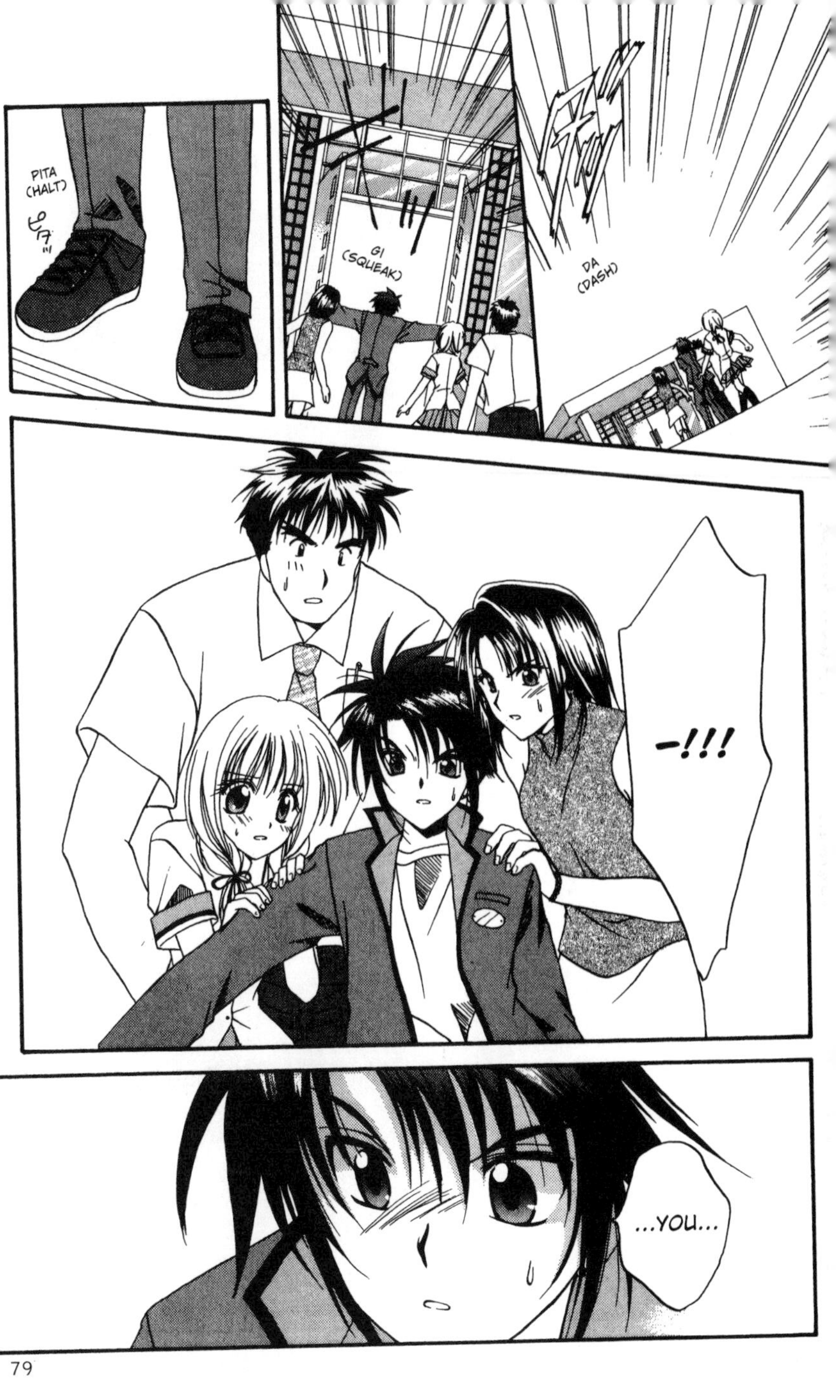
DA
(DASH)
GI
(SQUEAK)
PITA
(HALT)
ピタッ
—!!!
...YOU...

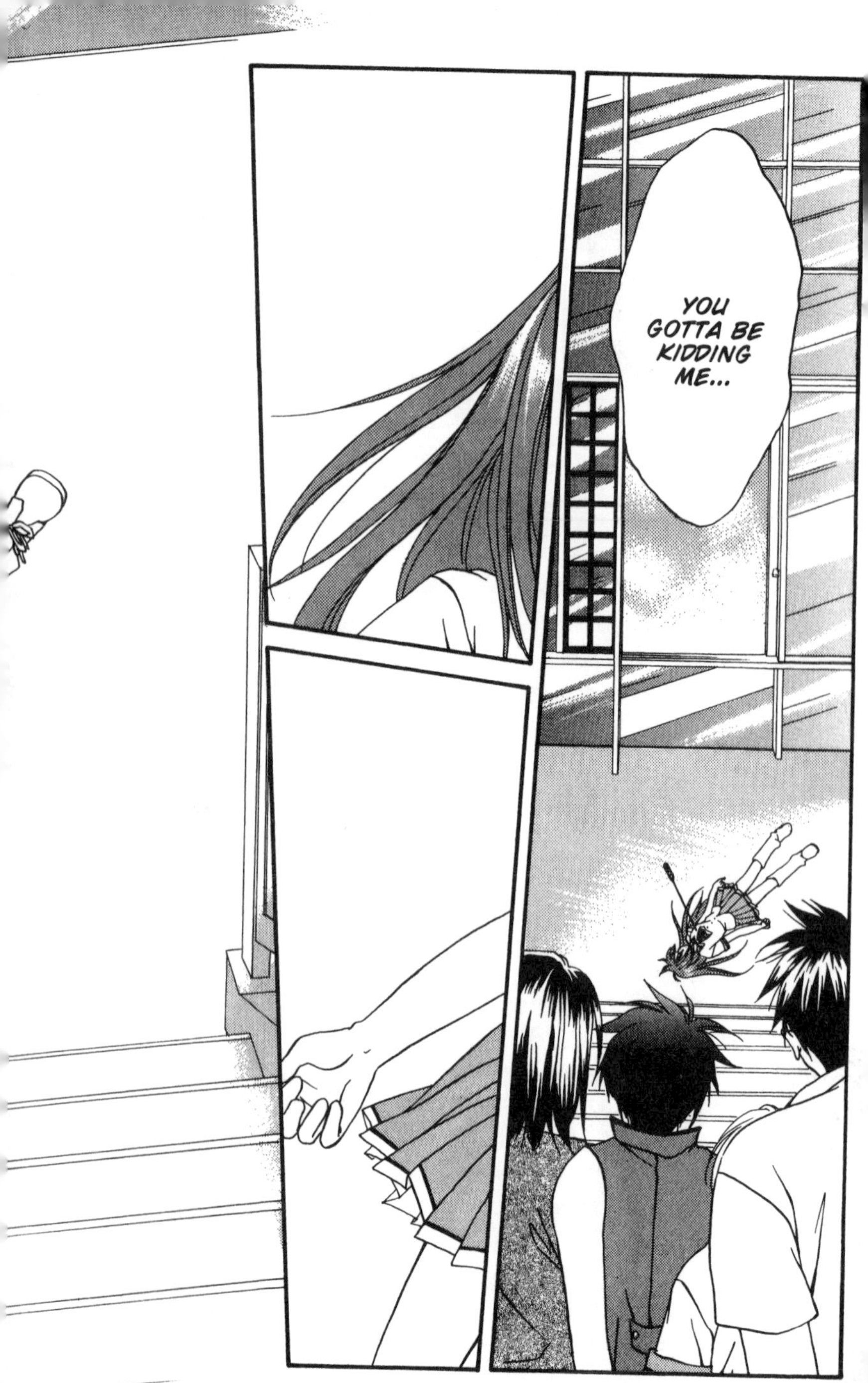
YOU GOTTA BE KIDDING ME...

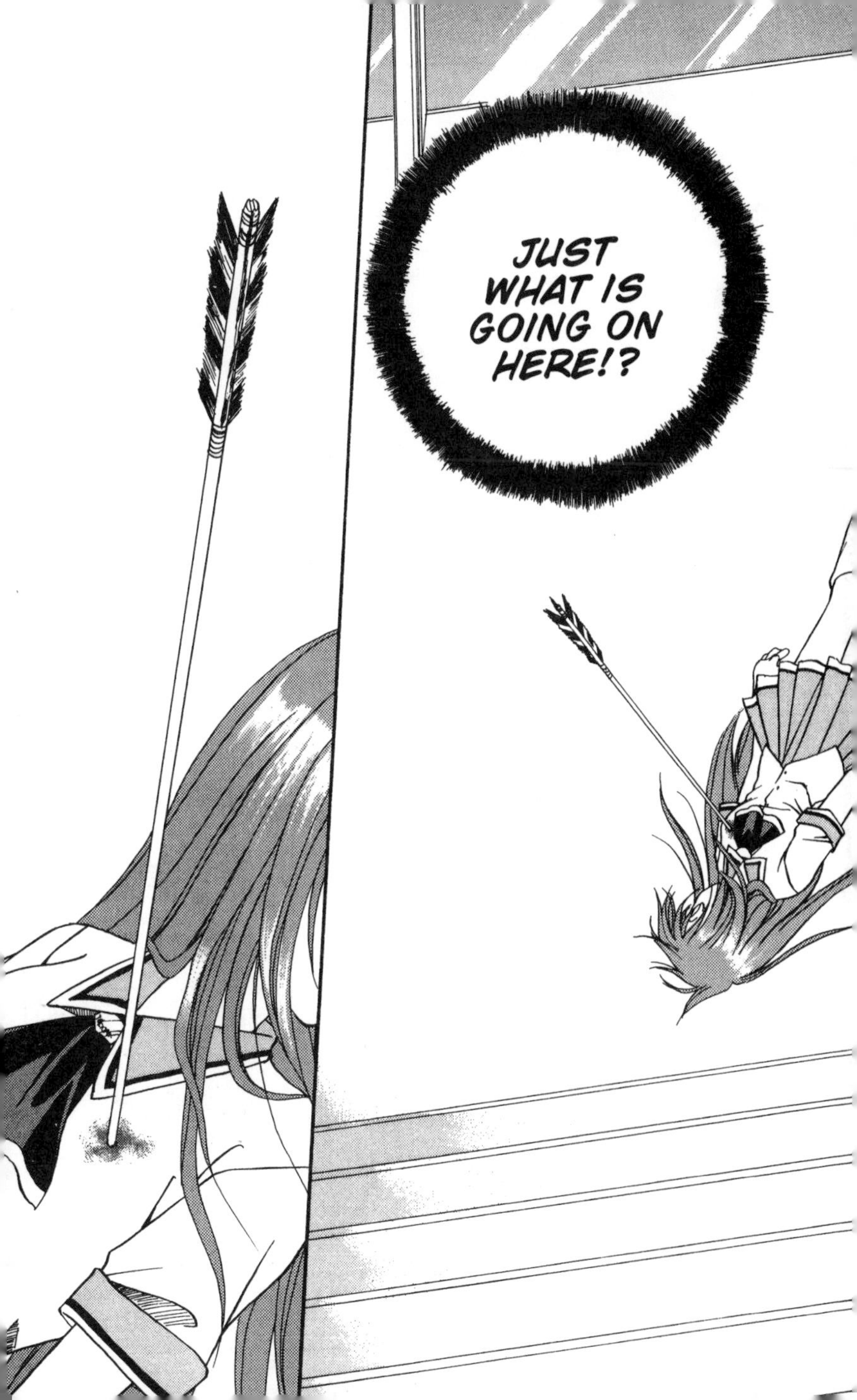
JUST WHAT IS GOING ON HERE!?

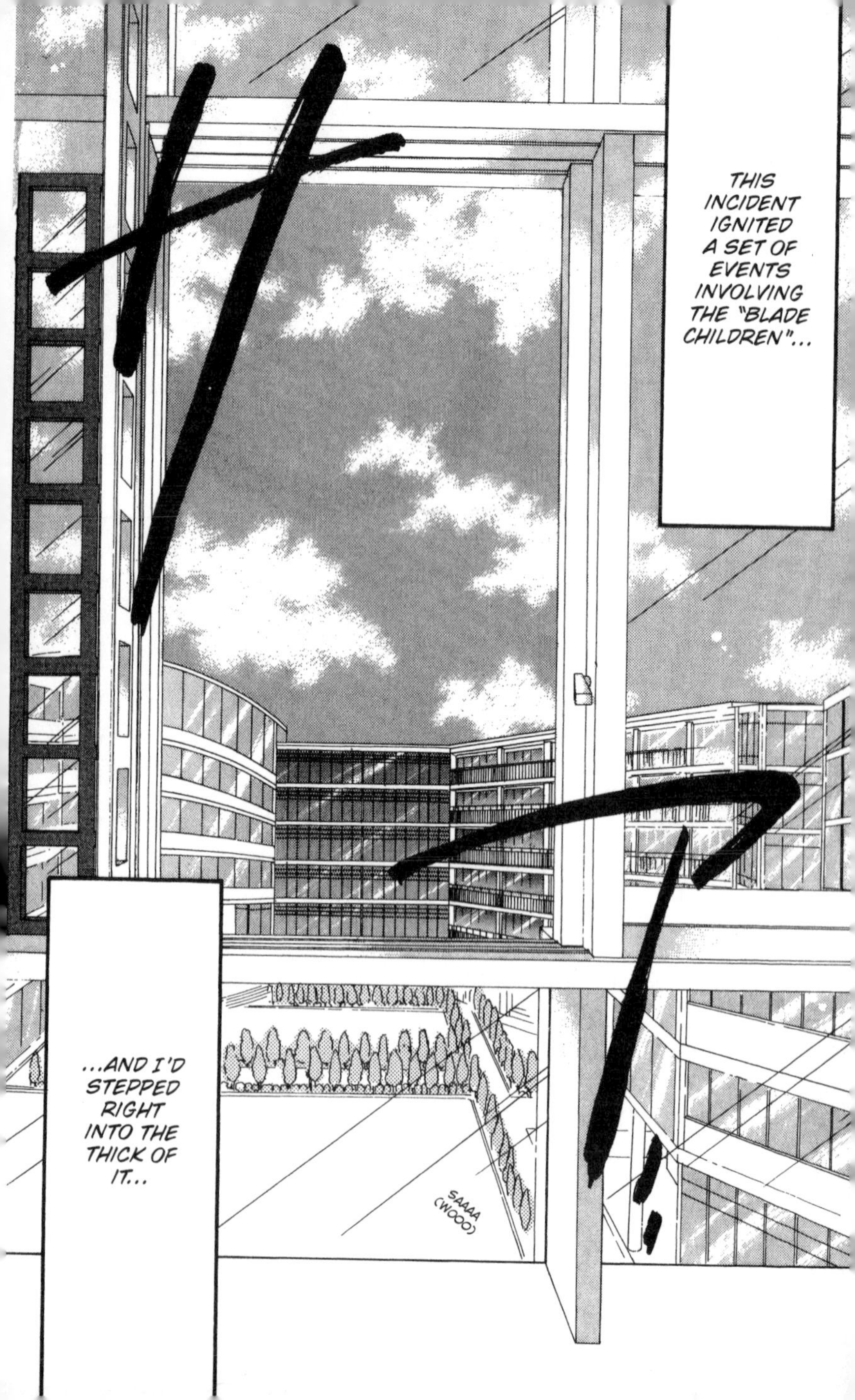
THIS INCIDENT IGNITED A SET OF EVENTS INVOLVING THE "BLADE CHILDREN"...
...AND I'D STEPPED RIGHT INTO THE THICK OF IT...
SAAAA (WOOO)

CHAPTER THREE

Apollo's Arrow

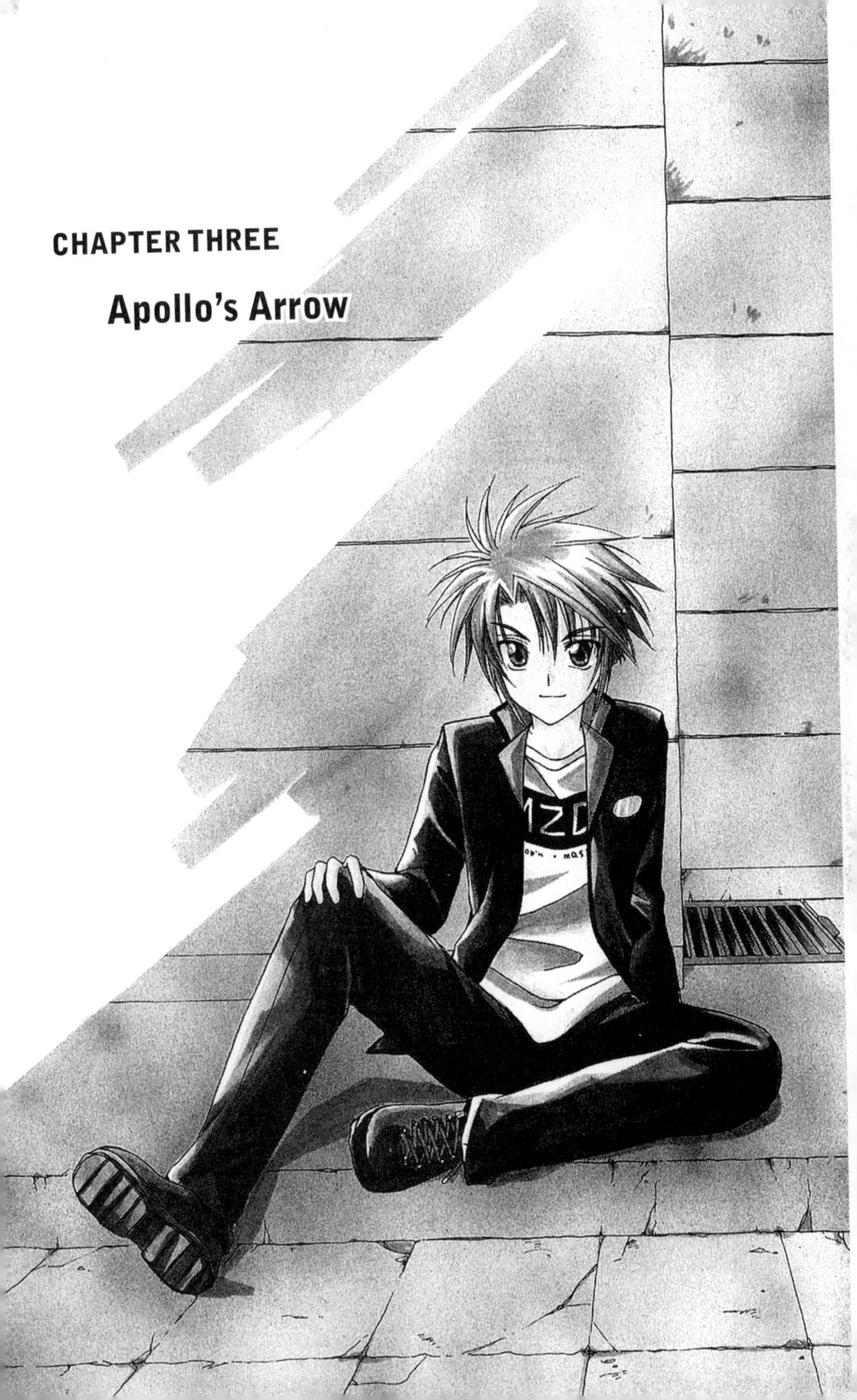

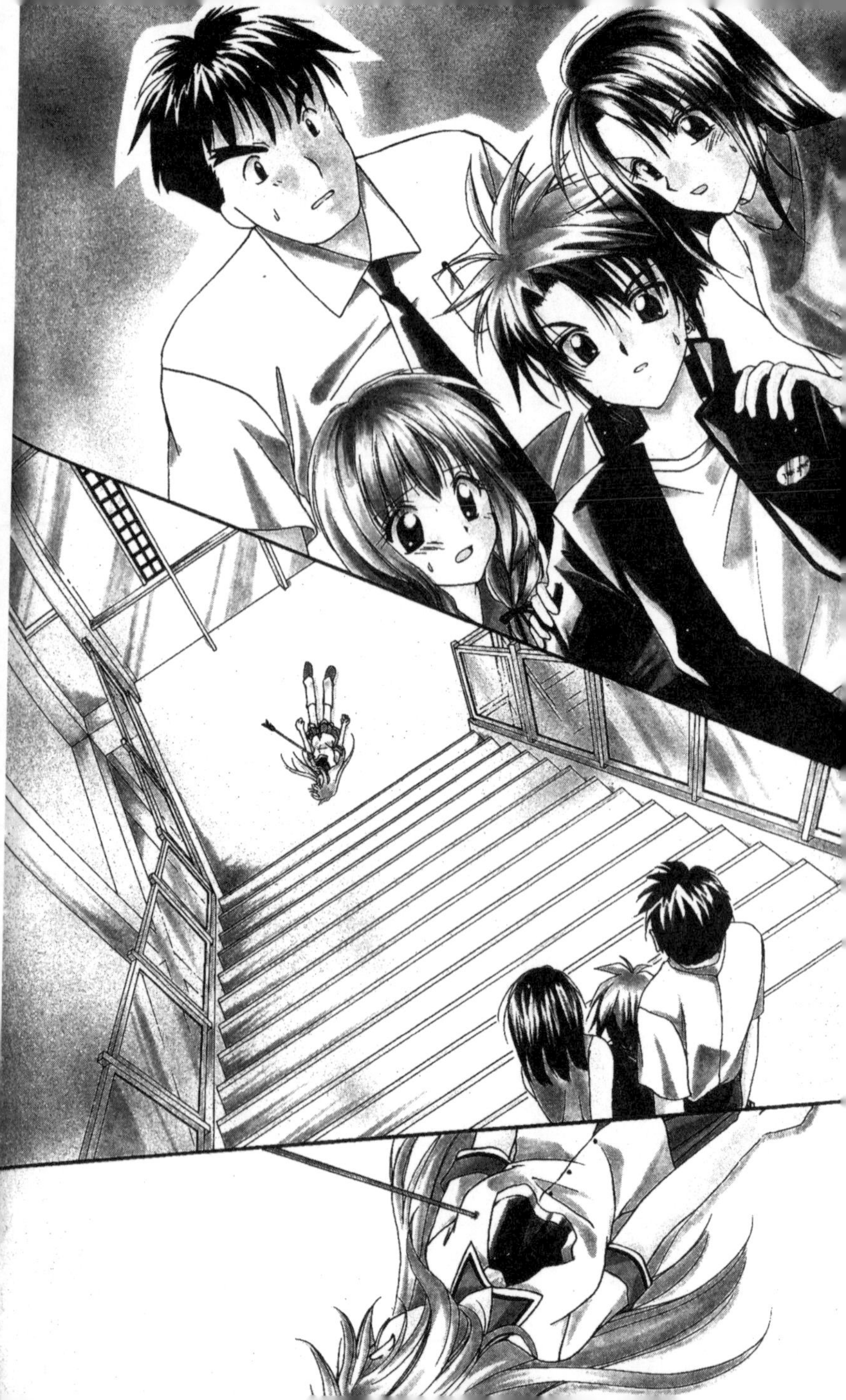

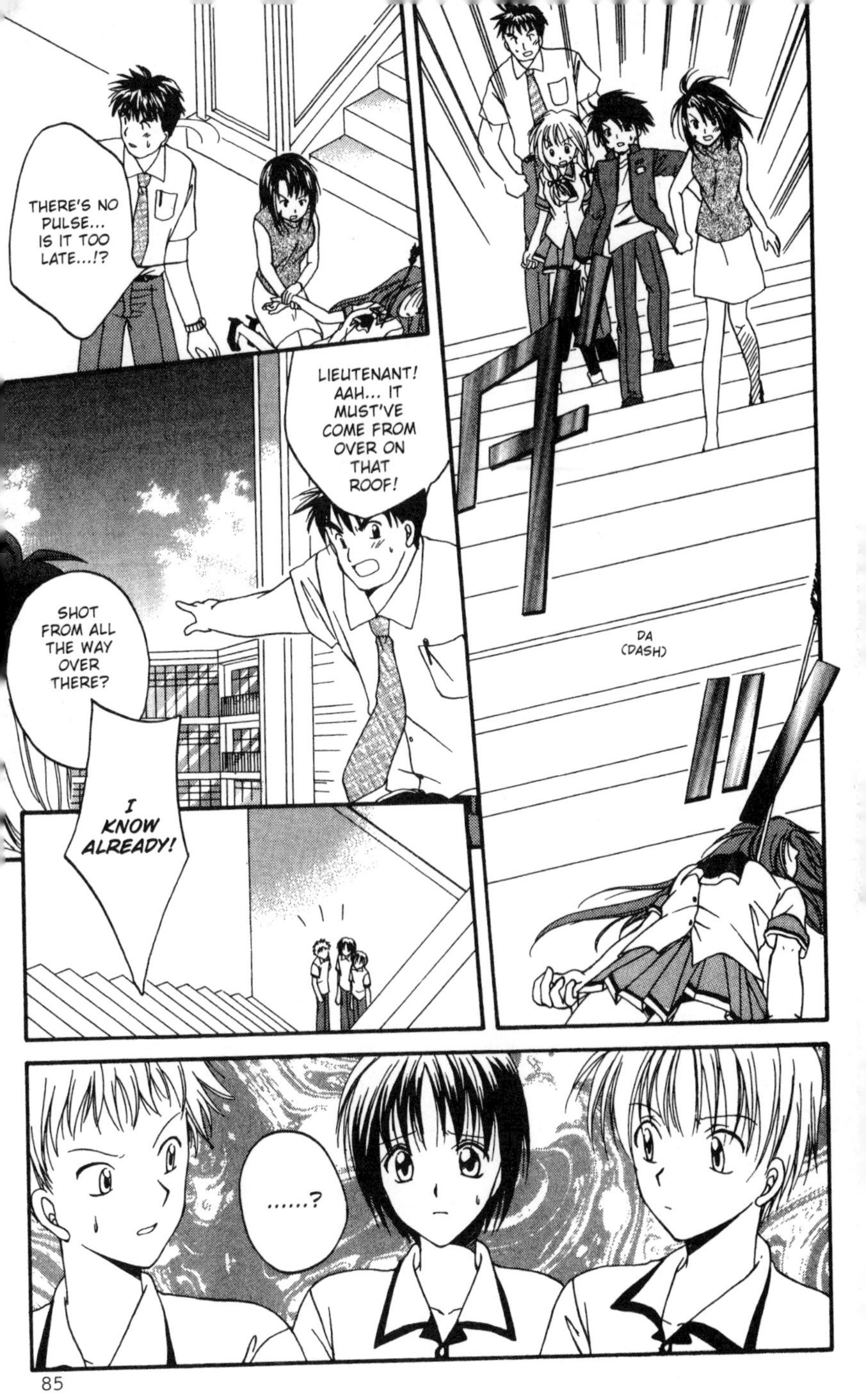
DA (DASH)
THERE'S NO PULSE... IS IT TOO LATE...!?
LIEUTENANT! AAH... IT MUST'VE COME FROM OVER ON THAT ROOF!
SHOT FROM ALL THE WAY OVER THERE?
I KNOW ALREADY!
......?

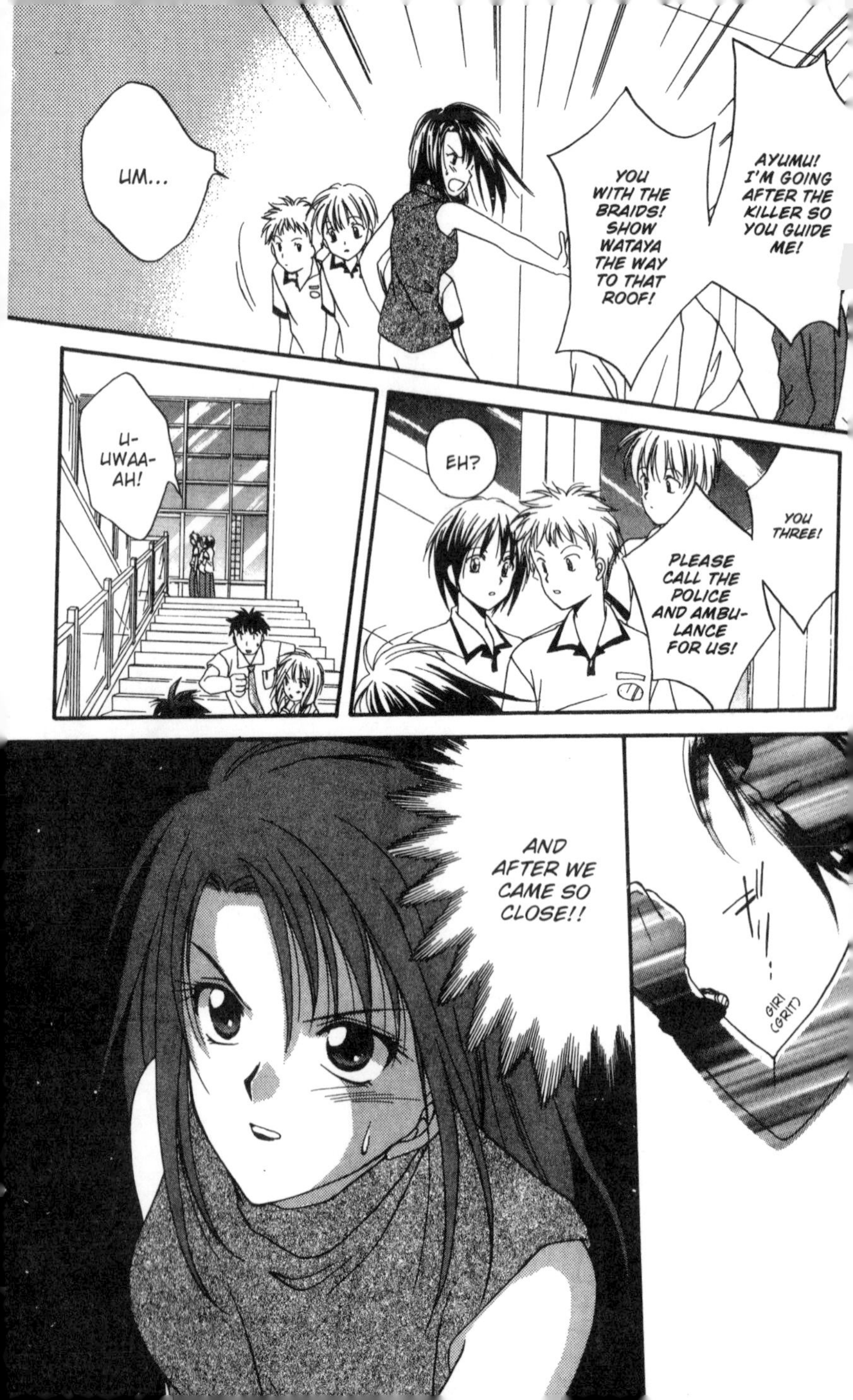
AYUMU! I'M GOING AFTER THE KILLER SO YOU GUIDE ME!
YOU WITH THE BRAIDS! SHOW WATAYA THE WAY TO THAT ROOF!
UM...
YOU THREE!
PLEASE CALL THE POLICE AND AMBULANCE FOR US!
EH?
U-UWAAA-AH!
GIRI (GRIT)
AND AFTER WE CAME SO CLOSE!!

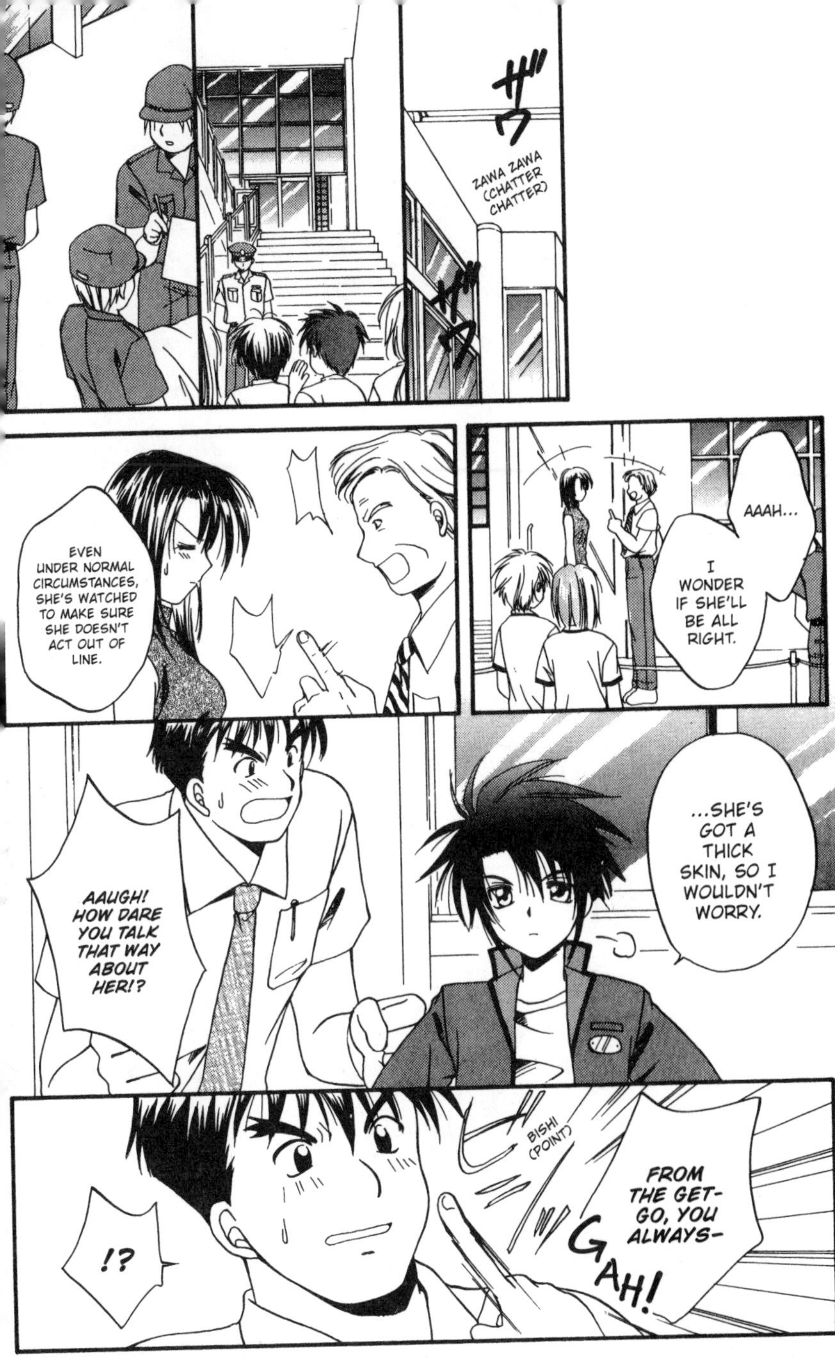
ZAWA ZAWA (CHATTER CHATTER)
AAAH...
I WONDER IF SHE'LL BE ALL RIGHT.
EVEN UNDER NORMAL CIRCUMSTANCES, SHE'S WATCHED TO MAKE SURE SHE DOESN'T ACT OUT OF LINE.
...SHE'S GOT A THICK SKIN, SO I WOULDN'T WORRY.
AAUGH! HOW DARE YOU TALK THAT WAY ABOUT HER!?
BISHI (POINT)
FROM THE GET-GO, YOU ALWAYS-
GAH!
!?

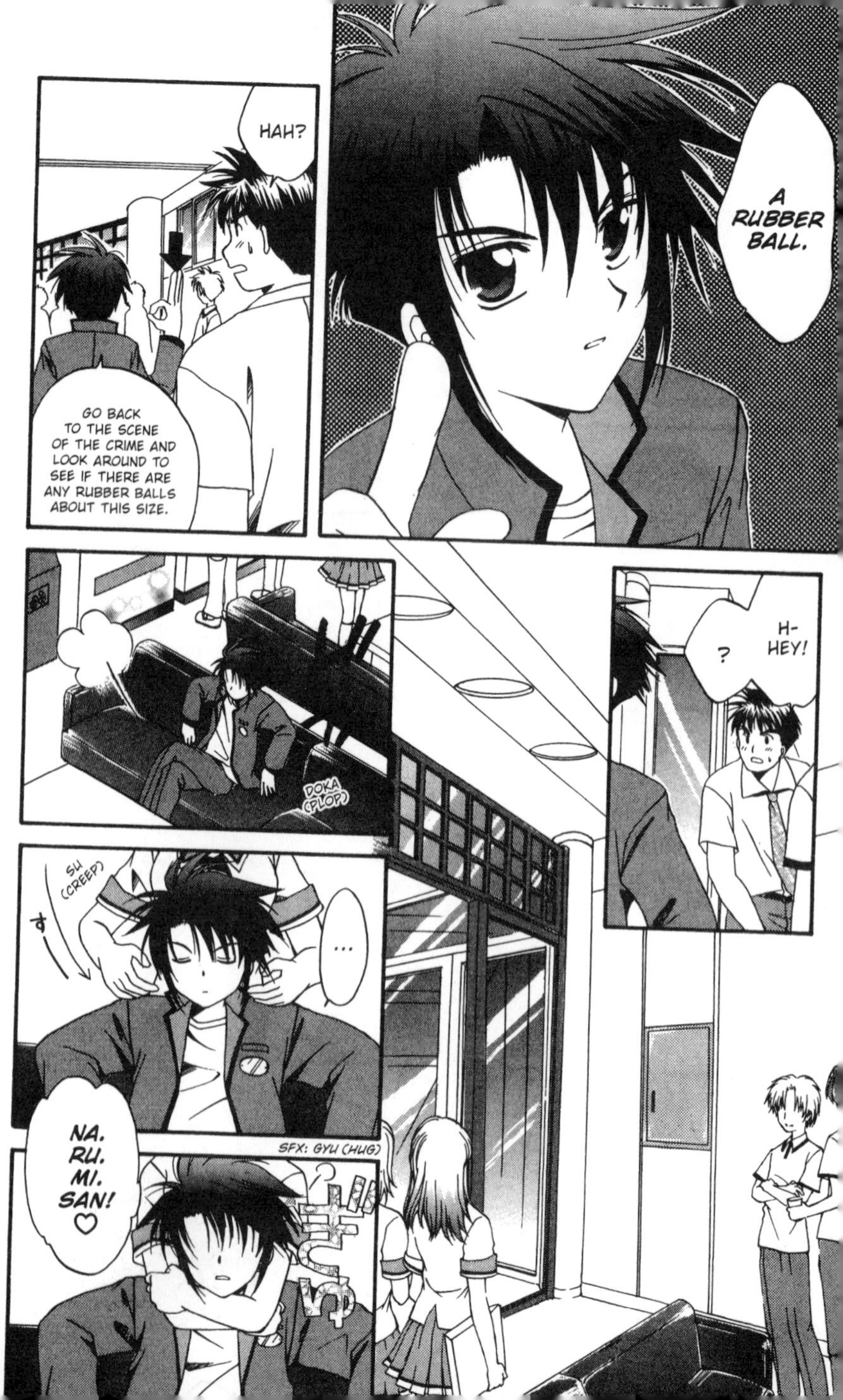
A RUBBER BALL.
HAH?
GO BACK TO THE SCENE OF THE CRIME AND LOOK AROUND TO SEE IF THERE ARE ANY RUBBER BALLS ABOUT THIS SIZE.
H- HEY!
?
DOKA (PLOP)
す
SU (CREEP)
...
NA. RU. MI. SAN! ♡
SFX: GYU (HUG)

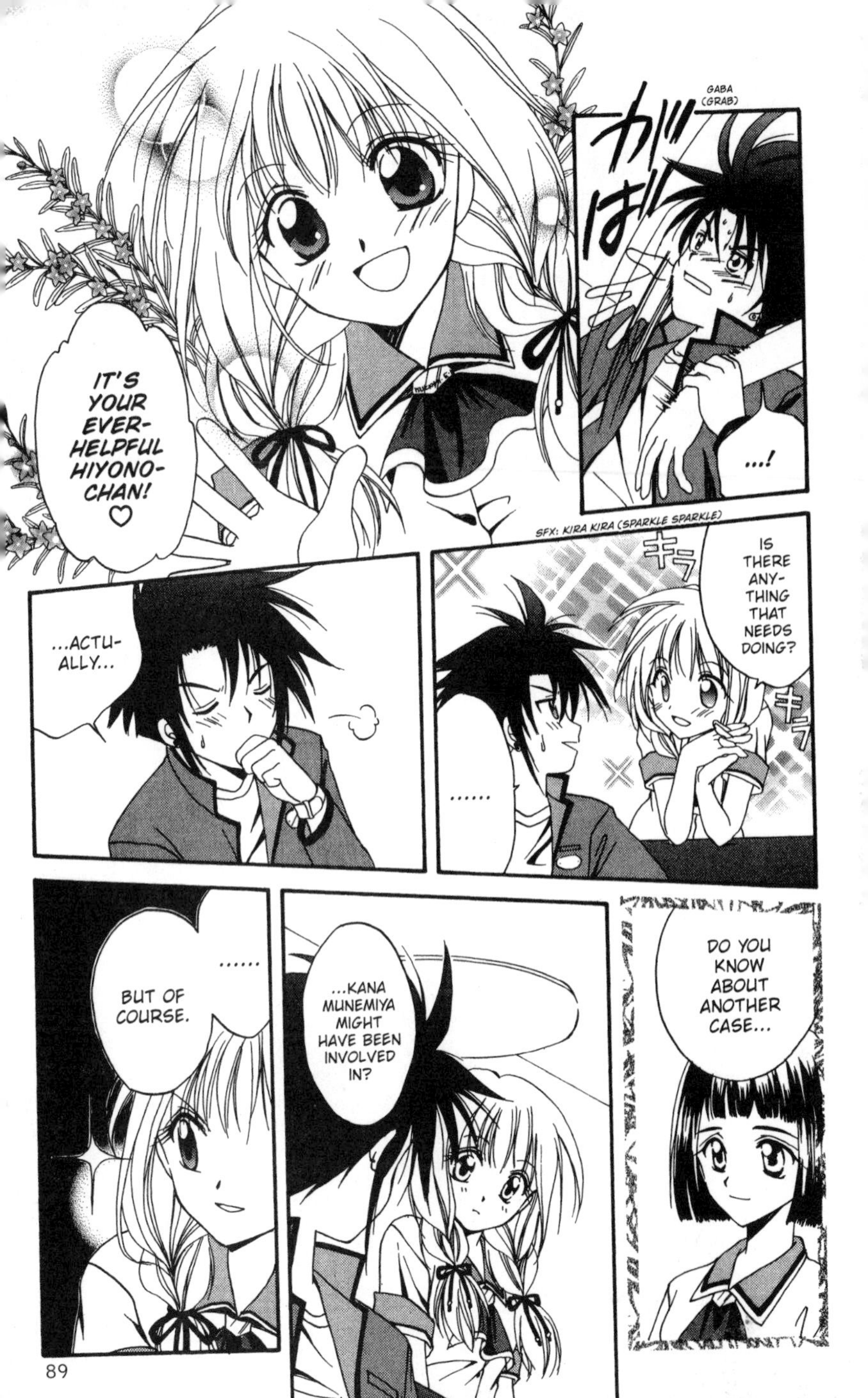
GABA (GRAB)
...!
IT'S YOUR EVER-HELPFUL HIYONO-CHAN! ♡
SFX: KIRA KIRA (SPARKLE SPARKLE)
IS THERE ANYTHING THAT NEEDS DOING?
......
...ACTUALLY...
DO YOU KNOW ABOUT ANOTHER CASE...
...KANA MUNEMIYA MIGHT HAVE BEEN INVOLVED IN?
......
BUT OF COURSE.

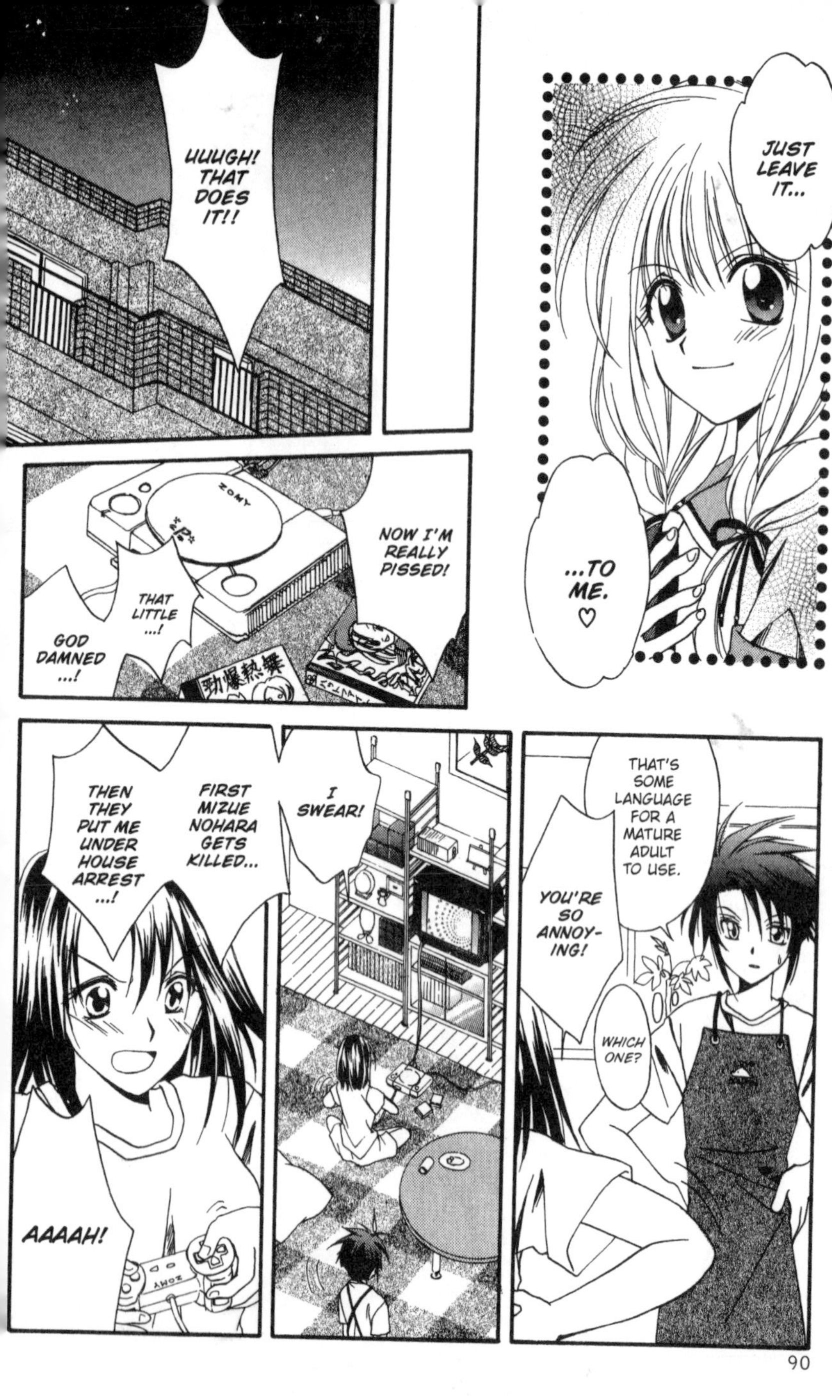
JUST LEAVE IT...
...TO ME. ♡
UUUGH! THAT DOES IT!!
NOW I'M REALLY PISSED!
THAT LITTLE ...!
GOD DAMNED ...!
THAT'S SOME LANGUAGE FOR A MATURE ADULT TO USE.
YOU'RE SO ANNOY-ING!
WHICH ONE?
I SWEAR!
FIRST MIZUE NOHARA GETS KILLED...
THEN THEY PUT ME UNDER HOUSE ARREST ...!
AAAAH!

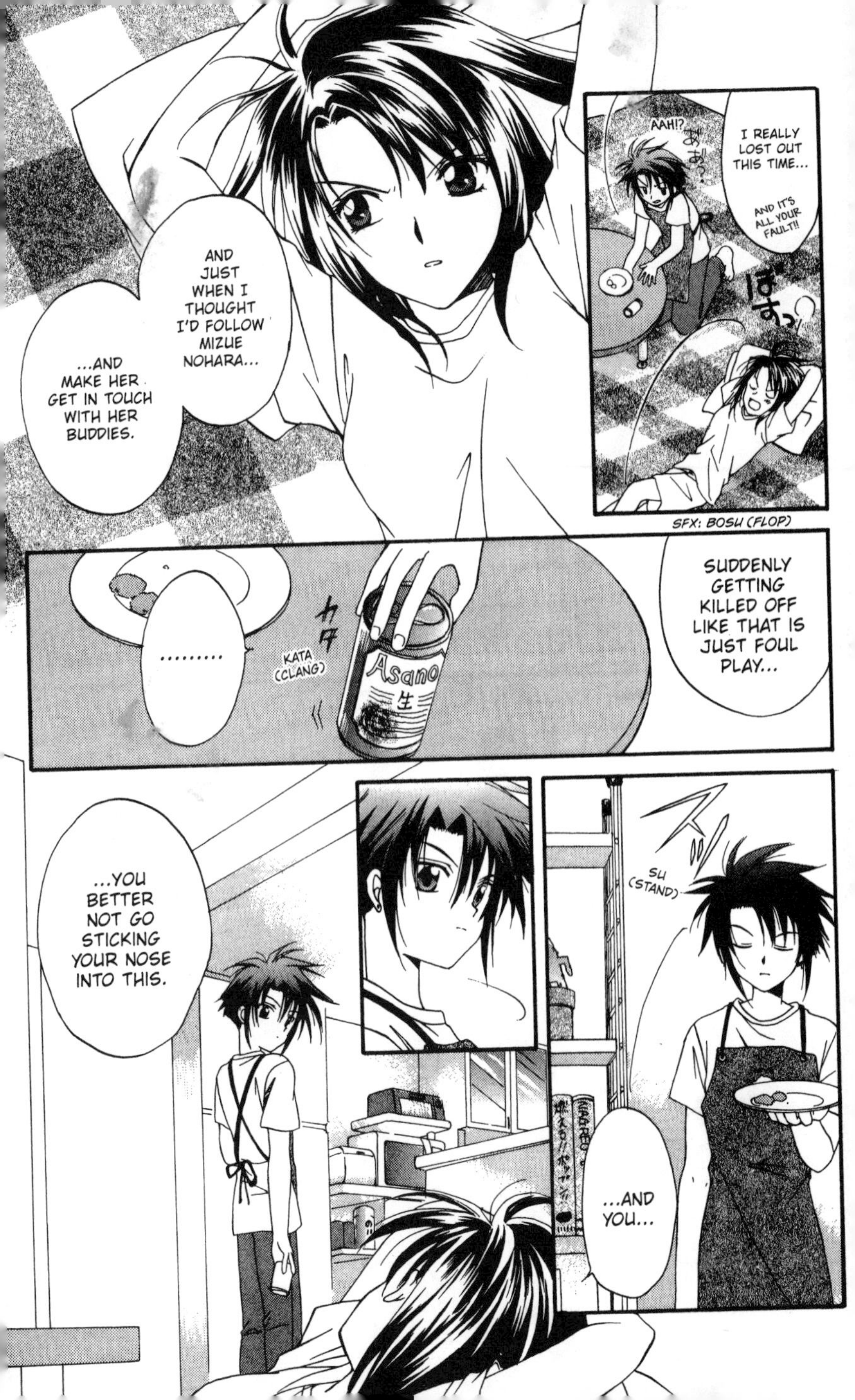
I REALLY LOST OUT THIS TIME...
AAH!?
AND IT'S ALL YOUR FAULT!!
SFX: BOSU (FLOP)
AND JUST WHEN I THOUGHT I'D FOLLOW MIZUE NOHARA...
...AND MAKE HER GET IN TOUCH WITH HER BUDDIES.
SUDDENLY GETTING KILLED OFF LIKE THAT IS JUST FOUL PLAY...
KATA (CLANG)
....
SU (STAND)
...AND YOU...
...YOU BETTER NOT GO STICKING YOUR NOSE INTO THIS.

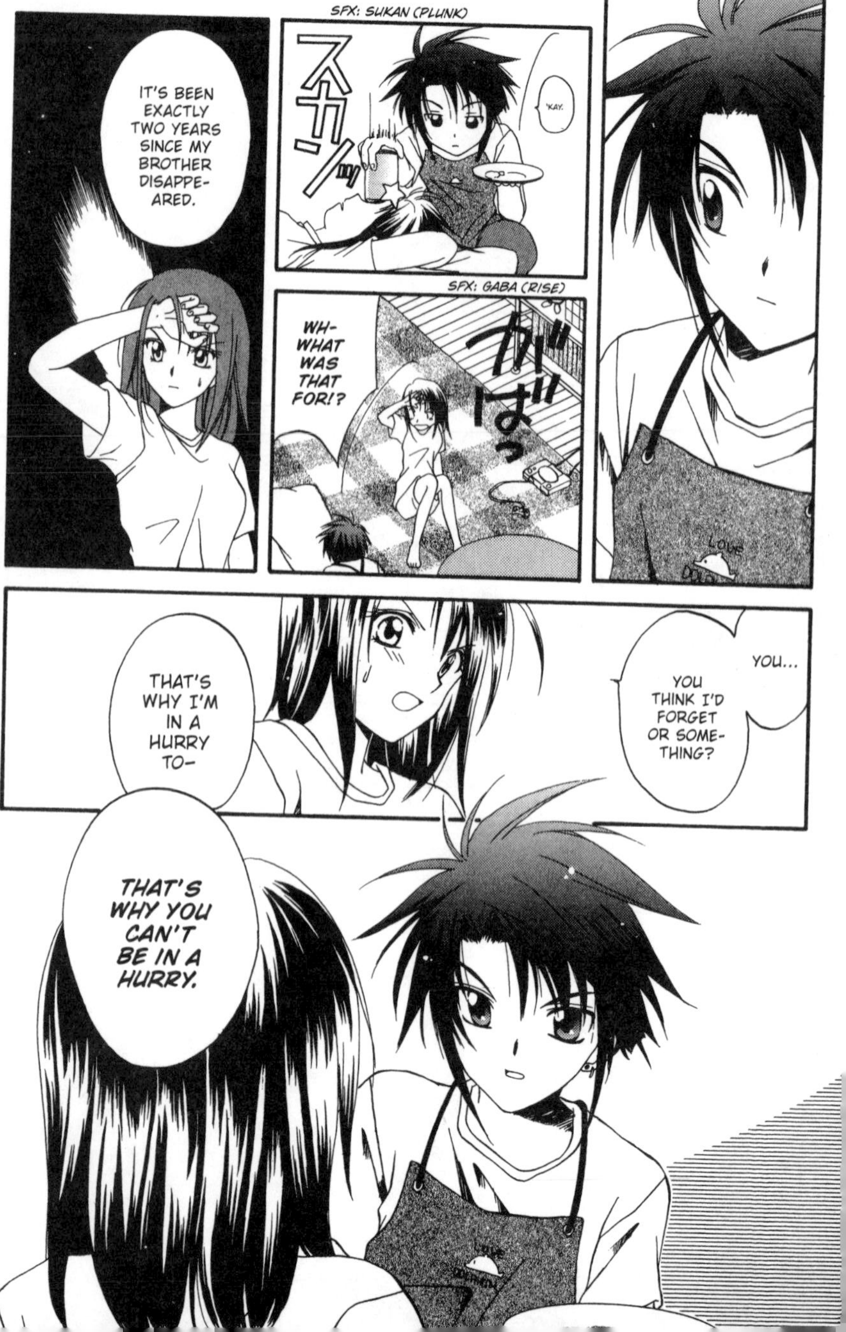
SFX: SUKAN (PLUNK)
'KAY.
SFX: GABA (RISE)
WH-WHAT WAS THAT FOR!?
IT'S BEEN EXACTLY TWO YEARS SINCE MY BROTHER DISAPPE-ARED.
YOU...
YOU THINK I'D FORGET OR SOME-THING?
THAT'S WHY I'M IN A HURRY TO-
THAT'S WHY YOU CAN'T BE IN A HURRY.

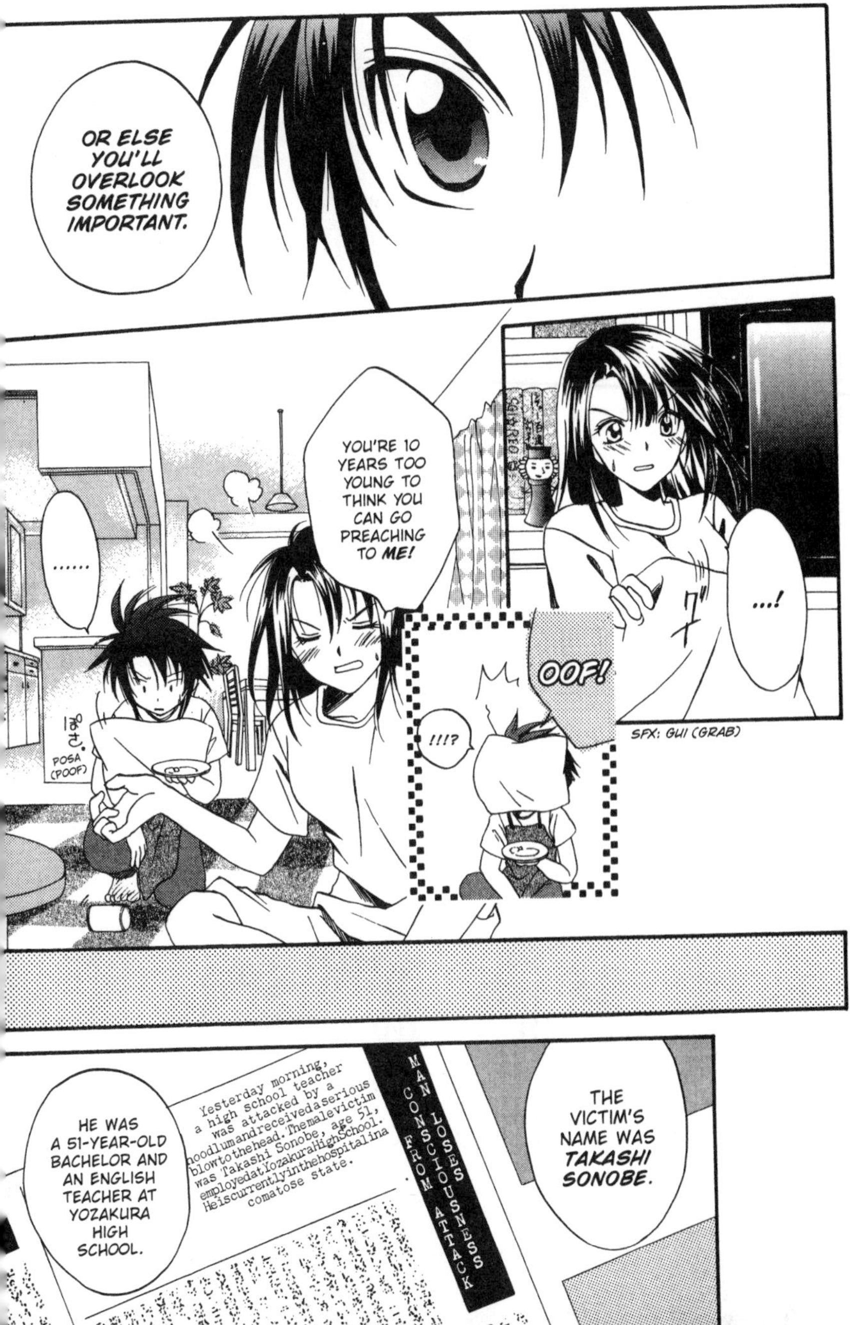
OR ELSE YOU'LL OVERLOOK SOMETHING IMPORTANT.
...!
SFX: GUI (GRAB)
YOU'RE 10 YEARS TOO YOUNG TO THINK YOU CAN GO PREACHING TO ME!
OOF!
!!!?
......
POSA (POOF)
THE VICTIM'S NAME WAS TAKASHI SONOBE.
MAN LOSES CONSCIOUSNESS FROM ATTACK
Yesterday morning, a high school teacher was attacked by a hoodlumandreceivedaserious blowtothehead.Themalevictim was Takashi Sonobe, age 51, employedatYozakuraHighSchool. Heiscurrentlyinthehospitalina comatose state.
HE WAS A 51-YEAR-OLD BACHELOR AND AN ENGLISH TEACHER AT YOZAKURA HIGH SCHOOL.

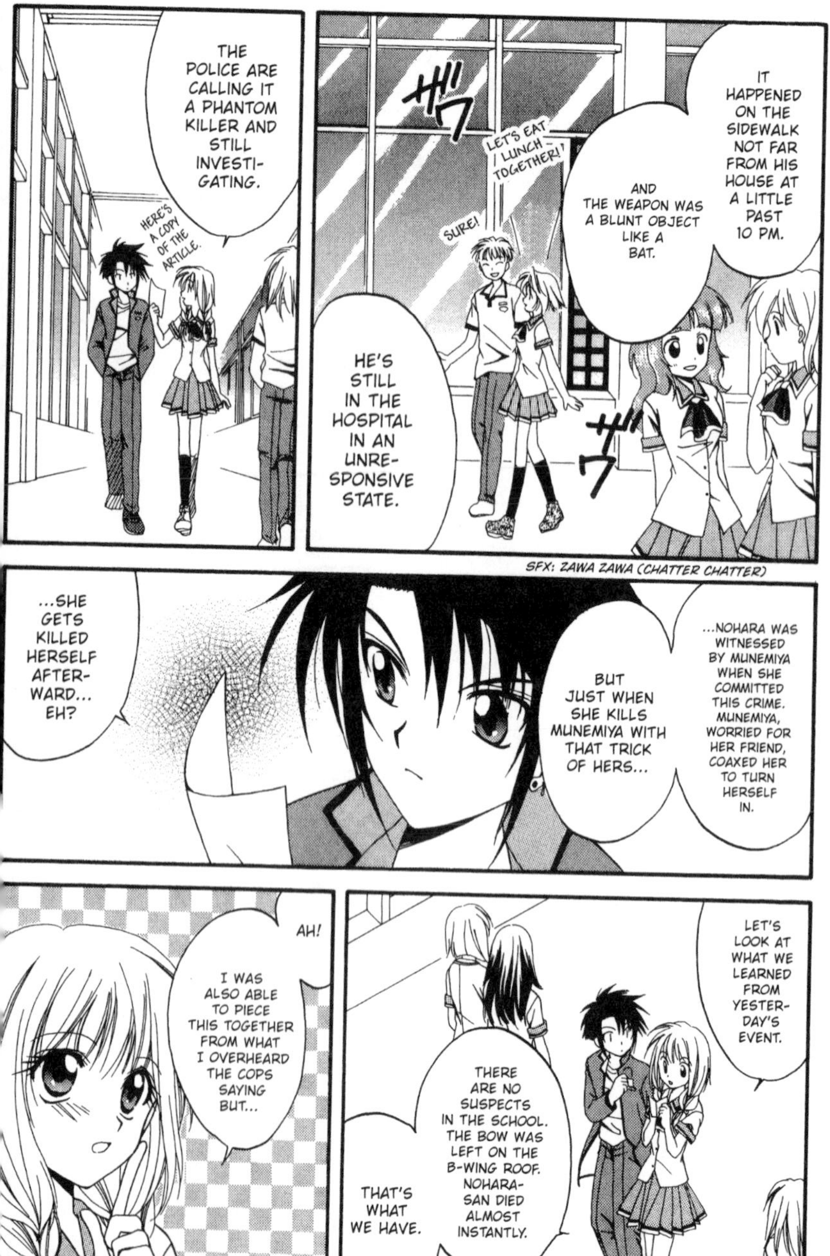
IT HAPPENED ON THE SIDEWALK NOT FAR FROM HIS HOUSE AT A LITTLE PAST 10 PM.
AND THE WEAPON WAS A BLUNT OBJECT LIKE A BAT.
LET'S EAT LUNCH TOGETHER!
SURE!
HE'S STILL IN THE HOSPITAL IN AN UNRESPONSIVE STATE.
THE POLICE ARE CALLING IT A PHANTOM KILLER AND STILL INVESTIGATING.
HERE'S A COPY OF THE ARTICLE.
SFX: ZAWA ZAWA (CHATTER CHATTER)
...NOHARA WAS WITNESSED BY MUNEMIYA WHEN SHE COMMITTED THIS CRIME. MUNEMIYA, WORRIED FOR HER FRIEND, COAXED HER TO TURN HERSELF IN.
BUT JUST WHEN SHE KILLS MUNEMIYA WITH THAT TRICK OF HERS...
...SHE GETS KILLED HERSELF AFTERWARD... EH?
LET'S LOOK AT WHAT WE LEARNED FROM YESTERDAY'S EVENT.
THERE ARE NO SUSPECTS IN THE SCHOOL. THE BOW WAS LEFT ON THE B-WING ROOF. NOHARA-SAN DIED ALMOST INSTANTLY.
THAT'S WHAT WE HAVE.
AH!
I WAS ALSO ABLE TO PIECE THIS TOGETHER FROM WHAT I OVERHEARD THE COPS SAYING BUT...

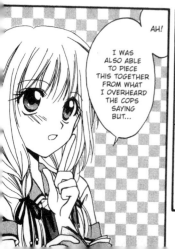

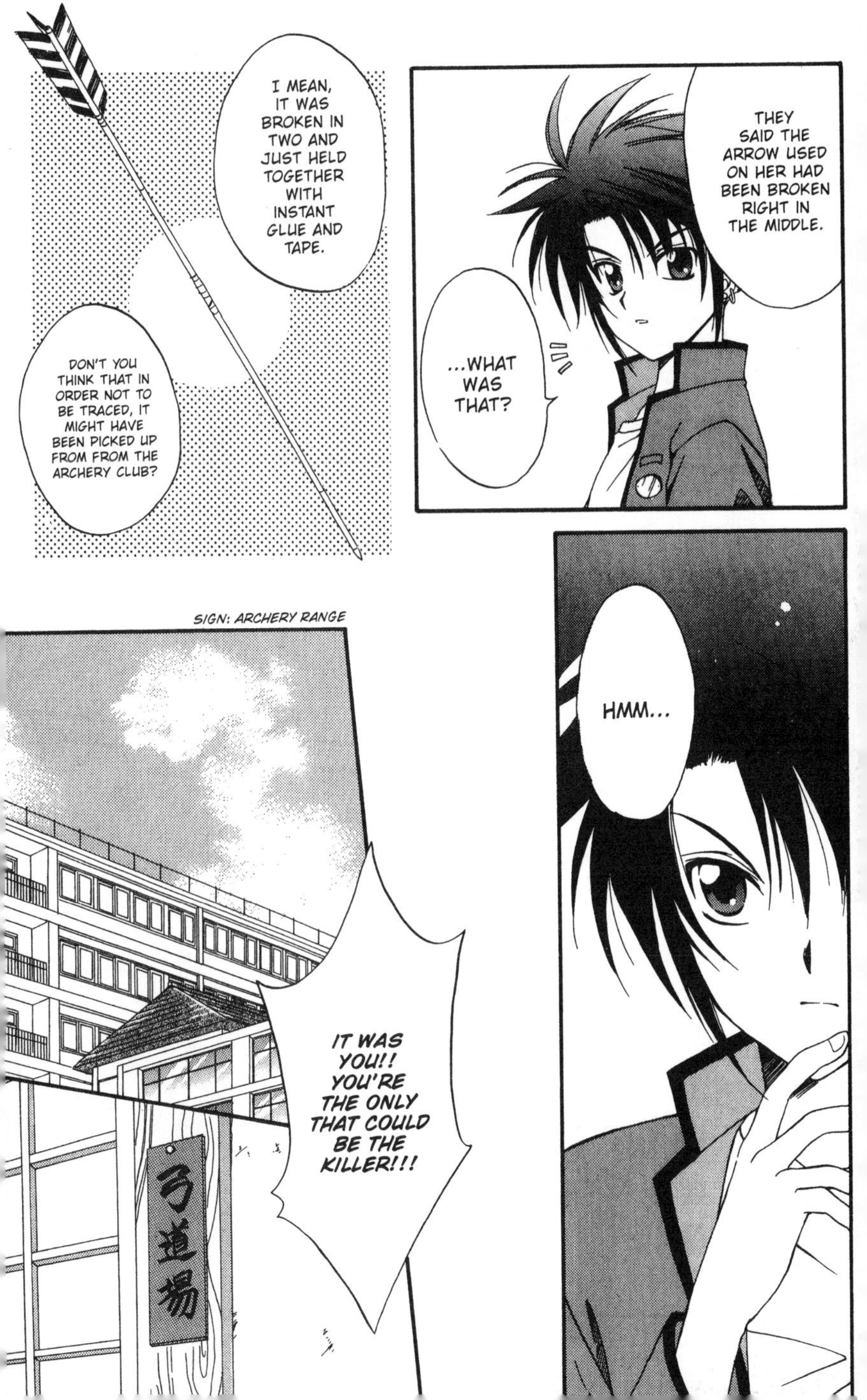
THEY SAID THE ARROW USED ON HER HAD BEEN BROKEN RIGHT IN THE MIDDLE.
...WHAT WAS THAT?
I MEAN, IT WAS BROKEN IN TWO AND JUST HELD TOGETHER WITH INSTANT GLUE AND TAPE.
DON'T YOU THINK THAT IN ORDER NOT TO BE TRACED, IT MIGHT HAVE BEEN PICKED UP FROM FROM THE ARCHERY CLUB?
HMM...
SIGN: ARCHERY RANGE
弓道場
IT WAS YOU!! YOU'RE THE ONLY THAT COULD BE THE KILLER!!!

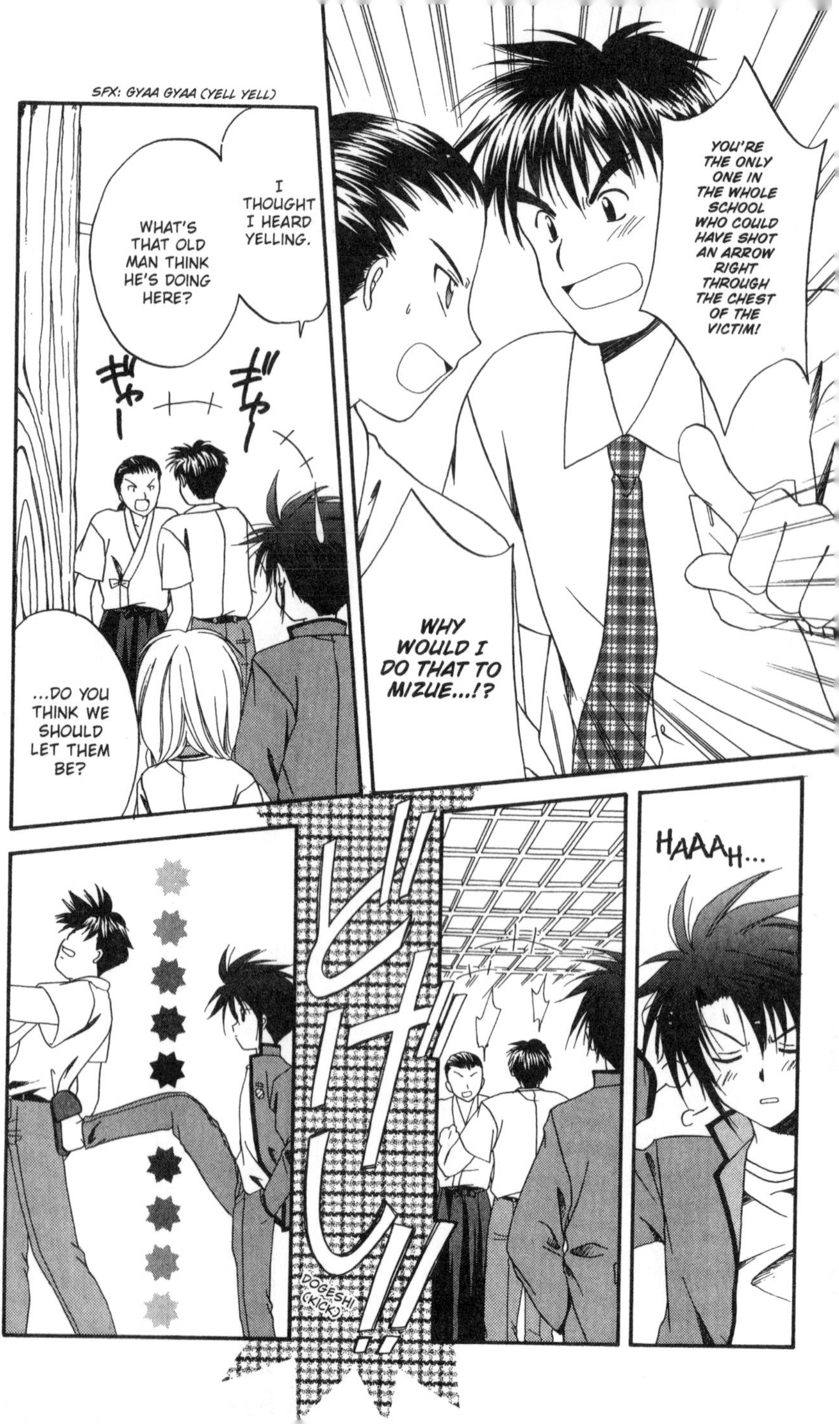
YOU'RE THE ONLY ONE IN THE WHOLE SCHOOL WHO COULD HAVE SHOT AN ARROW RIGHT THROUGH THE CHEST OF THE VICTIM!
WHY WOULD I DO THAT TO MIZUE...!?
SFX: GYAA GYAA (YELL YELL)
I THOUGHT I HEARD YELLING.
WHAT'S THAT OLD MAN THINK HE'S DOING HERE?
ぎゃー ぎゃー
...DO YOU THINK WE SHOULD LET THEM BE?
HAAAH...
DOGESHI (KICK)

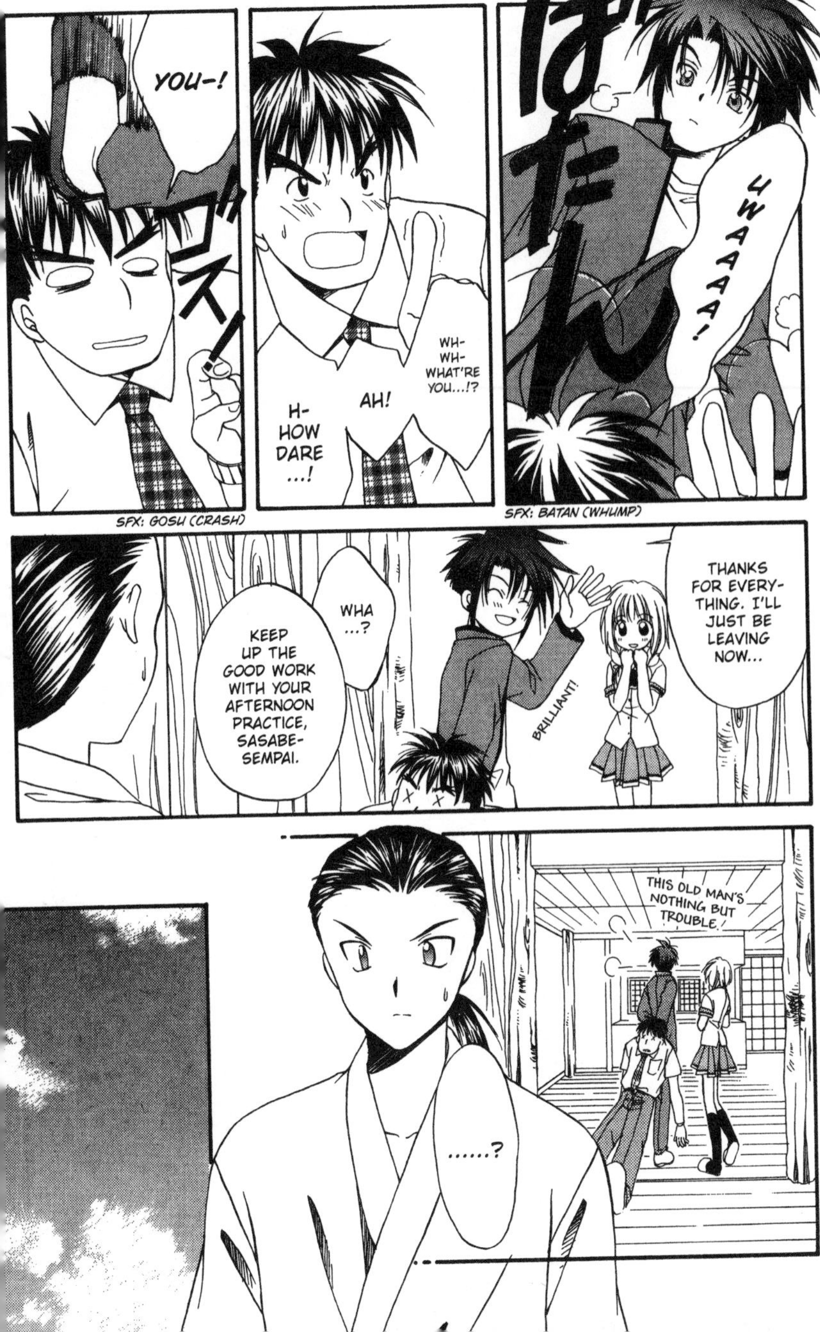
ばたん
UWAAAAAA!
SFX: BATAN (WHUMP)
WH-WH-WHAT'RE YOU...!?
AH!
H-HOW DARE ...!
YOU-!
ゴス!
SFX: GOSU (CRASH)
THANKS FOR EVERY-THING. I'LL JUST BE LEAVING NOW...
BRILLIANT!
WHA ...?
KEEP UP THE GOOD WORK WITH YOUR AFTERNOON PRACTICE, SASABE-SEMPAI.
THIS OLD MAN'S NOTHING BUT TROUBLE.
......?

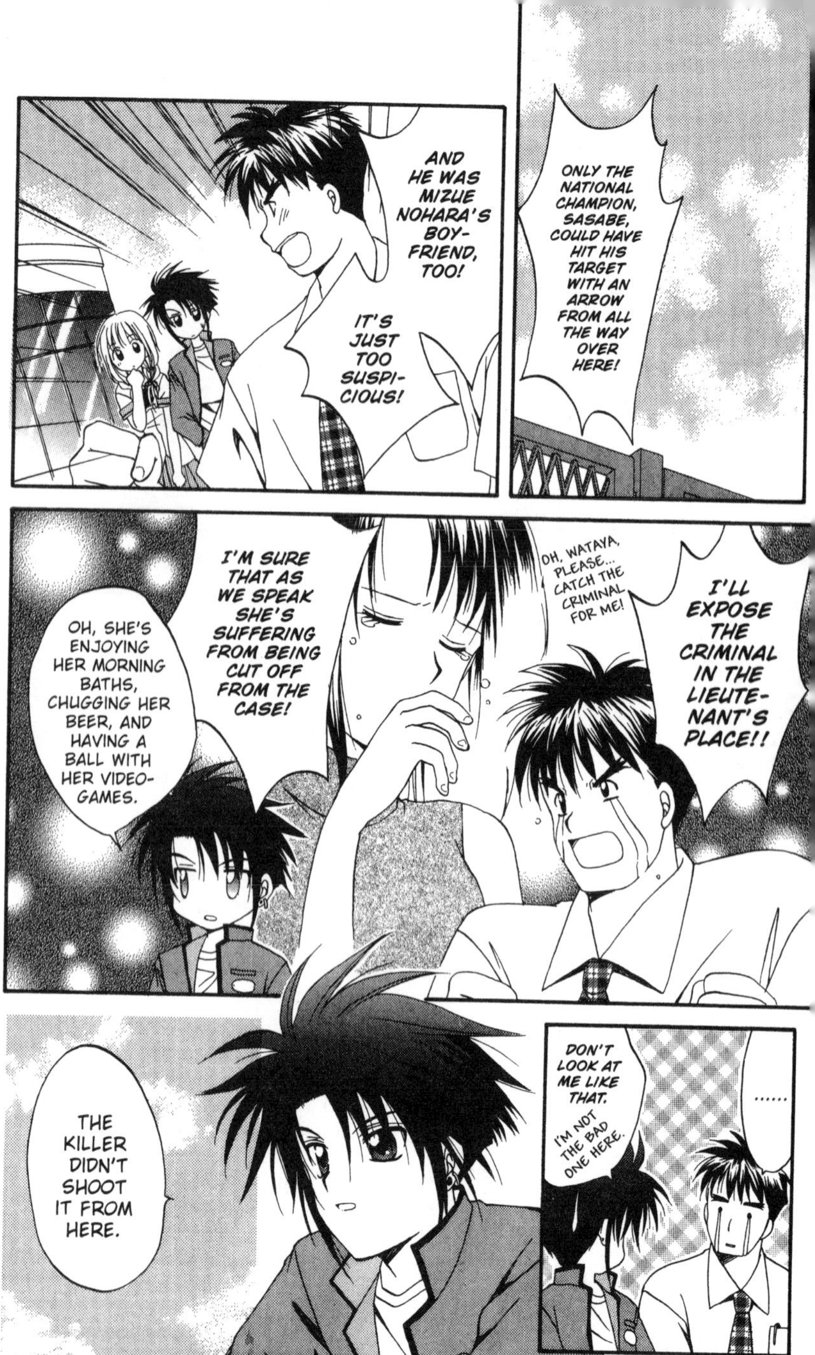
ONLY THE NATIONAL CHAMPION, SASABE, COULD HAVE HIT HIS TARGET WITH AN ARROW FROM ALL THE WAY OVER HERE!
AND HE WAS MIZUE NOHARA'S BOY-FRIEND, TOO!
IT'S JUST TOO SUSPI-CIOUS!
I'LL EXPOSE THE CRIMINAL IN THE LIEUTE-NANT'S PLACE!!
OH, WATAYA, PLEASE... CATCH THE CRIMINAL FOR ME!
I'M SURE THAT AS WE SPEAK SHE'S SUFFERING FROM BEING CUT OFF FROM THE CASE!
OH, SHE'S ENJOYING HER MORNING BATHS, CHUGGING HER BEER, AND HAVING A BALL WITH HER VIDEO-GAMES.
......
DON'T LOOK AT ME LIKE THAT.
I'M NOT THE BAD ONE HERE.
THE KILLER DIDN'T SHOOT IT FROM HERE.

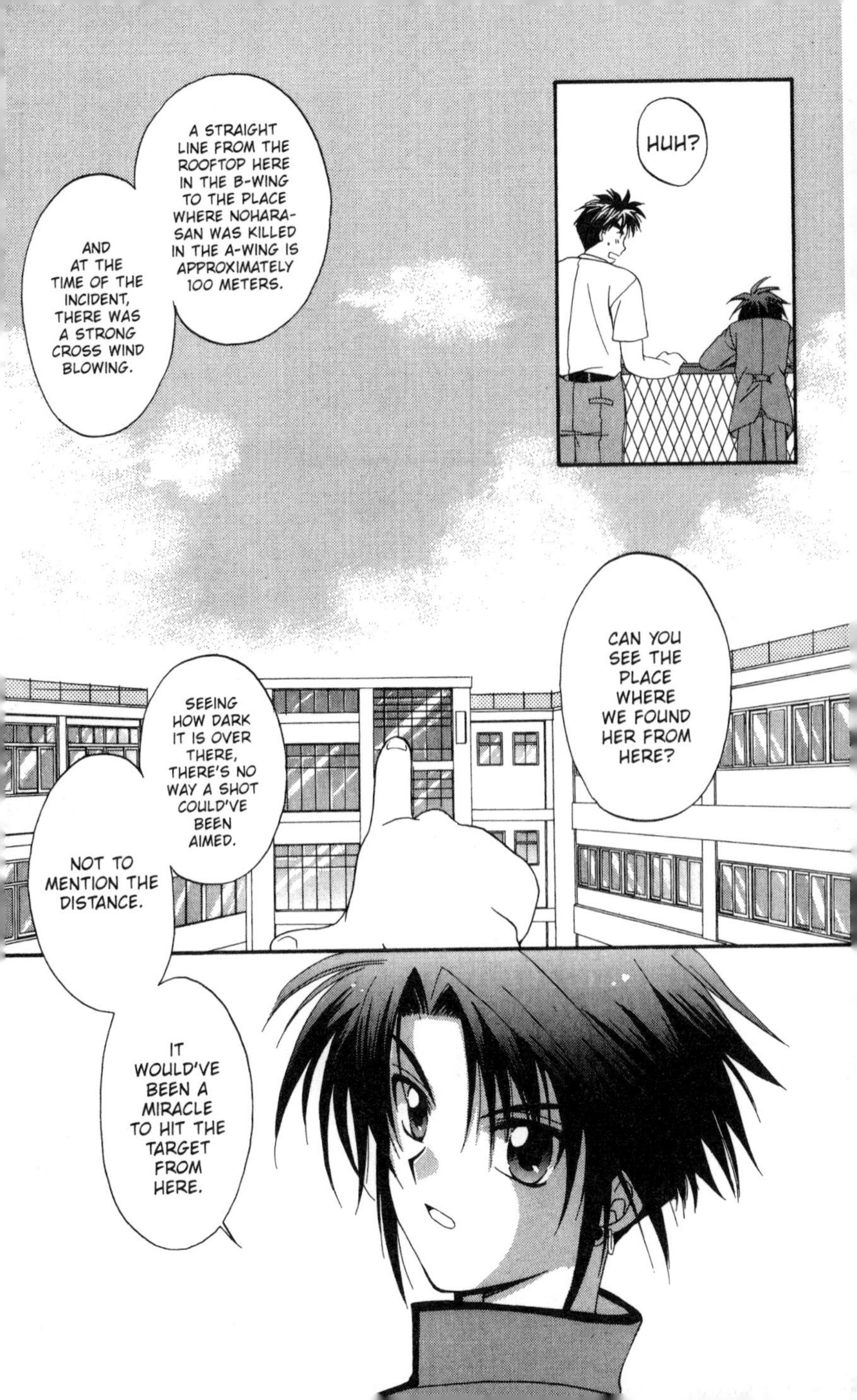
HUH?
A STRAIGHT LINE FROM THE ROOFTOP HERE IN THE B-WING TO THE PLACE WHERE NOHARA-SAN WAS KILLED IN THE A-WING IS APPROXIMATELY 100 METERS.
AND AT THE TIME OF THE INCIDENT, THERE WAS A STRONG CROSS WIND BLOWING.
CAN YOU SEE THE PLACE WHERE WE FOUND HER FROM HERE?
SEEING HOW DARK IT IS OVER THERE, THERE'S NO WAY A SHOT COULD'VE BEEN AIMED.
NOT TO MENTION THE DISTANCE.
IT WOULD'VE BEEN A MIRACLE TO HIT THE TARGET FROM HERE.

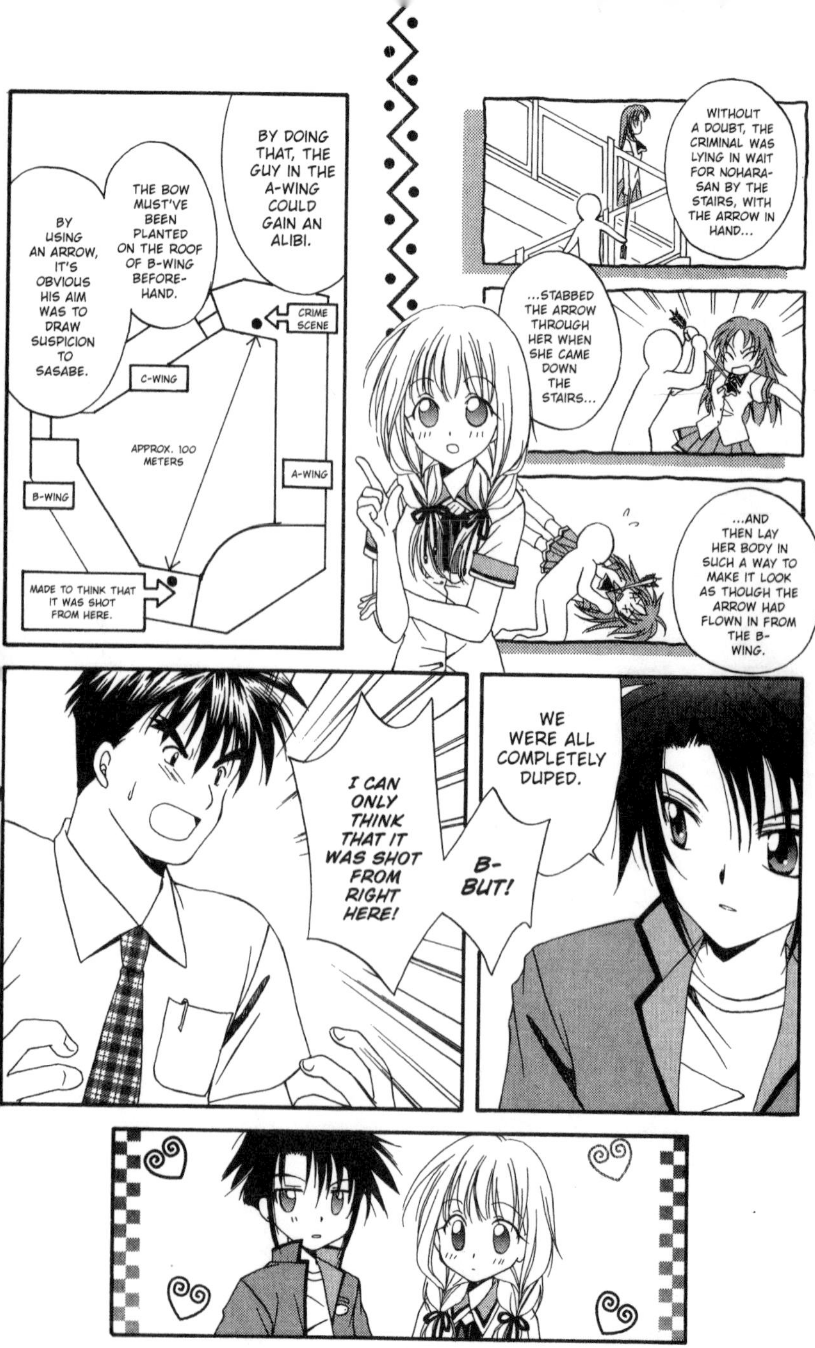
WITHOUT A DOUBT, THE CRIMINAL WAS LYING IN WAIT FOR NOHARA-SAN BY THE STAIRS, WITH THE ARROW IN HAND...
...STABBED THE ARROW THROUGH HER WHEN SHE CAME DOWN THE STAIRS...
...AND THEN LAY HER BODY IN SUCH A WAY TO MAKE IT LOOK AS THOUGH THE ARROW HAD FLOWN IN FROM THE B-WING.
BY DOING THAT, THE GUY IN THE A-WING COULD GAIN AN ALIBI.
THE BOW MUST'VE BEEN PLANTED ON THE ROOF OF B-WING BEFORE-HAND.
BY USING AN ARROW, IT'S OBVIOUS HIS AIM WAS TO DRAW SUSPICION TO SASABE.
CRIME SCENE
C-WING
APPROX. 100 METERS
A-WING
B-WING
MADE TO THINK THAT IT WAS SHOT FROM HERE.
WE WERE ALL COMPLETELY DUPED.
B-BUT!
I CAN ONLY THINK THAT IT WAS SHOT FROM RIGHT HERE!

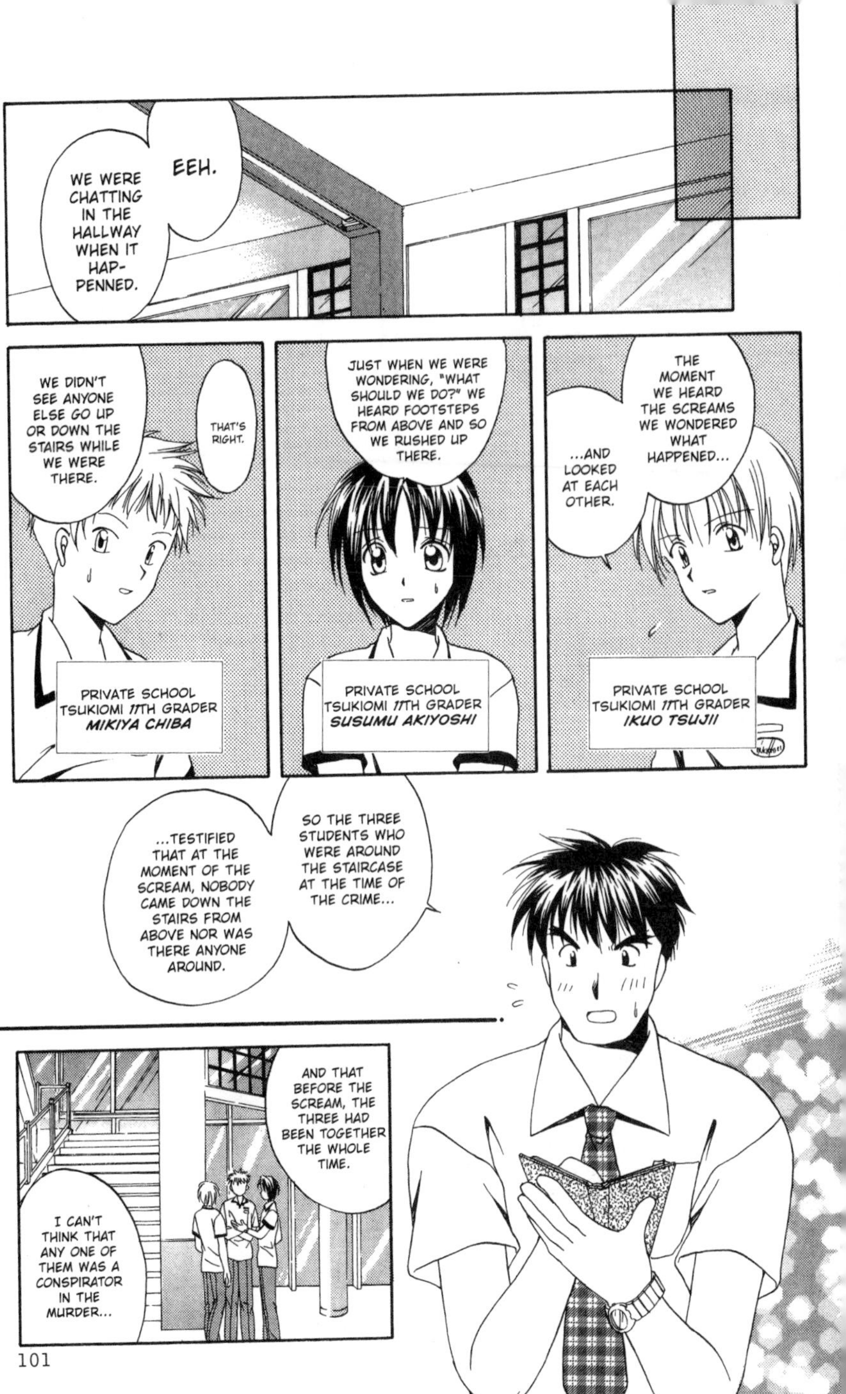
EEH.
WE WERE CHATTING IN THE HALLWAY WHEN IT HAP-PENNED.
THE MOMENT WE HEARD THE SCREAMS WE WONDERED WHAT HAPPENED...
...AND LOOKED AT EACH OTHER.
PRIVATE SCHOOL TSUKIOMI 11TH GRADER IKUO TSUJII
JUST WHEN WE WERE WONDERING, "WHAT SHOULD WE DO?" WE HEARD FOOTSTEPS FROM ABOVE AND SO WE RUSHED UP THERE.
PRIVATE SCHOOL TSUKIOMI 11TH GRADER SUSUMU AKIYOSHI
THAT'S RIGHT.
WE DIDN'T SEE ANYONE ELSE GO UP OR DOWN THE STAIRS WHILE WE WERE THERE.
PRIVATE SCHOOL TSUKIOMI 11TH GRADER MIKIYA CHIBA
SO THE THREE STUDENTS WHO WERE AROUND THE STAIRCASE AT THE TIME OF THE CRIME...
...TESTIFIED THAT AT THE MOMENT OF THE SCREAM, NOBODY CAME DOWN THE STAIRS FROM ABOVE NOR WAS THERE ANYONE AROUND.
AND THAT BEFORE THE SCREAM, THE THREE HAD BEEN TOGETHER THE WHOLE TIME.
I CAN'T THINK THAT ANY ONE OF THEM WAS A CONSPIRATOR IN THE MURDER...

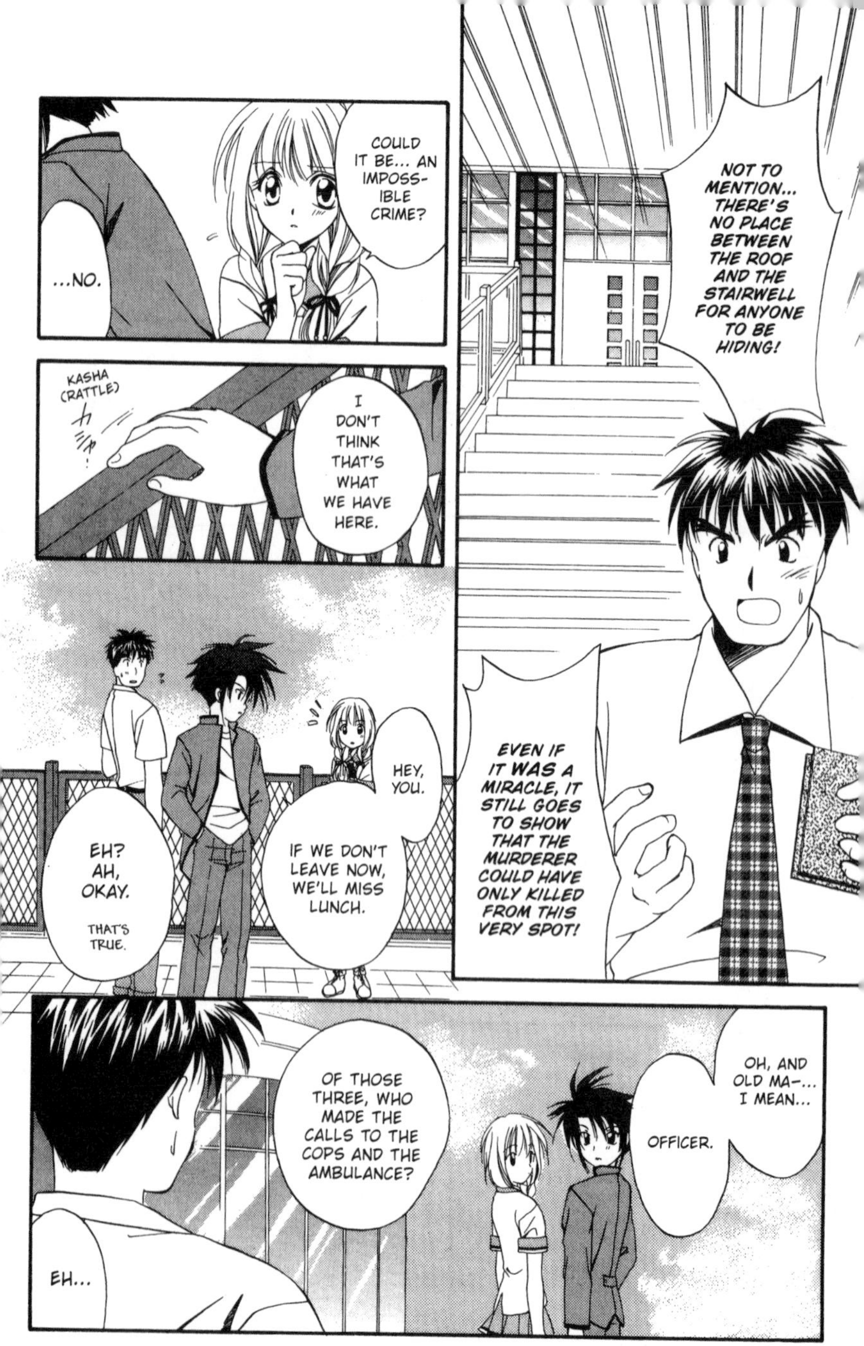
NOT TO MENTION... THERE'S NO PLACE BETWEEN THE ROOF AND THE STAIRWELL FOR ANYONE TO BE HIDING!
EVEN IF IT WAS A MIRACLE, IT STILL GOES TO SHOW THAT THE MURDERER COULD HAVE ONLY KILLED FROM THIS VERY SPOT!
COULD IT BE... AN IMPOSS-IBLE CRIME?
...NO.
KASHA (RATTLE)
I DON'T THINK THAT'S WHAT WE HAVE HERE.
HEY, YOU.
IF WE DON'T LEAVE NOW, WE'LL MISS LUNCH.
EH? AH, OKAY.
THAT'S TRUE.
OH, AND OLD MA-... I MEAN...
OFFICER.
OF THOSE THREE, WHO MADE THE CALLS TO THE COPS AND THE AMBULANCE?
EH...

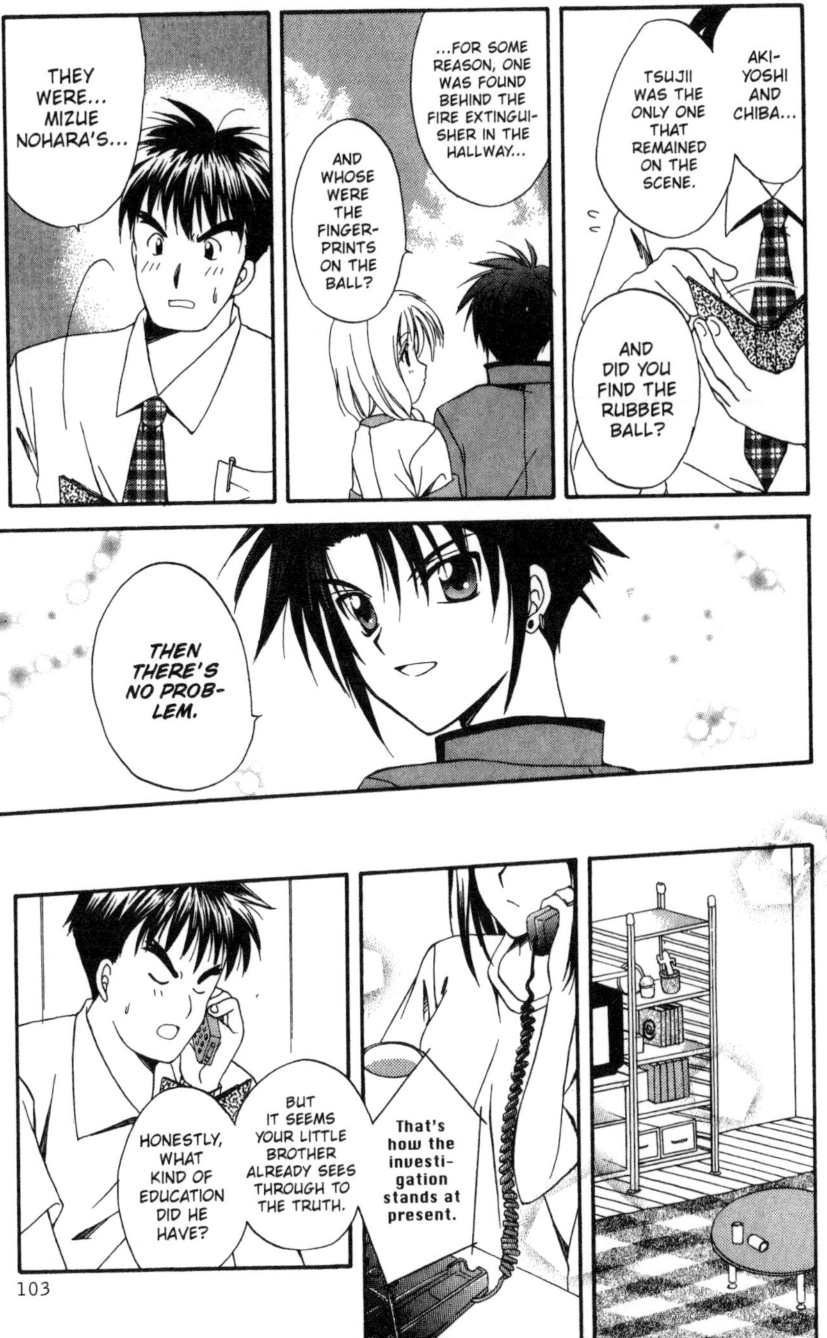
AKI-YOSHI AND CHIBA...
TSUJII WAS THE ONLY ONE THAT REMAINED ON THE SCENE.
AND DID YOU FIND THE RUBBER BALL?
...FOR SOME REASON, ONE WAS FOUND BEHIND THE FIRE EXTINGUISHER IN THE HALLWAY...
AND WHOSE WERE THE FINGERPRINTS ON THE BALL?
THEY WERE... MIZUE NOHARA'S...
THEN THERE'S NO PROBLEM.
That's how the investigation stands at present.
BUT IT SEEMS YOUR LITTLE BROTHER ALREADY SEES THROUGH TO THE TRUTH.
HONESTLY, WHAT KIND OF EDUCATION DID HE HAVE?

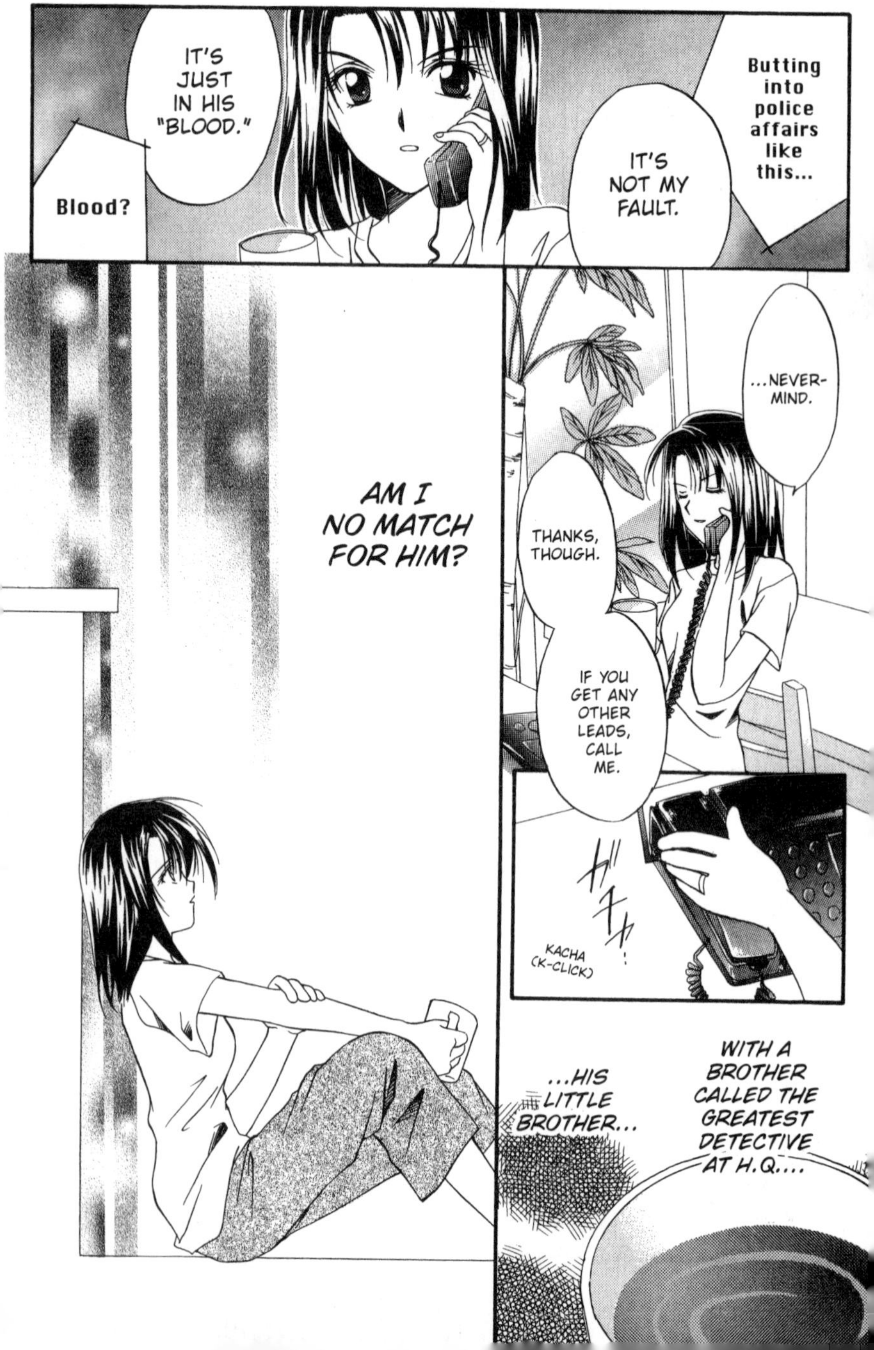
Butting into police affairs like this...
IT'S NOT MY FAULT.
IT'S JUST IN HIS "BLOOD."
Blood?
...NEVER-MIND.
THANKS, THOUGH.
IF YOU GET ANY OTHER LEADS, CALL ME.
KACHA (K-CLICK)
WITH A BROTHER CALLED THE GREATEST DETECTIVE AT H.Q....
...HIS LITTLE BROTHER...
AM I NO MATCH FOR HIM?

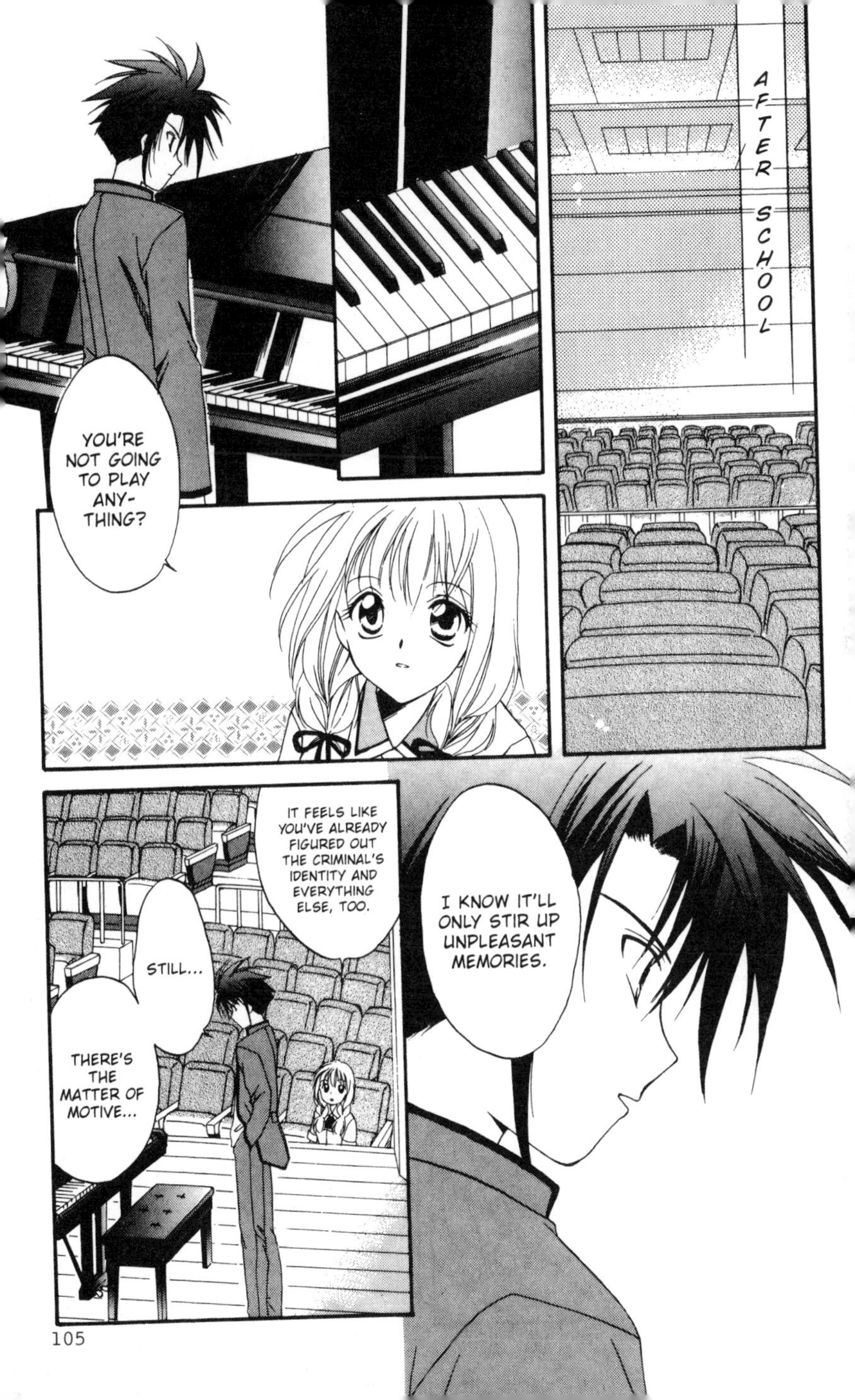
AFTER SCHOOL
YOU'RE NOT GOING TO PLAY ANY-THING?
I KNOW IT'LL ONLY STIR UP UNPLEASANT MEMORIES.
IT FEELS LIKE YOU'VE ALREADY FIGURED OUT THE CRIMINAL'S IDENTITY AND EVERYTHING ELSE, TOO.
STILL...
THERE'S THE MATTER OF MOTIVE...

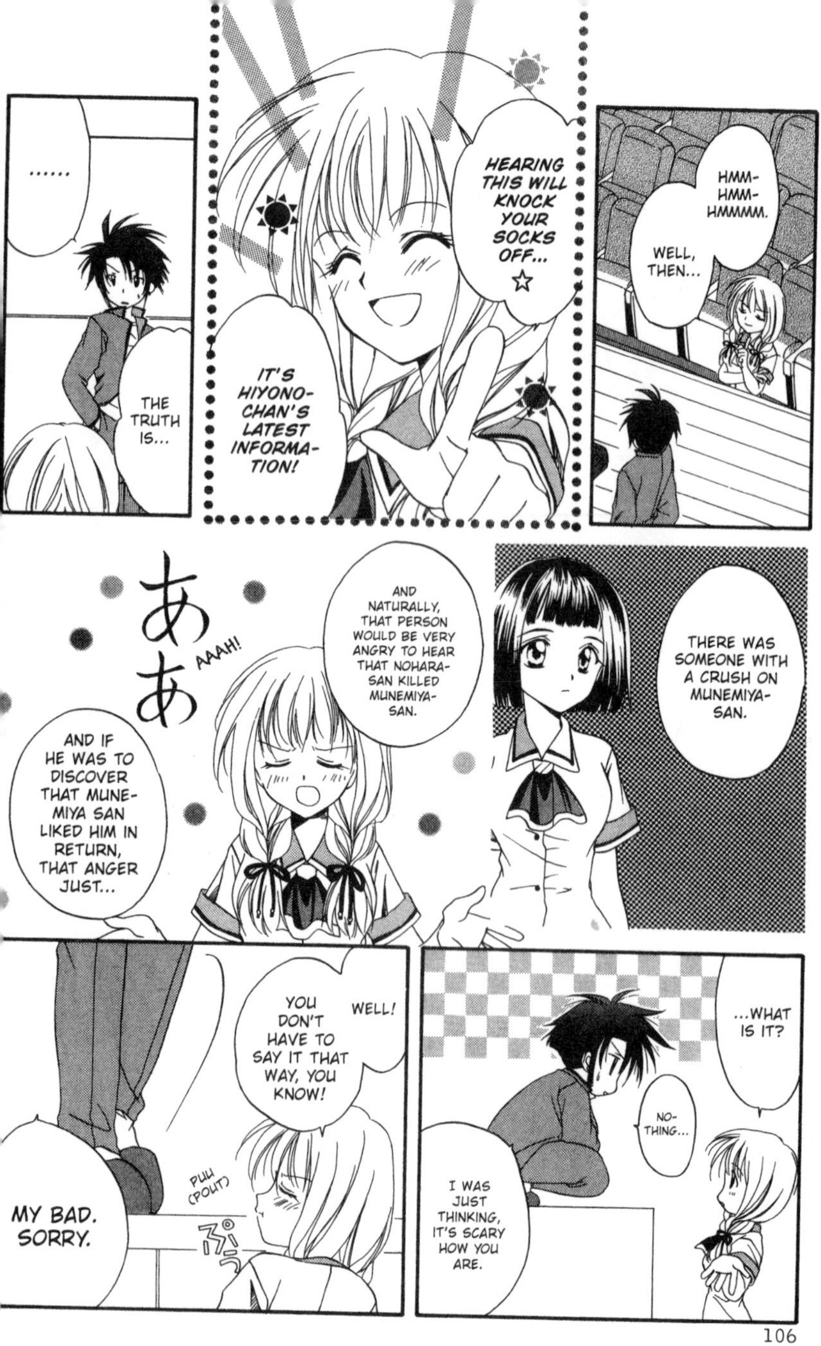
HMM-HMM-HMMMM.
WELL, THEN...
HEARING THIS WILL KNOCK YOUR SOCKS OFF... ☆
IT'S HIYONO-CHAN'S LATEST INFORMATION!
......
THE TRUTH IS...
THERE WAS SOMEONE WITH A CRUSH ON MUNEMIYA-SAN.
AND NATURALLY, THAT PERSON WOULD BE VERY ANGRY TO HEAR THAT NOHARA-SAN KILLED MUNEMIYA-SAN.
ああ
AAAH!
AND IF HE WAS TO DISCOVER THAT MUNE-MIYA SAN LIKED HIM IN RETURN, THAT ANGER JUST...
...WHAT IS IT?
NO-THING...
I WAS JUST THINKING, IT'S SCARY HOW YOU ARE.
WELL!
YOU DON'T HAVE TO SAY IT THAT WAY, YOU KNOW!
PUU (POUT)
ぷぅ
MY BAD. SORRY.

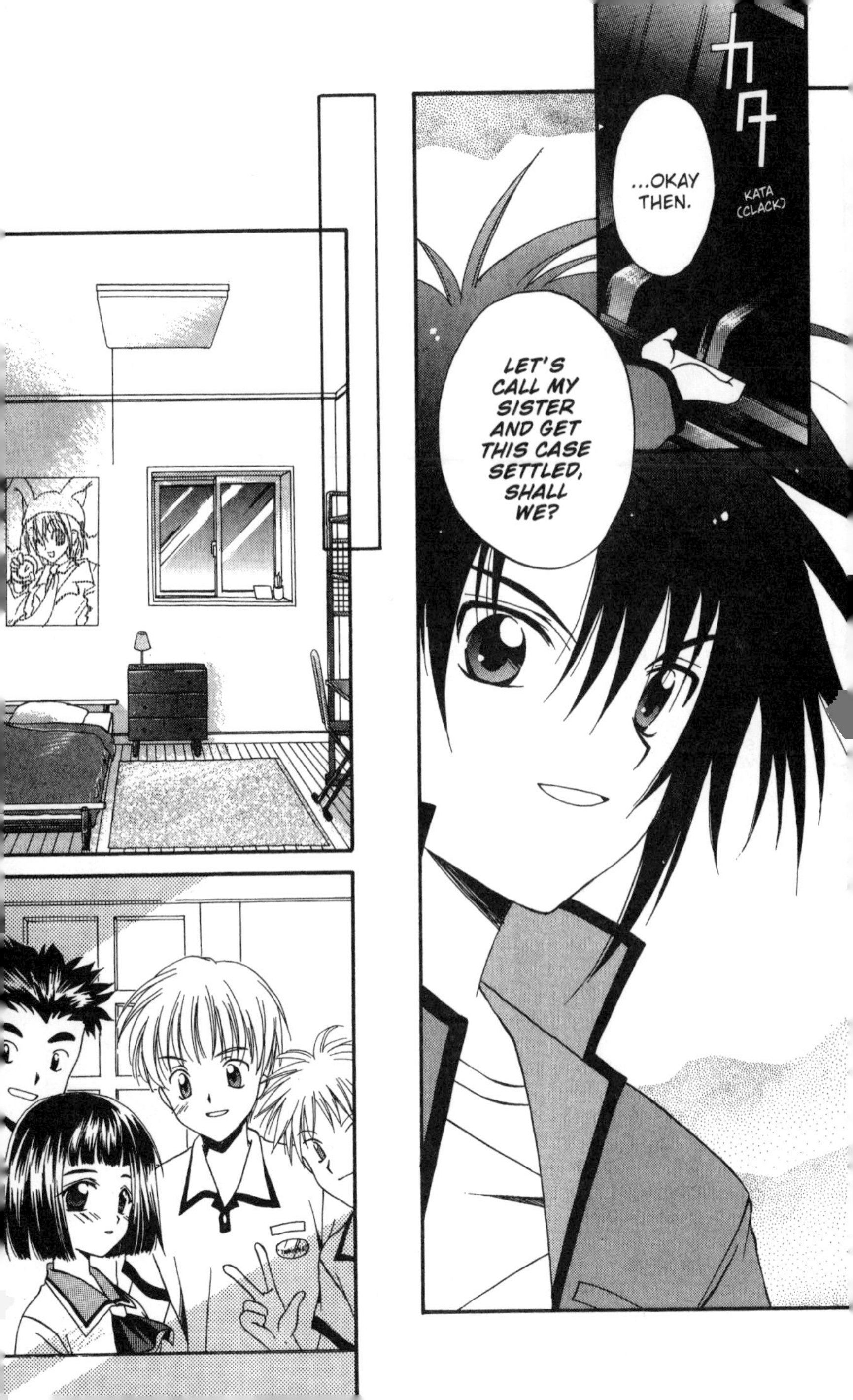
カタ
KATA (CLACK)
...OKAY THEN.
LET'S CALL MY SISTER AND GET THIS CASE SETTLED, SHALL WE?

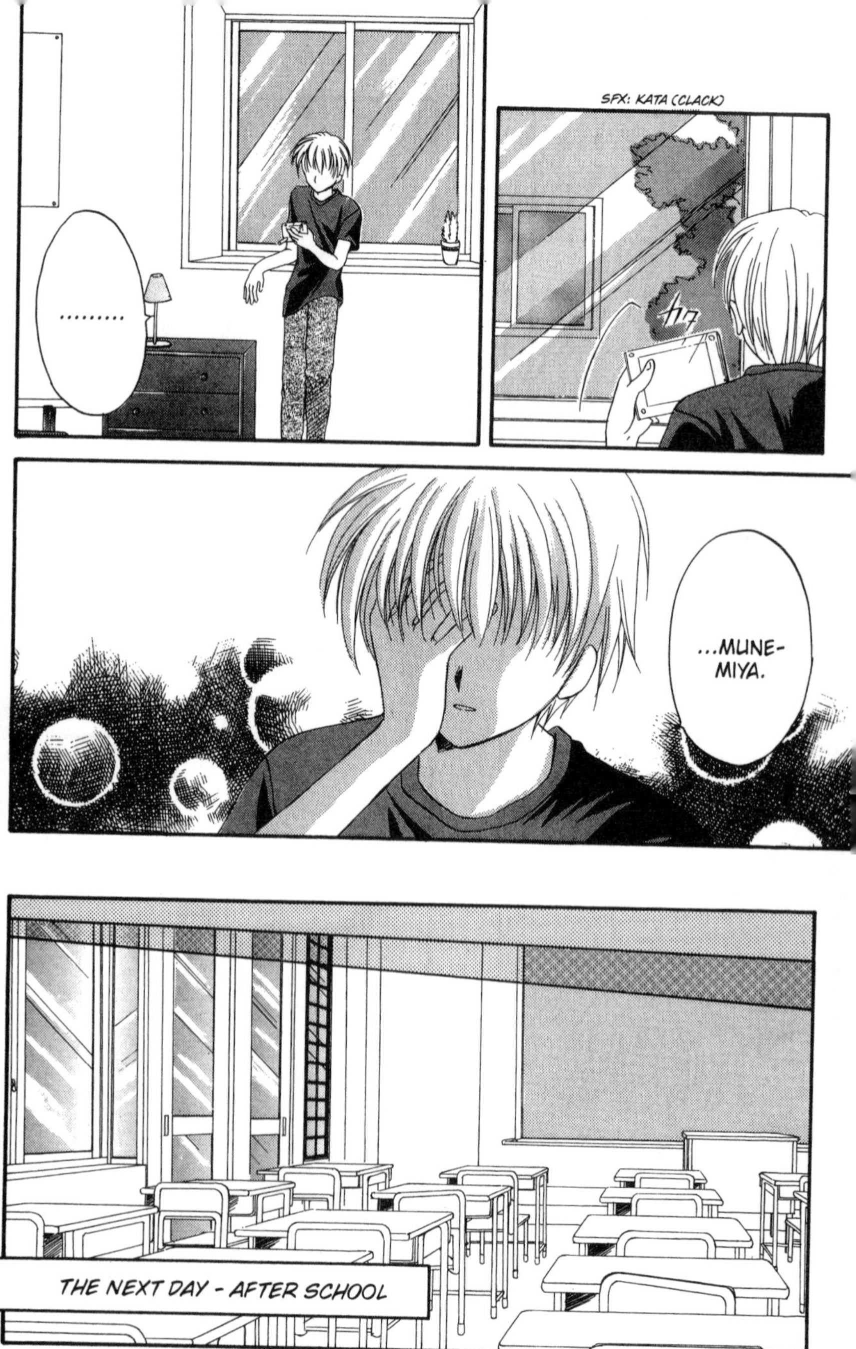
SFX: KATA (CLACK)
....
...MUNE-MIYA.
THE NEXT DAY - AFTER SCHOOL

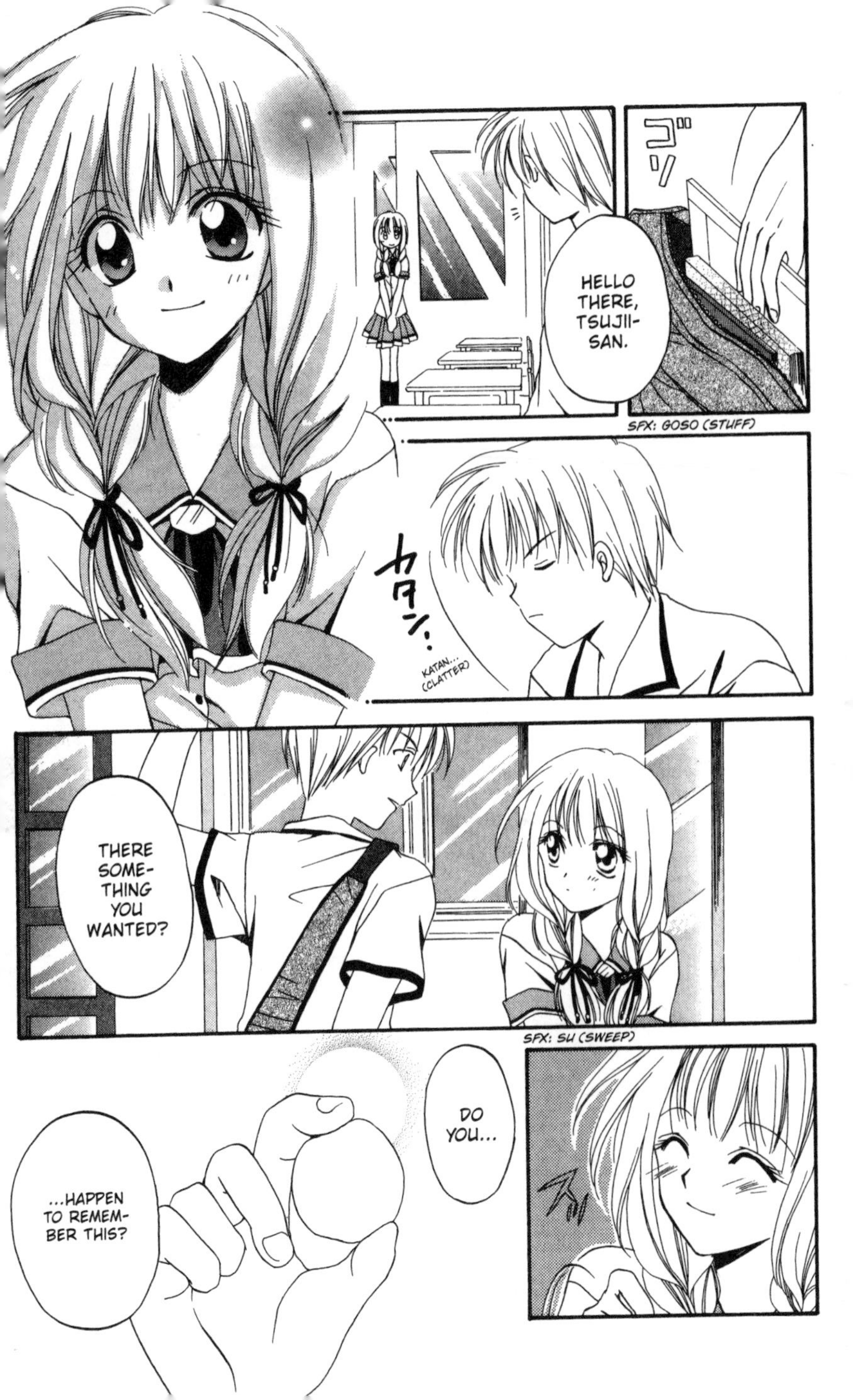
ゴソ
SFX: GOSO (STUFF)
HELLO THERE, TSUJII-SAN.
カタン
KATAN... (CLATTER)
THERE SOME-THING YOU WANTED?
SFX: SU (SWEEP)
DO YOU...
...HAPPEN TO REMEM-BER THIS?

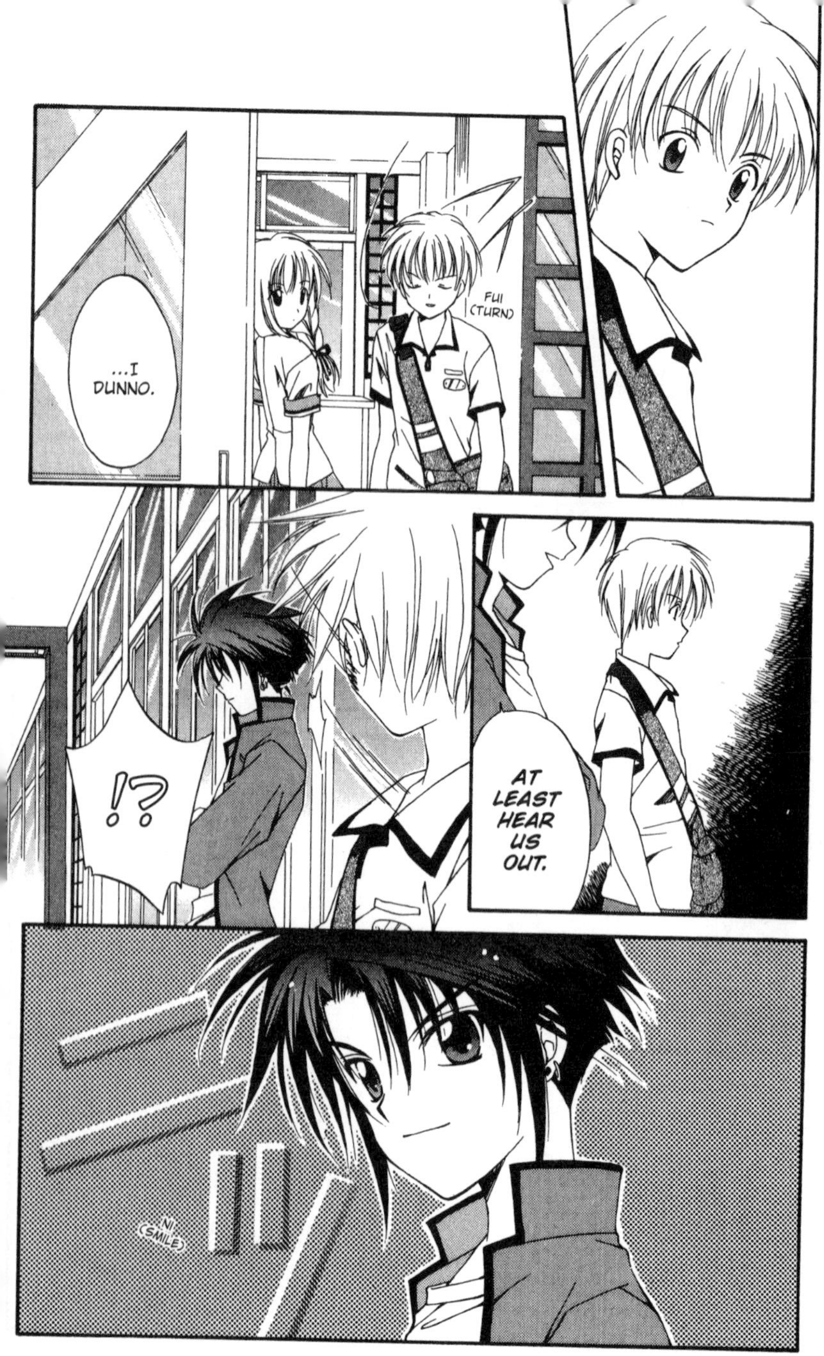
FUI (TURN)
...I DUNNO.
AT LEAST HEAR US OUT.
!?
NI (SMILE)

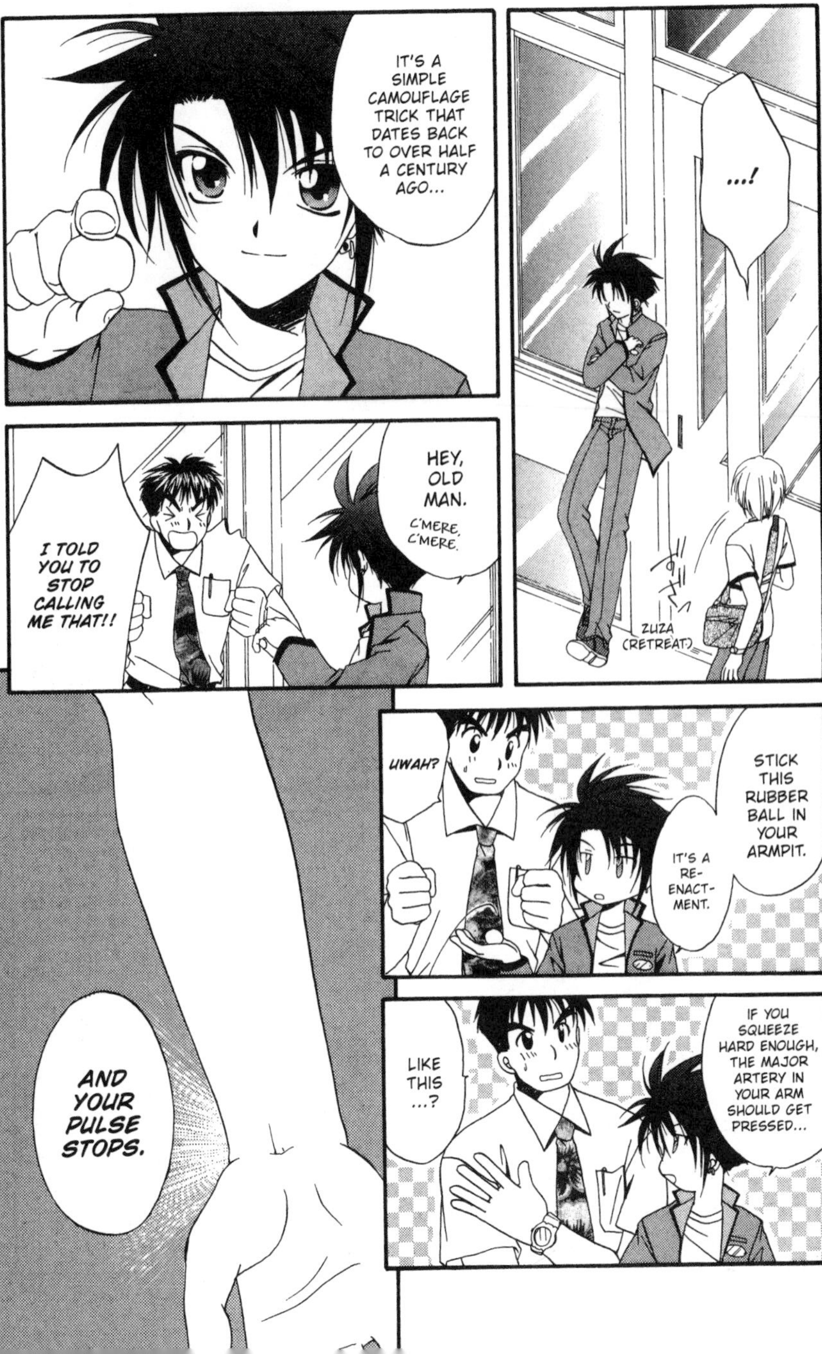
...!
ZUZA (RETREAT)
IT'S A SIMPLE CAMOUFLAGE TRICK THAT DATES BACK TO OVER HALF A CENTURY AGO...
HEY, OLD MAN.
C'MERE, C'MERE.
I TOLD YOU TO STOP CALLING ME THAT!!
STICK THIS RUBBER BALL IN YOUR ARMPIT.
IT'S A RE-ENACT-MENT.
UWAH?
IF YOU SQUEEZE HARD ENOUGH, THE MAJOR ARTERY IN YOUR ARM SHOULD GET PRESSED...
LIKE THIS ...?
AND YOUR PULSE STOPS.

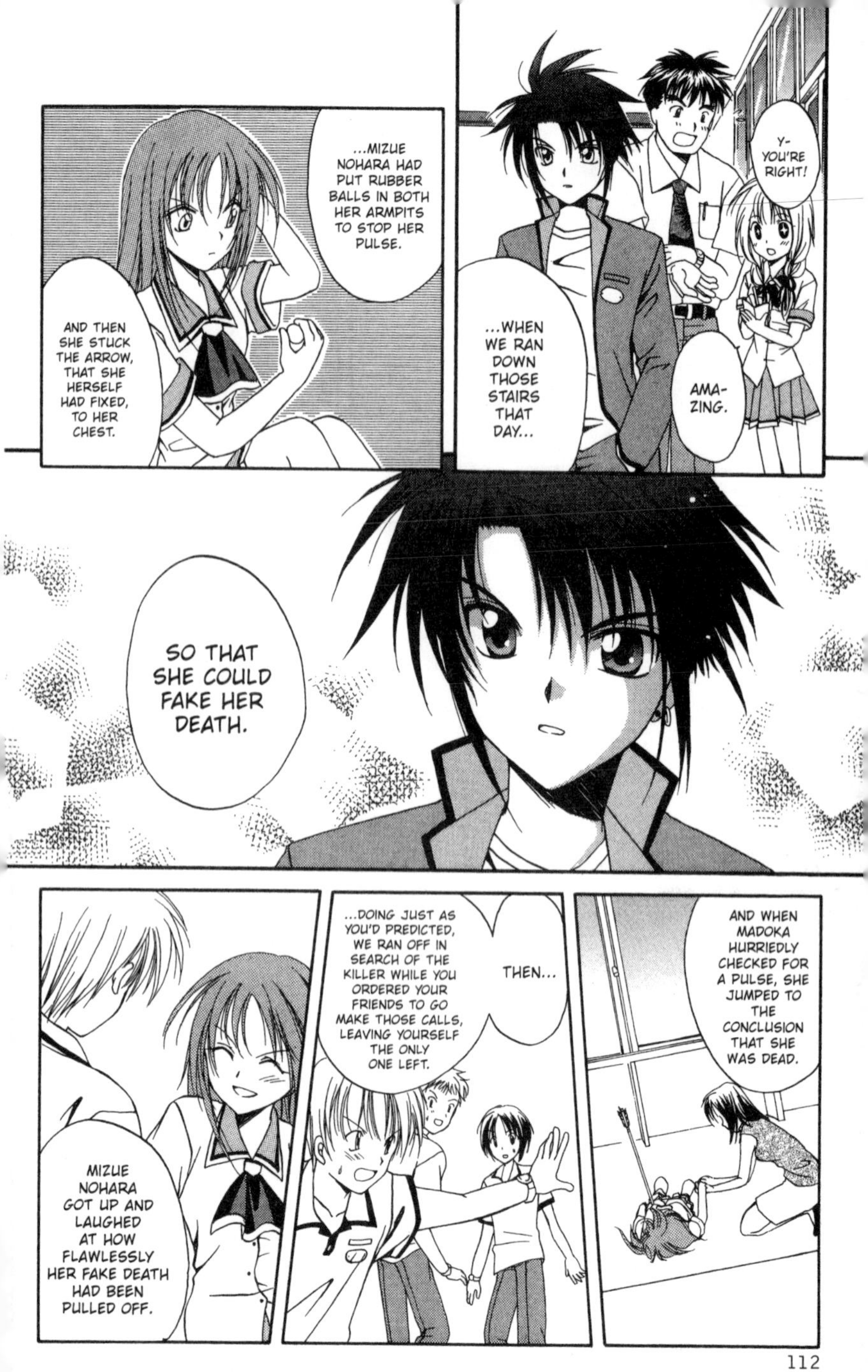

Y- YOU'RE RIGHT!
AMA- ZING.
...WHEN WE RAN DOWN THOSE STAIRS THAT DAY...
...MIZUE NOHARA HAD PUT RUBBER BALLS IN BOTH HER ARMPITS TO STOP HER PULSE.
AND THEN SHE STUCK THE ARROW, THAT SHE HERSELF HAD FIXED, TO HER CHEST.
SO THAT SHE COULD FAKE HER DEATH.
AND WHEN MADOKA HURRIEDLY CHECKED FOR A PULSE, SHE JUMPED TO THE CONCLUSION THAT SHE WAS DEAD.
THEN...
...DOING JUST AS YOU'D PREDICTED, WE RAN OFF IN SEARCH OF THE KILLER WHILE YOU ORDERED YOUR FRIENDS TO GO MAKE THOSE CALLS, LEAVING YOURSELF THE ONLY ONE LEFT.
MIZUE NOHARA GOT UP AND LAUGHED AT HOW FLAWLESSLY HER FAKE DEATH HAD BEEN PULLED OFF.

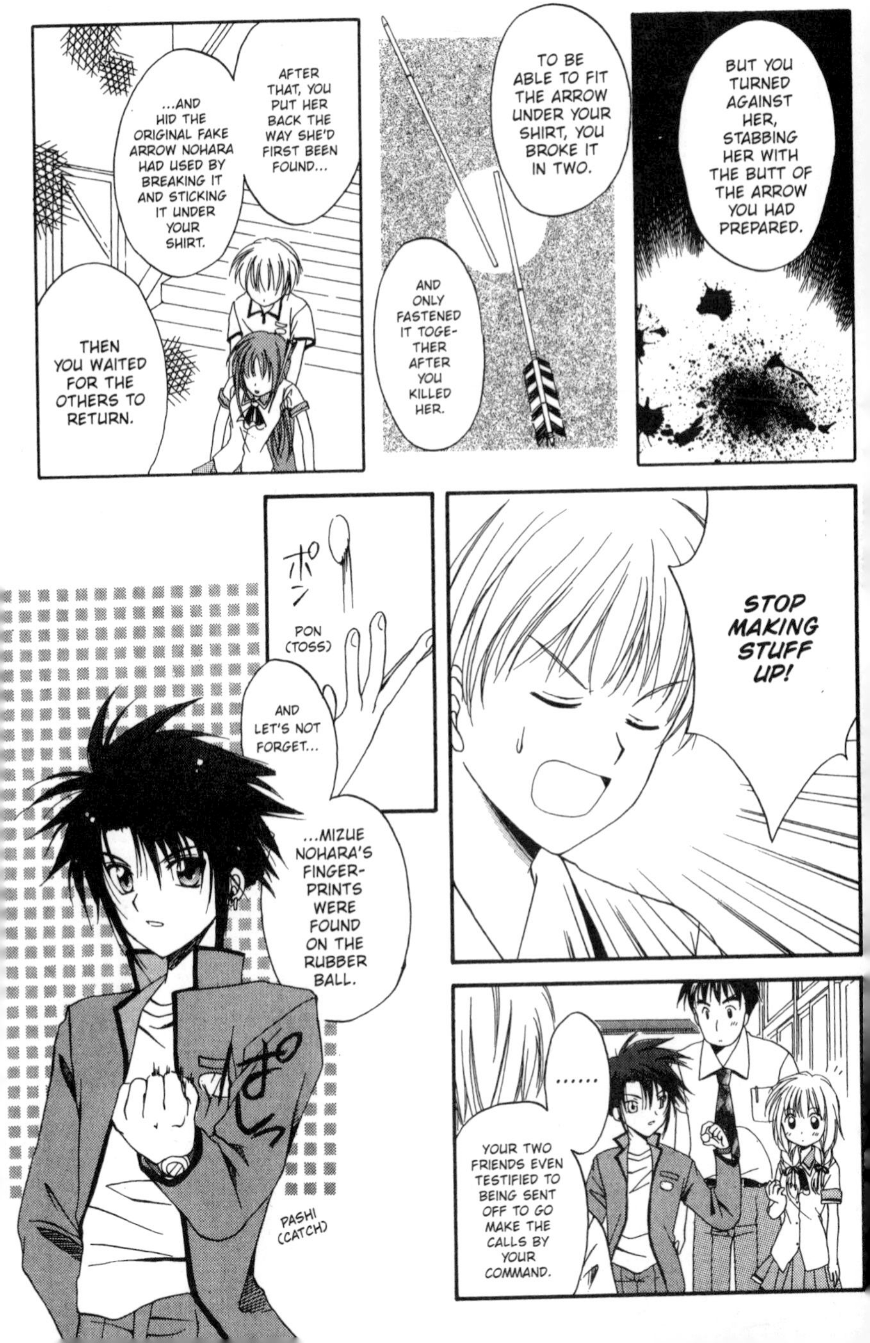

BUT YOU TURNED AGAINST HER, STABBING HER WITH THE BUTT OF THE ARROW YOU HAD PREPARED.
TO BE ABLE TO FIT THE ARROW UNDER YOUR SHIRT, YOU BROKE IT IN TWO.
AND ONLY FASTENED IT TOGE-THER AFTER YOU KILLED HER.
...AND HID THE ORIGINAL FAKE ARROW NOHARA HAD USED BY BREAKING IT AND STICKING IT UNDER YOUR SHIRT.
AFTER THAT, YOU PUT HER BACK THE WAY SHE'D FIRST BEEN FOUND...
THEN YOU WAITED FOR THE OTHERS TO RETURN.
STOP MAKING STUFF UP!
ポン
PON (TOSS)
AND LET'S NOT FORGET...
...MIZUE NOHARA'S FINGER-PRINTS WERE FOUND ON THE RUBBER BALL.
PASHI (CATCH)
......
YOUR TWO FRIENDS EVEN TESTIFIED TO BEING SENT OFF TO GO MAKE THE CALLS BY YOUR COMMAND.

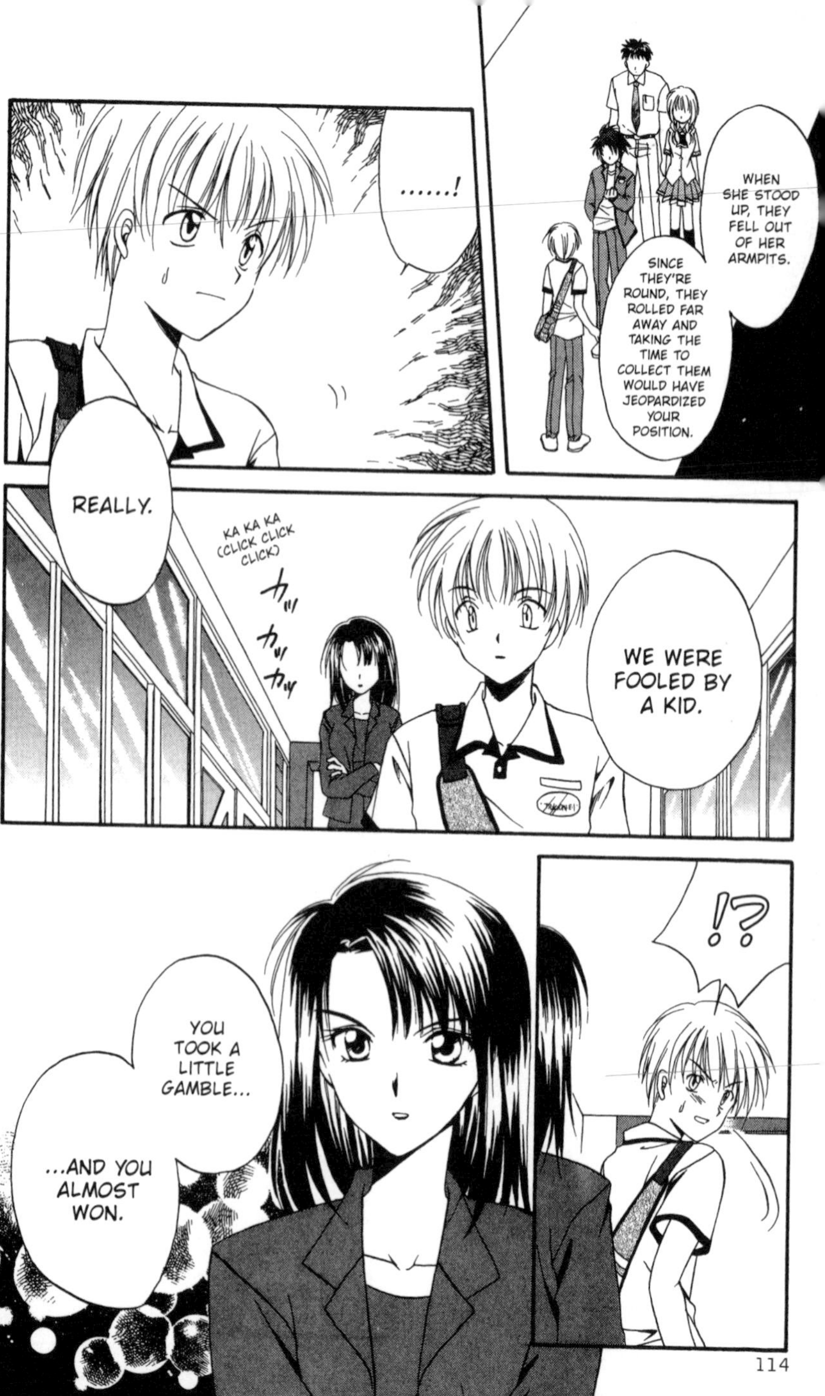

WHEN SHE STOOD UP, THEY FELL OUT OF HER ARMPITS.
SINCE THEY'RE ROUND, THEY ROLLED FAR AWAY AND TAKING THE TIME TO COLLECT THEM WOULD HAVE JEOPARDIZED YOUR POSITION.
......!
REALLY.
WE WERE FOOLED BY A KID.
KA KA KA (CLICK CLICK CLICK)
!?
YOU TOOK A LITTLE GAMBLE...
...AND YOU ALMOST WON.

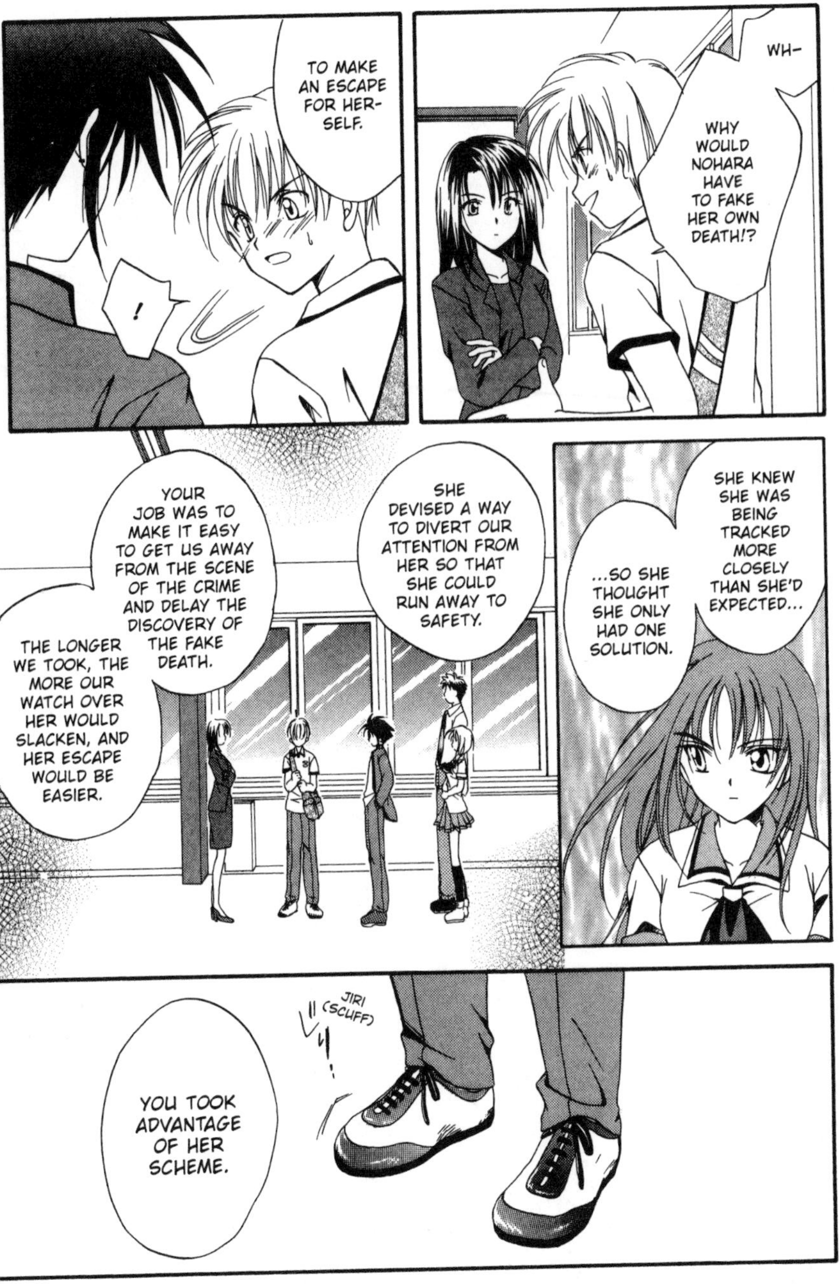
WH-
WHY WOULD NOHARA HAVE TO FAKE HER OWN DEATH!?
TO MAKE AN ESCAPE FOR HER-SELF.
!
SHE KNEW SHE WAS BEING TRACKED MORE CLOSELY THAN SHE'D EXPECTED...
...SO SHE THOUGHT SHE ONLY HAD ONE SOLUTION.
SHE DEVISED A WAY TO DIVERT OUR ATTENTION FROM HER SO THAT SHE COULD RUN AWAY TO SAFETY.
YOUR JOB WAS TO MAKE IT EASY TO GET US AWAY FROM THE SCENE OF THE CRIME AND DELAY THE DISCOVERY OF THE FAKE DEATH.
THE LONGER WE TOOK, THE MORE OUR WATCH OVER HER WOULD SLACKEN, AND HER ESCAPE WOULD BE EASIER.
JIRI (SCUFF)
YOU TOOK ADVANTAGE OF HER SCHEME.

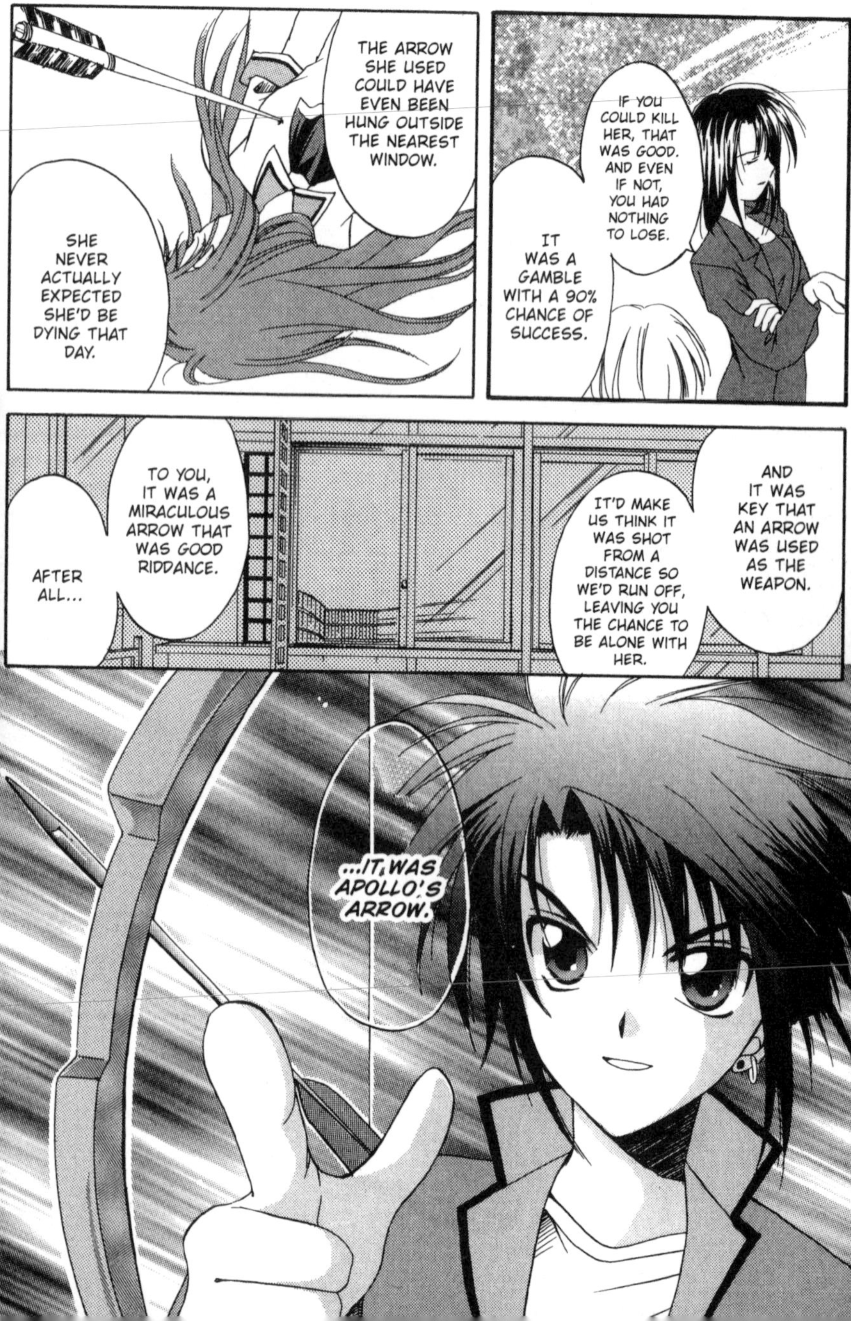
IF YOU COULD KILL HER, THAT WAS GOOD. AND EVEN IF NOT, YOU HAD NOTHING TO LOSE.
IT WAS A GAMBLE WITH A 90% CHANCE OF SUCCESS.
THE ARROW SHE USED COULD HAVE EVEN BEEN HUNG OUTSIDE THE NEAREST WINDOW.
SHE NEVER ACTUALLY EXPECTED SHE'D BE DYING THAT DAY.
AND IT WAS KEY THAT AN ARROW WAS USED AS THE WEAPON.
IT'D MAKE US THINK IT WAS SHOT FROM A DISTANCE SO WE'D RUN OFF, LEAVING YOU THE CHANCE TO BE ALONE WITH HER.
TO YOU, IT WAS A MIRACULOUS ARROW THAT WAS GOOD RIDDANCE.
AFTER ALL...
...IT WAS APOLLO'S ARROW.

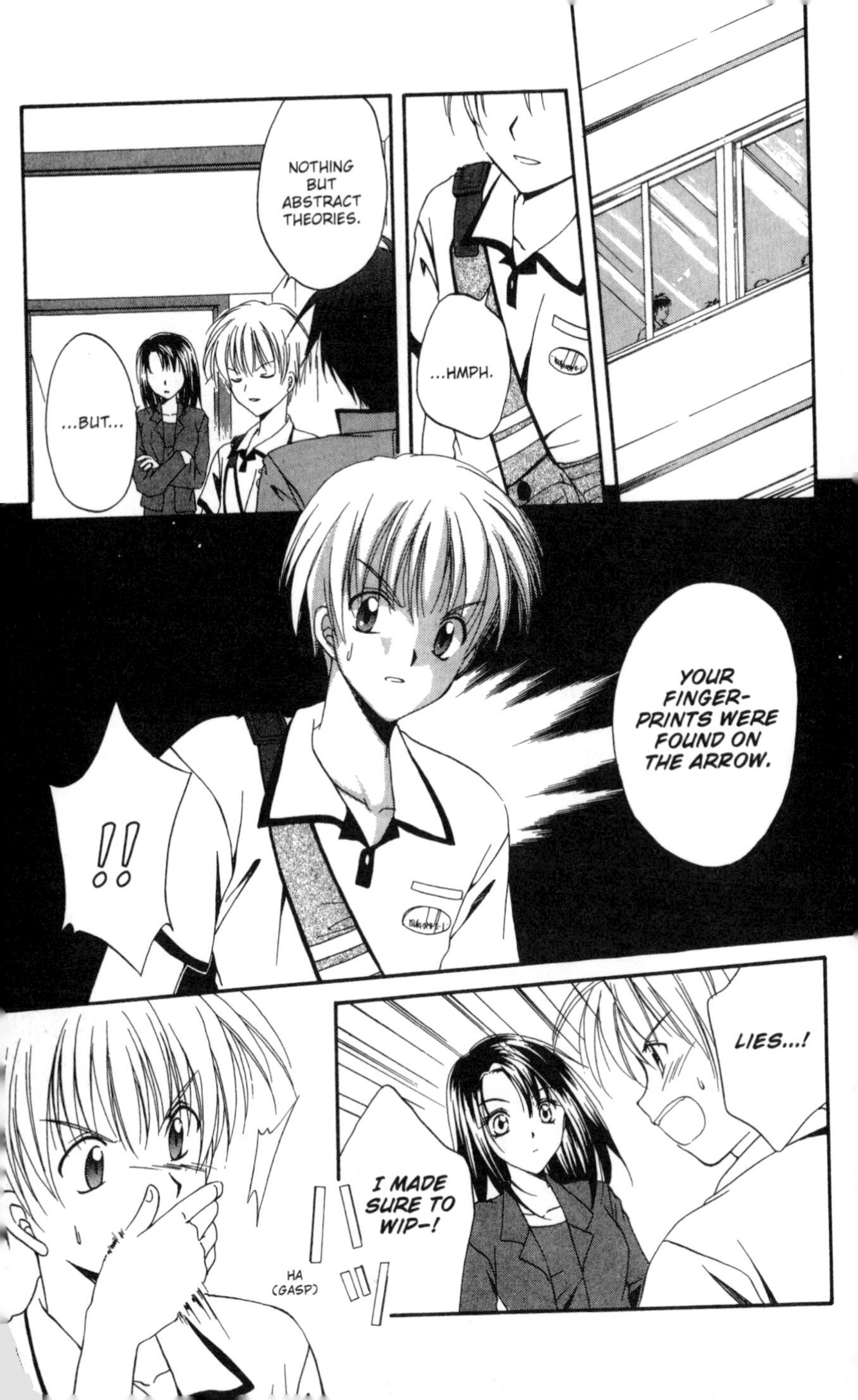
...HMPH.
NOTHING BUT ABSTRACT THEORIES.
...BUT...
YOUR FINGER-PRINTS WERE FOUND ON THE ARROW.
!!
LIES...!
I MADE SURE TO WIP-!
HA (GASP)

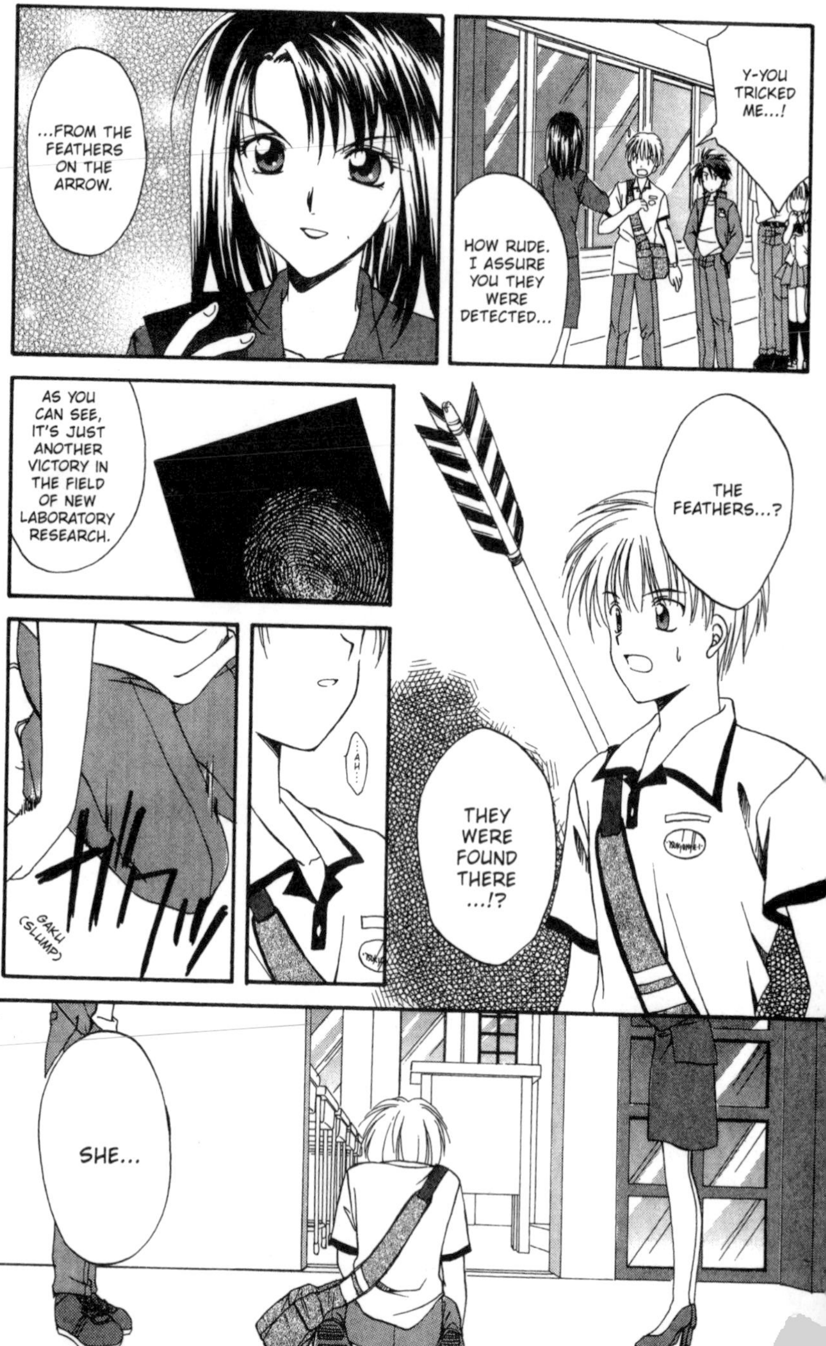
Y-YOU TRICKED ME...!
HOW RUDE. I ASSURE YOU THEY WERE DETECTED...
...FROM THE FEATHERS ON THE ARROW.
THE FEATHERS...?
THEY WERE FOUND THERE ...!?
AS YOU CAN SEE, IT'S JUST ANOTHER VICTORY IN THE FIELD OF NEW LABORATORY RESEARCH.
...AH...
GAKU (SLUMP)
SHE...

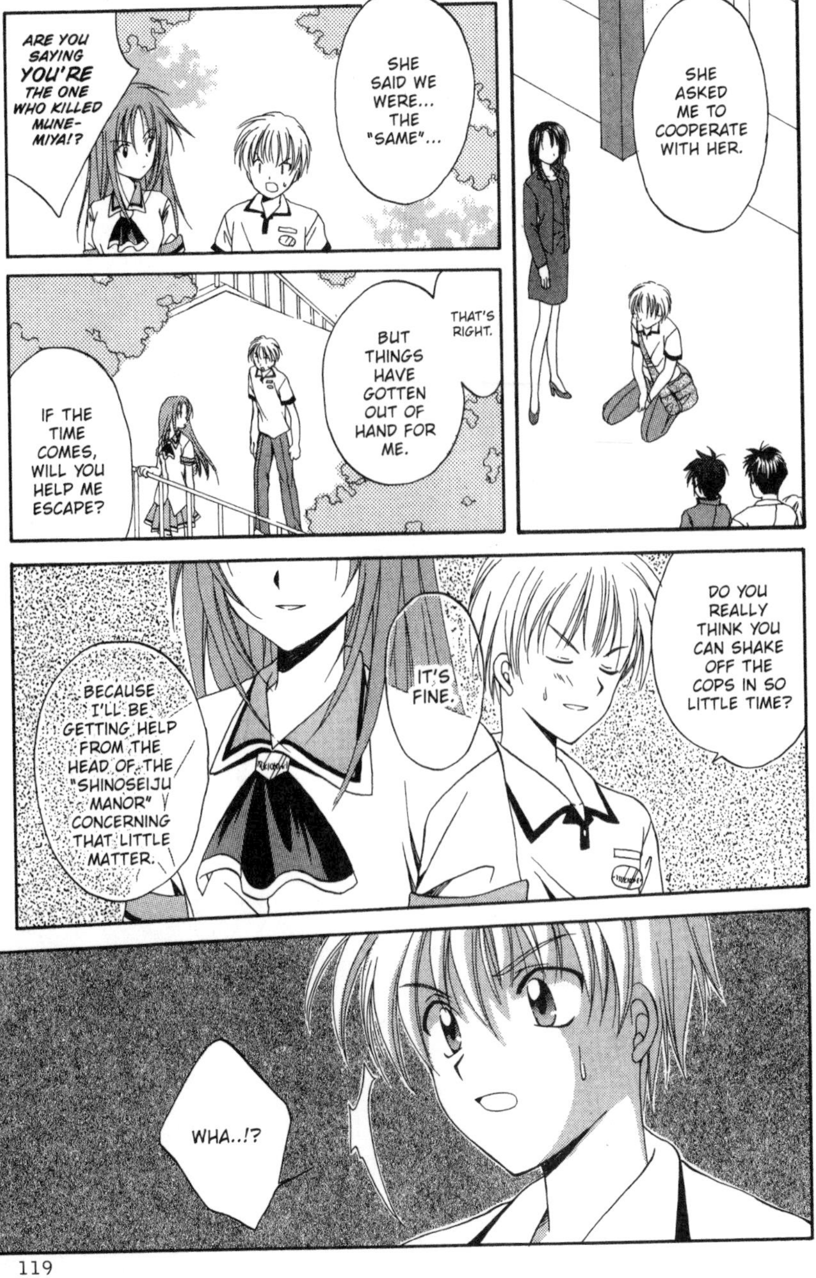
SHE ASKED ME TO COOPERATE WITH HER.
SHE SAID WE WERE... THE "SAME"...
ARE YOU SAYING YOU'RE THE ONE WHO KILLED MUNE-MIYA!?
THAT'S RIGHT.
BUT THINGS HAVE GOTTEN OUT OF HAND FOR ME.
IF THE TIME COMES, WILL YOU HELP ME ESCAPE?
DO YOU REALLY THINK YOU CAN SHAKE OFF THE COPS IN SO LITTLE TIME?
IT'S FINE.
BECAUSE I'LL BE GETTING HELP FROM THE HEAD OF THE "SHINOSEIJU MANOR" CONCERNING THAT LITTLE MATTER.
WHA..!?

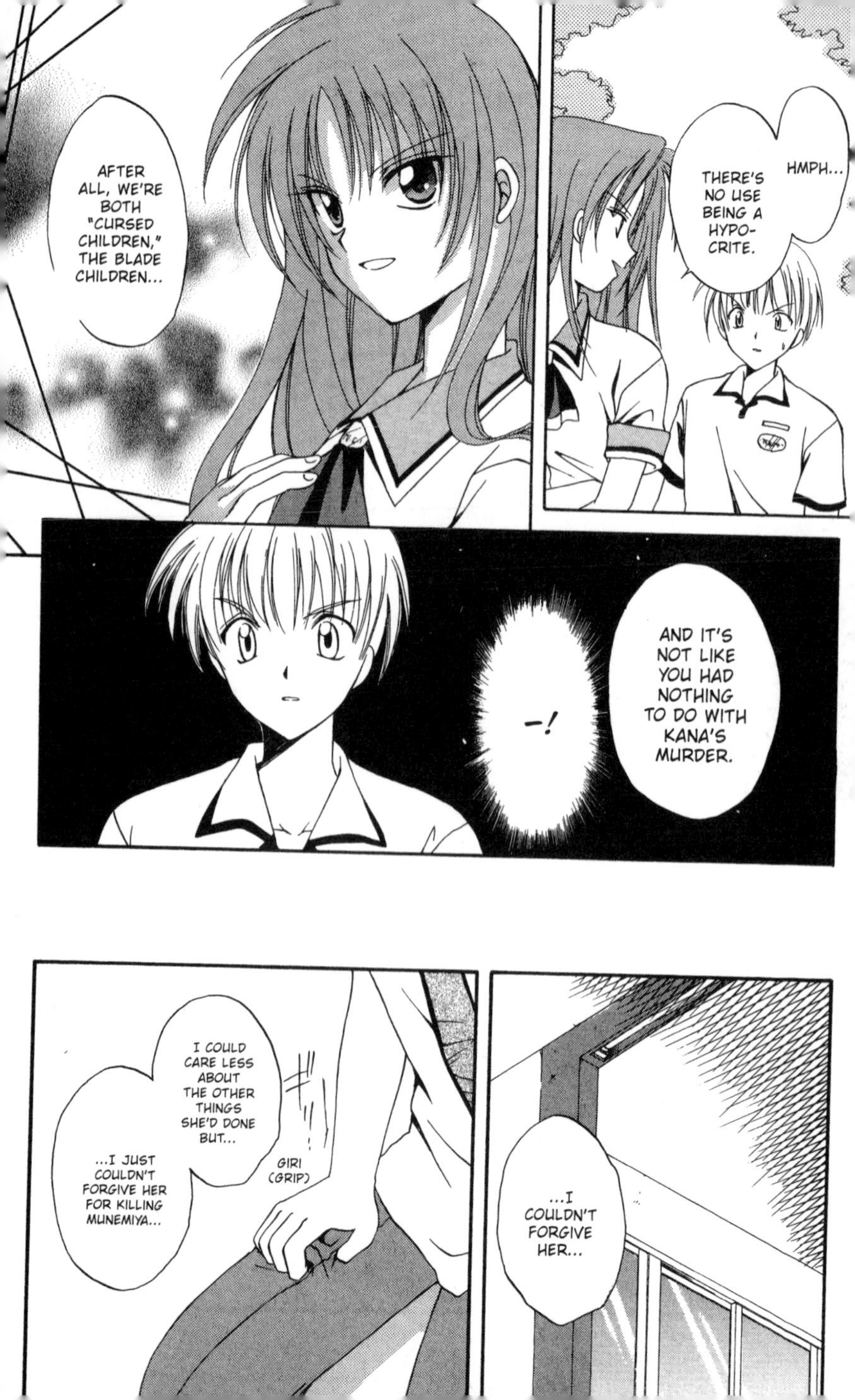
HMPH...
THERE'S NO USE BEING A HYPOCRITE.
AFTER ALL, WE'RE BOTH "CURSED CHILDREN," THE BLADE CHILDREN...
AND IT'S NOT LIKE YOU HAD NOTHING TO DO WITH KANA'S MURDER.
–!
...I COULDN'T FORGIVE HER...
I COULD CARE LESS ABOUT THE OTHER THINGS SHE'D DONE BUT...
GIRI (GRIP)
...I JUST COULDN'T FORGIVE HER FOR KILLING MUNEMIYA...

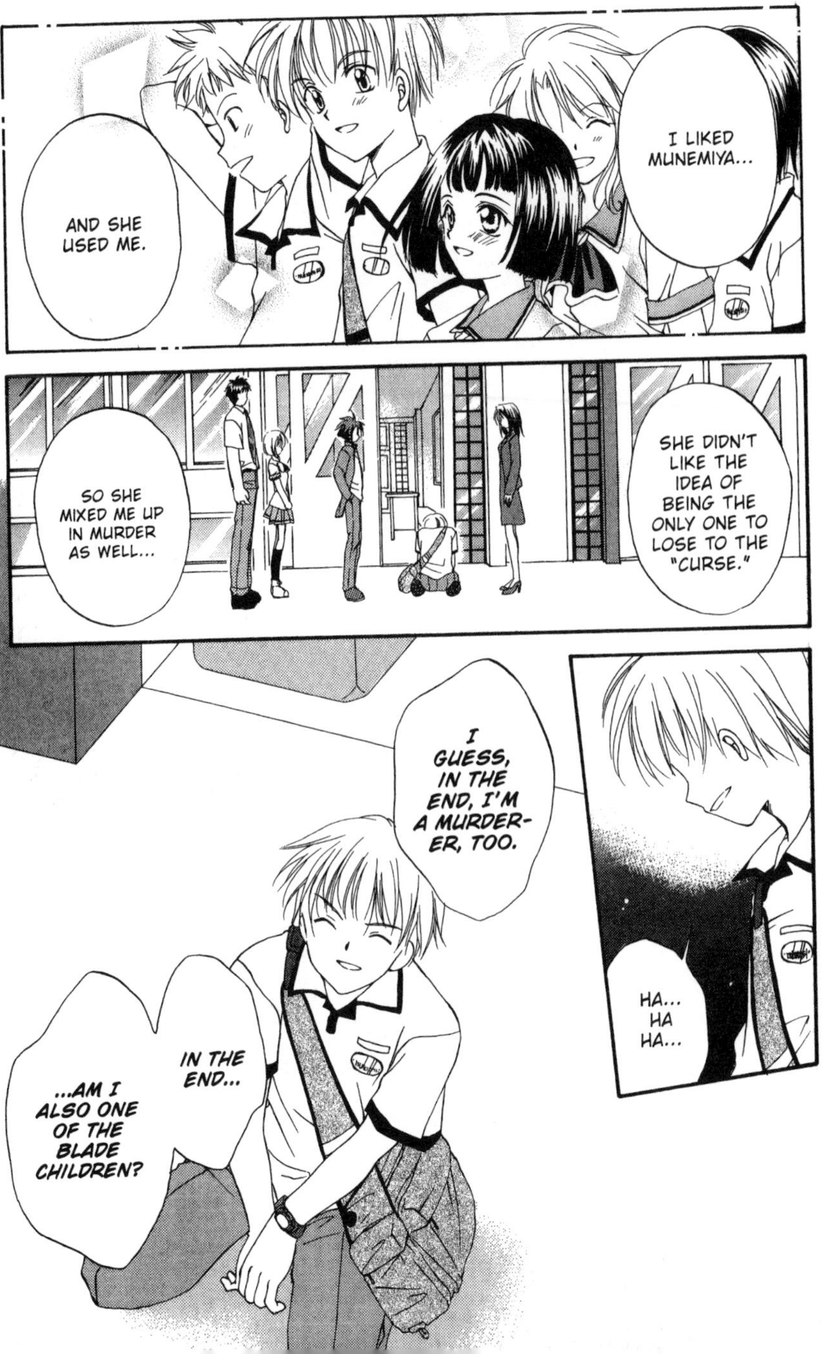
I LIKED MUNEMIYA...
AND SHE USED ME.
SHE DIDN'T LIKE THE IDEA OF BEING THE ONLY ONE TO LOSE TO THE "CURSE."
SO SHE MIXED ME UP IN MURDER AS WELL...
HA... HA HA...
I GUESS, IN THE END, I'M A MURDER-ER, TOO.
IN THE END...
...AM I ALSO ONE OF THE BLADE CHILDREN?

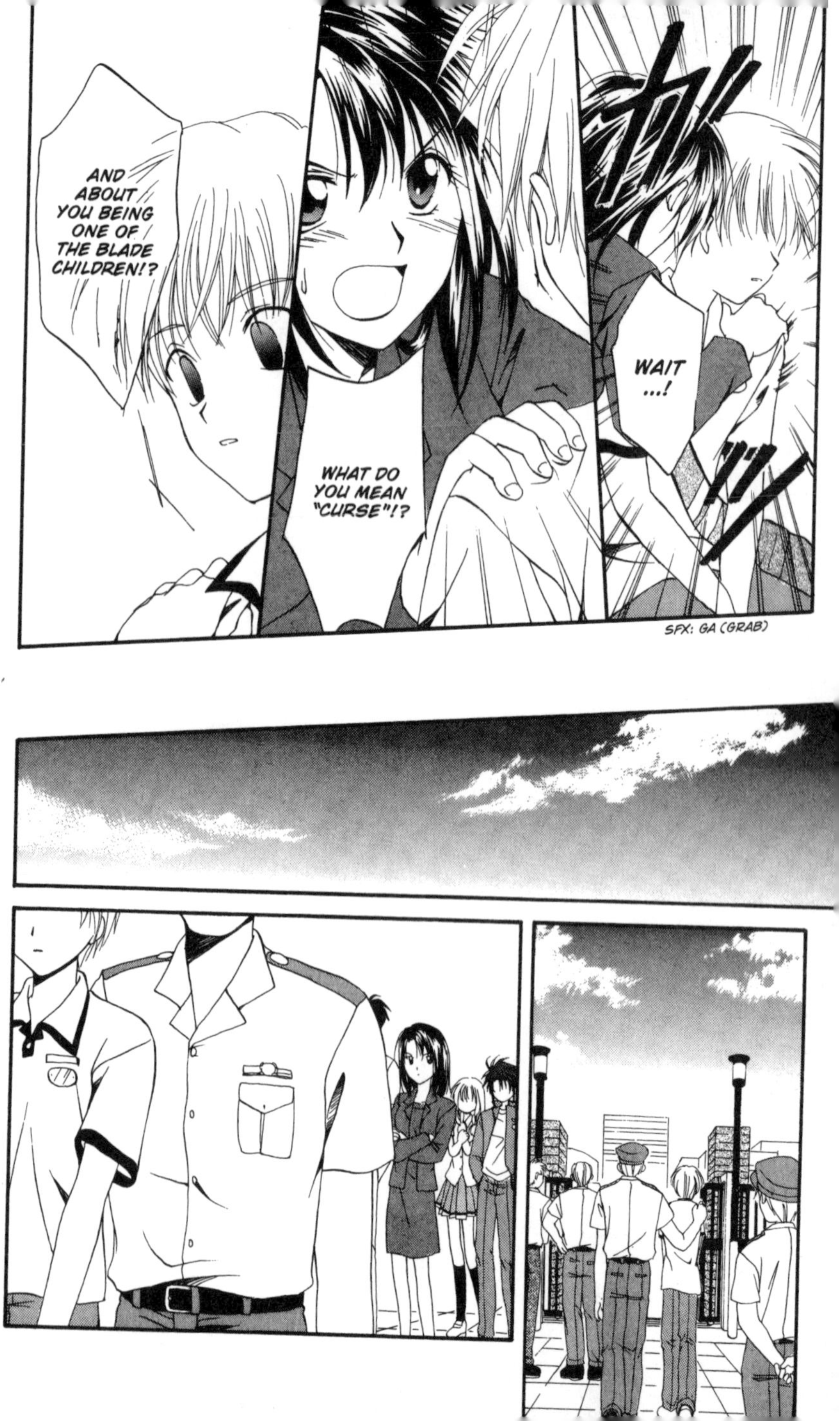
WAIT ...!
WHAT DO YOU MEAN "CURSE"!?
AND ABOUT YOU BEING ONE OF THE BLADE CHILDREN!?
SFX: GA (GRAB)

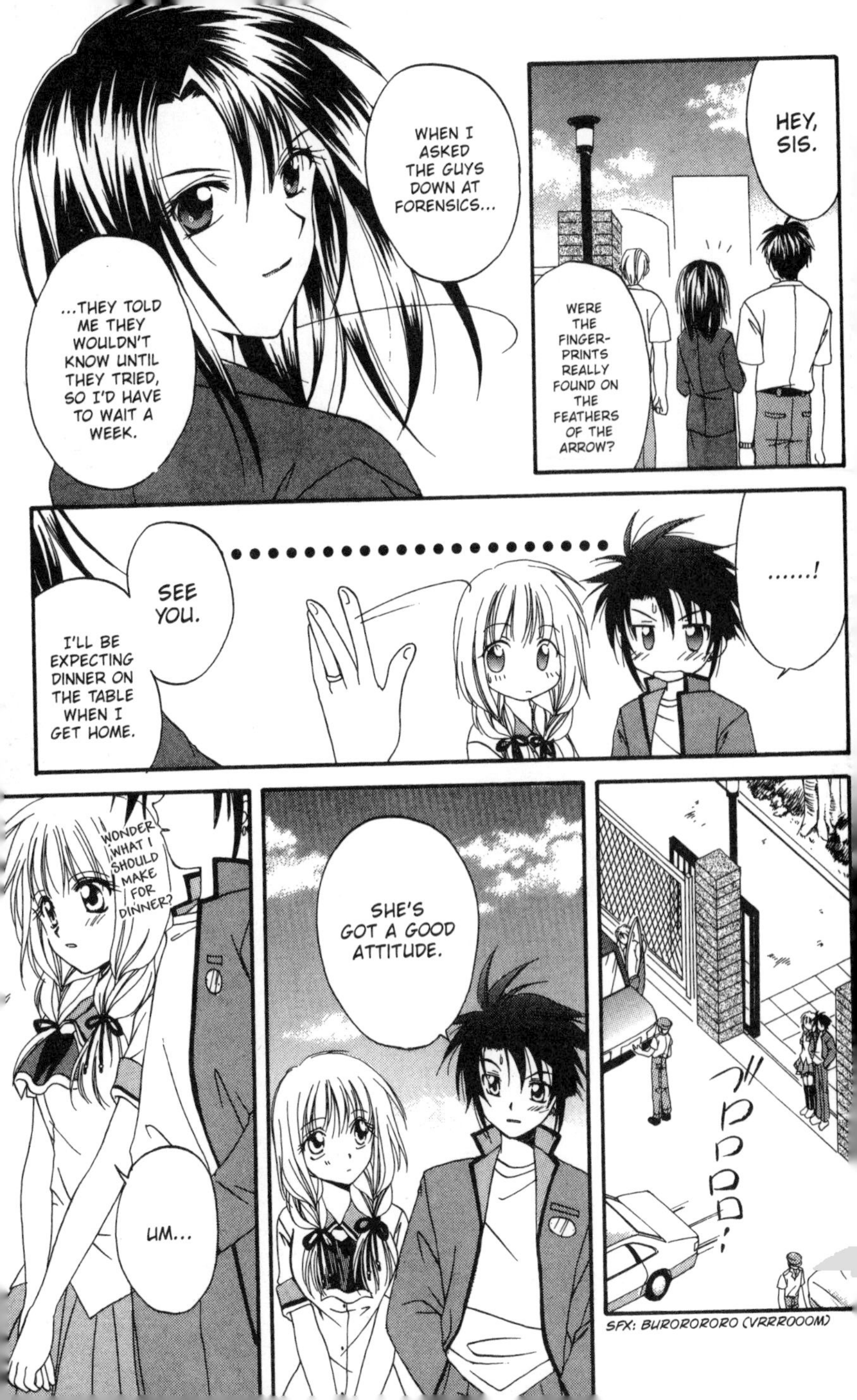
HEY, SIS.
WERE THE FINGER-PRINTS REALLY FOUND ON THE FEATHERS OF THE ARROW?
WHEN I ASKED THE GUYS DOWN AT FORENSICS...
...THEY TOLD ME THEY WOULDN'T KNOW UNTIL THEY TRIED, SO I'D HAVE TO WAIT A WEEK.
......!
••••••••••••••••••••••••
SEE YOU.
I'LL BE EXPECTING DINNER ON THE TABLE WHEN I GET HOME.
SFX: BURORORORO (VRRROOOM)
SHE'S GOT A GOOD ATTITUDE.
WONDER WHAT I SHOULD MAKE FOR DINNER?
UM...

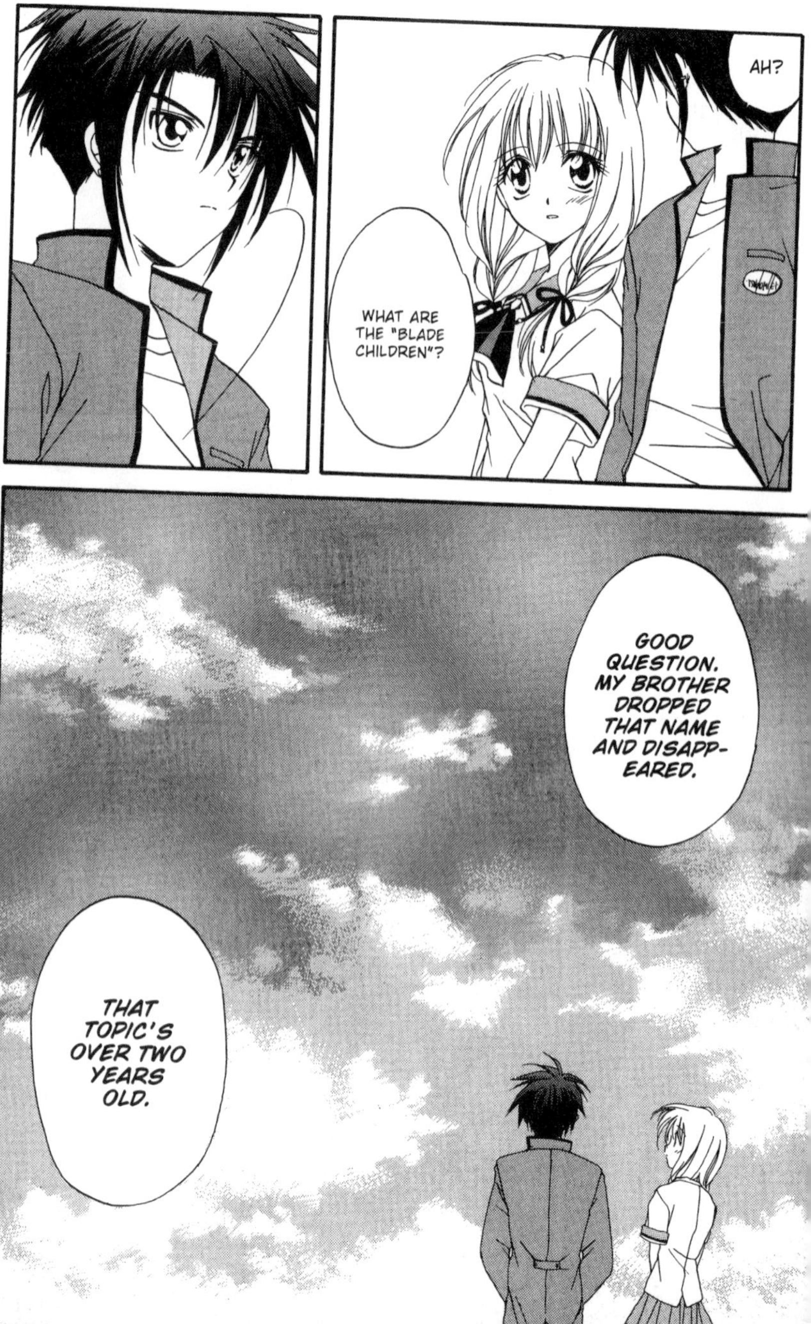
AH?
WHAT ARE THE "BLADE CHILDREN"?
GOOD QUESTION. MY BROTHER DROPPED THAT NAME AND DISAPP-EARED.
THAT TOPIC'S OVER TWO YEARS OLD.

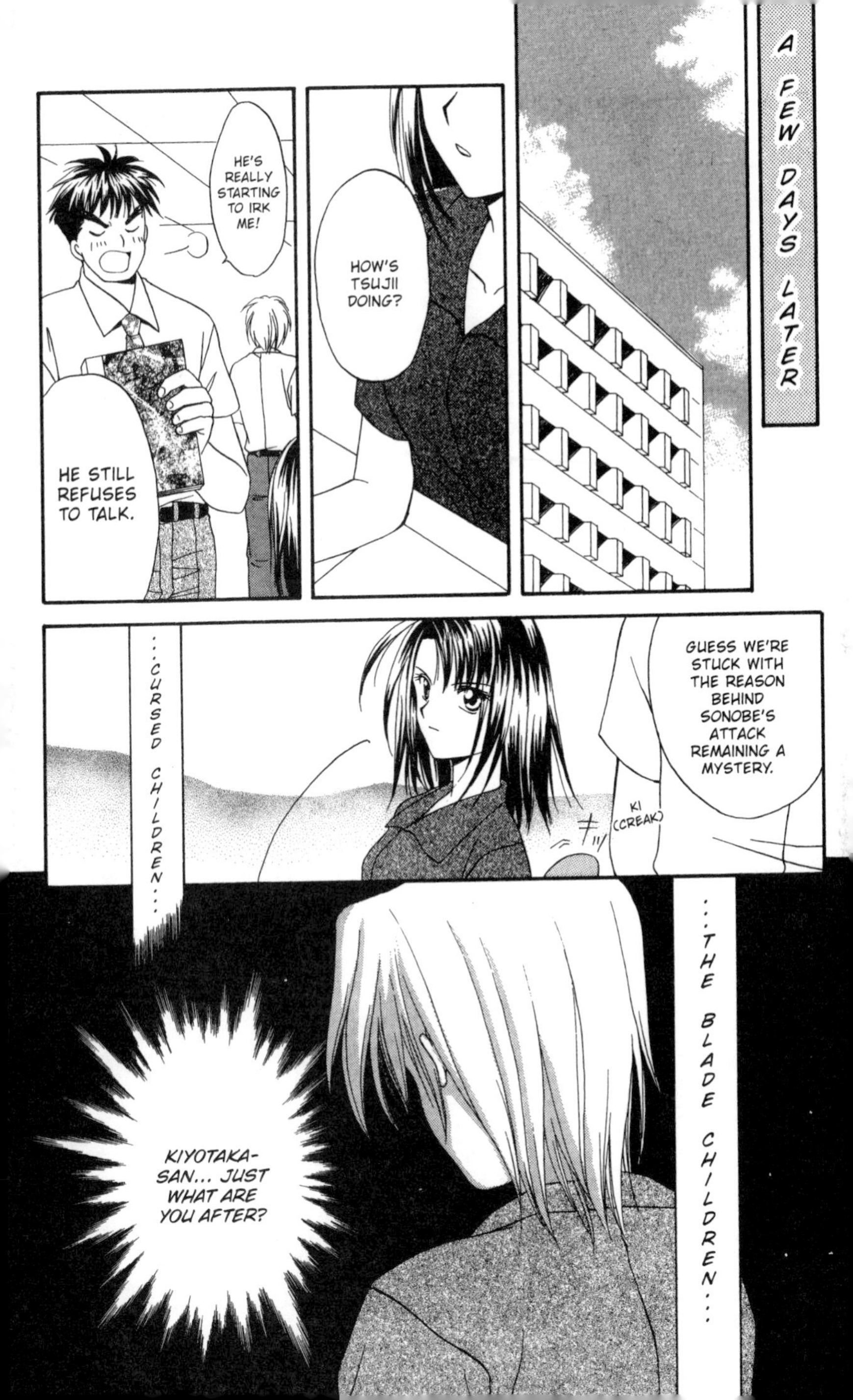
A FEW DAYS LATER
HOW'S TSUJII DOING?
HE'S REALLY STARTING TO IRK ME!
HE STILL REFUSES TO TALK.
GUESS WE'RE STUCK WITH THE REASON BEHIND SONOBE'S ATTACK REMAINING A MYSTERY.
KI (CREAK)
...CURSED CHILDREN...
...THE BLADE CHILDREN...
KIYOTAKA-SAN... JUST WHAT ARE YOU AFTER?

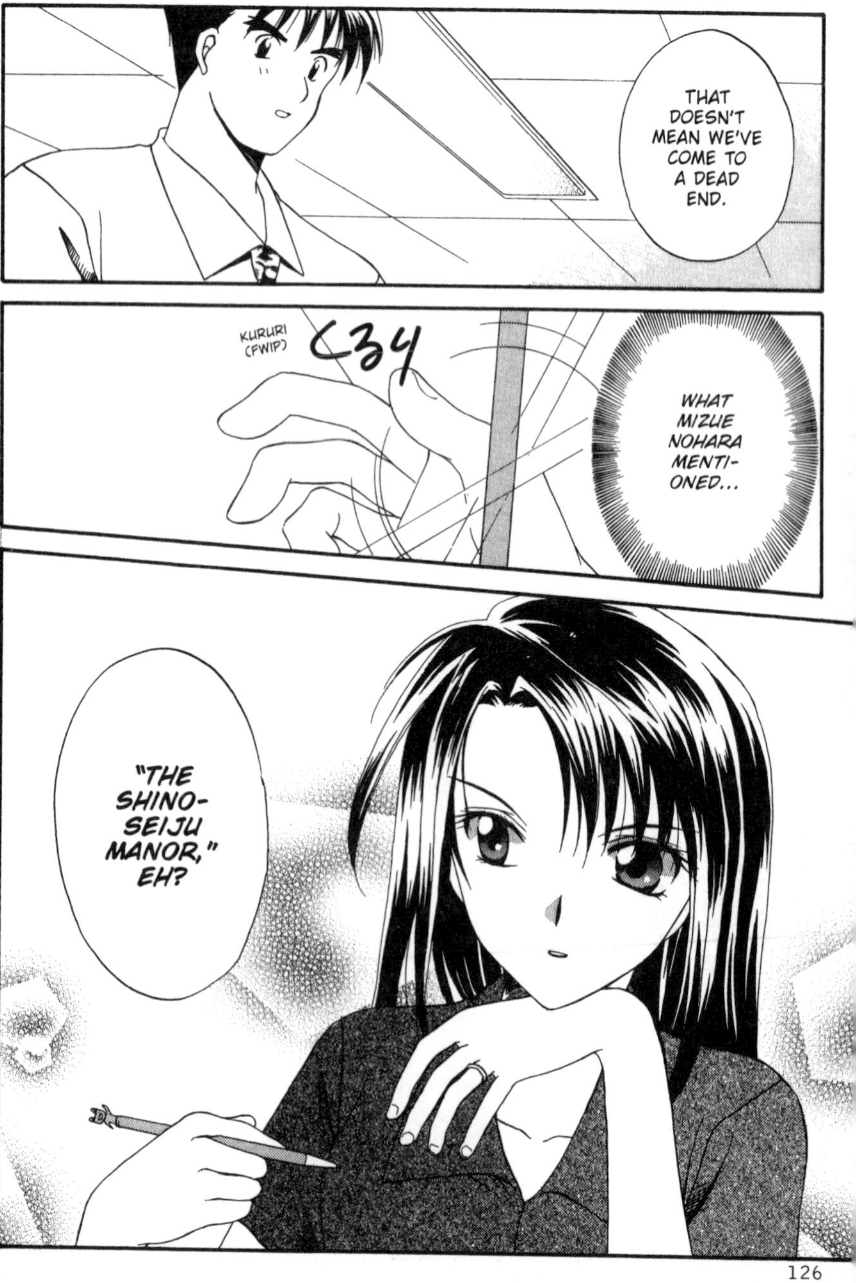
THAT DOESN'T MEAN WE'VE COME TO A DEAD END.
WHAT MIZUE NOHARA MENTI-ONED...
KURURI (FWIP)
くるり
"THE SHINO-SEIJU MANOR," EH?

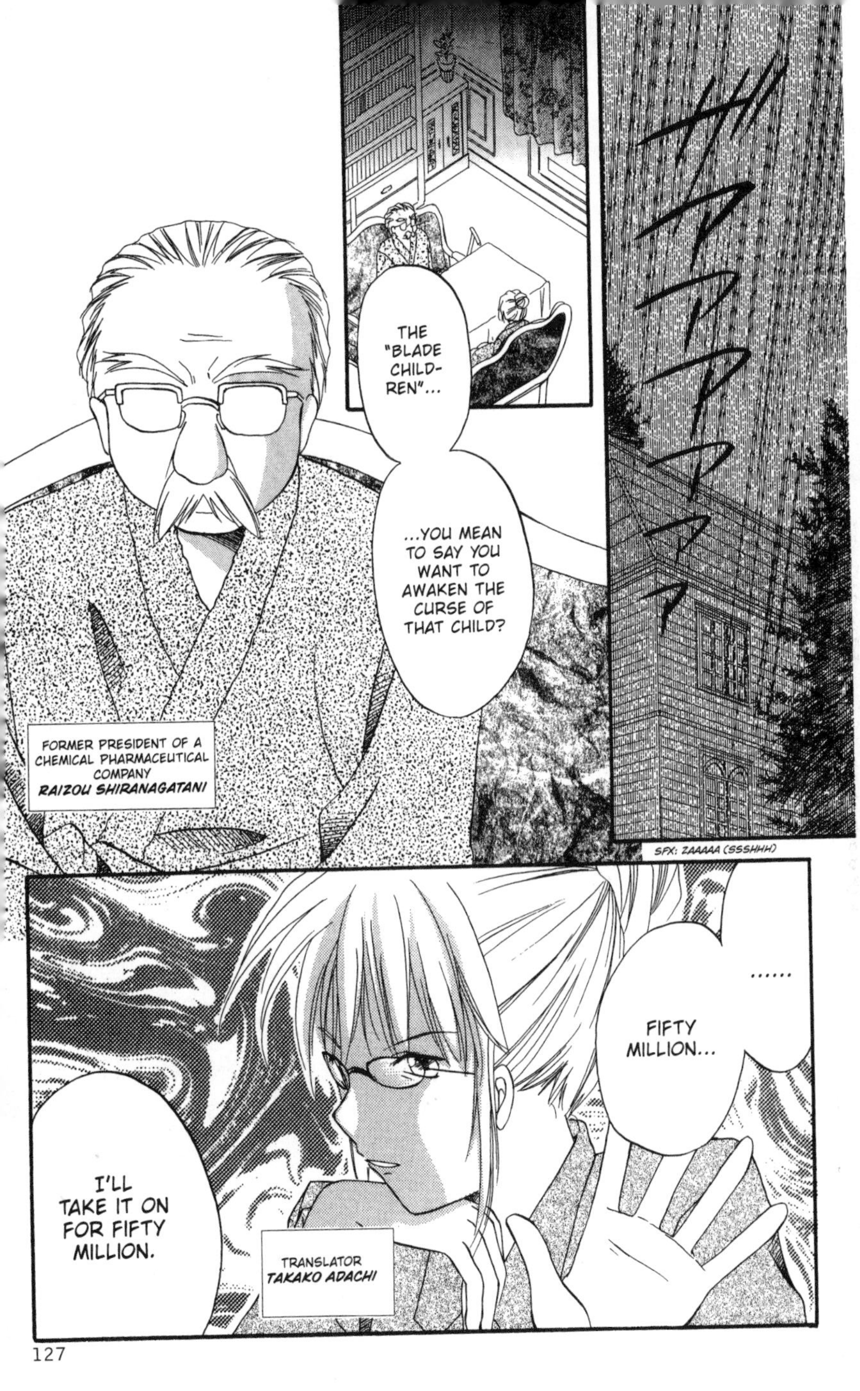
SFX: ZAAAAA (SSSHHH)
THE "BLADE CHILD-REN"...
...YOU MEAN TO SAY YOU WANT TO AWAKEN THE CURSE OF THAT CHILD?
FORMER PRESIDENT OF A CHEMICAL PHARMACEUTICAL COMPANY
RAIZOU SHIRANAGATANI
......
FIFTY MILLION...
I'LL TAKE IT ON FOR FIFTY MILLION.
TRANSLATOR
TAKAKO ADACHI

CHAPTER FOUR

Room Behind the Ward Lock (Part I)

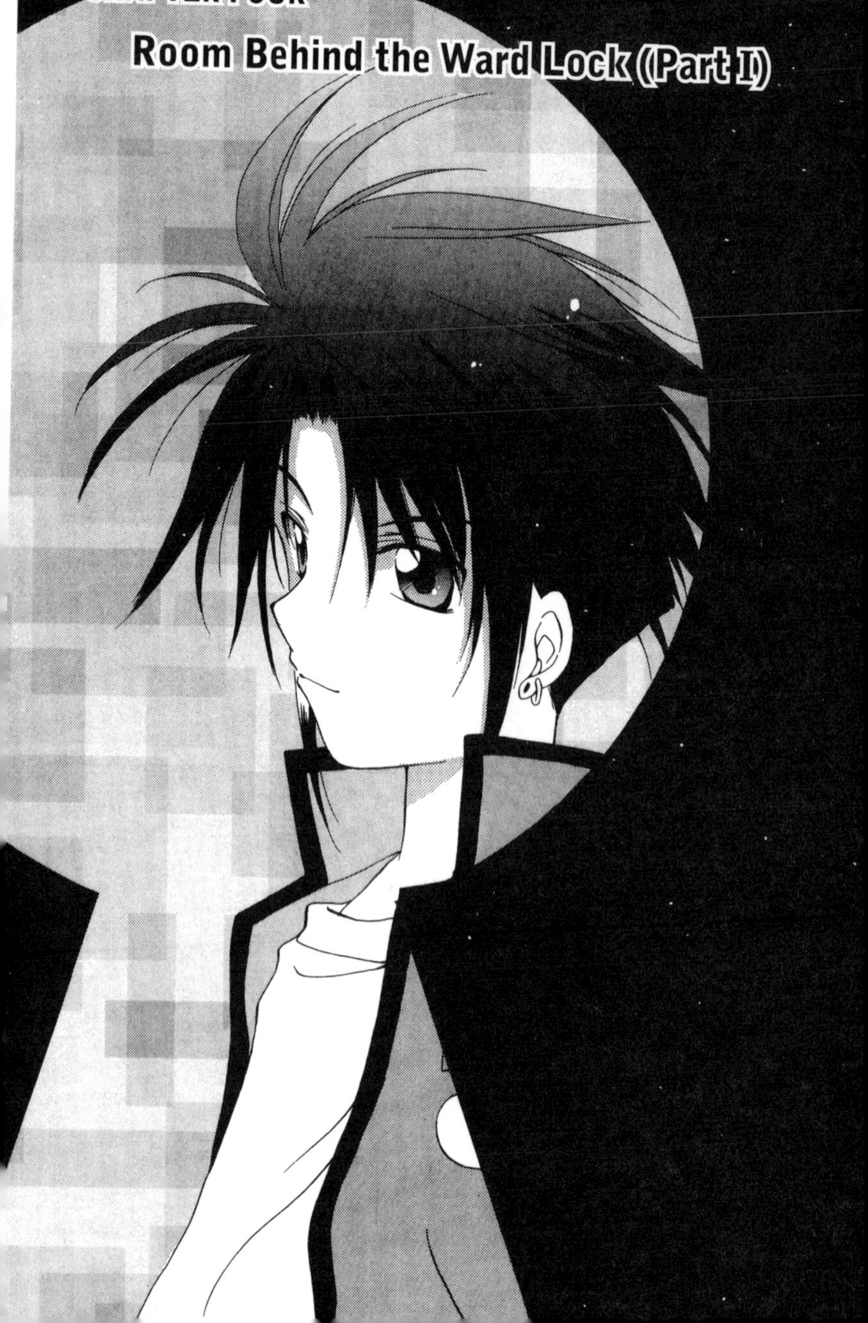

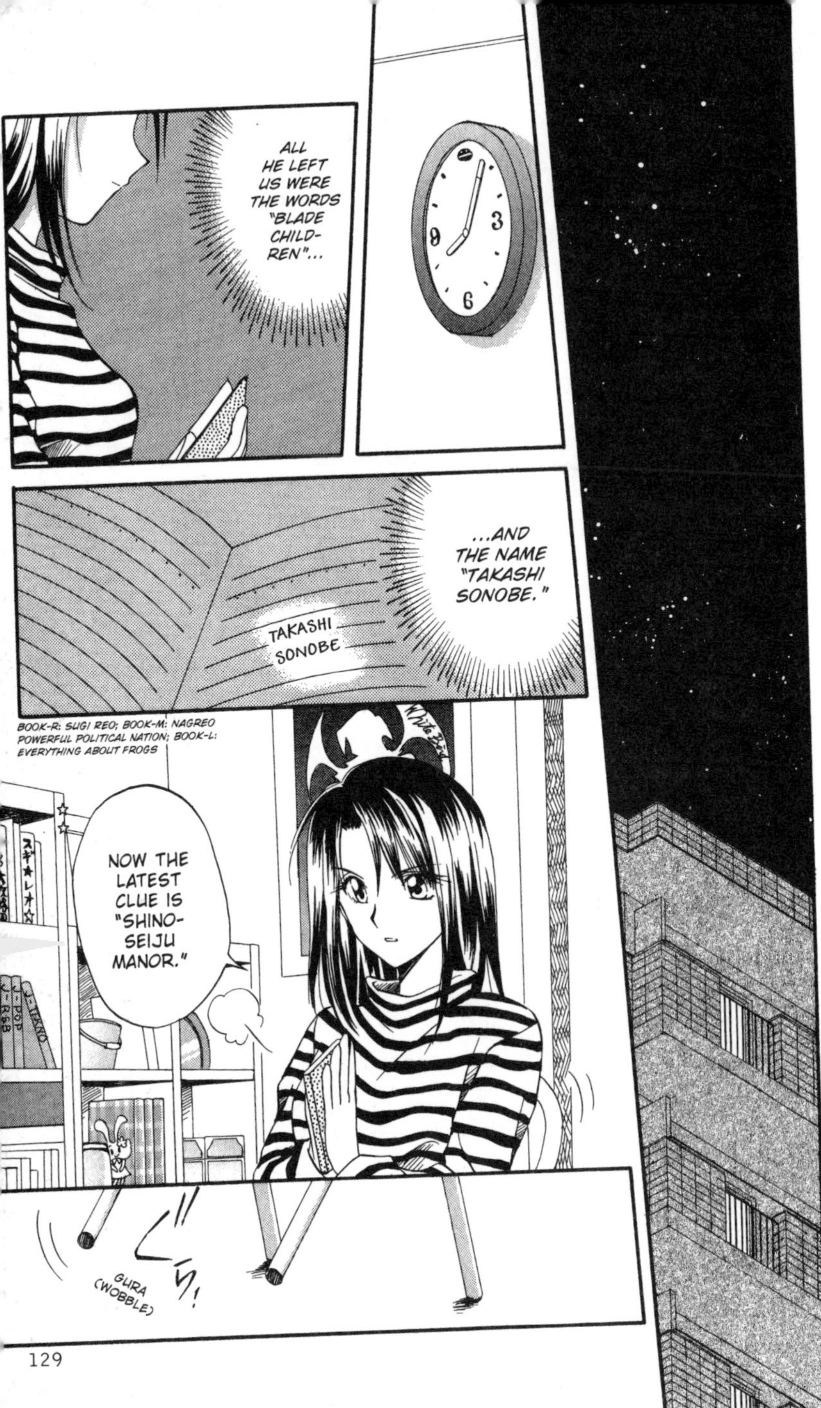
ALL HE LEFT US WERE THE WORDS "BLADE CHILD-REN"...
...AND THE NAME "TAKASHI SONOBE."
TAKASHI SONOBE
BOOK-R: SUGI REO; BOOK-M: NAGREO POWERFUL POLITICAL NATION; BOOK-L: EVERYTHING ABOUT FROGS
NOW THE LATEST CLUE IS "SHINO-SEIJU MANOR."
GURA (WOBBLE)

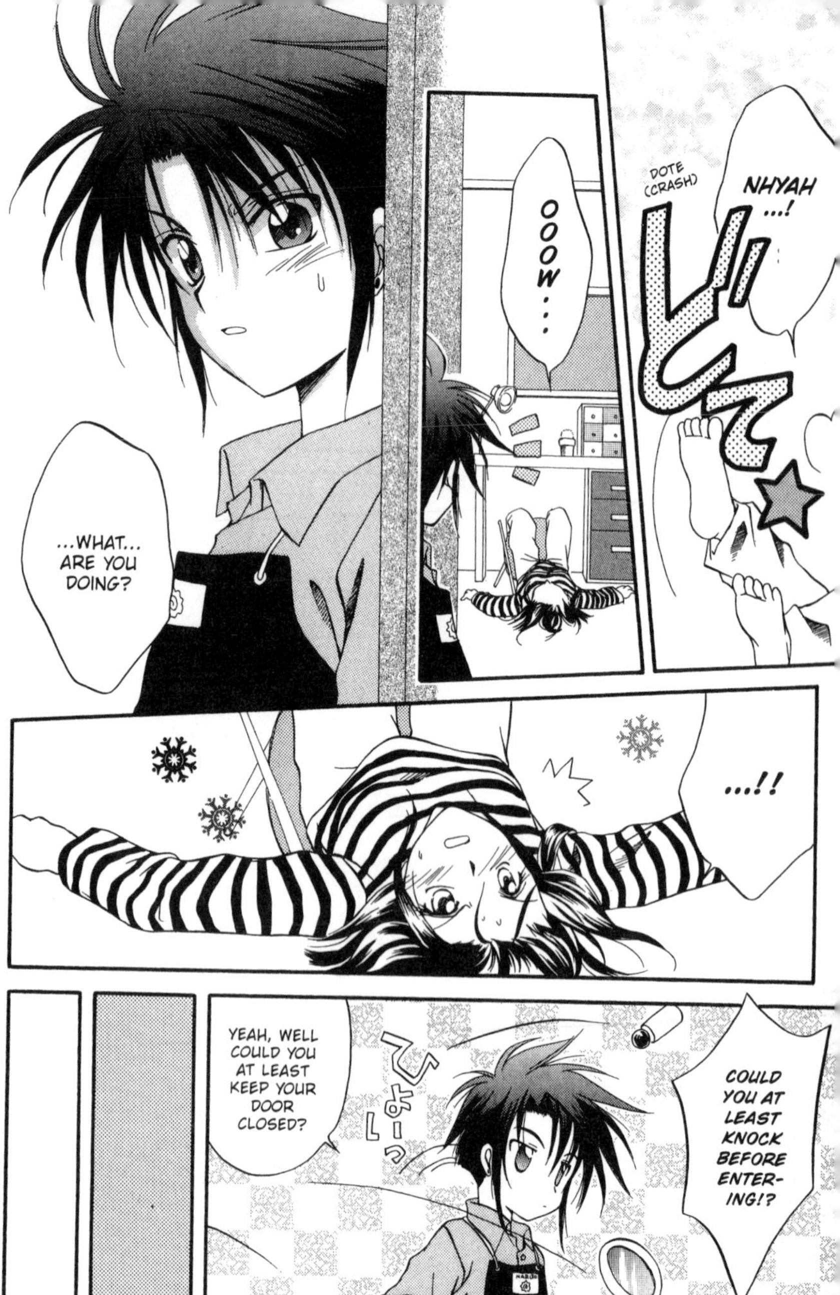
NHYAH ...!
DOTE (CRASH)
OOOW...
...WHAT... ARE YOU DOING?
...!!
COULD YOU AT LEAST KNOCK BEFORE ENTER-ING!?
YEAH, WELL COULD YOU AT LEAST KEEP YOUR DOOR CLOSED?
ひょいっ

SFX: HYOI (DUCK)

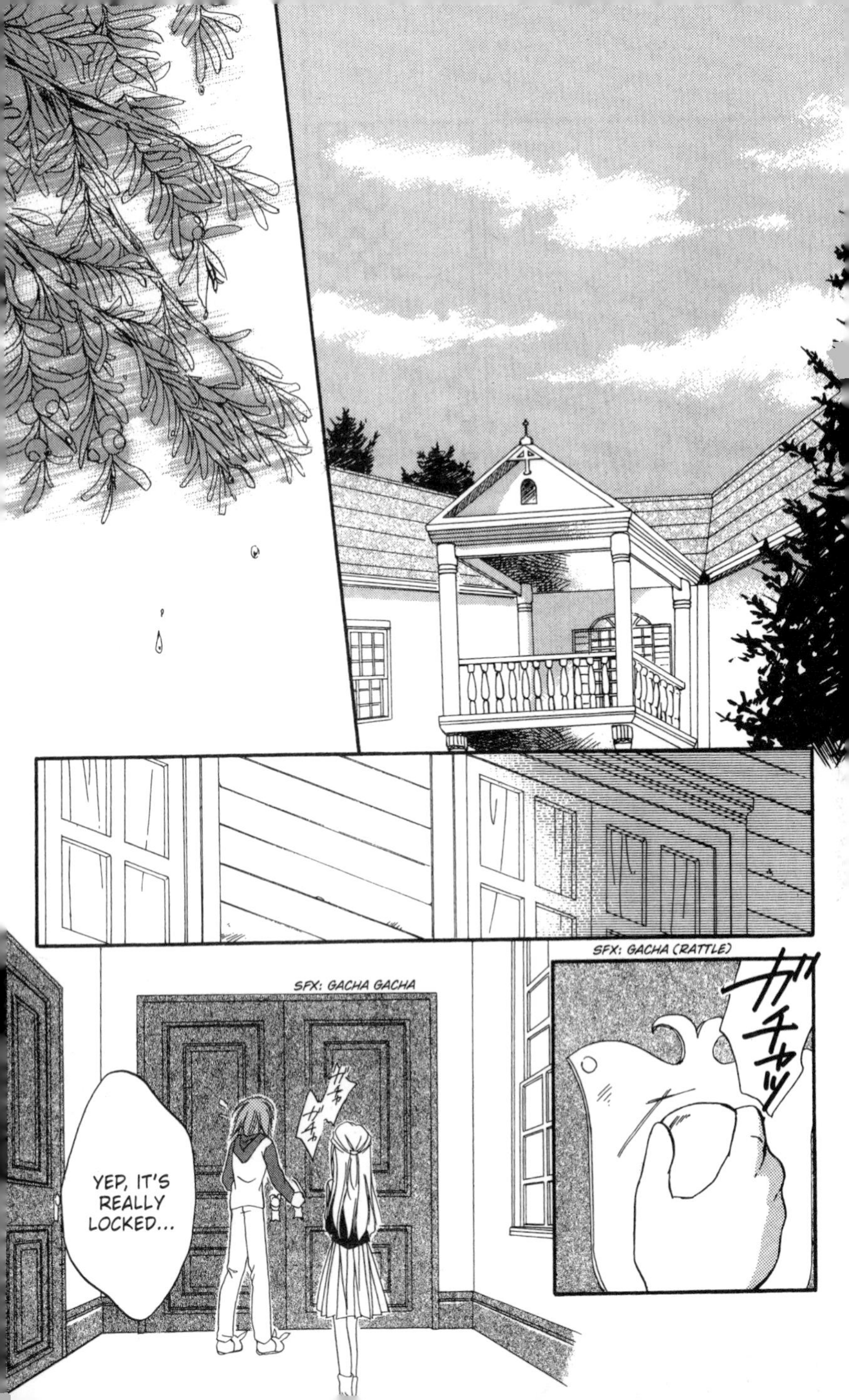
SFX: GACHA (RATTLE)
ガチャッ
SFX: GACHA GACHA
ガチャガチャ
YEP, IT'S REALLY LOCKED...

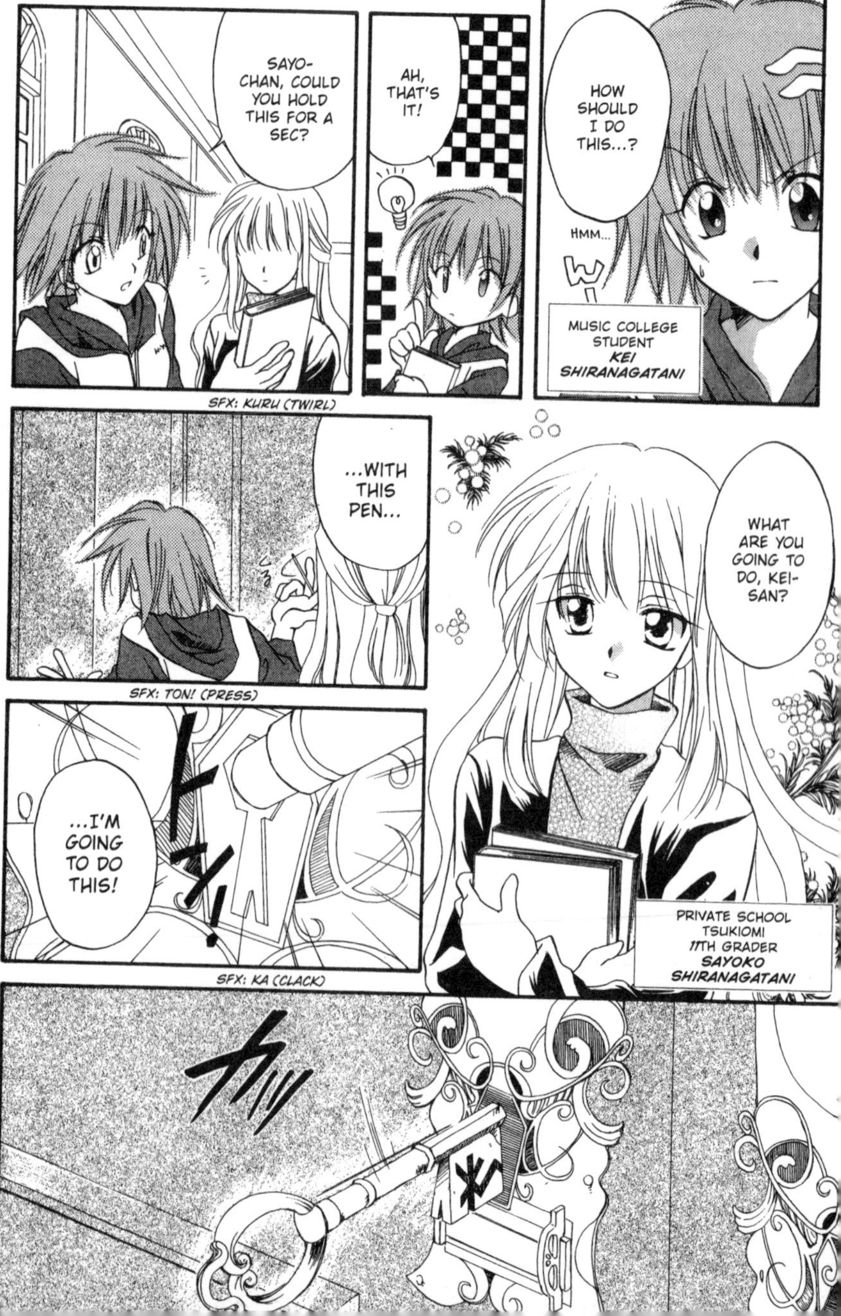
HOW SHOULD I DO THIS...?
HMM...
MUSIC COLLEGE STUDENT KEI SHIRANAGATANI
AH, THAT'S IT!
SAYO-CHAN, COULD YOU HOLD THIS FOR A SEC?
SFX: KURU (TWIRL)
WHAT ARE YOU GOING TO DO, KEI-SAN?
PRIVATE SCHOOL TSUKIOMI 11TH GRADER SAYOKO SHIRANAGATANI
...WITH THIS PEN...
SFX: TON! (PRESS)
...I'M GOING TO DO THIS!
SFX: KA (CLACK)

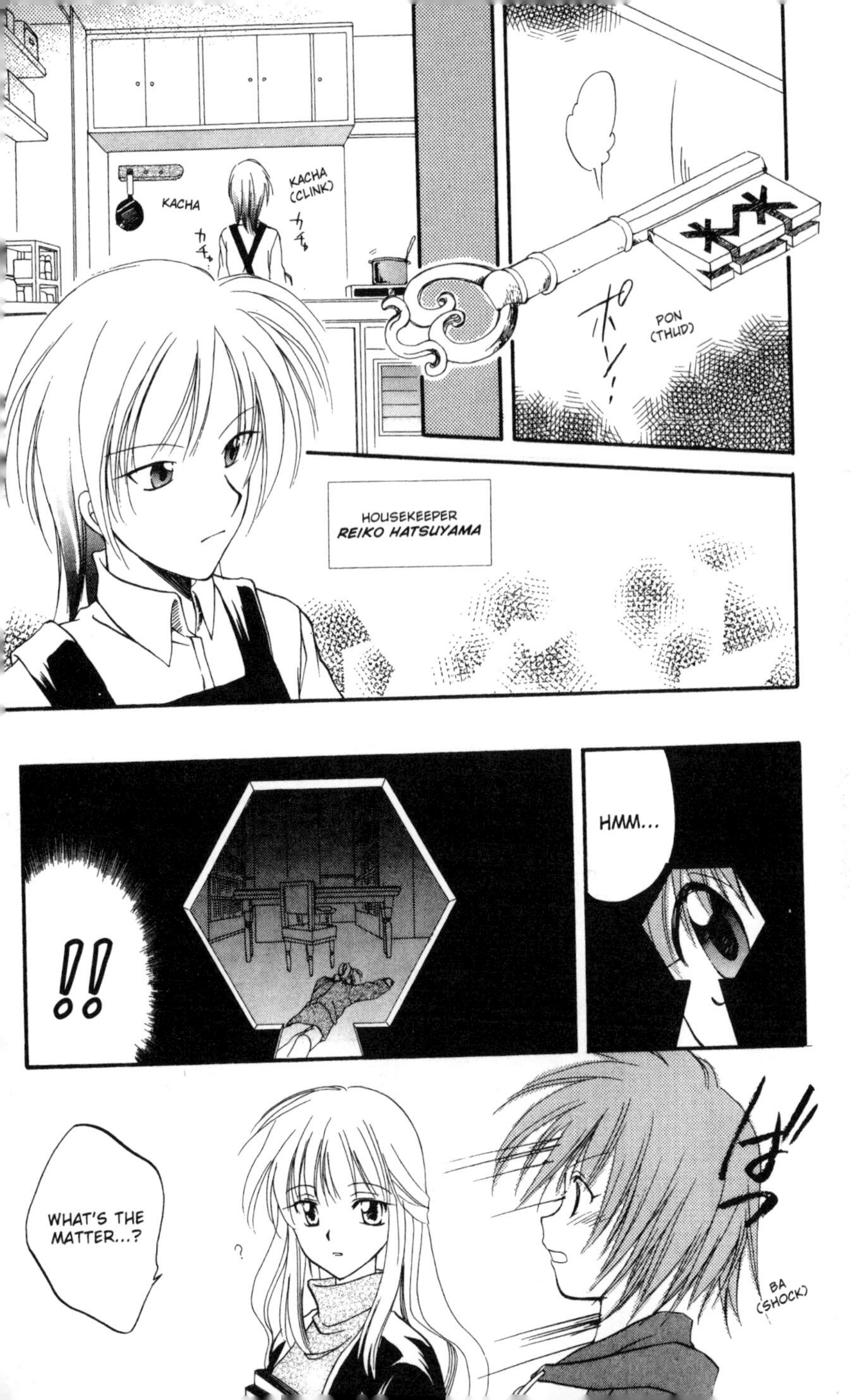
PON (THUD)
KACHA (CLINK)
KACHA
HOUSEKEEPER REIKO HATSUYAMA
HMM...
!!
BA (SHOCK)
WHAT'S THE MATTER...?
?

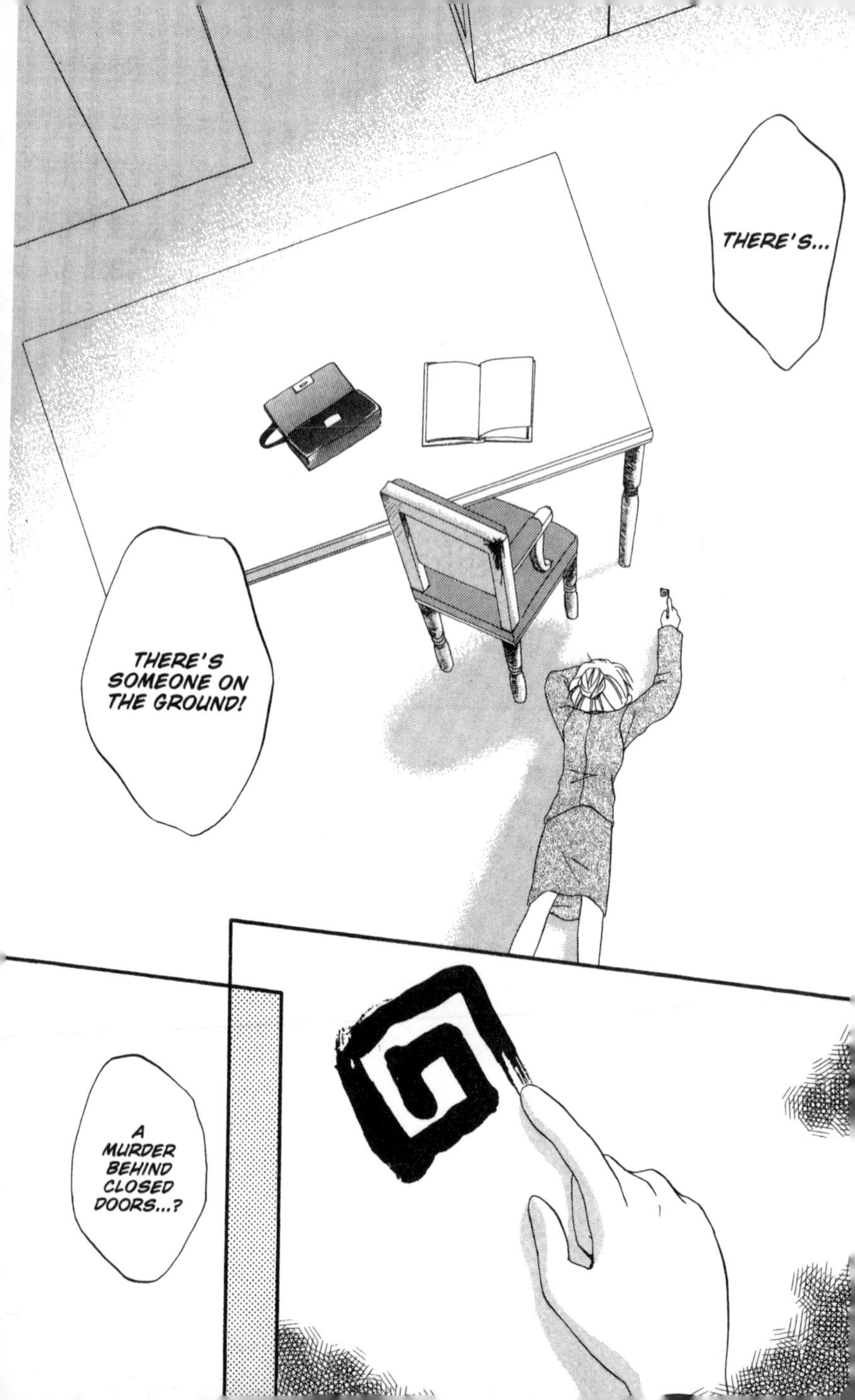
THERE'S...
THERE'S SOMEONE ON THE GROUND!
A MURDER BEHIND CLOSED DOORS...?

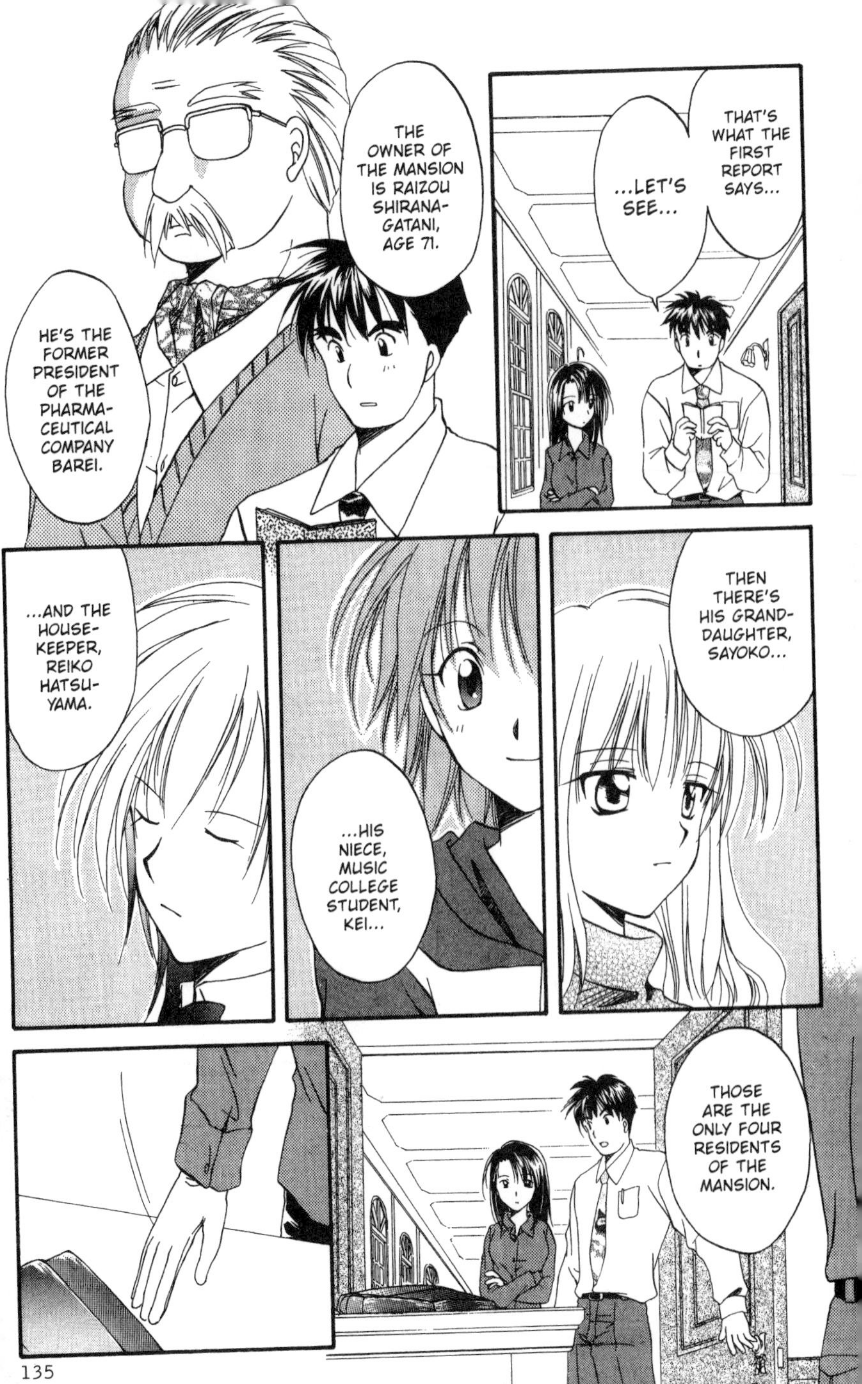
THAT'S WHAT THE FIRST REPORT SAYS...
...LET'S SEE...
THE OWNER OF THE MANSION IS RAIZOU SHIRANA-GATANI, AGE 71.
HE'S THE FORMER PRESIDENT OF THE PHARMA-CEUTICAL COMPANY BAREI.
THEN THERE'S HIS GRAND-DAUGHTER, SAYOKO...
...HIS NIECE, MUSIC COLLEGE STUDENT, KEI...
...AND THE HOUSE-KEEPER, REIKO HATSU-YAMA.
THOSE ARE THE ONLY FOUR RESIDENTS OF THE MANSION.

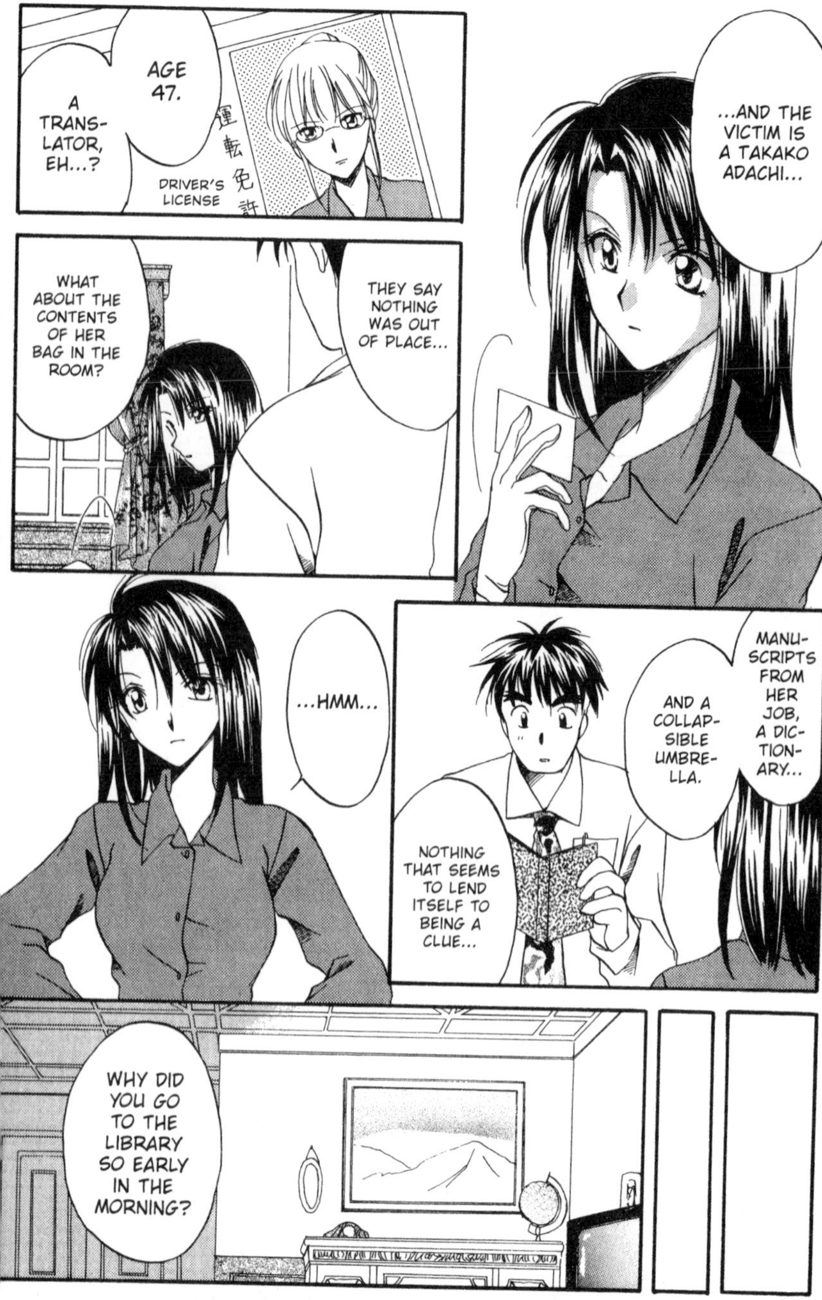
...AND THE VICTIM IS A TAKAKO ADACHI...
AGE 47.
A TRANS-LATOR, EH...?
DRIVER'S LICENSE
運転免許
THEY SAY NOTHING WAS OUT OF PLACE...
WHAT ABOUT THE CONTENTS OF HER BAG IN THE ROOM?
MANU-SCRIPTS FROM HER JOB, A DIC-TION-ARY...
AND A COLLAP-SIBLE UMBRE-LLA.
NOTHING THAT SEEMS TO LEND ITSELF TO BEING A CLUE...
...HMM...
WHY DID YOU GO TO THE LIBRARY SO EARLY IN THE MORNING?

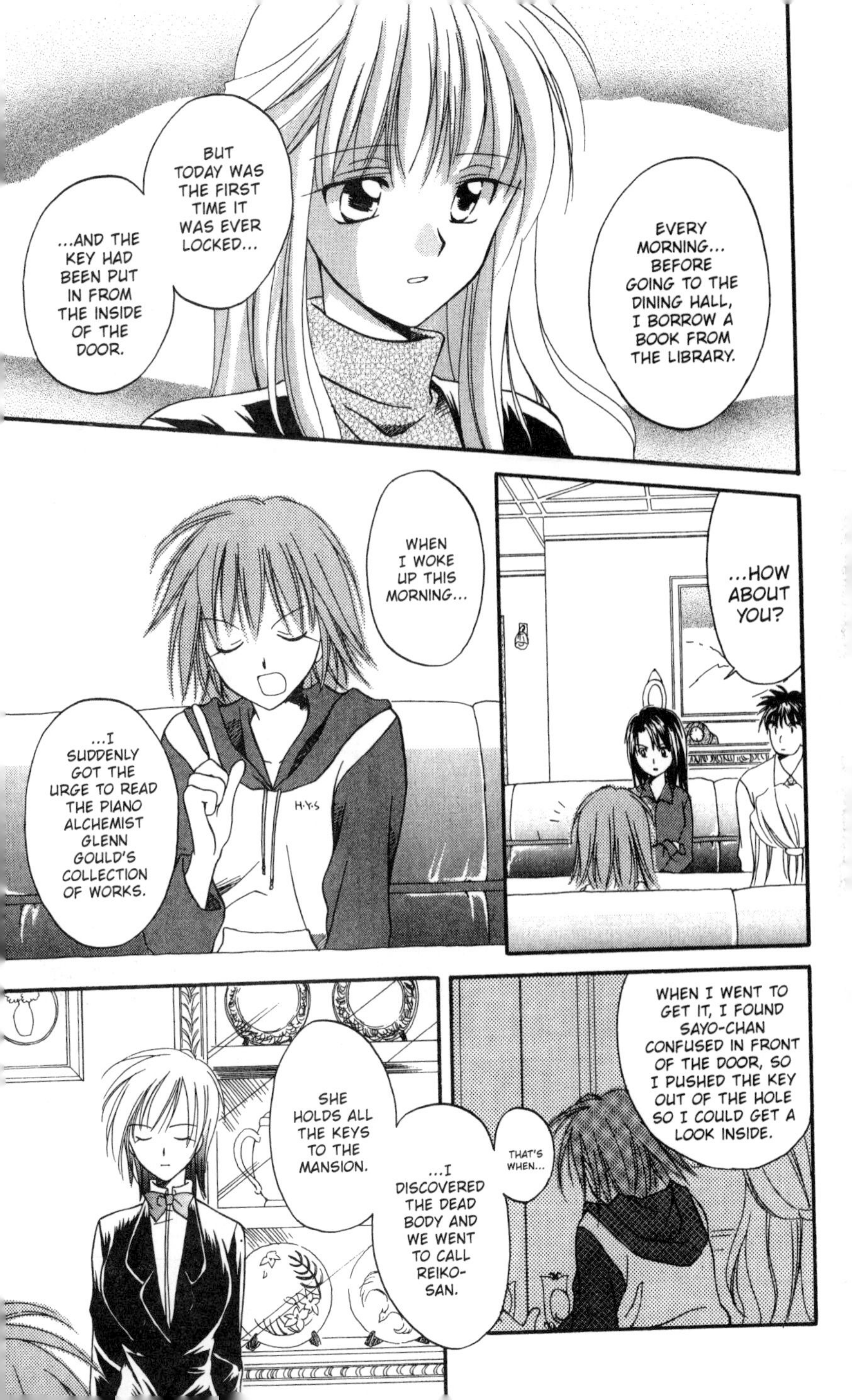
EVERY MORNING... BEFORE GOING TO THE DINING HALL, I BORROW A BOOK FROM THE LIBRARY.
BUT TODAY WAS THE FIRST TIME IT WAS EVER LOCKED...
...AND THE KEY HAD BEEN PUT IN FROM THE INSIDE OF THE DOOR.
...HOW ABOUT YOU?
WHEN I WOKE UP THIS MORNING...
...I SUDDENLY GOT THE URGE TO READ THE PIANO ALCHEMIST GLENN GOULD'S COLLECTION OF WORKS.
H·Y·S
WHEN I WENT TO GET IT, I FOUND SAYO-CHAN CONFUSED IN FRONT OF THE DOOR, SO I PUSHED THE KEY OUT OF THE HOLE SO I COULD GET A LOOK INSIDE.
THAT'S WHEN...
...I DISCOVERED THE DEAD BODY AND WE WENT TO CALL REIKO-SAN.
SHE HOLDS ALL THE KEYS TO THE MANSION.

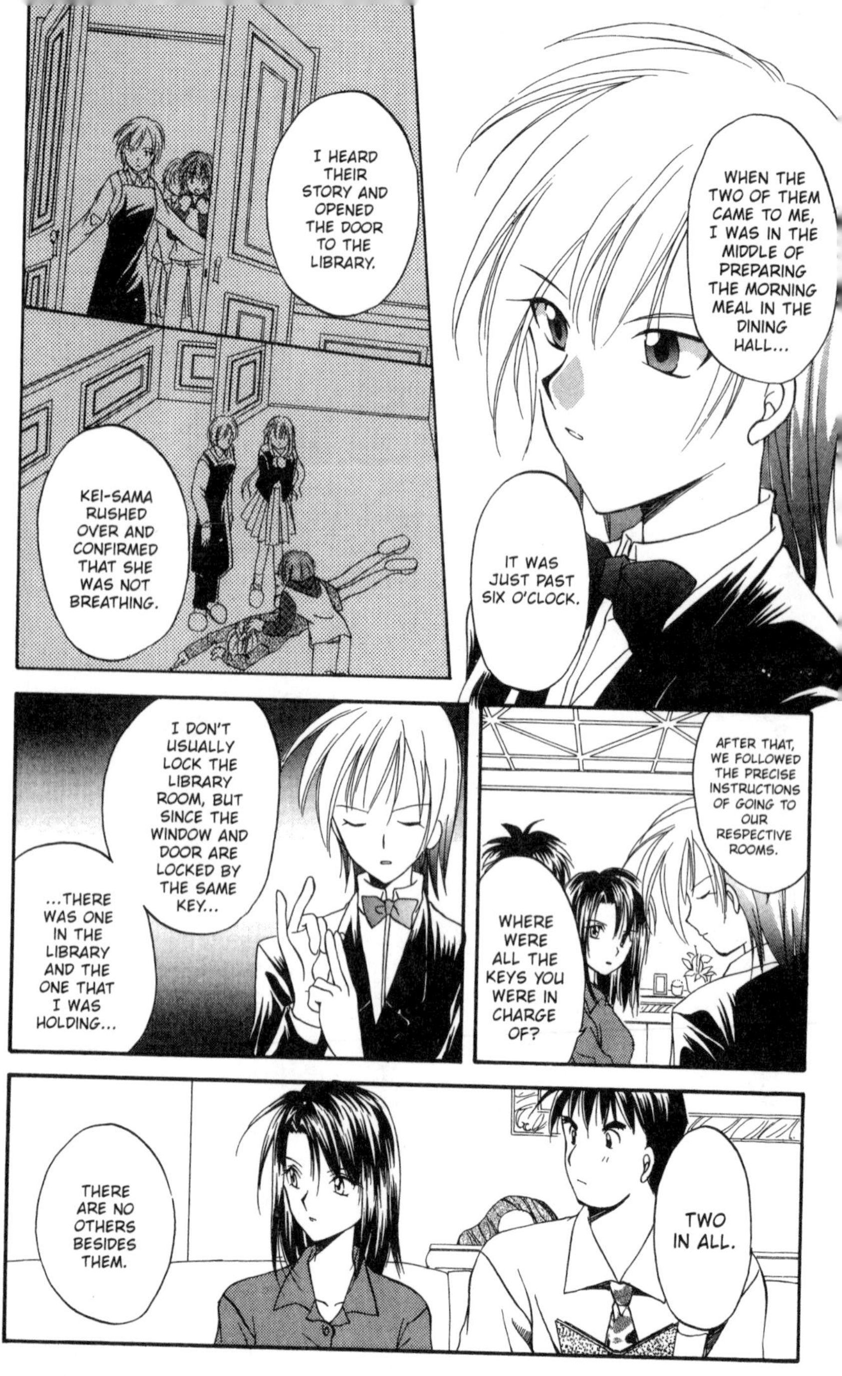
WHEN THE TWO OF THEM CAME TO ME, I WAS IN THE MIDDLE OF PREPARING THE MORNING MEAL IN THE DINING HALL...
IT WAS JUST PAST SIX O'CLOCK.
I HEARD THEIR STORY AND OPENED THE DOOR TO THE LIBRARY.
KEI-SAMA RUSHED OVER AND CONFIRMED THAT SHE WAS NOT BREATHING.
AFTER THAT, WE FOLLOWED THE PRECISE INSTRUCTIONS OF GOING TO OUR RESPECTIVE ROOMS.
WHERE WERE ALL THE KEYS YOU WERE IN CHARGE OF?
I DON'T USUALLY LOCK THE LIBRARY ROOM, BUT SINCE THE WINDOW AND DOOR ARE LOCKED BY THE SAME KEY...
...THERE WAS ONE IN THE LIBRARY AND THE ONE THAT I WAS HOLDING...
TWO IN ALL.
THERE ARE NO OTHERS BESIDES THEM.

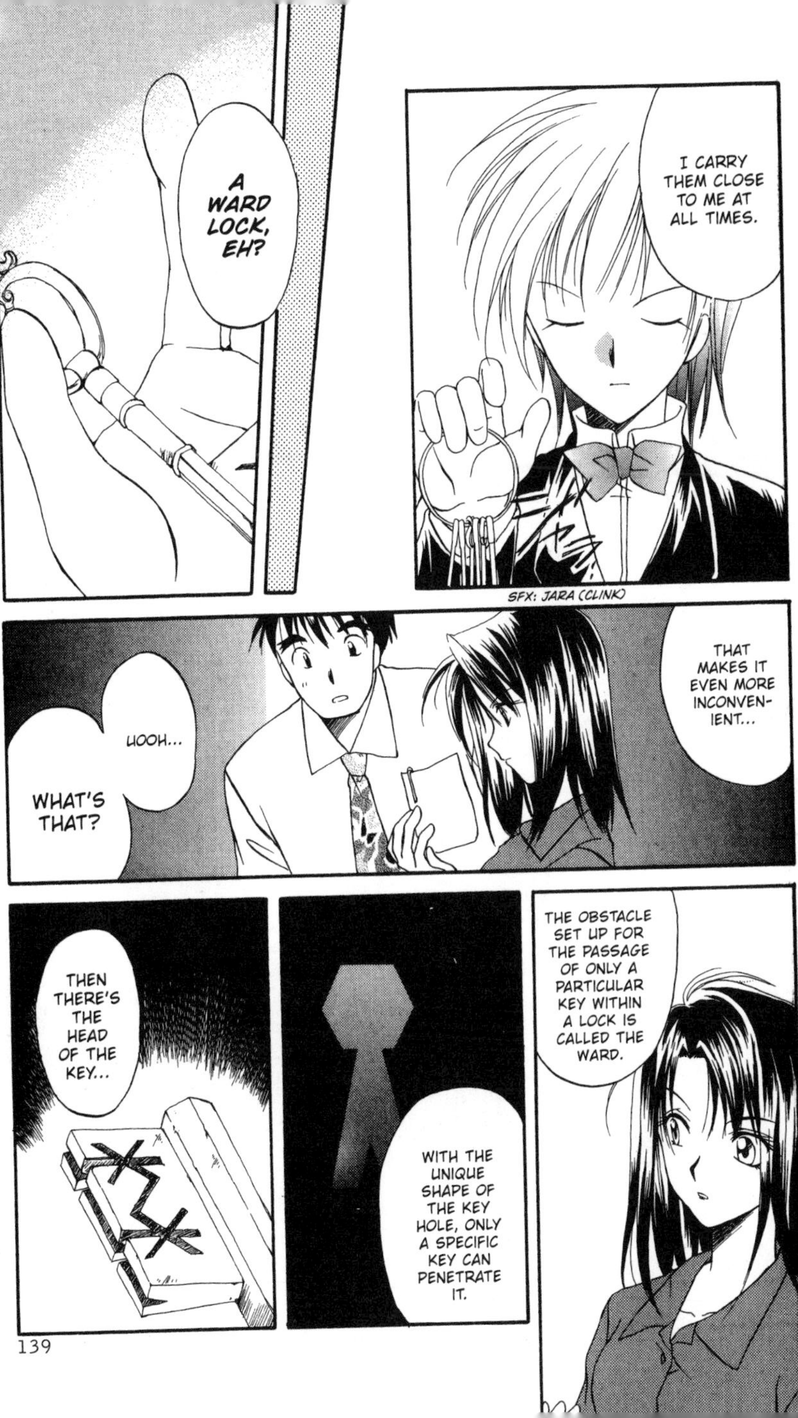
I CARRY THEM CLOSE TO ME AT ALL TIMES.
SFX: JARA (CLINK)
A WARD LOCK, EH?
THAT MAKES IT EVEN MORE INCONVEN-IENT...
UOOH...
WHAT'S THAT?
THE OBSTACLE SET UP FOR THE PASSAGE OF ONLY A PARTICULAR KEY WITHIN A LOCK IS CALLED THE WARD.
WITH THE UNIQUE SHAPE OF THE KEY HOLE, ONLY A SPECIFIC KEY CAN PENETRATE IT.
THEN THERE'S THE HEAD OF THE KEY...

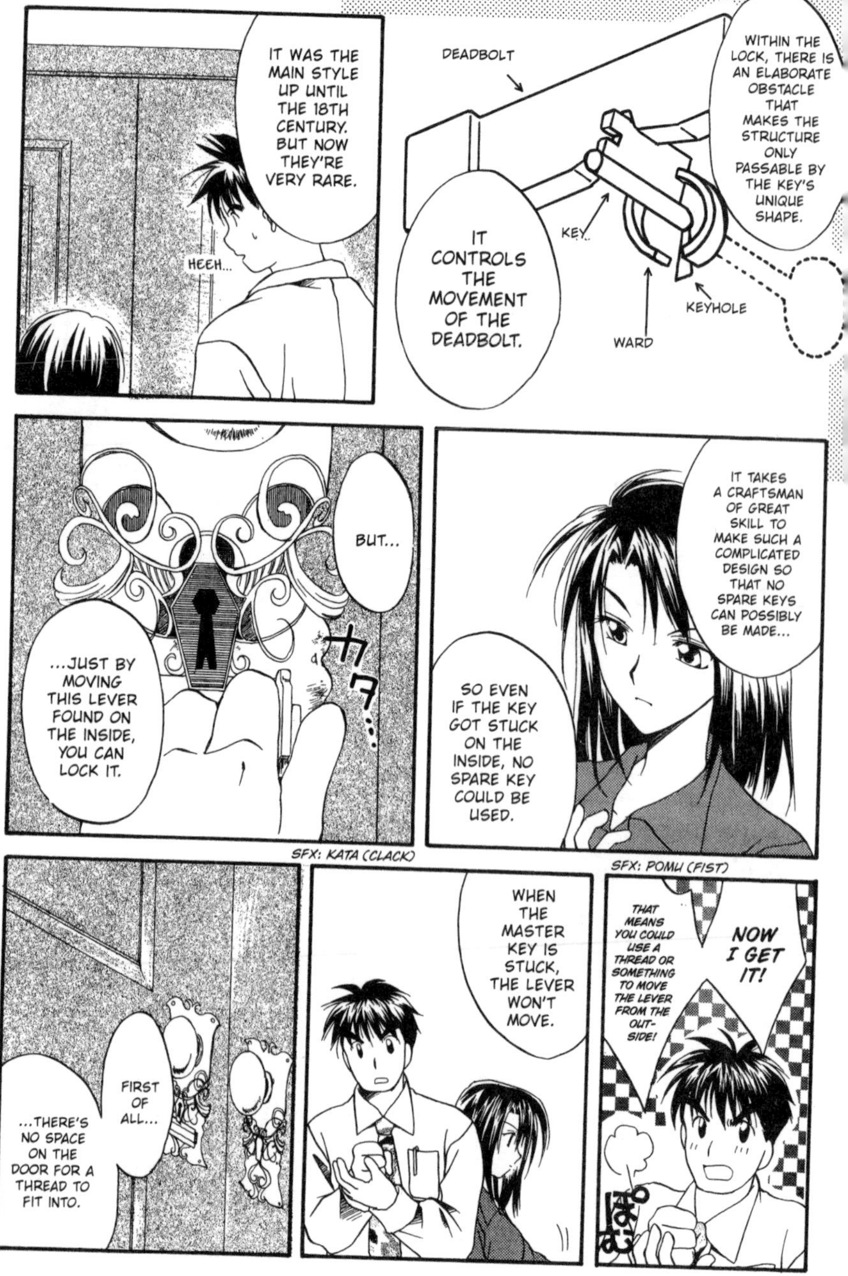
WITHIN THE LOCK, THERE IS AN ELABORATE OBSTACLE THAT MAKES THE STRUCTURE ONLY PASSABLE BY THE KEY'S UNIQUE SHAPE.
DEADBOLT
KEY
KEYHOLE
WARD
IT CONTROLS THE MOVEMENT OF THE DEADBOLT.
IT WAS THE MAIN STYLE UP UNTIL THE 18TH CENTURY. BUT NOW THEY'RE VERY RARE.
HEEH...
IT TAKES A CRAFTSMAN OF GREAT SKILL TO MAKE SUCH A COMPLICATED DESIGN SO THAT NO SPARE KEYS CAN POSSIBLY BE MADE...
SO EVEN IF THE KEY GOT STUCK ON THE INSIDE, NO SPARE KEY COULD BE USED.
BUT...
...JUST BY MOVING THIS LEVER FOUND ON THE INSIDE, YOU CAN LOCK IT.
SFX: KATA (CLACK)
SFX: POMU (FIST)
NOW I GET IT!
THAT MEANS YOU COULD USE A THREAD OR SOMETHING TO MOVE THE LEVER FROM THE OUT-SIDE!
WHEN THE MASTER KEY IS STUCK, THE LEVER WON'T MOVE.
FIRST OF ALL...
...THERE'S NO SPACE ON THE DOOR FOR A THREAD TO FIT INTO.

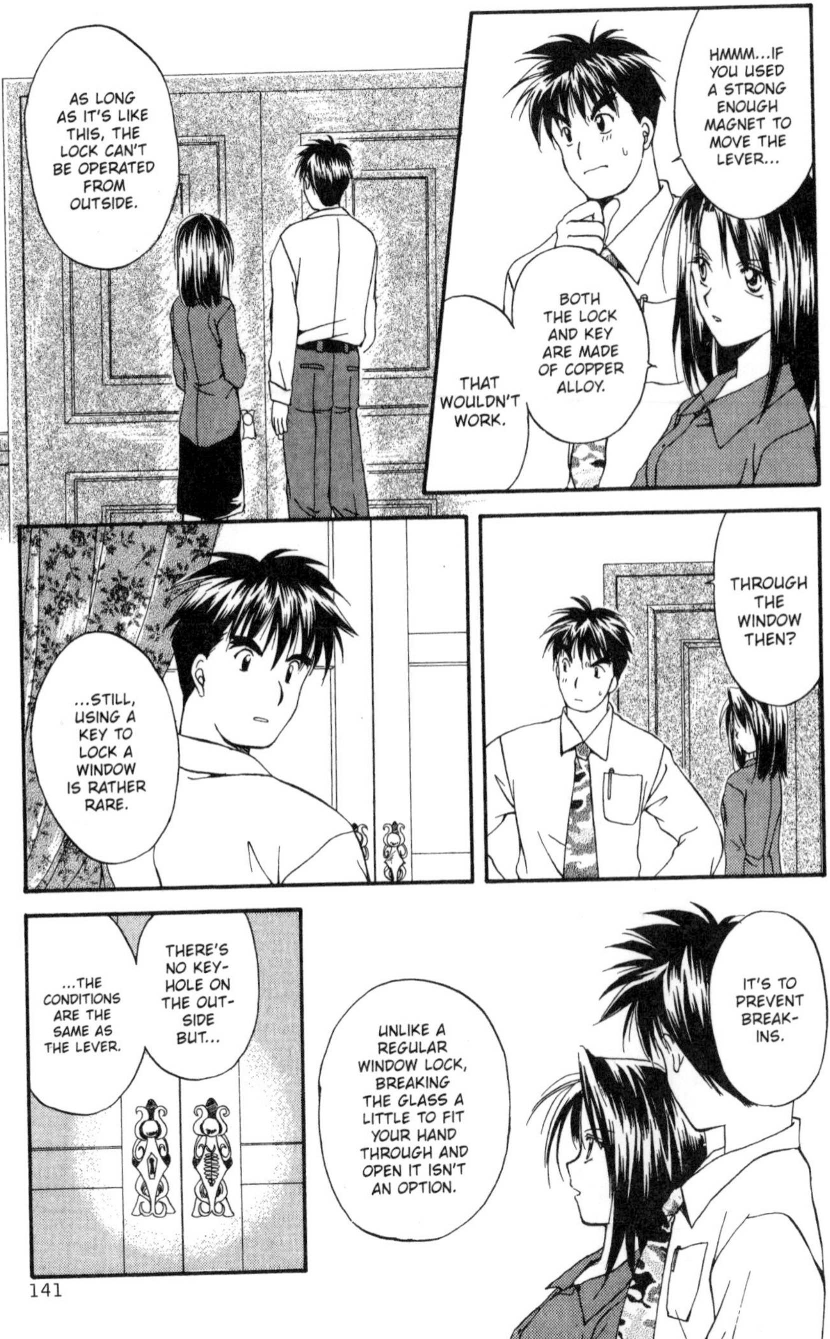
HMMM...IF YOU USED A STRONG ENOUGH MAGNET TO MOVE THE LEVER...
BOTH THE LOCK AND KEY ARE MADE OF COPPER ALLOY.
THAT WOULDN'T WORK.
AS LONG AS IT'S LIKE THIS, THE LOCK CAN'T BE OPERATED FROM OUTSIDE.
THROUGH THE WINDOW THEN?
...STILL, USING A KEY TO LOCK A WINDOW IS RATHER RARE.
IT'S TO PREVENT BREAK-INS.
UNLIKE A REGULAR WINDOW LOCK, BREAKING THE GLASS A LITTLE TO FIT YOUR HAND THROUGH AND OPEN IT ISN'T AN OPTION.
THERE'S NO KEY-HOLE ON THE OUT-SIDE BUT...
...THE CONDITIONS ARE THE SAME AS THE LEVER.

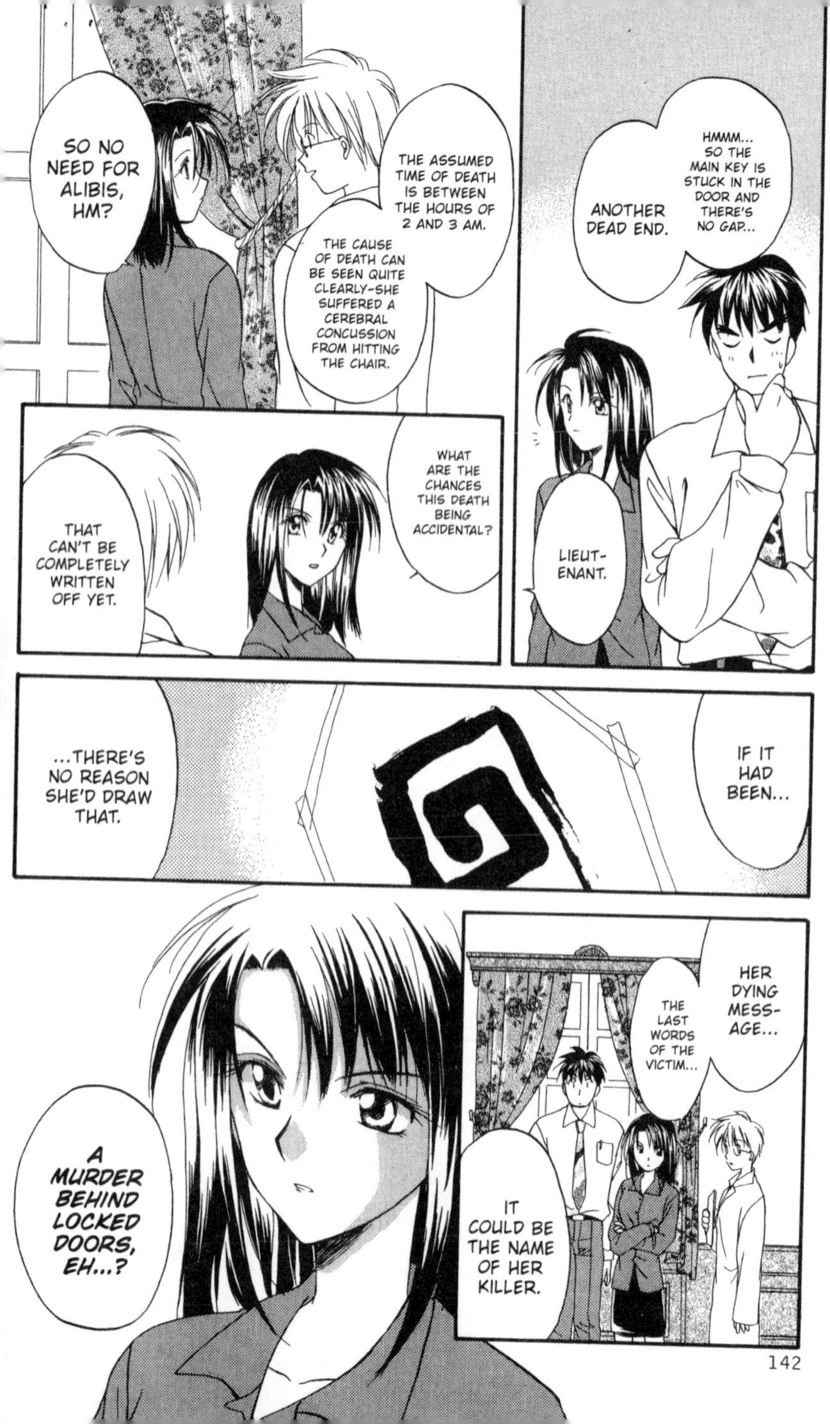
HMMM... SO THE MAIN KEY IS STUCK IN THE DOOR AND THERE'S NO GAP...
ANOTHER DEAD END.
LIEUT-ENANT.
THE ASSUMED TIME OF DEATH IS BETWEEN THE HOURS OF 2 AND 3 AM.
THE CAUSE OF DEATH CAN BE SEEN QUITE CLEARLY-SHE SUFFERED A CEREBRAL CONCUSSION FROM HITTING THE CHAIR.
SO NO NEED FOR ALIBIS, HM?
WHAT ARE THE CHANCES THIS DEATH BEING ACCIDENTAL?
THAT CAN'T BE COMPLETELY WRITTEN OFF YET.
IF IT HAD BEEN...
...THERE'S NO REASON SHE'D DRAW THAT.
HER DYING MESS-AGE...
THE LAST WORDS OF THE VICTIM...
IT COULD BE THE NAME OF HER KILLER.
A MURDER BEHIND LOCKED DOORS, EH...?

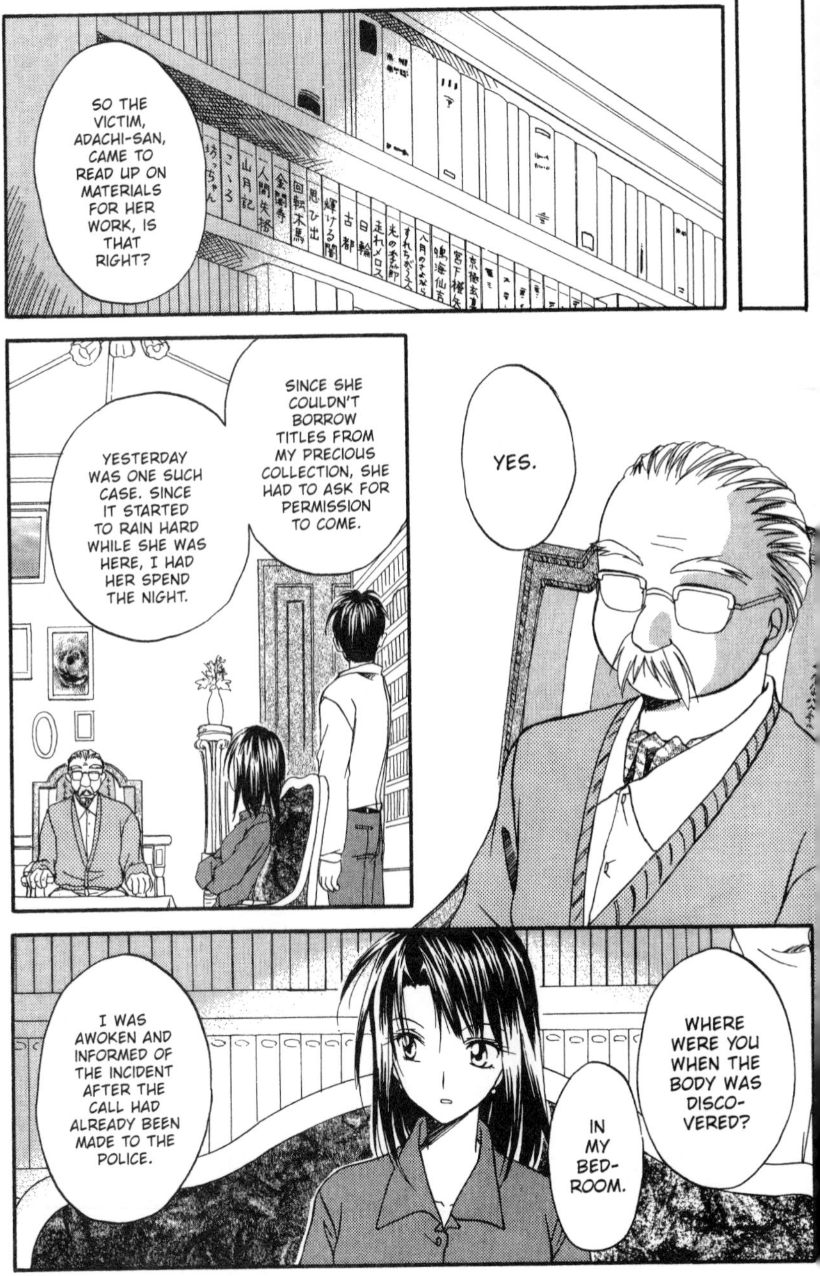
SO THE VICTIM, ADACHI-SAN, CAME TO READ UP ON MATERIALS FOR HER WORK, IS THAT RIGHT?
YES.
SINCE SHE COULDN'T BORROW TITLES FROM MY PRECIOUS COLLECTION, SHE HAD TO ASK FOR PERMISSION TO COME.
YESTERDAY WAS ONE SUCH CASE. SINCE IT STARTED TO RAIN HARD WHILE SHE WAS HERE, I HAD HER SPEND THE NIGHT.
WHERE WERE YOU WHEN THE BODY WAS DISCO-VERED?
IN MY BED-ROOM.
I WAS AWOKEN AND INFORMED OF THE INCIDENT AFTER THE CALL HAD ALREADY BEEN MADE TO THE POLICE.

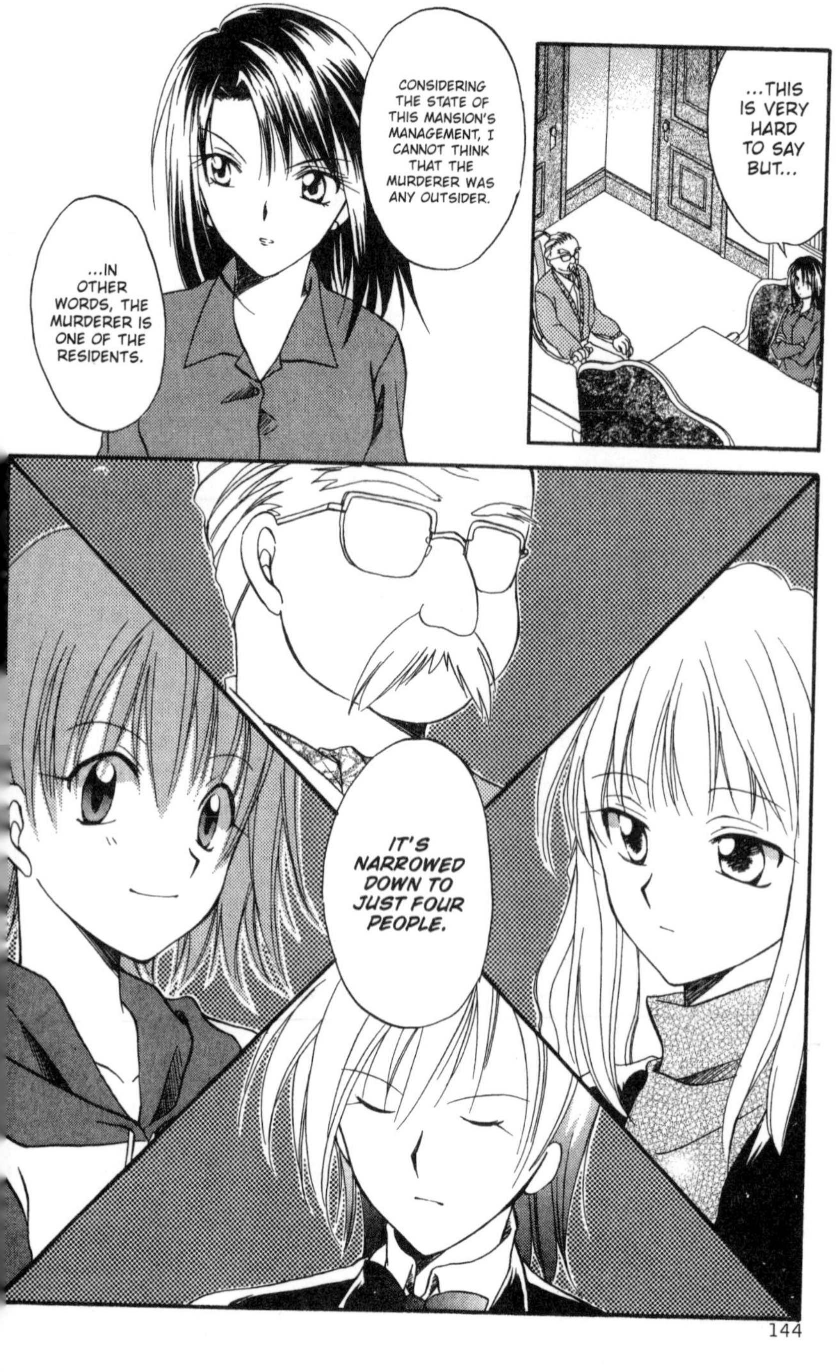
...THIS IS VERY HARD TO SAY BUT...
CONSIDERING THE STATE OF THIS MANSION'S MANAGEMENT, I CANNOT THINK THAT THE MURDERER WAS ANY OUTSIDER.
...IN OTHER WORDS, THE MURDERER IS ONE OF THE RESIDENTS.
IT'S NARROWED DOWN TO JUST FOUR PEOPLE.

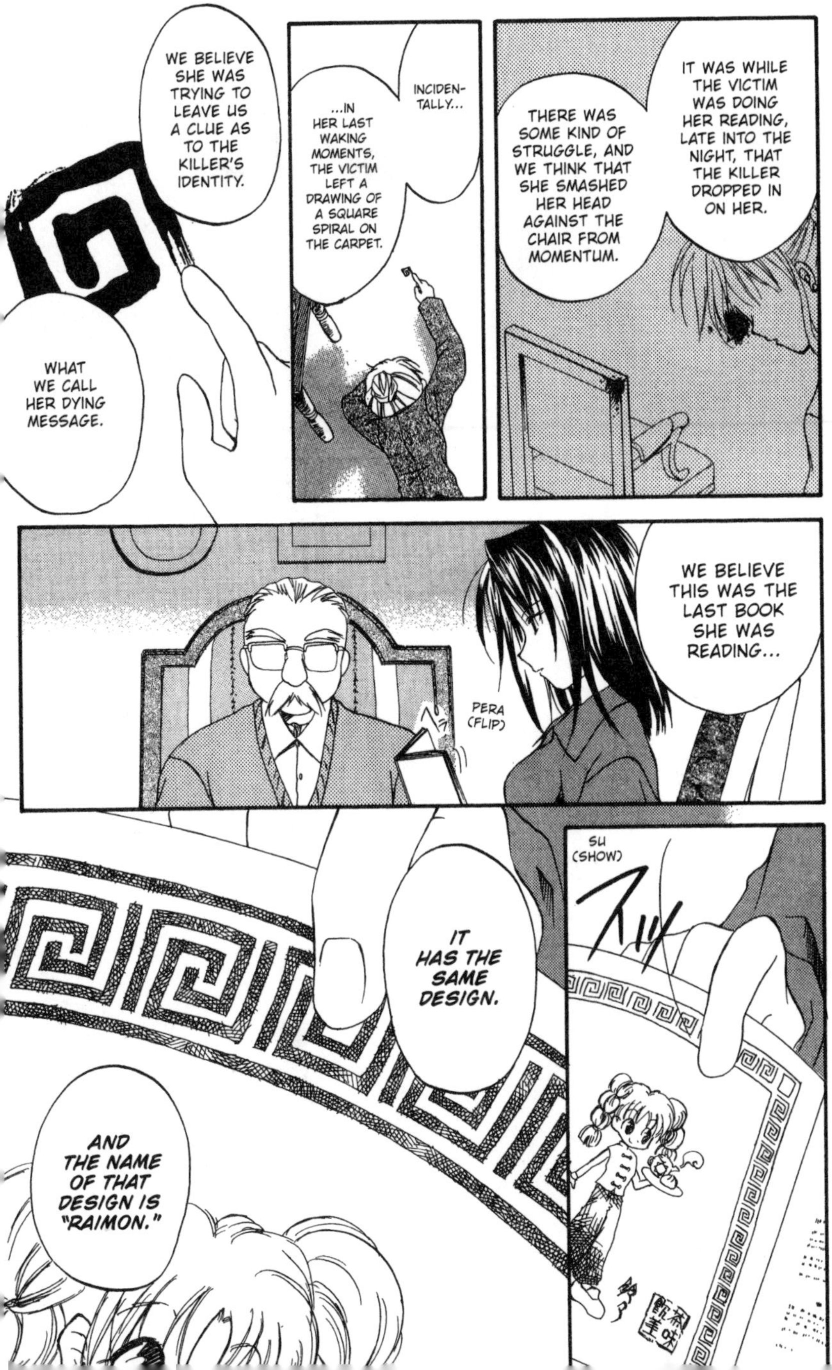
IT WAS WHILE THE VICTIM WAS DOING HER READING, LATE INTO THE NIGHT, THAT THE KILLER DROPPED IN ON HER.
THERE WAS SOME KIND OF STRUGGLE, AND WE THINK THAT SHE SMASHED HER HEAD AGAINST THE CHAIR FROM MOMENTUM.
INCIDEN-TALLY...
...IN HER LAST WAKING MOMENTS, THE VICTIM LEFT A DRAWING OF A SQUARE SPIRAL ON THE CARPET.
WE BELIEVE SHE WAS TRYING TO LEAVE US A CLUE AS TO THE KILLER'S IDENTITY.
WHAT WE CALL HER DYING MESSAGE.
WE BELIEVE THIS WAS THE LAST BOOK SHE WAS READING...
PERA (FLIP)
SU (SHOW)
IT HAS THE SAME DESIGN.
AND THE NAME OF THAT DESIGN IS "RAIMON."

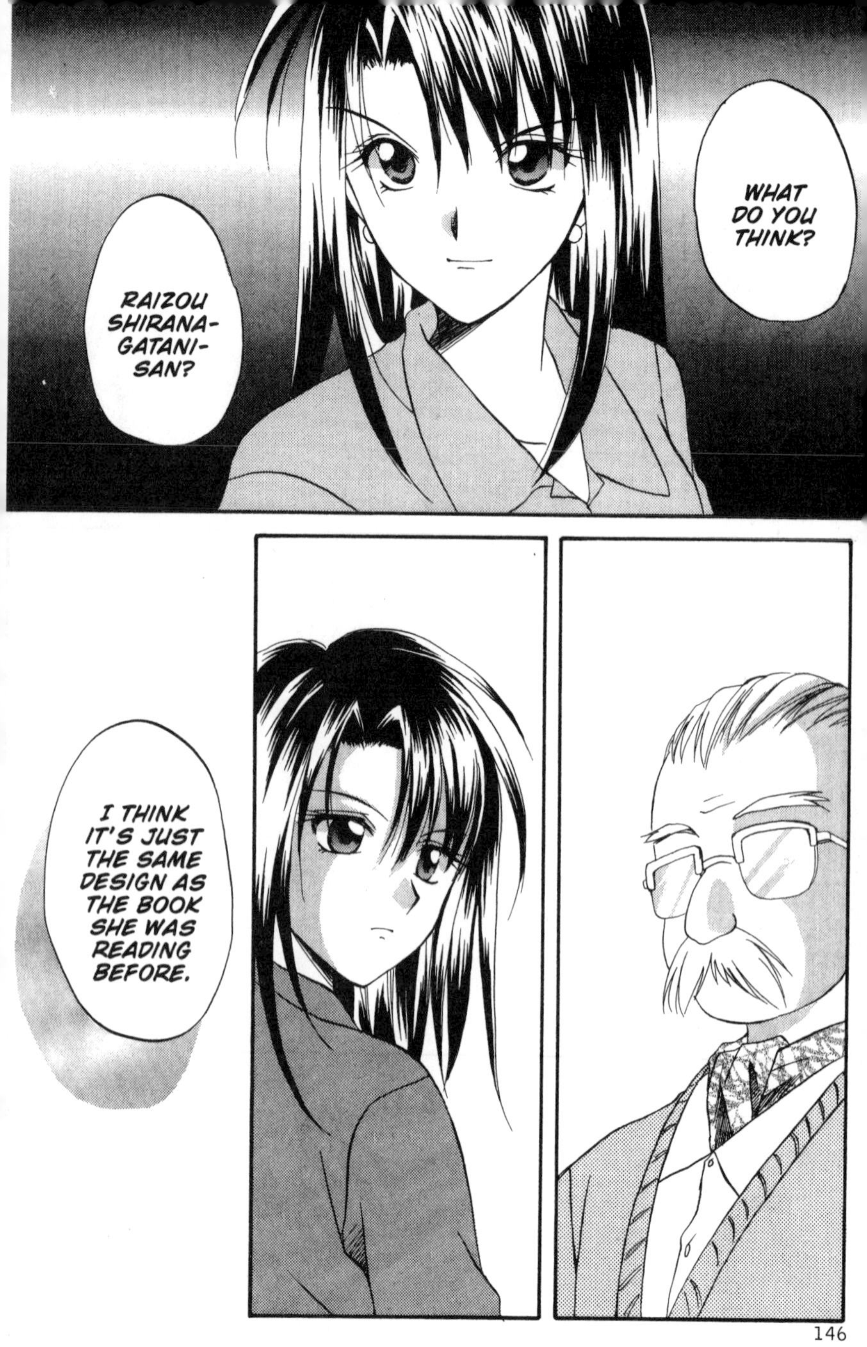
WHAT DO YOU THINK?
RAIZOU SHIRANA-GATANI-SAN?
I THINK IT'S JUST THE SAME DESIGN AS THE BOOK SHE WAS READING BEFORE.

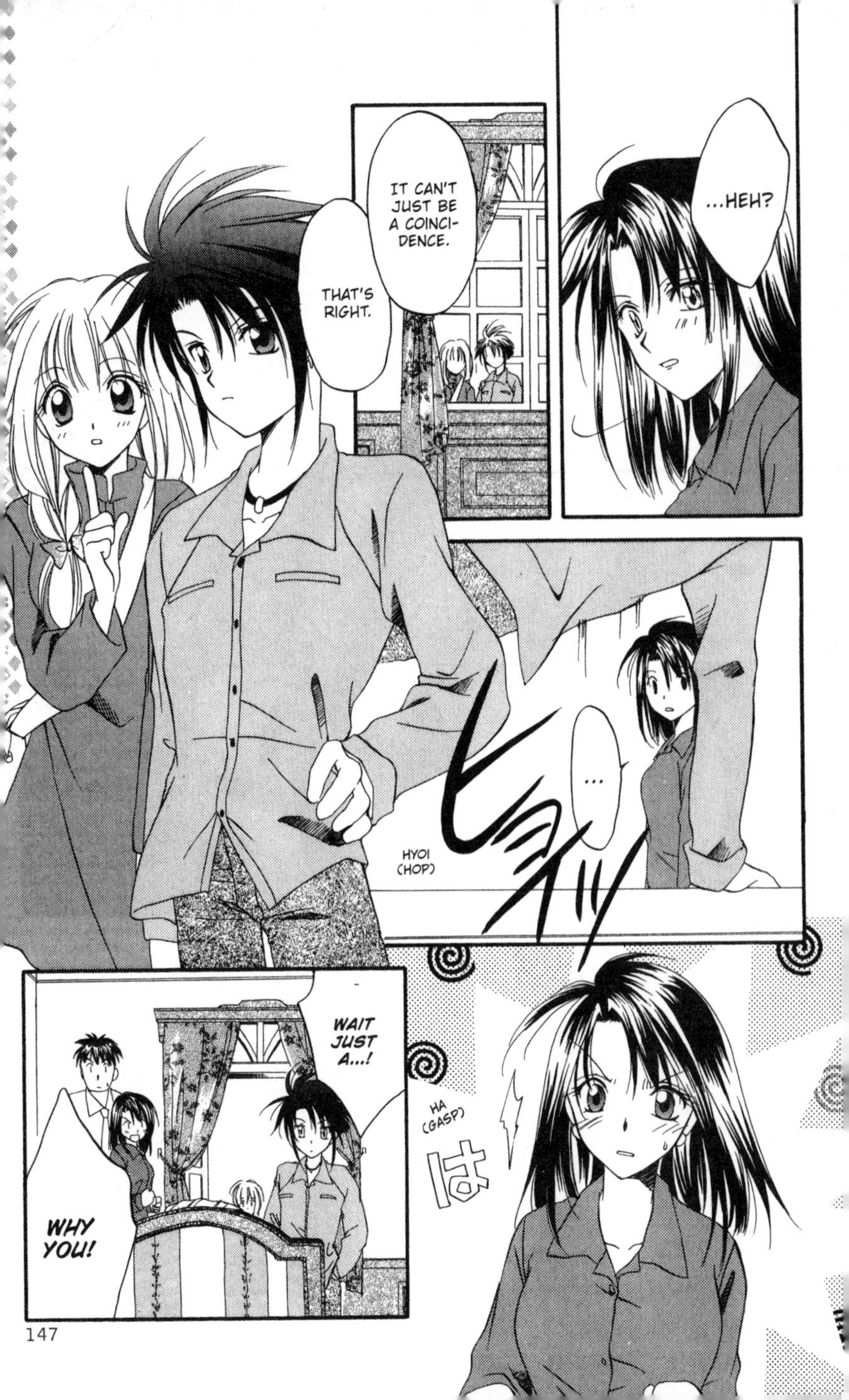
...HEH?
IT CAN'T JUST BE A COINCIDENCE.
THAT'S RIGHT.
...
HYOI (HOP)
HA (GASP)
は
WAIT JUST A...!
WHY YOU!

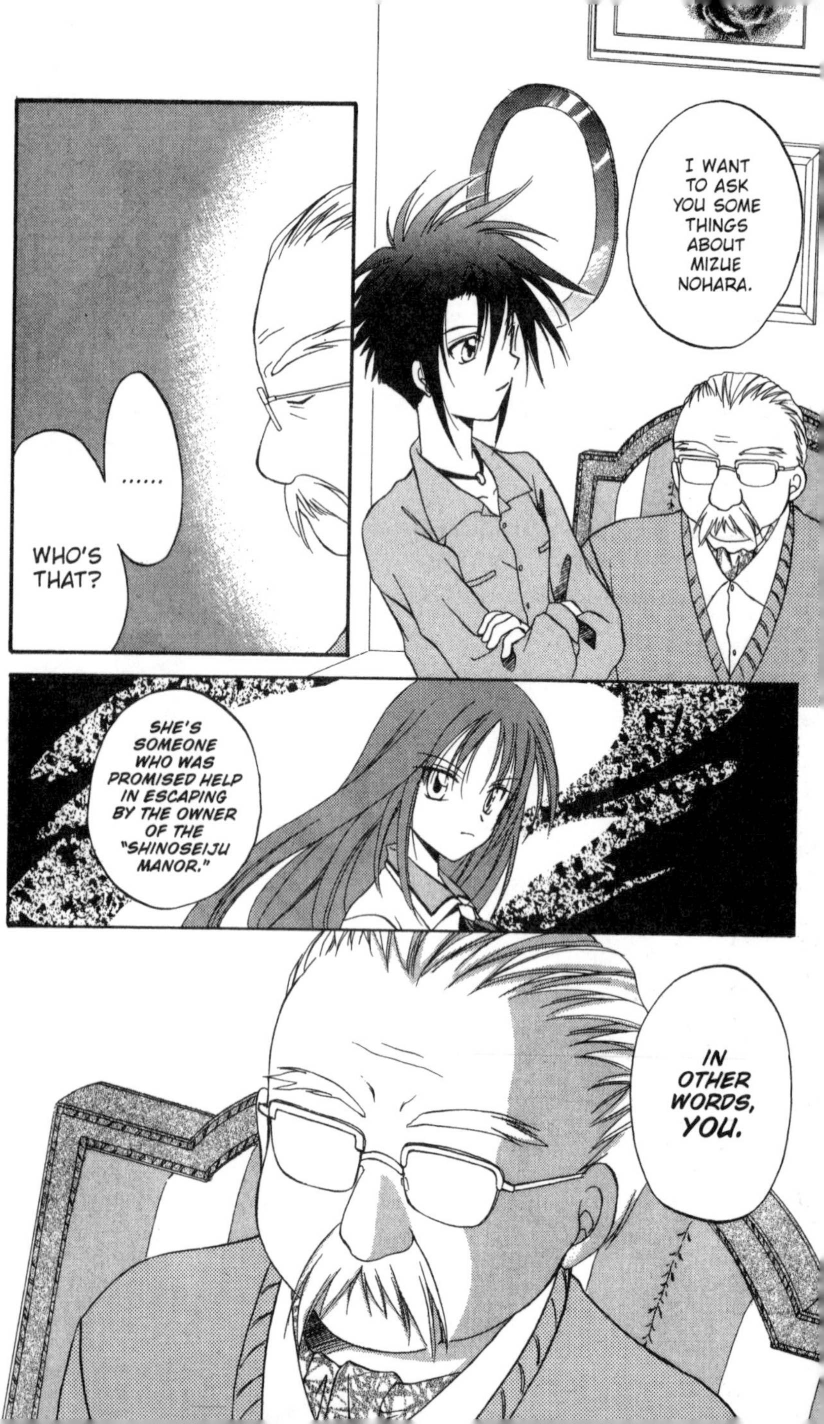
I WANT TO ASK YOU SOME THINGS ABOUT MIZUE NOHARA.
......
WHO'S THAT?
SHE'S SOMEONE WHO WAS PROMISED HELP IN ESCAPING BY THE OWNER OF THE "SHINOSEIJU MANOR."
IN OTHER WORDS, YOU.

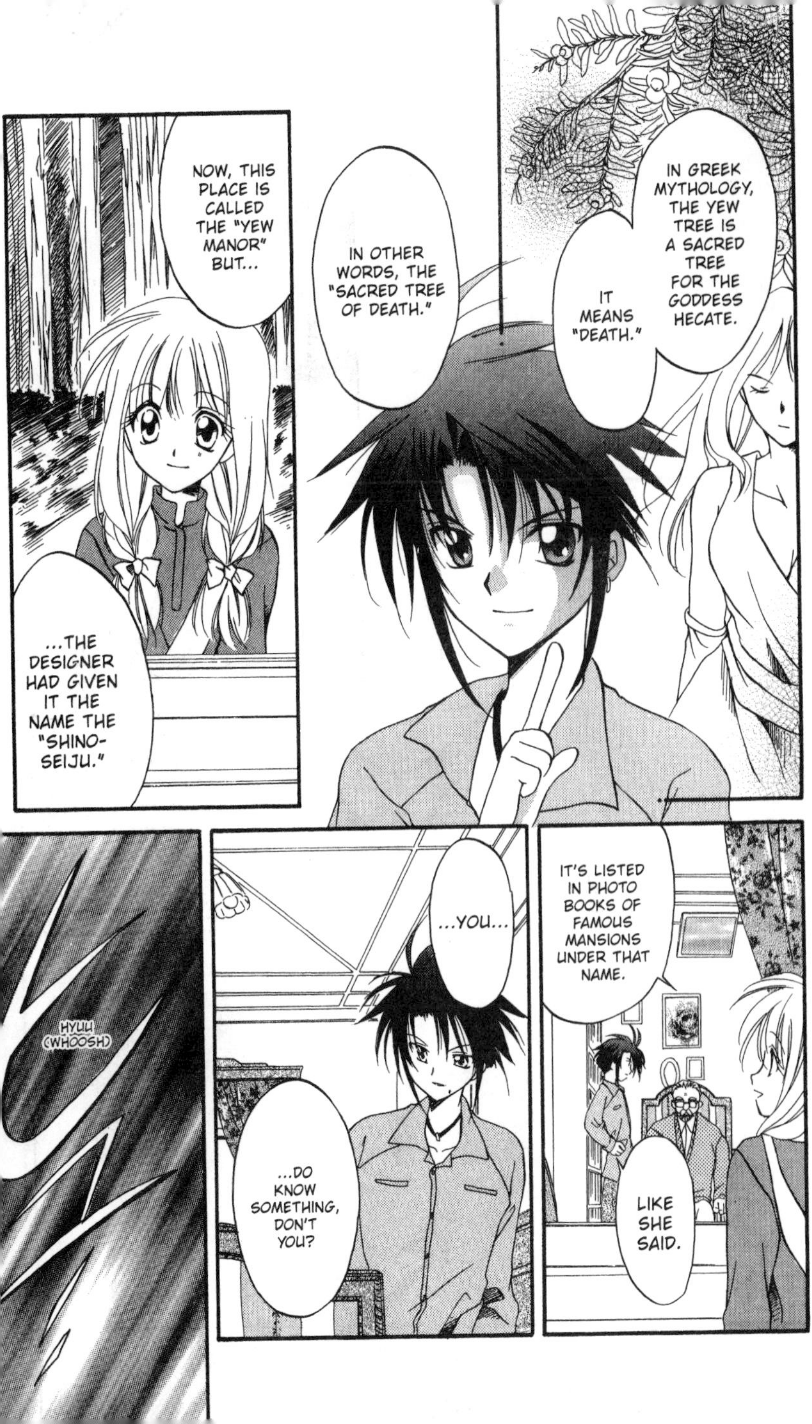
IN GREEK MYTHOLOGY, THE YEW TREE IS A SACRED TREE FOR THE GODDESS HECATE.
IT MEANS "DEATH."
IN OTHER WORDS, THE "SACRED TREE OF DEATH."
NOW, THIS PLACE IS CALLED THE "YEW MANOR" BUT...
...THE DESIGNER HAD GIVEN IT THE NAME THE "SHINO-SEIJU."
IT'S LISTED IN PHOTO BOOKS OF FAMOUS MANSIONS UNDER THAT NAME.
LIKE SHE SAID.
...YOU...
...DO KNOW SOMETHING, DON'T YOU?
HYUU (WHOOSH)

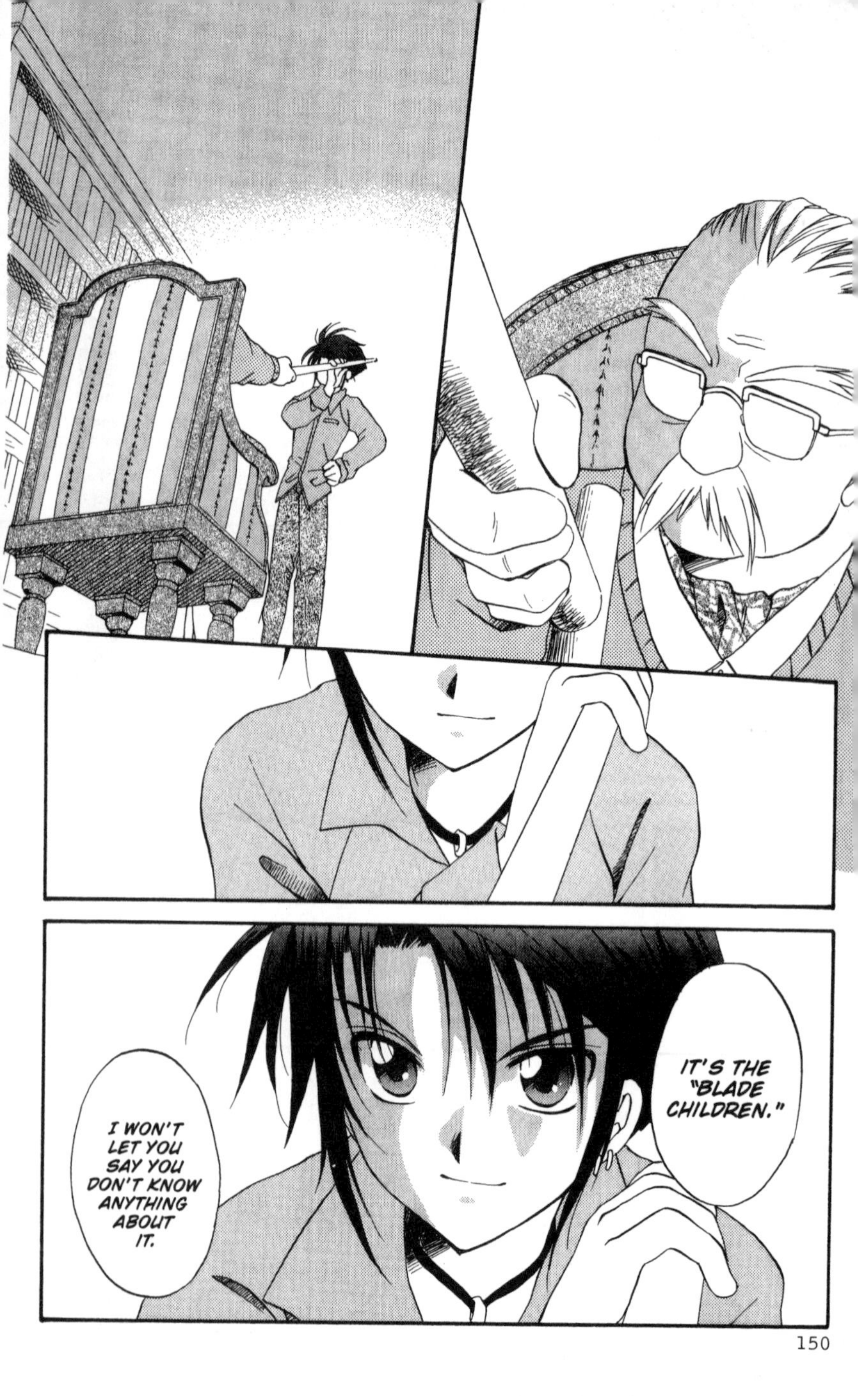
IT'S THE "BLADE CHILDREN."
I WON'T LET YOU SAY YOU DON'T KNOW ANYTHING ABOUT IT.

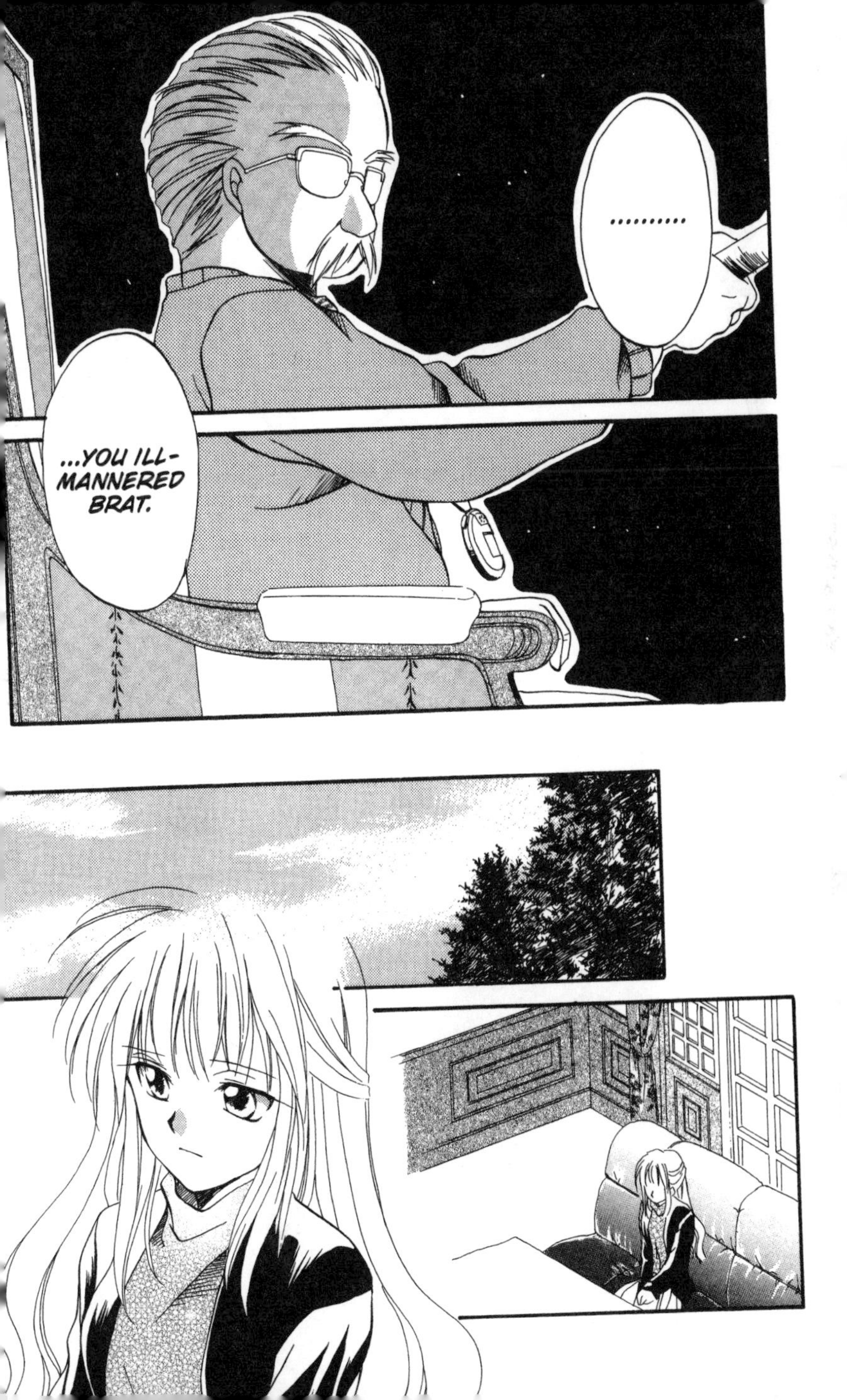
....
...YOU ILL-MANNERED BRAT.

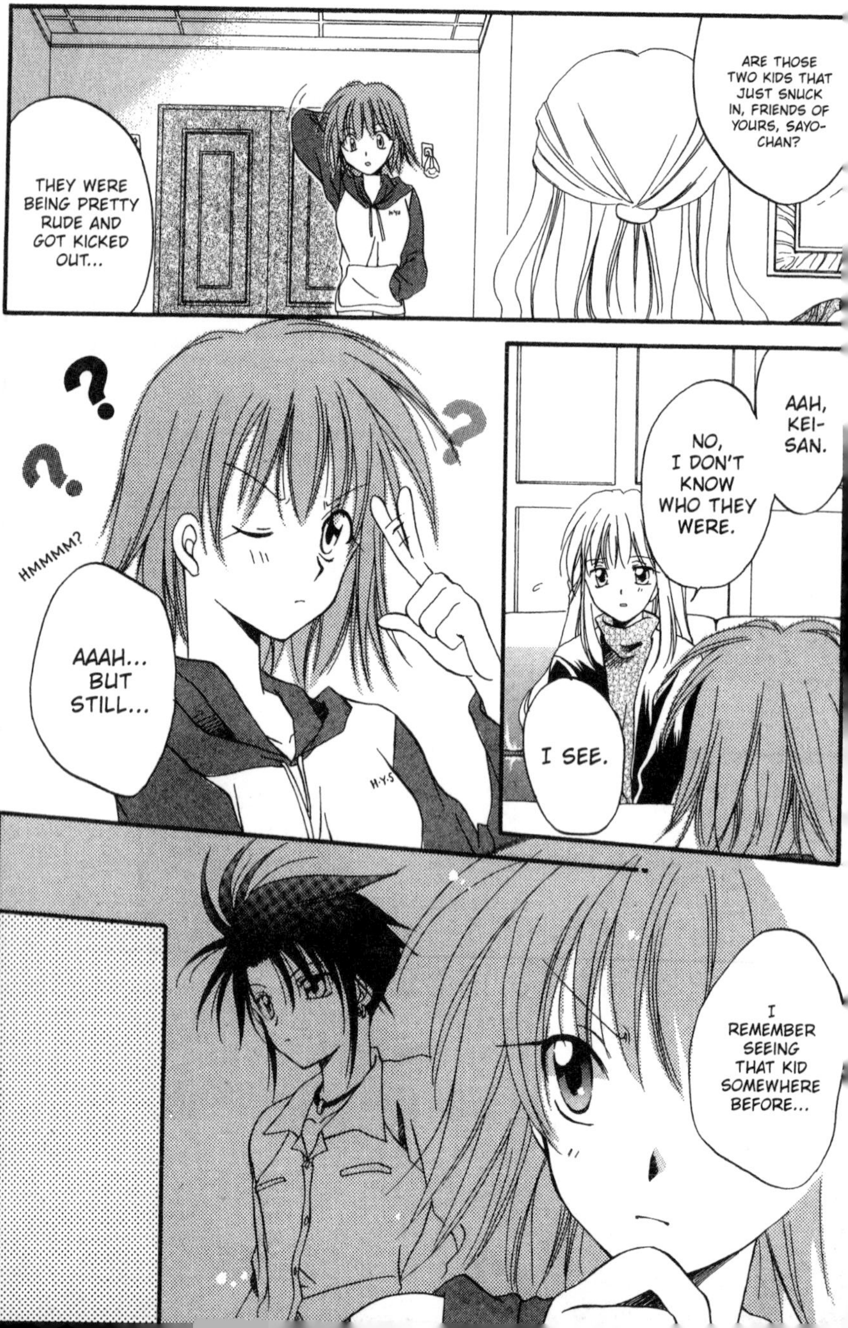
ARE THOSE TWO KIDS THAT JUST SNUCK IN, FRIENDS OF YOURS, SAYO-CHAN?
THEY WERE BEING PRETTY RUDE AND GOT KICKED OUT...
AAH, KEI-SAN.
NO, I DON'T KNOW WHO THEY WERE.
I SEE.
HMMMM?
AAAH... BUT STILL...
I REMEMBER SEEING THAT KID SOMEWHERE BEFORE...

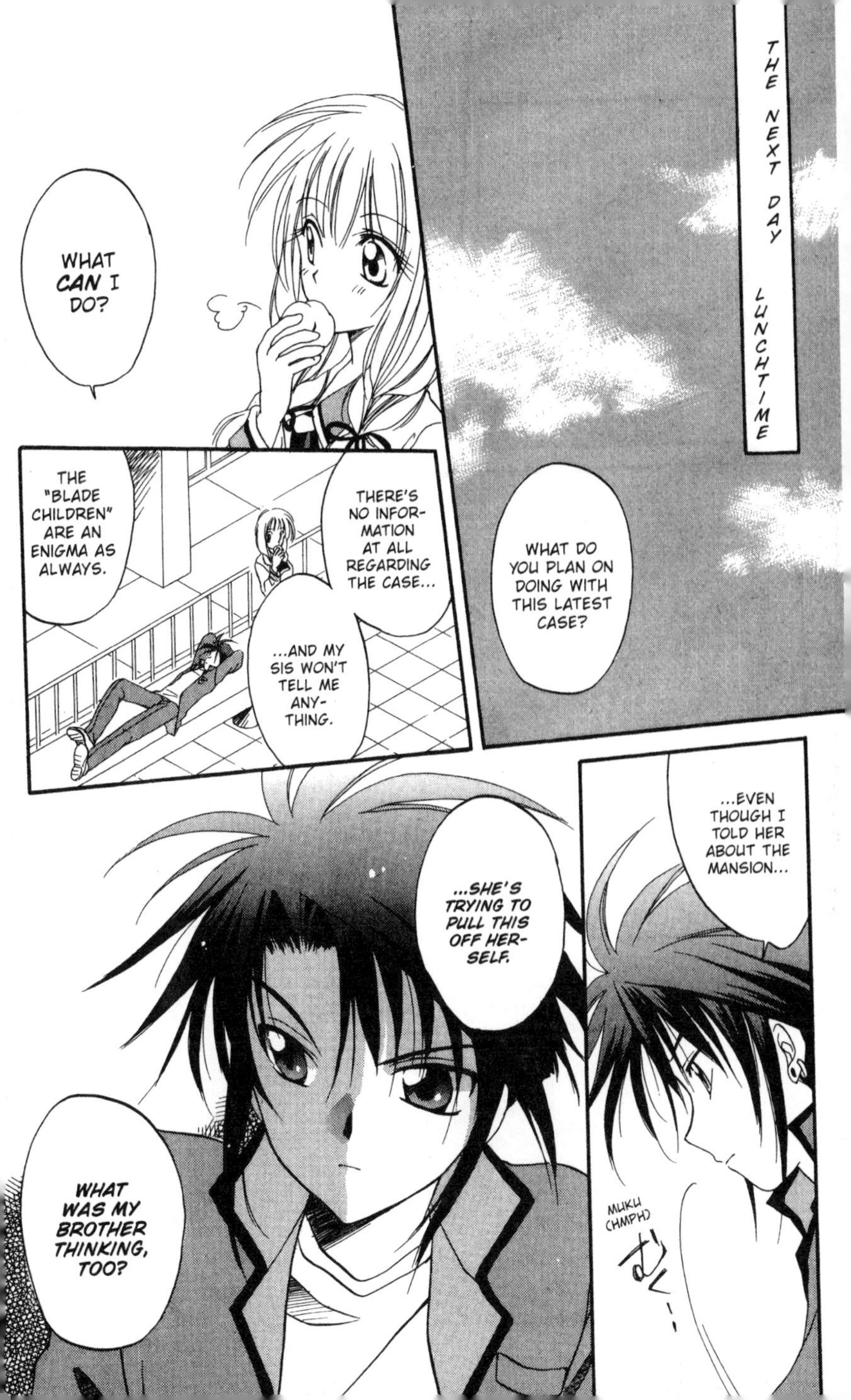
THE NEXT DAY LUNCHTIME
WHAT DO YOU PLAN ON DOING WITH THIS LATEST CASE?
WHAT *CAN* I DO?
THERE'S NO INFOR-MATION AT ALL REGARDING THE CASE...
...AND MY SIS WON'T TELL ME ANY-THING.
THE "BLADE CHILDREN" ARE AN ENIGMA AS ALWAYS.
...EVEN THOUGH I TOLD HER ABOUT THE MANSION...
MUKU (HMPH)
...SHE'S TRYING TO PULL THIS OFF HER-SELF.
WHAT WAS MY BROTHER THINKING, TOO?

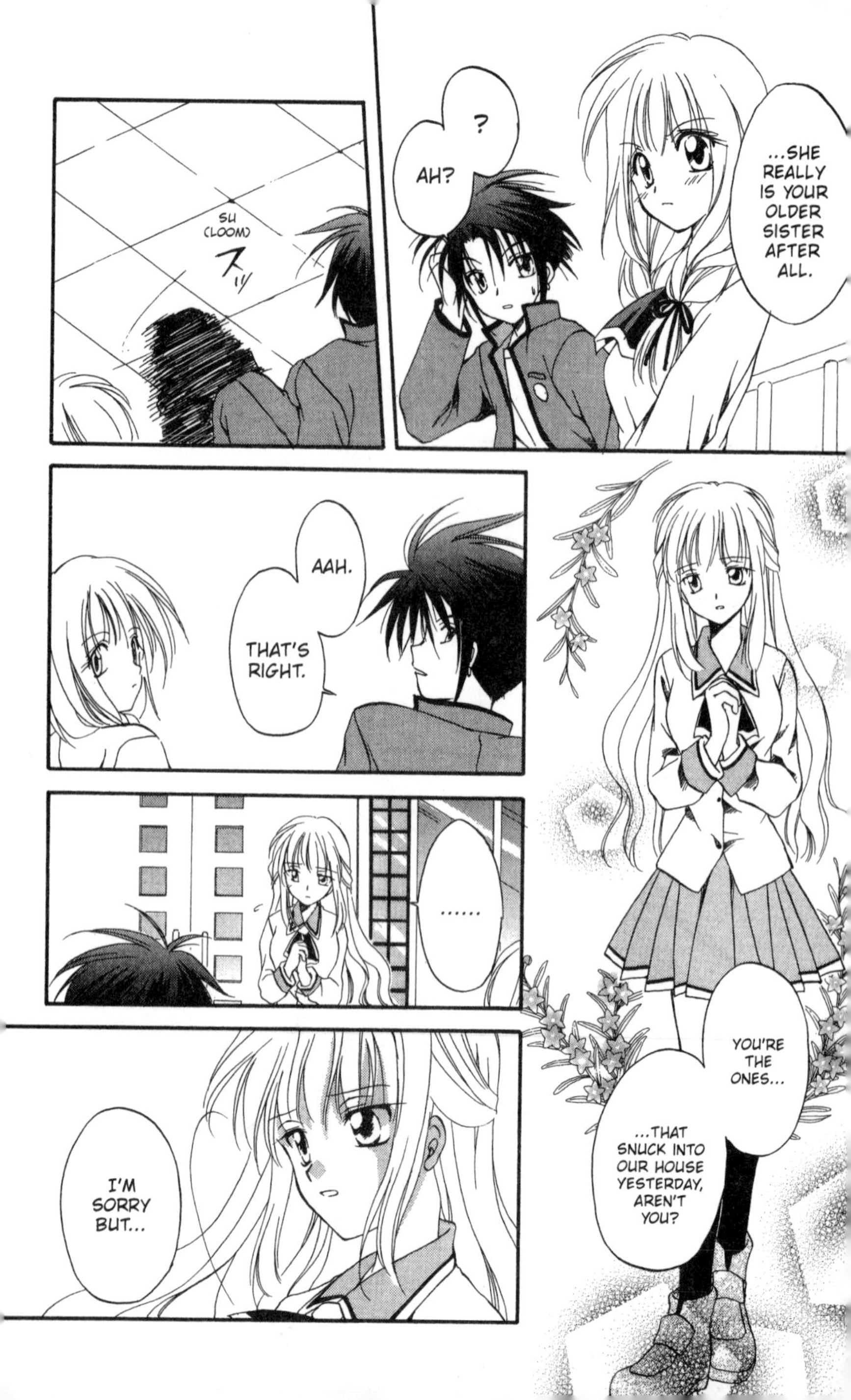

...SHE REALLY IS YOUR OLDER SISTER AFTER ALL.
?
AH?
SU (LOOM)
スッ
YOU'RE THE ONES...
...THAT SNUCK INTO OUR HOUSE YESTERDAY, AREN'T YOU?
AAH.
THAT'S RIGHT.
......
I'M SORRY BUT...

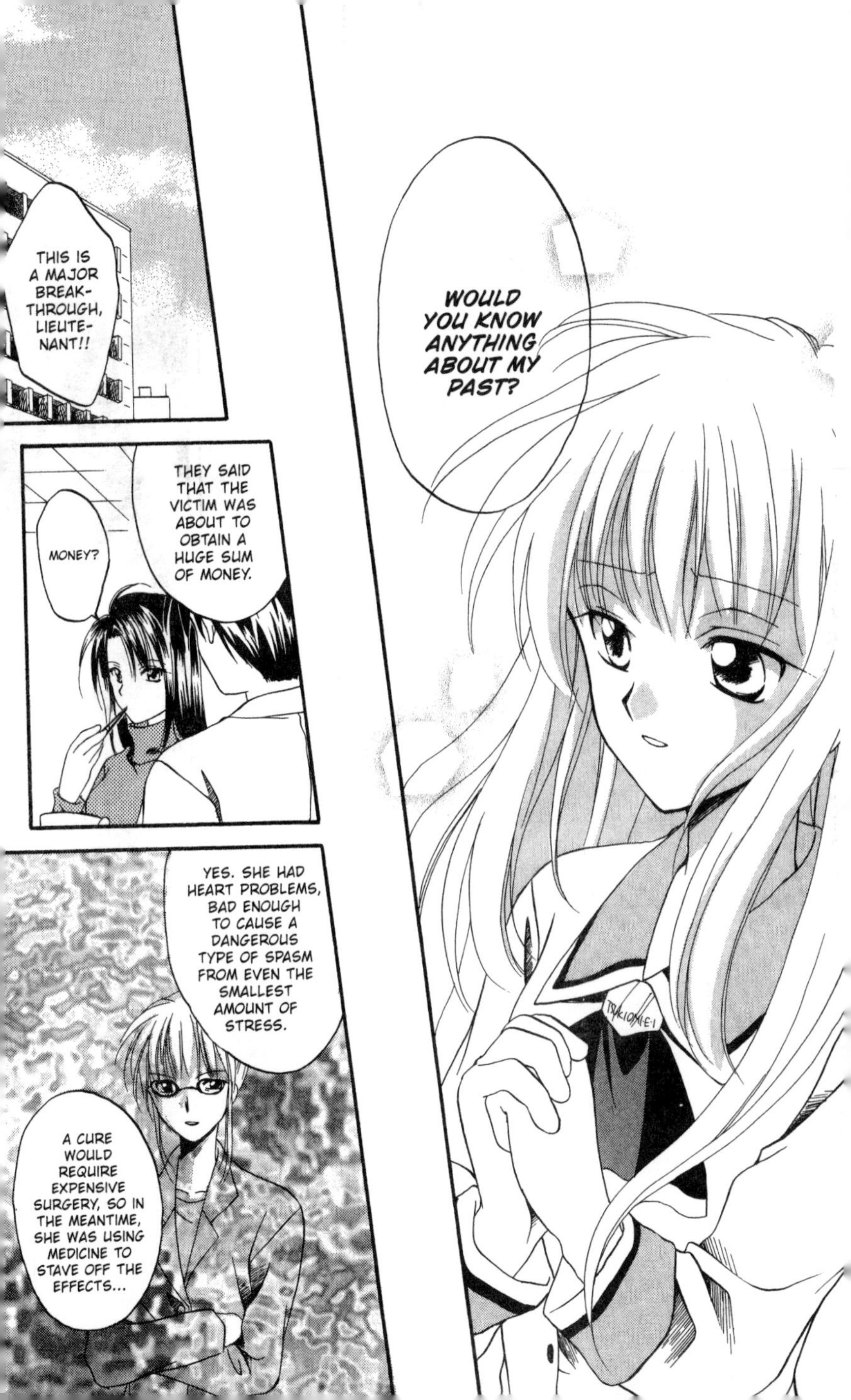
WOULD YOU KNOW ANYTHING ABOUT MY PAST?
THIS IS A MAJOR BREAK-THROUGH, LIEUTE-NANT!!
THEY SAID THAT THE VICTIM WAS ABOUT TO OBTAIN A HUGE SUM OF MONEY.
MONEY?
YES. SHE HAD HEART PROBLEMS, BAD ENOUGH TO CAUSE A DANGEROUS TYPE OF SPASM FROM EVEN THE SMALLEST AMOUNT OF STRESS.
A CURE WOULD REQUIRE EXPENSIVE SURGERY, SO IN THE MEANTIME, SHE WAS USING MEDICINE TO STAVE OFF THE EFFECTS...

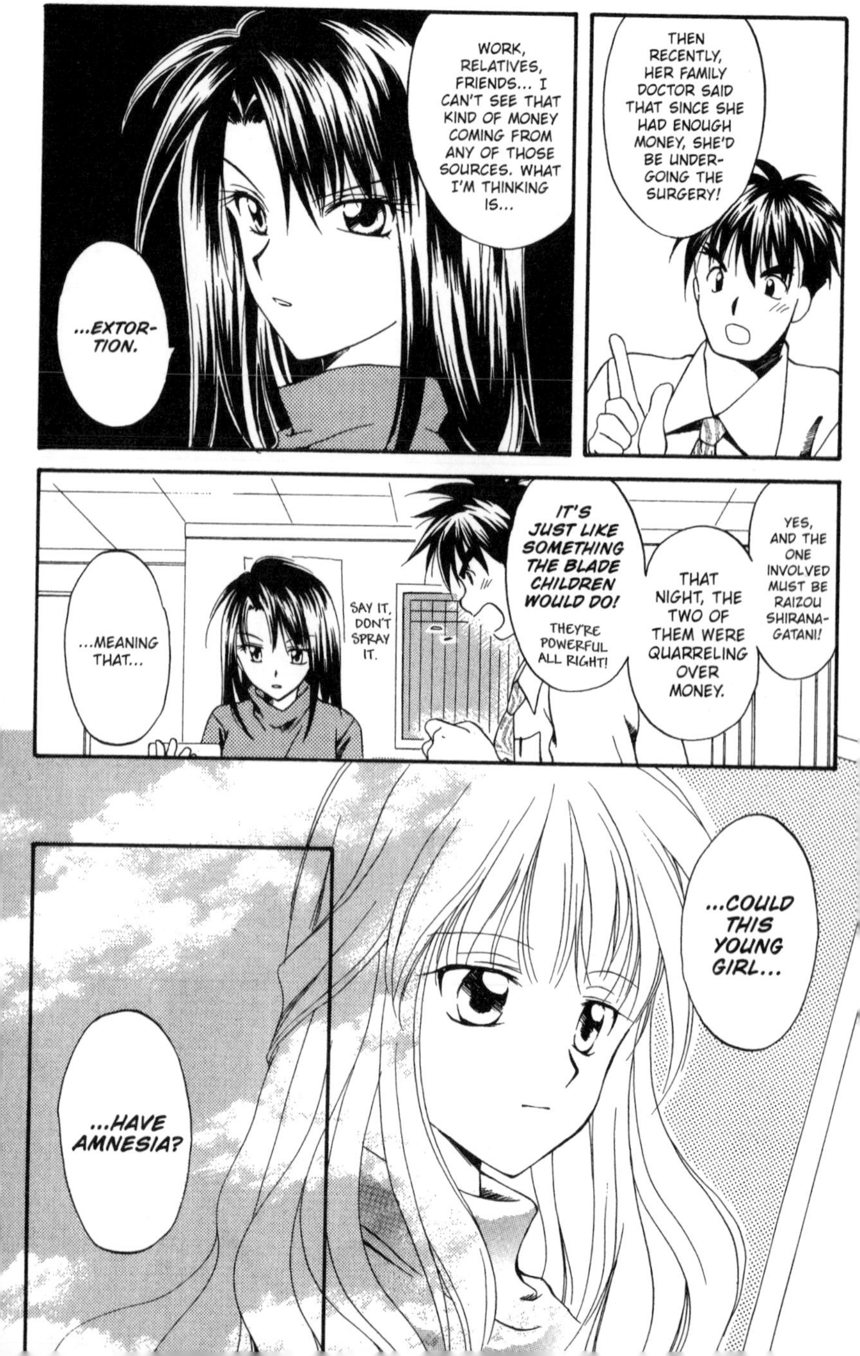
THEN RECENTLY, HER FAMILY DOCTOR SAID THAT SINCE SHE HAD ENOUGH MONEY, SHE'D BE UNDER-GOING THE SURGERY!
WORK, RELATIVES, FRIENDS... I CAN'T SEE THAT KIND OF MONEY COMING FROM ANY OF THOSE SOURCES. WHAT I'M THINKING IS...
...EXTOR-TION.
YES, AND THE ONE INVOLVED MUST BE RAIZOU SHIRANA-GATANI!
THAT NIGHT, THE TWO OF THEM WERE QUARRELING OVER MONEY.
IT'S JUST LIKE SOMETHING THE BLADE CHILDREN WOULD DO!
THEY'RE POWERFUL ALL RIGHT!
SAY IT, DON'T SPRAY IT.
...MEANING THAT...
...COULD THIS YOUNG GIRL...
...HAVE AMNESIA?

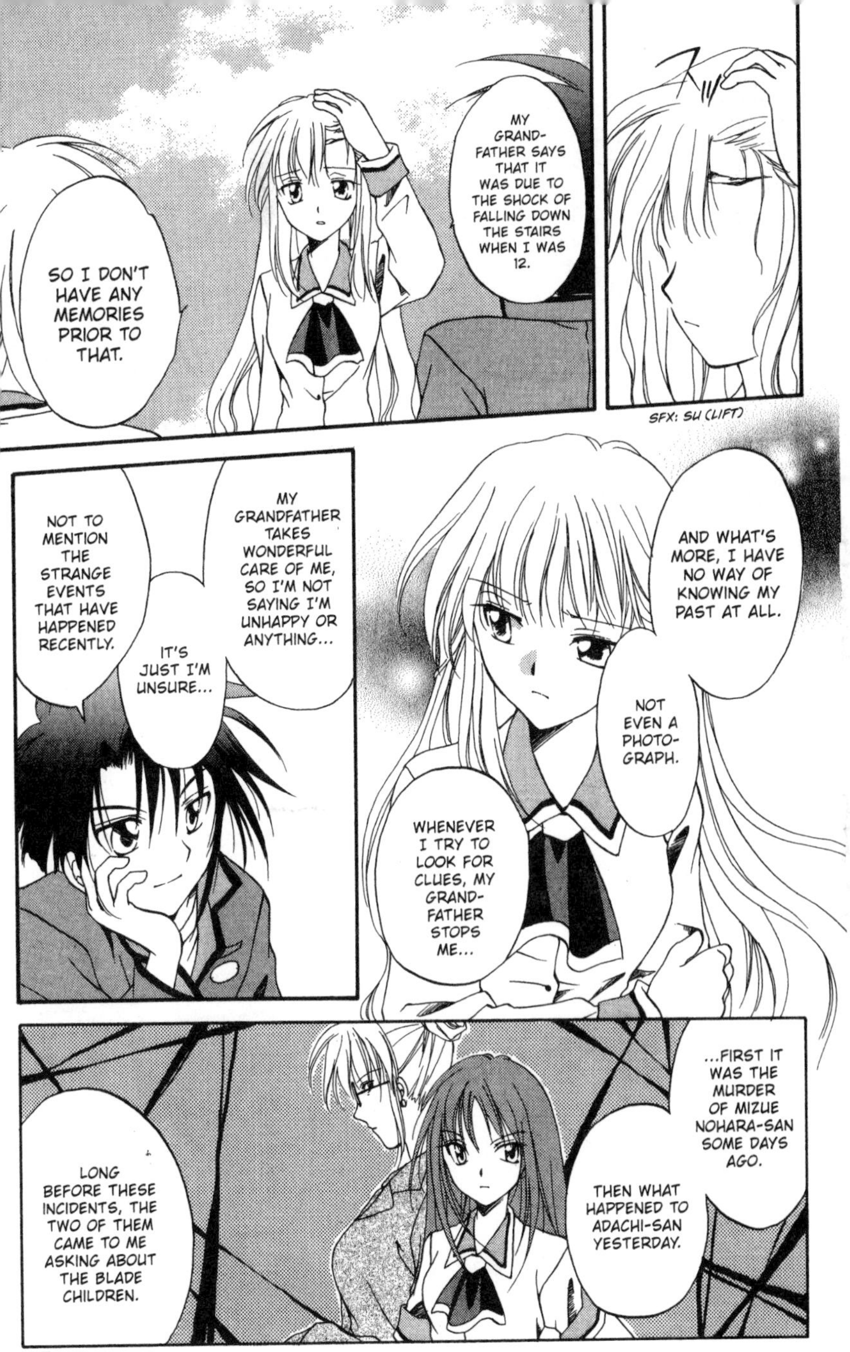
SFX: SU (LIFT)
MY GRANDFATHER SAYS THAT IT WAS DUE TO THE SHOCK OF FALLING DOWN THE STAIRS WHEN I WAS 12.
SO I DON'T HAVE ANY MEMORIES PRIOR TO THAT.
AND WHAT'S MORE, I HAVE NO WAY OF KNOWING MY PAST AT ALL.
NOT EVEN A PHOTOGRAPH.
WHENEVER I TRY TO LOOK FOR CLUES, MY GRANDFATHER STOPS ME...
MY GRANDFATHER TAKES WONDERFUL CARE OF ME, SO I'M NOT SAYING I'M UNHAPPY OR ANYTHING...
IT'S JUST I'M UNSURE...
NOT TO MENTION THE STRANGE EVENTS THAT HAVE HAPPENED RECENTLY.
...FIRST IT WAS THE MURDER OF MIZUE NOHARA-SAN SOME DAYS AGO.
THEN WHAT HAPPENED TO ADACHI-SAN YESTERDAY.
LONG BEFORE THESE INCIDENTS, THE TWO OF THEM CAME TO ME ASKING ABOUT THE BLADE CHILDREN.

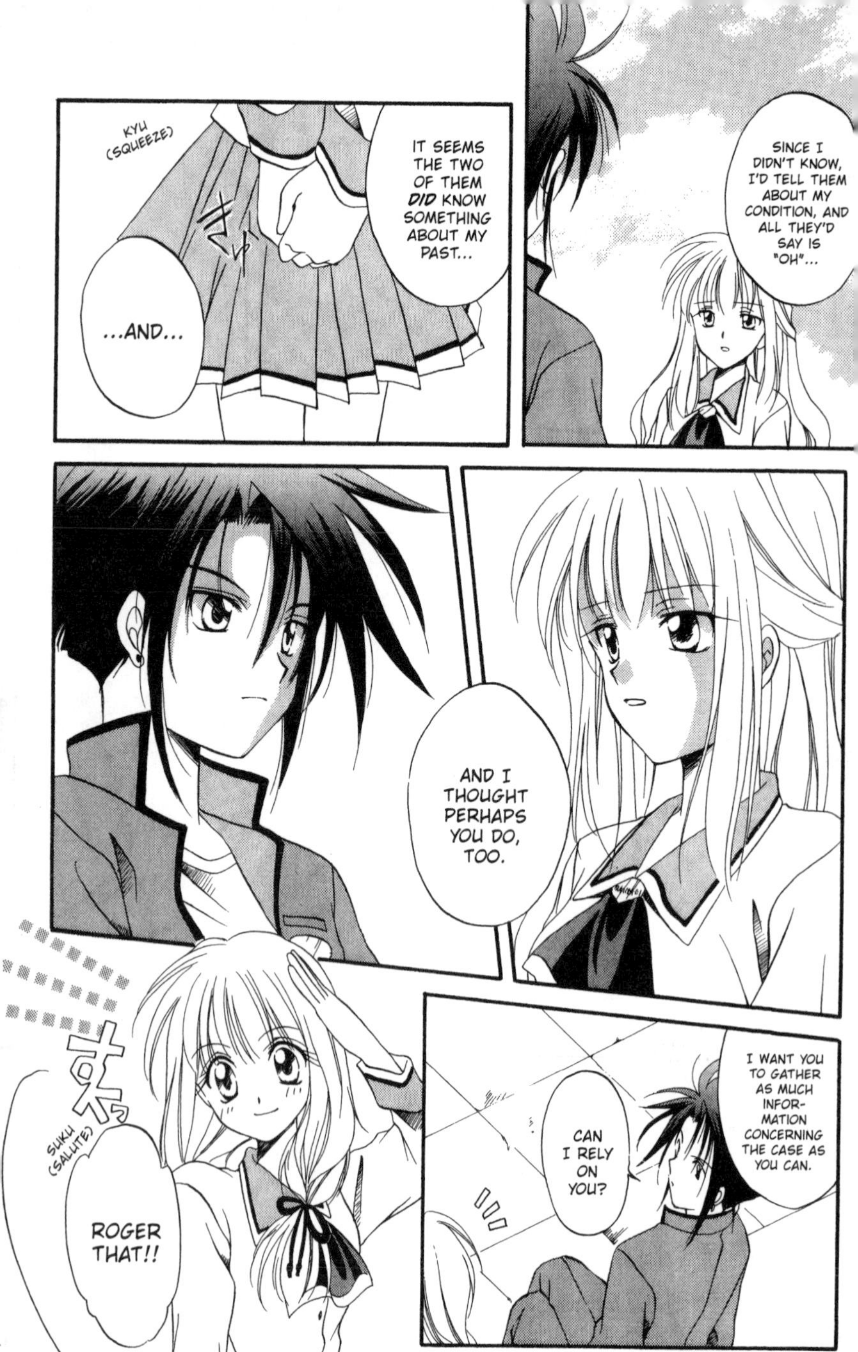
SINCE I DIDN'T KNOW, I'D TELL THEM ABOUT MY CONDITION, AND ALL THEY'D SAY IS "OH"...
IT SEEMS THE TWO OF THEM DID KNOW SOMETHING ABOUT MY PAST...
KYU (SQUEEZE)
...AND...
AND I THOUGHT PERHAPS YOU DO, TOO.
I WANT YOU TO GATHER AS MUCH INFORMATION CONCERNING THE CASE AS YOU CAN.
CAN I RELY ON YOU?
SUKU (SALUTE)
ROGER THAT!!

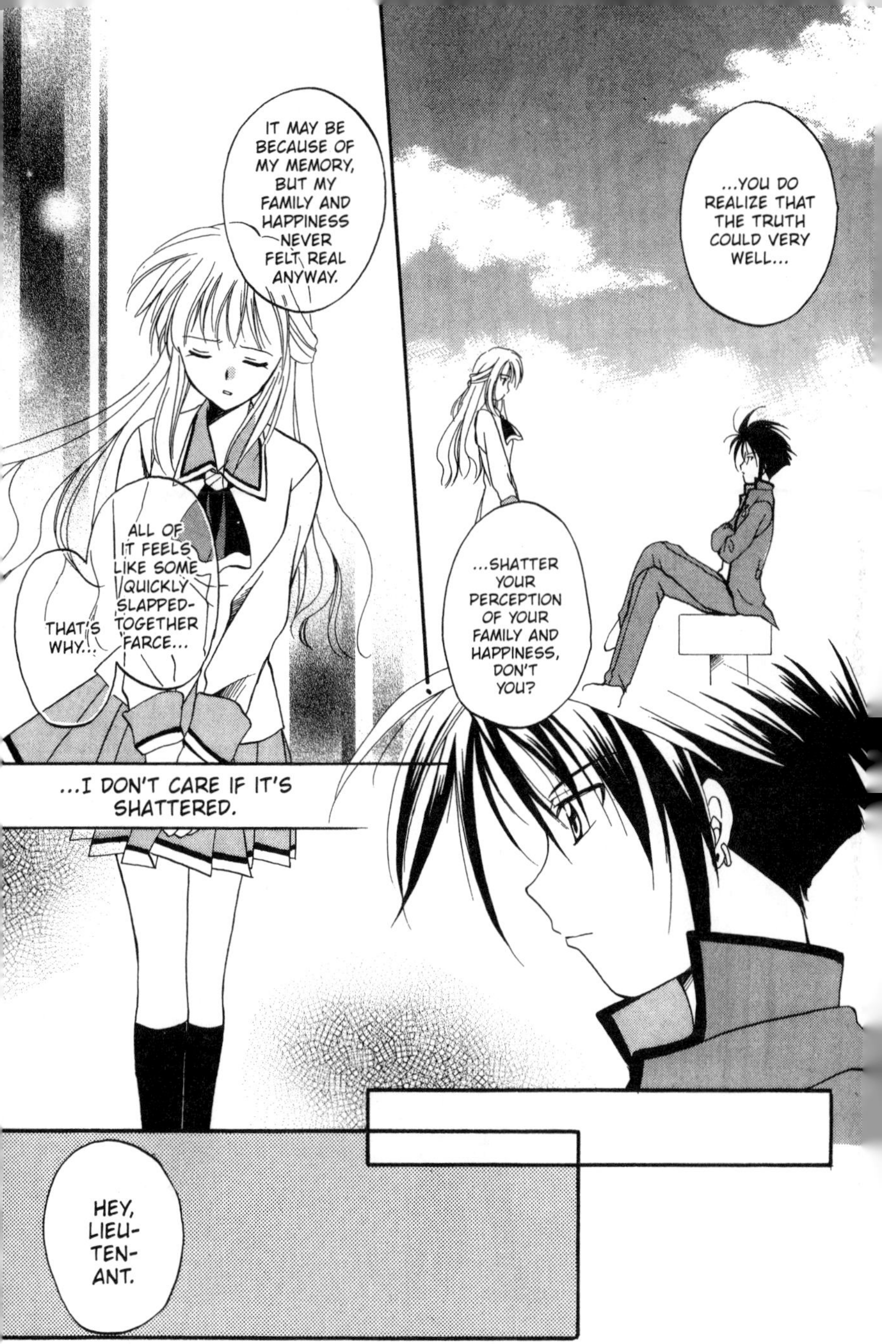
...YOU DO REALIZE THAT THE TRUTH COULD VERY WELL...
...SHATTER YOUR PERCEPTION OF YOUR FAMILY AND HAPPINESS, DON'T YOU?
IT MAY BE BECAUSE OF MY MEMORY, BUT MY FAMILY AND HAPPINESS NEVER FELT REAL ANYWAY.
ALL OF IT FEELS LIKE SOME QUICKLY SLAPPED-TOGETHER FARCE...
THAT'S WHY...
...I DON'T CARE IF IT'S SHATTERED.
HEY, LIEU-TEN-ANT.

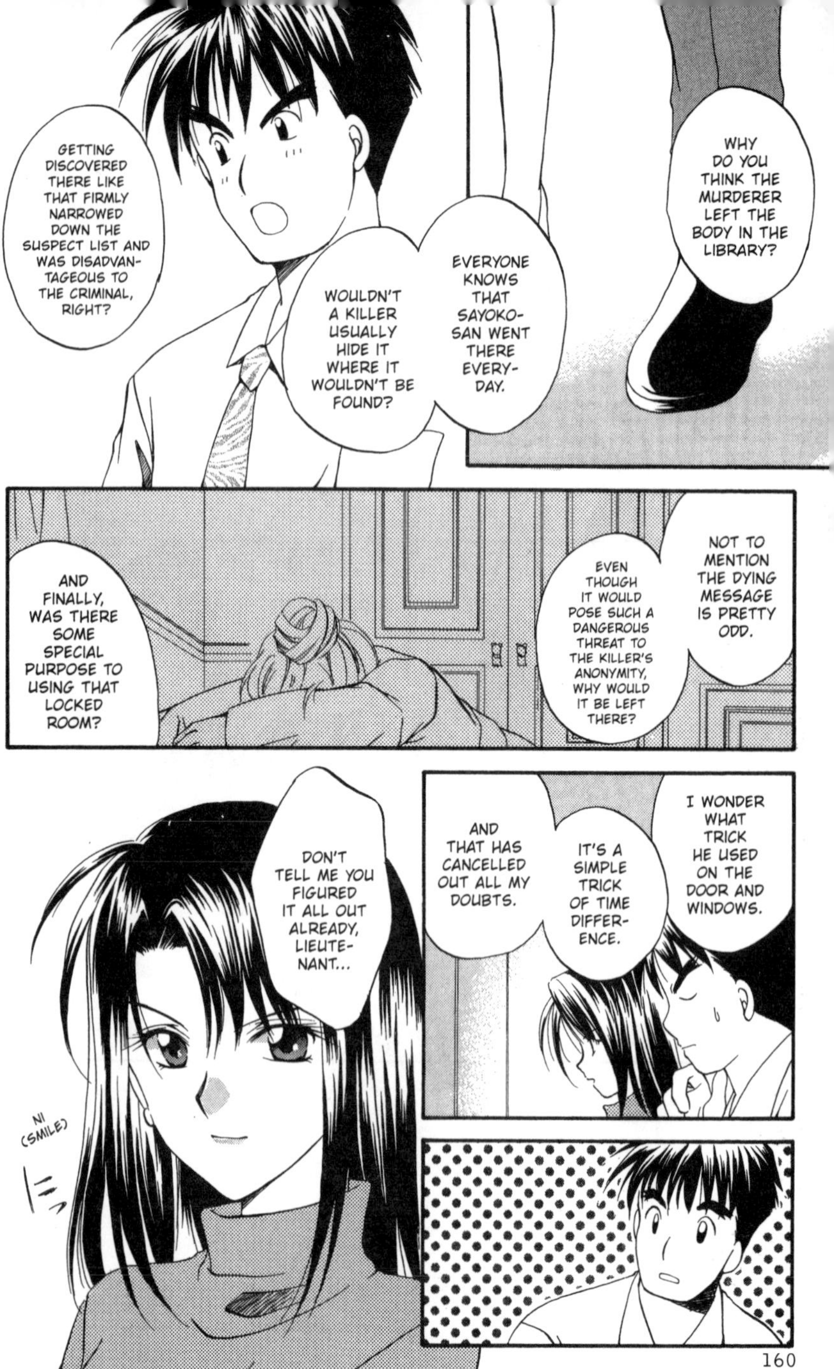
WHY DO YOU THINK THE MURDERER LEFT THE BODY IN THE LIBRARY?
EVERYONE KNOWS THAT SAYOKO-SAN WENT THERE EVERY-DAY.
WOULDN'T A KILLER USUALLY HIDE IT WHERE IT WOULDN'T BE FOUND?
GETTING DISCOVERED THERE LIKE THAT FIRMLY NARROWED DOWN THE SUSPECT LIST AND WAS DISADVAN-TAGEOUS TO THE CRIMINAL, RIGHT?
NOT TO MENTION THE DYING MESSAGE IS PRETTY ODD.
EVEN THOUGH IT WOULD POSE SUCH A DANGEROUS THREAT TO THE KILLER'S ANONYMITY, WHY WOULD IT BE LEFT THERE?
AND FINALLY, WAS THERE SOME SPECIAL PURPOSE TO USING THAT LOCKED ROOM?
I WONDER WHAT TRICK HE USED ON THE DOOR AND WINDOWS.
IT'S A SIMPLE TRICK OF TIME DIFFER-ENCE.
AND THAT HAS CANCELLED OUT ALL MY DOUBTS.
DON'T TELL ME YOU FIGURED IT ALL OUT ALREADY, LIEUTE-NANT...
NI (SMILE)

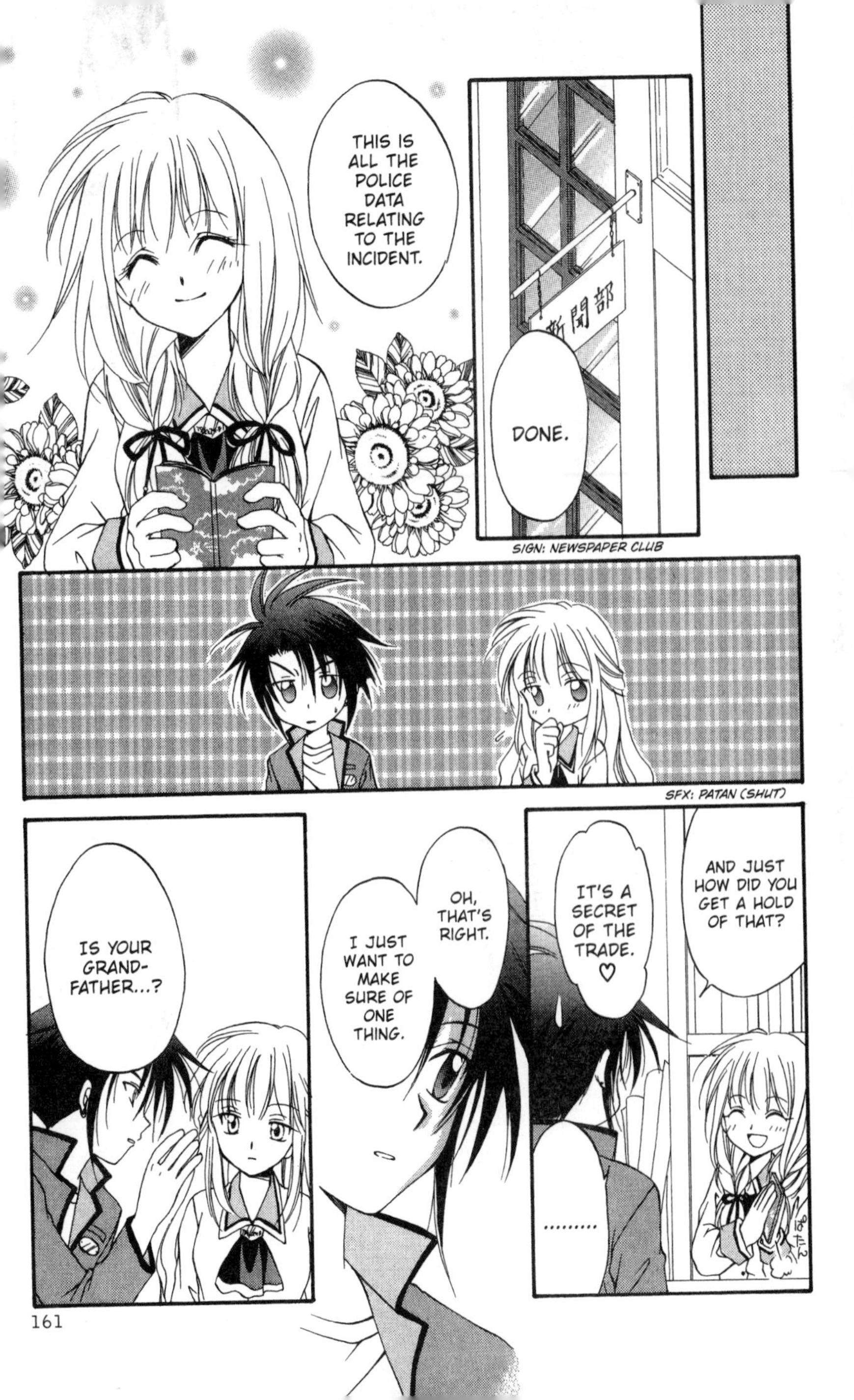
新聞部
DONE.
SIGN: NEWSPAPER CLUB
THIS IS ALL THE POLICE DATA RELATING TO THE INCIDENT.
SFX: PATAN (SHUT)
ぱたん
AND JUST HOW DID YOU GET A HOLD OF THAT?
IT'S A SECRET OF THE TRADE. ♡
....
OH, THAT'S RIGHT.
I JUST WANT TO MAKE SURE OF ONE THING.
IS YOUR GRAND-FATHER...?

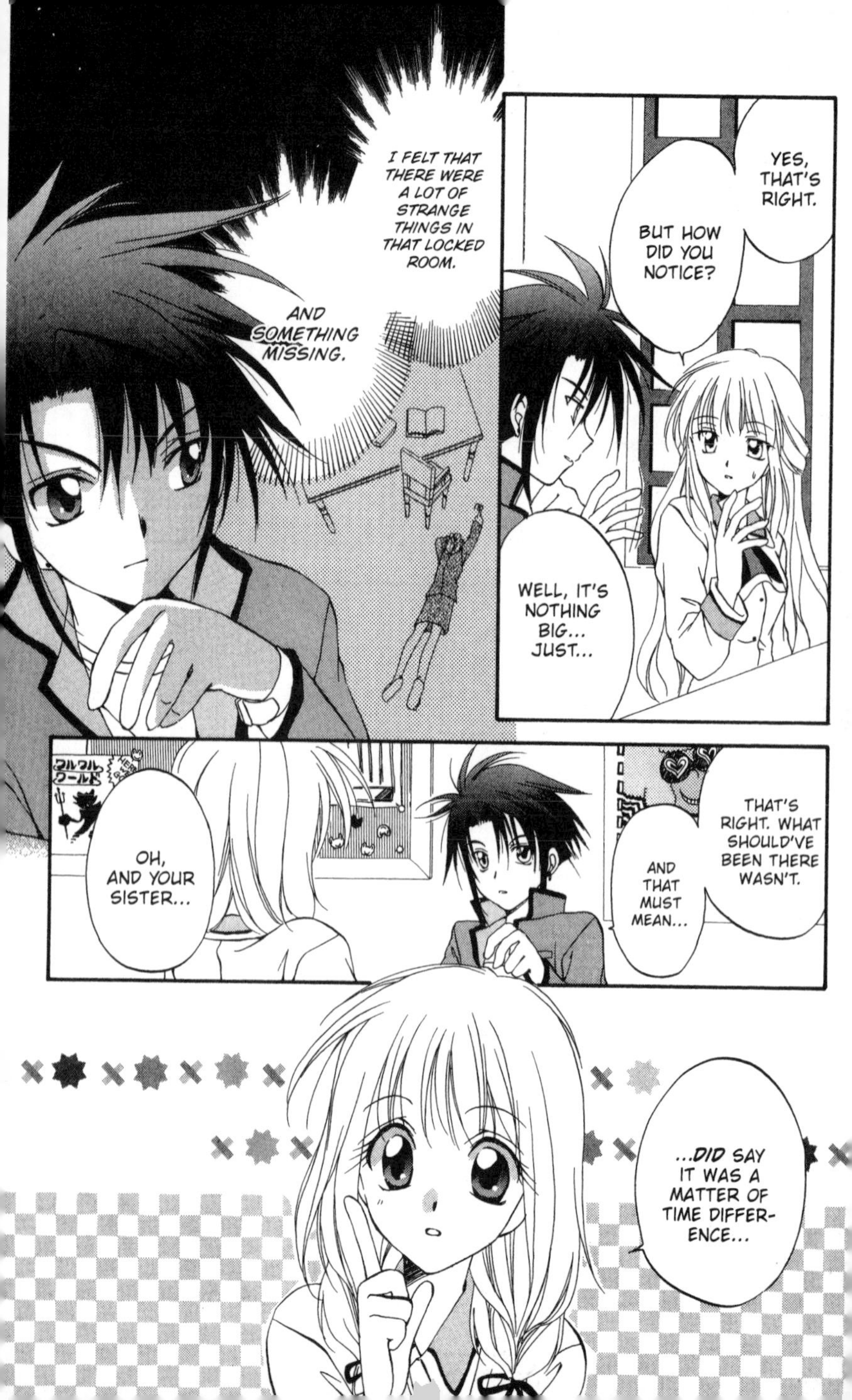
YES, THAT'S RIGHT.
BUT HOW DID YOU NOTICE?
WELL, IT'S NOTHING BIG... JUST...
I FELT THAT THERE WERE A LOT OF STRANGE THINGS IN THAT LOCKED ROOM.
AND SOMETHING MISSING.
THAT'S RIGHT. WHAT SHOULD'VE BEEN THERE WASN'T.
AND THAT MUST MEAN...
OH, AND YOUR SISTER...
...**DID** SAY IT WAS A MATTER OF TIME DIFFER-ENCE...

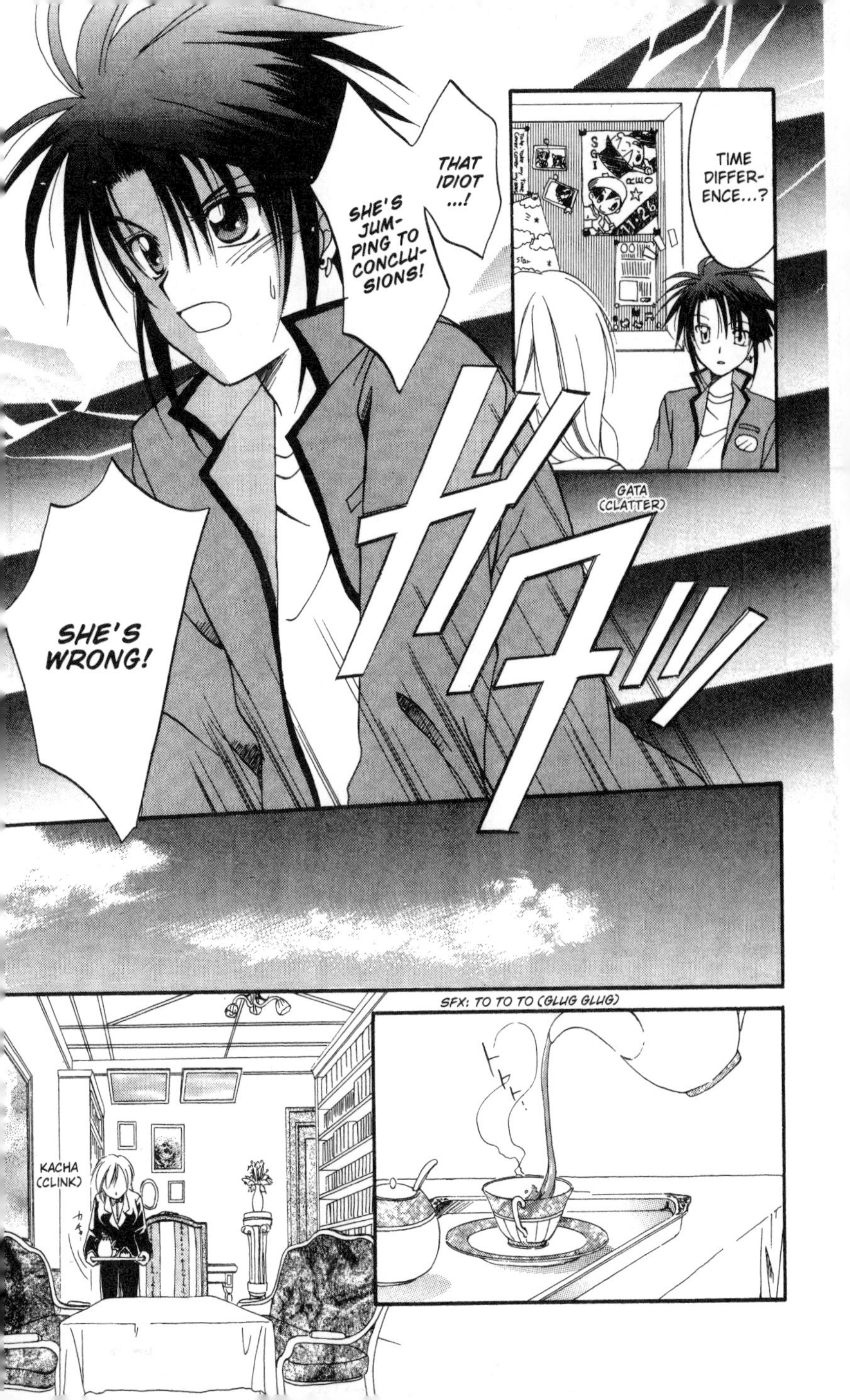
TIME DIFFERENCE...?
THAT IDIOT...!
SHE'S JUMPING TO CONCLUSIONS!
GATA (CLATTER)
SHE'S WRONG!
SFX: TO TO TO (GLUG GLUG)
KACHA (CLINK)

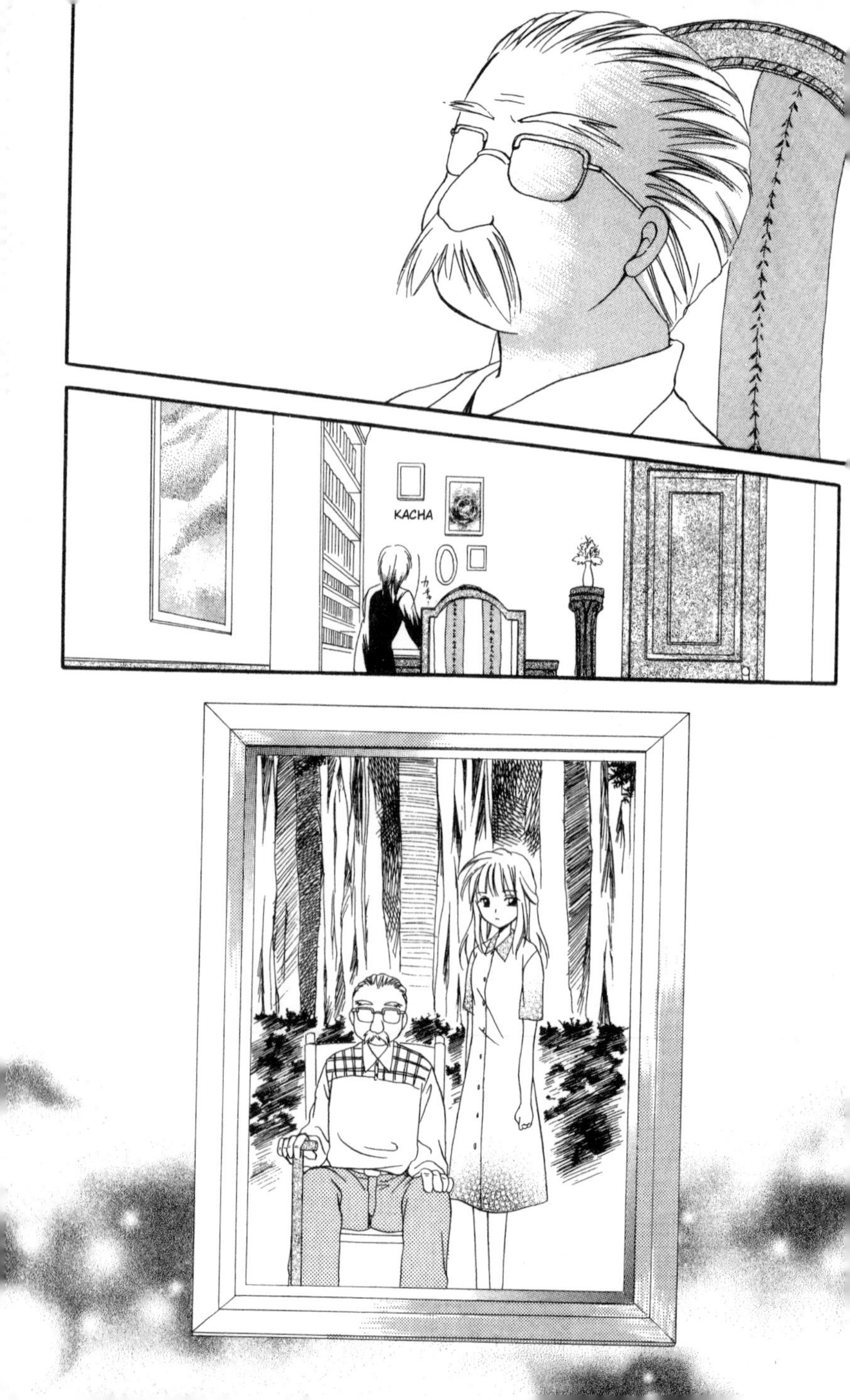
KACHA
カチャ

CHAPTER FIVE

Room Behind the Ward Lock (Part II)

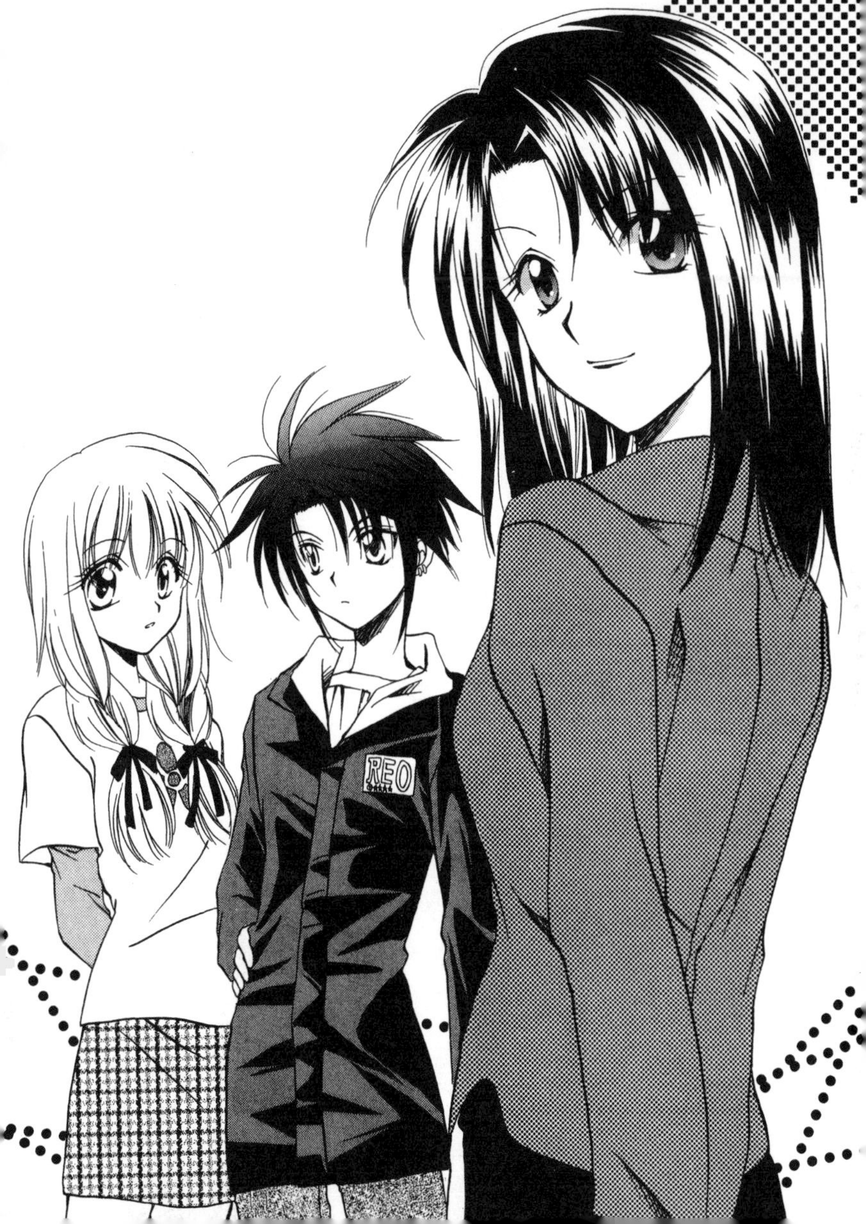
REO

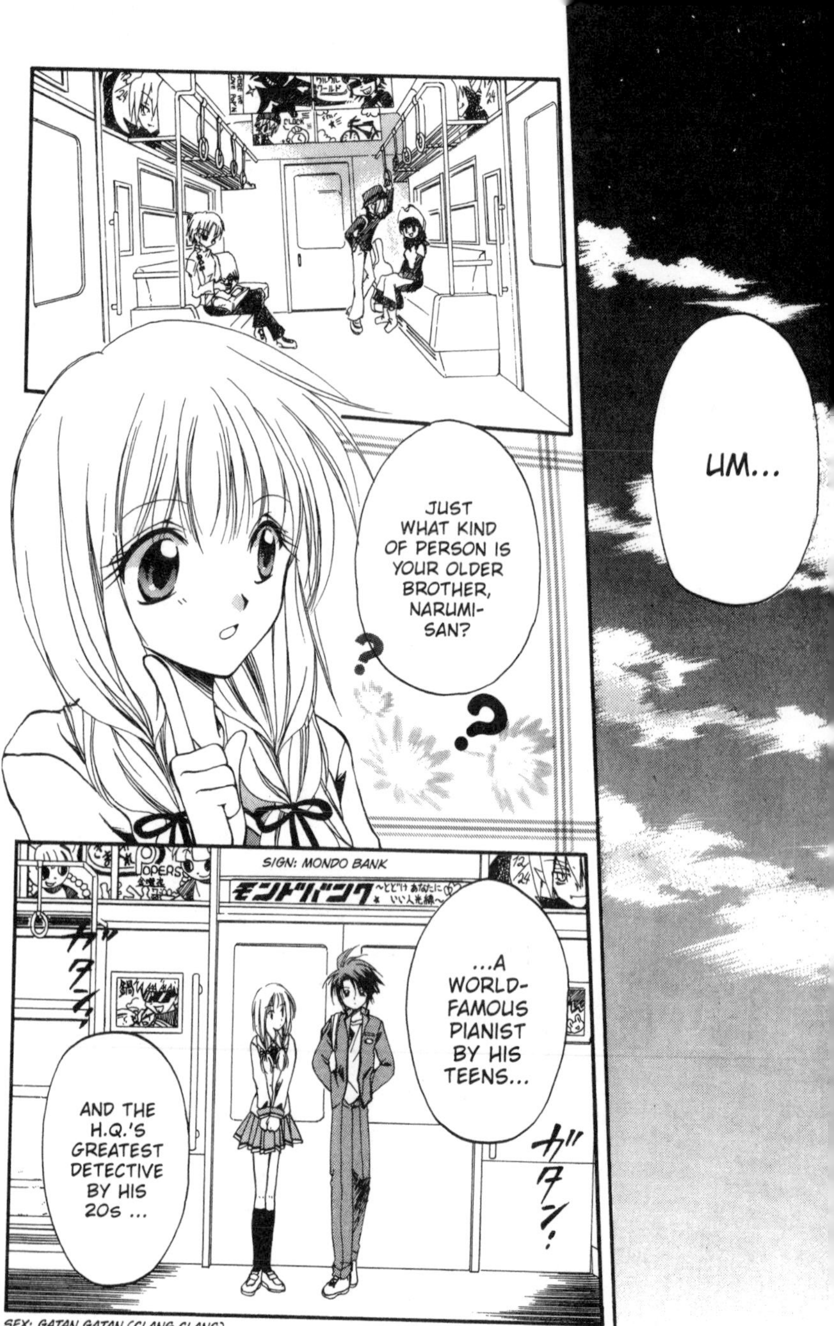
UM...
JUST WHAT KIND OF PERSON IS YOUR OLDER BROTHER, NARUMI-SAN?
SIGN: MONDO BANK
モンドバンク
ガタン
...A WORLD-FAMOUS PIANIST BY HIS TEENS...
AND THE H.Q.'S GREATEST DETECTIVE BY HIS 20s ...
ガタン
SFX: GATAN GATAN (CLANG CLANG)

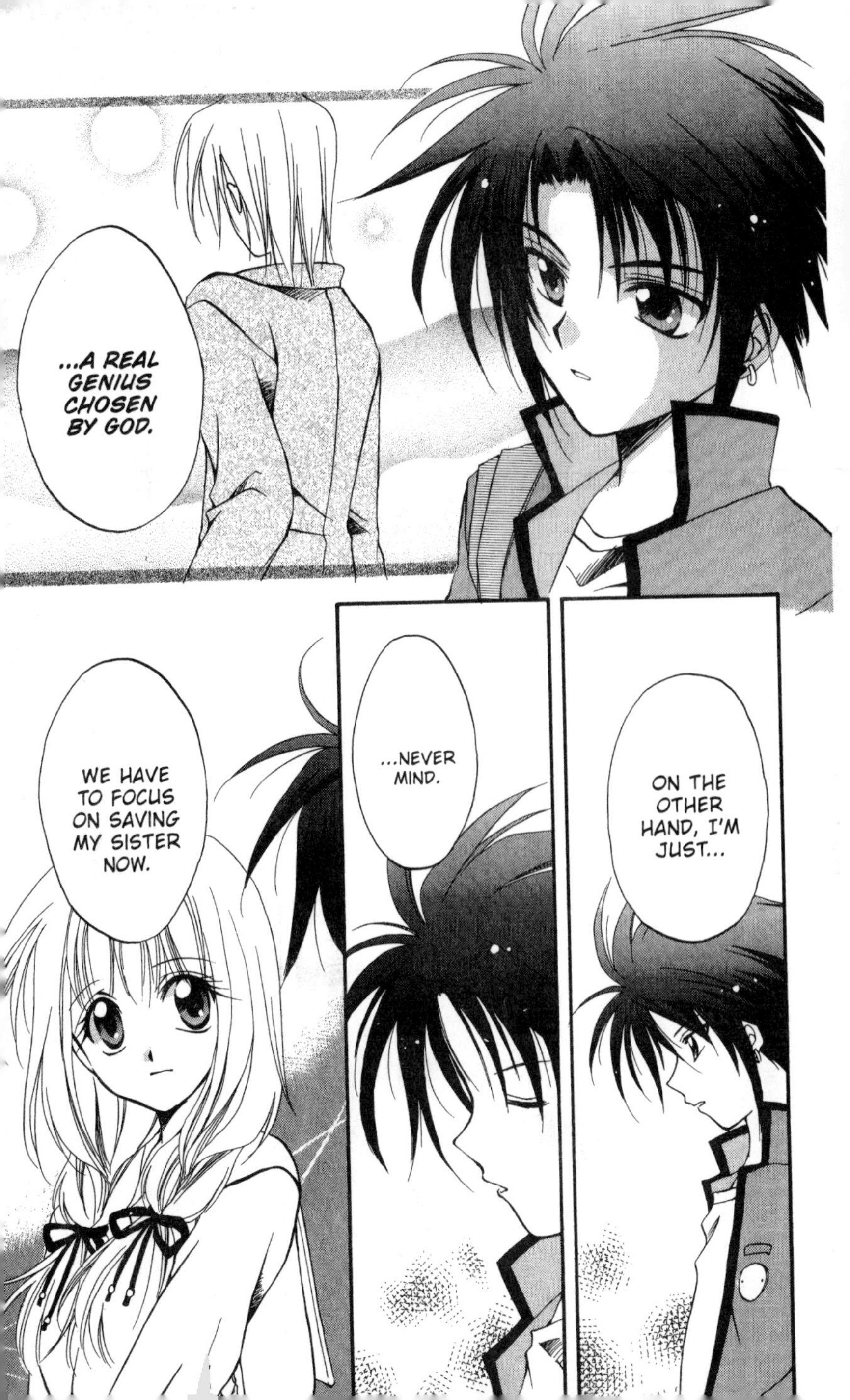
...A REAL GENIUS CHOSEN BY GOD.
ON THE OTHER HAND, I'M JUST...
...NEVER MIND.
WE HAVE TO FOCUS ON SAVING MY SISTER NOW.

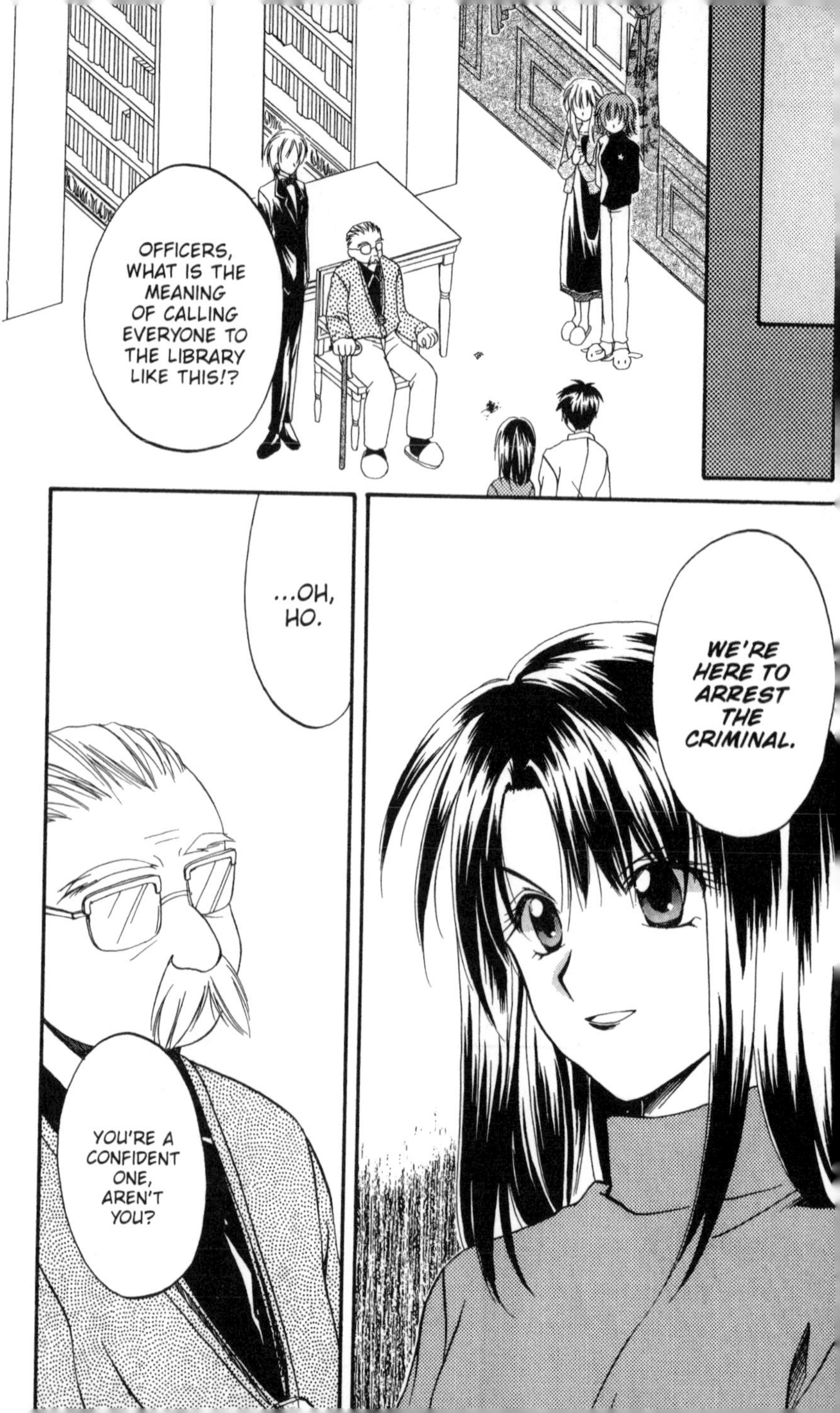
OFFICERS, WHAT IS THE MEANING OF CALLING EVERYONE TO THE LIBRARY LIKE THIS!?
WE'RE HERE TO ARREST THE CRIMINAL.
...OH, HO.
YOU'RE A CONFIDENT ONE, AREN'T YOU?

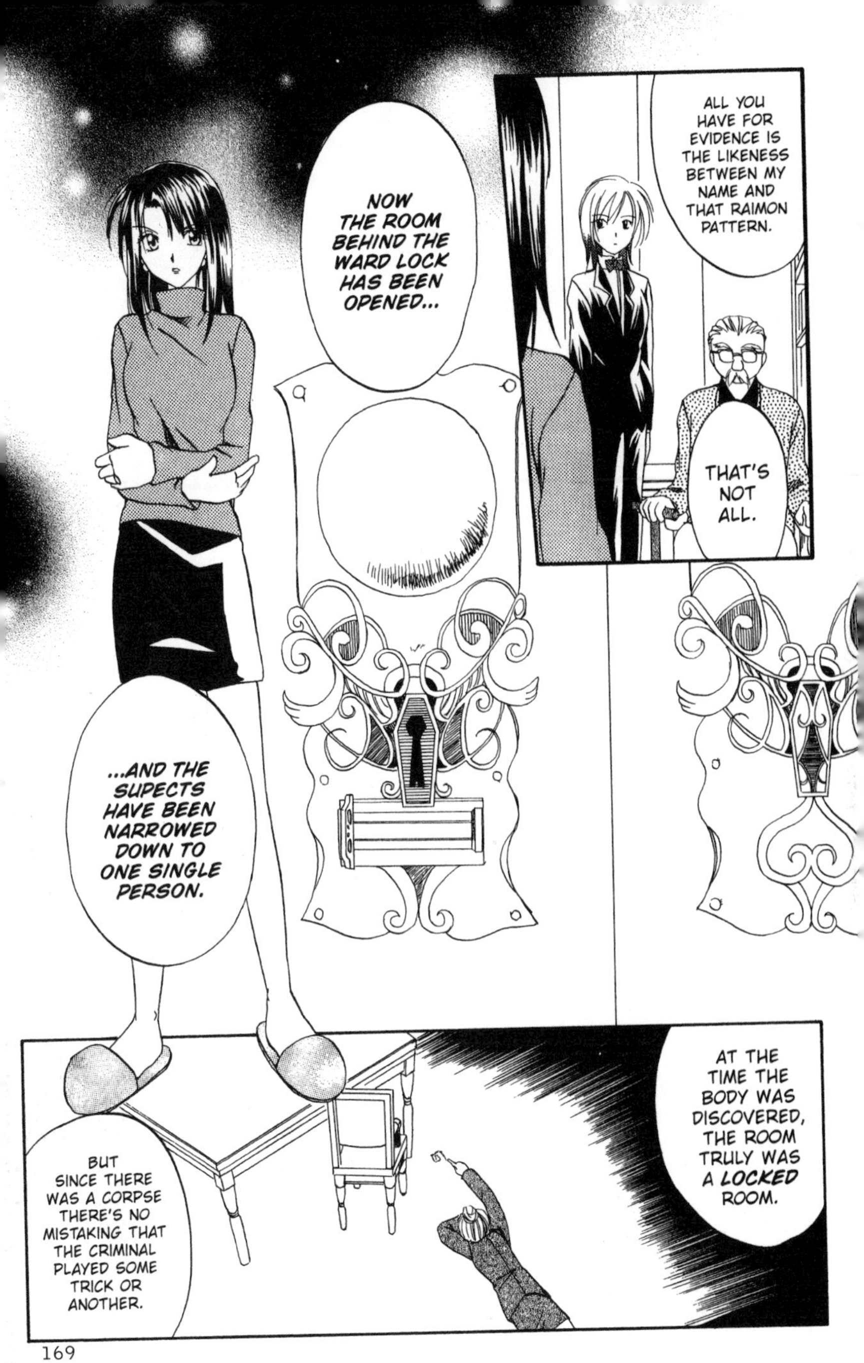
ALL YOU HAVE FOR EVIDENCE IS THE LIKENESS BETWEEN MY NAME AND THAT RAIMON PATTERN.
THAT'S NOT ALL.
NOW THE ROOM BEHIND THE WARD LOCK HAS BEEN OPENED...
...AND THE SUPECTS HAVE BEEN NARROWED DOWN TO ONE SINGLE PERSON.
AT THE TIME THE BODY WAS DISCOVERED, THE ROOM TRULY WAS A *LOCKED* ROOM.
BUT SINCE THERE WAS A CORPSE THERE'S NO MISTAKING THAT THE CRIMINAL PLAYED SOME TRICK OR ANOTHER.

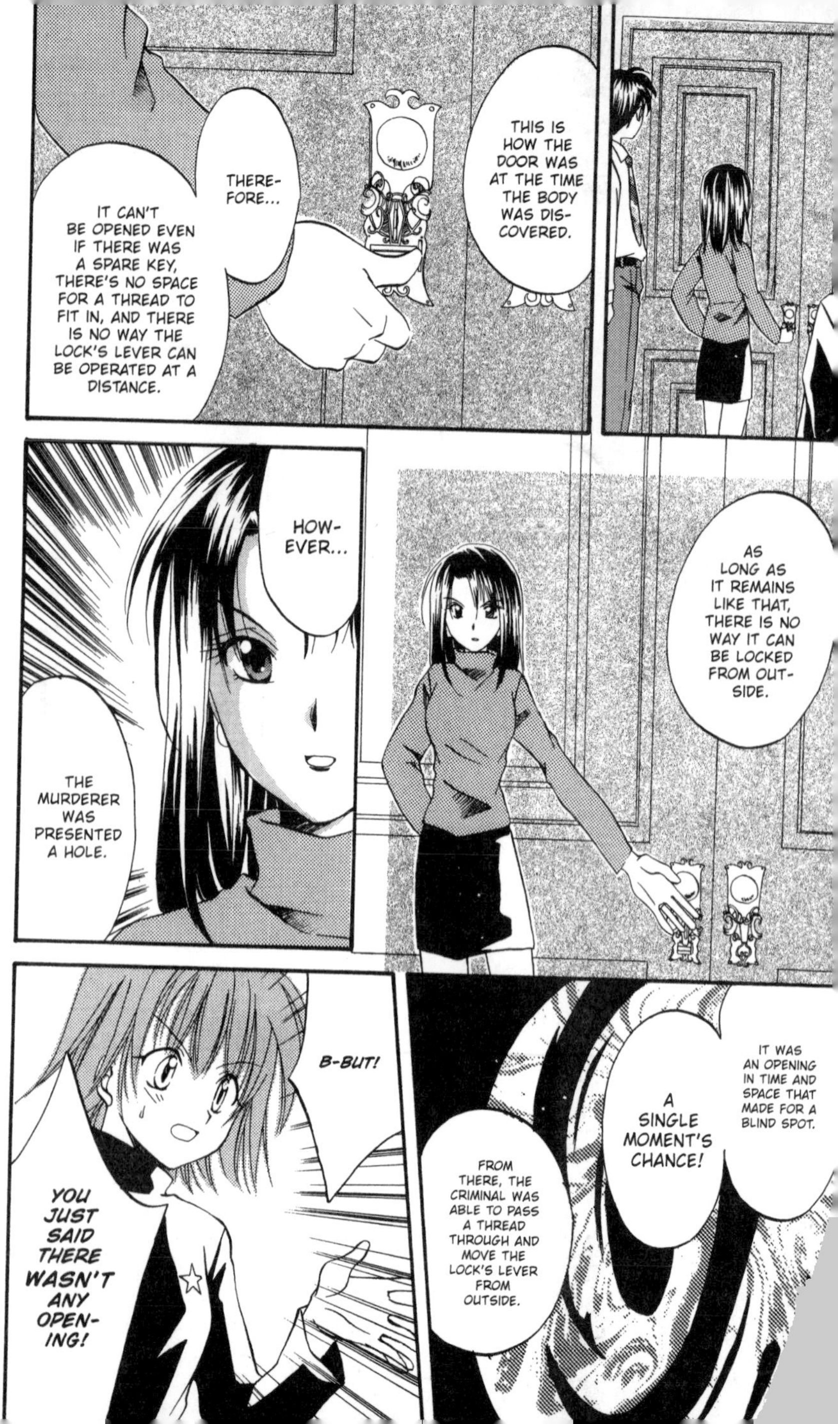
THIS IS HOW THE DOOR WAS AT THE TIME THE BODY WAS DISCOVERED.
THEREFORE...
IT CAN'T BE OPENED EVEN IF THERE WAS A SPARE KEY, THERE'S NO SPACE FOR A THREAD TO FIT IN, AND THERE IS NO WAY THE LOCK'S LEVER CAN BE OPERATED AT A DISTANCE.
AS LONG AS IT REMAINS LIKE THAT, THERE IS NO WAY IT CAN BE LOCKED FROM OUTSIDE.
HOWEVER...
THE MURDERER WAS PRESENTED A HOLE.
IT WAS AN OPENING IN TIME AND SPACE THAT MADE FOR A BLIND SPOT.
A SINGLE MOMENT'S CHANCE!
FROM THERE, THE CRIMINAL WAS ABLE TO PASS A THREAD THROUGH AND MOVE THE LOCK'S LEVER FROM OUTSIDE.
B-BUT!
YOU JUST SAID THERE WASN'T ANY OPENING!

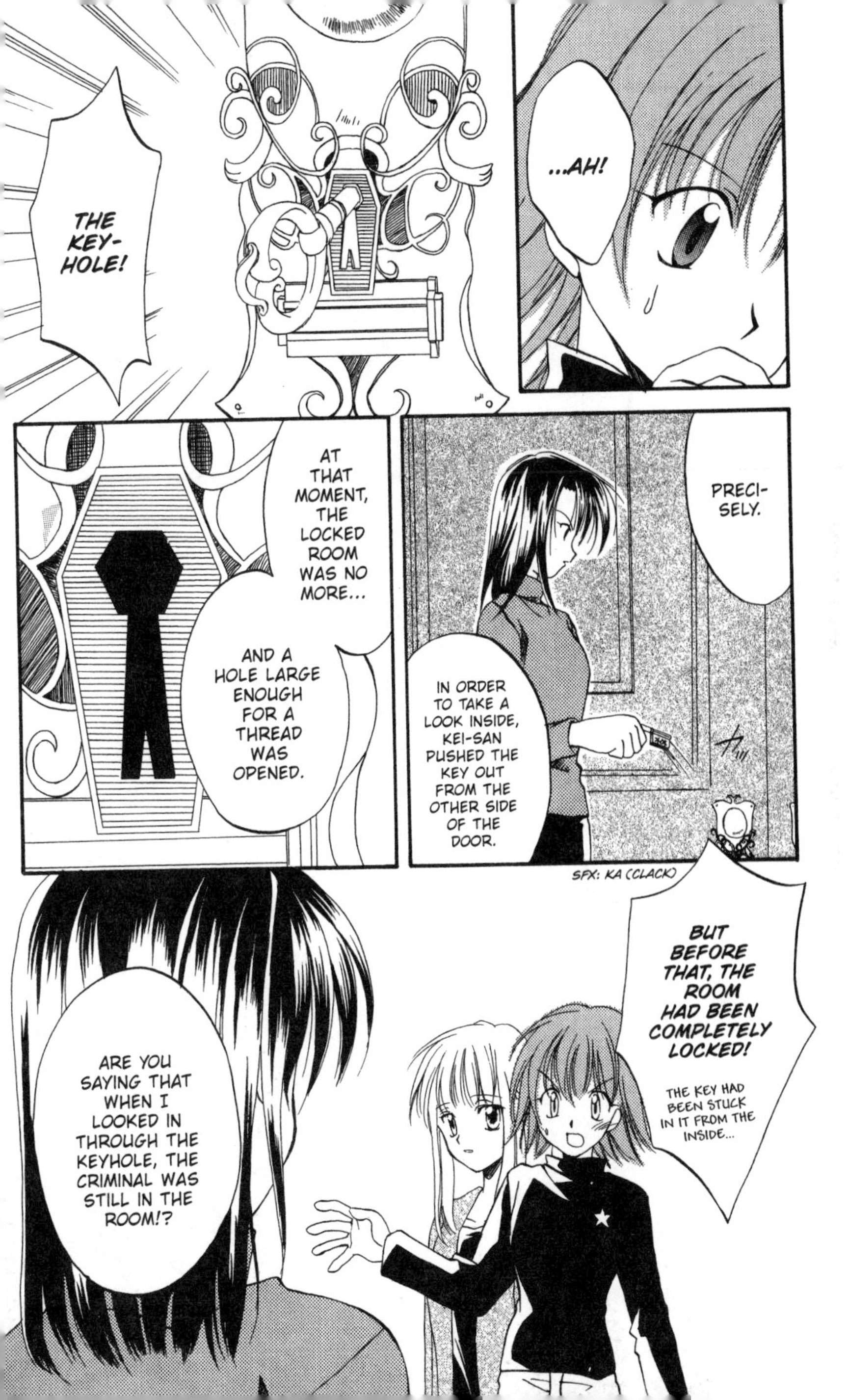

...AH!
THE KEY-HOLE!
PRECISELY.
IN ORDER TO TAKE A LOOK INSIDE, KEI-SAN PUSHED THE KEY OUT FROM THE OTHER SIDE OF THE DOOR.
SFX: KA (CLACK)
AT THAT MOMENT, THE LOCKED ROOM WAS NO MORE...
AND A HOLE LARGE ENOUGH FOR A THREAD WAS OPENED.
BUT BEFORE THAT, THE ROOM HAD BEEN COMPLETELY LOCKED!
THE KEY HAD BEEN STUCK IN IT FROM THE INSIDE...
ARE YOU SAYING THAT WHEN I LOOKED IN THROUGH THE KEYHOLE, THE CRIMINAL WAS STILL IN THE ROOM!?

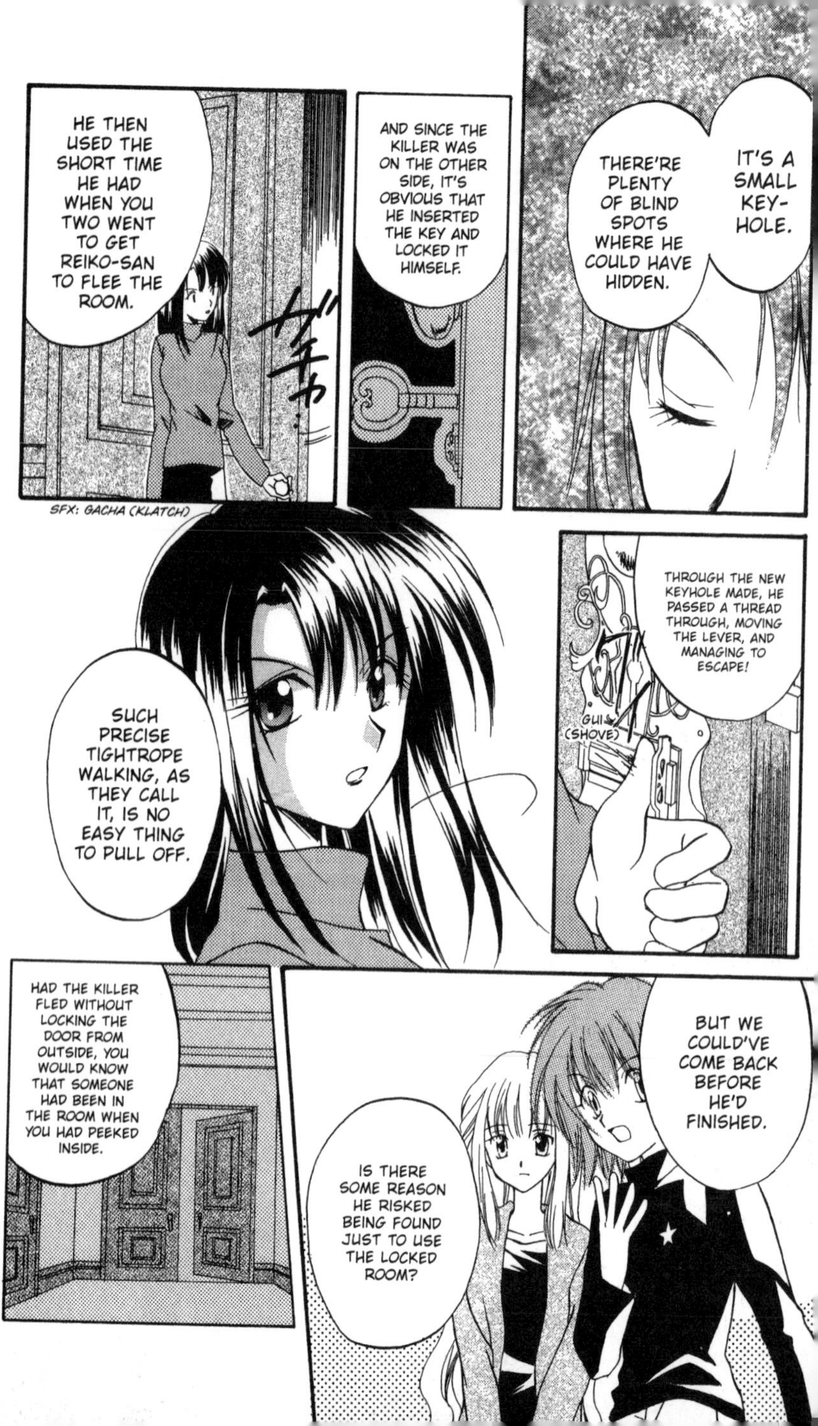
IT'S A SMALL KEY-HOLE.
THERE'RE PLENTY OF BLIND SPOTS WHERE HE COULD HAVE HIDDEN.
AND SINCE THE KILLER WAS ON THE OTHER SIDE, IT'S OBVIOUS THAT HE INSERTED THE KEY AND LOCKED IT HIMSELF.
HE THEN USED THE SHORT TIME HE HAD WHEN YOU TWO WENT TO GET REIKO-SAN TO FLEE THE ROOM.
SFX: GACHA (KLATCH)
THROUGH THE NEW KEYHOLE MADE, HE PASSED A THREAD THROUGH, MOVING THE LEVER, AND MANAGING TO ESCAPE!
GUI (SHOVE)
SUCH PRECISE TIGHTROPE WALKING, AS THEY CALL IT, IS NO EASY THING TO PULL OFF.
BUT WE COULD'VE COME BACK BEFORE HE'D FINISHED.
IS THERE SOME REASON HE RISKED BEING FOUND JUST TO USE THE LOCKED ROOM?
HAD THE KILLER FLED WITHOUT LOCKING THE DOOR FROM OUTSIDE, YOU WOULD KNOW THAT SOMEONE HAD BEEN IN THE ROOM WHEN YOU HAD PEEKED INSIDE.

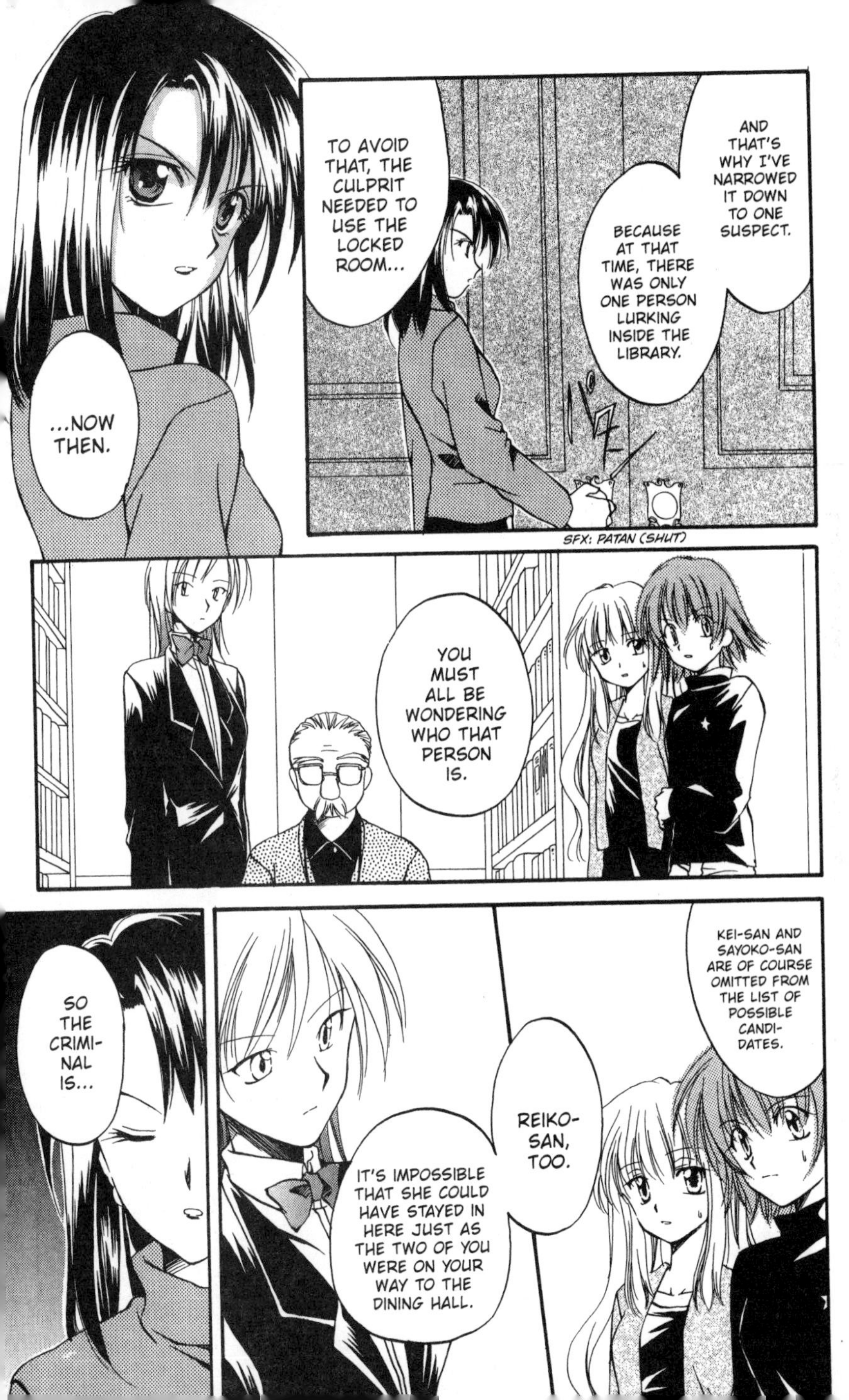

AND THAT'S WHY I'VE NARROWED IT DOWN TO ONE SUSPECT.
BECAUSE AT THAT TIME, THERE WAS ONLY ONE PERSON LURKING INSIDE THE LIBRARY.
TO AVOID THAT, THE CULPRIT NEEDED TO USE THE LOCKED ROOM...
SFX: PATAN (SHUT)
...NOW THEN.
YOU MUST ALL BE WONDERING WHO THAT PERSON IS.
KEI-SAN AND SAYOKO-SAN ARE OF COURSE OMITTED FROM THE LIST OF POSSIBLE CANDI-DATES.
REIKO-SAN, TOO.
IT'S IMPOSSIBLE THAT SHE COULD HAVE STAYED IN HERE JUST AS THE TWO OF YOU WERE ON YOUR WAY TO THE DINING HALL.
SO THE CRIMI-NAL IS...

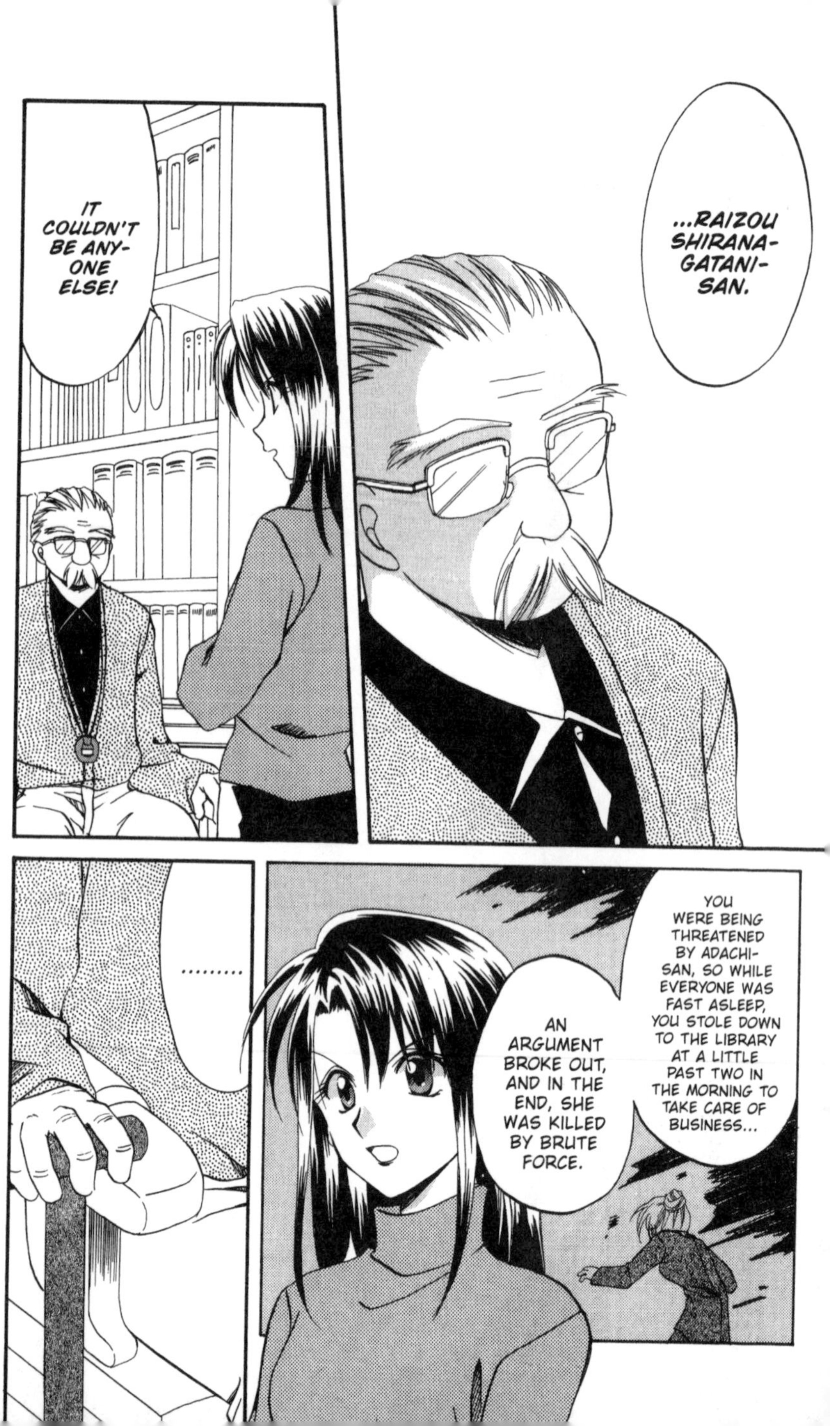
...RAIZOU SHIRANA-GATANI-SAN.
IT COULDN'T BE ANY-ONE ELSE!
YOU WERE BEING THREATENED BY ADACHI-SAN, SO WHILE EVERYONE WAS FAST ASLEEP, YOU STOLE DOWN TO THE LIBRARY AT A LITTLE PAST TWO IN THE MORNING TO TAKE CARE OF BUSINESS...
AN ARGUMENT BROKE OUT, AND IN THE END, SHE WAS KILLED BY BRUTE FORCE.
....

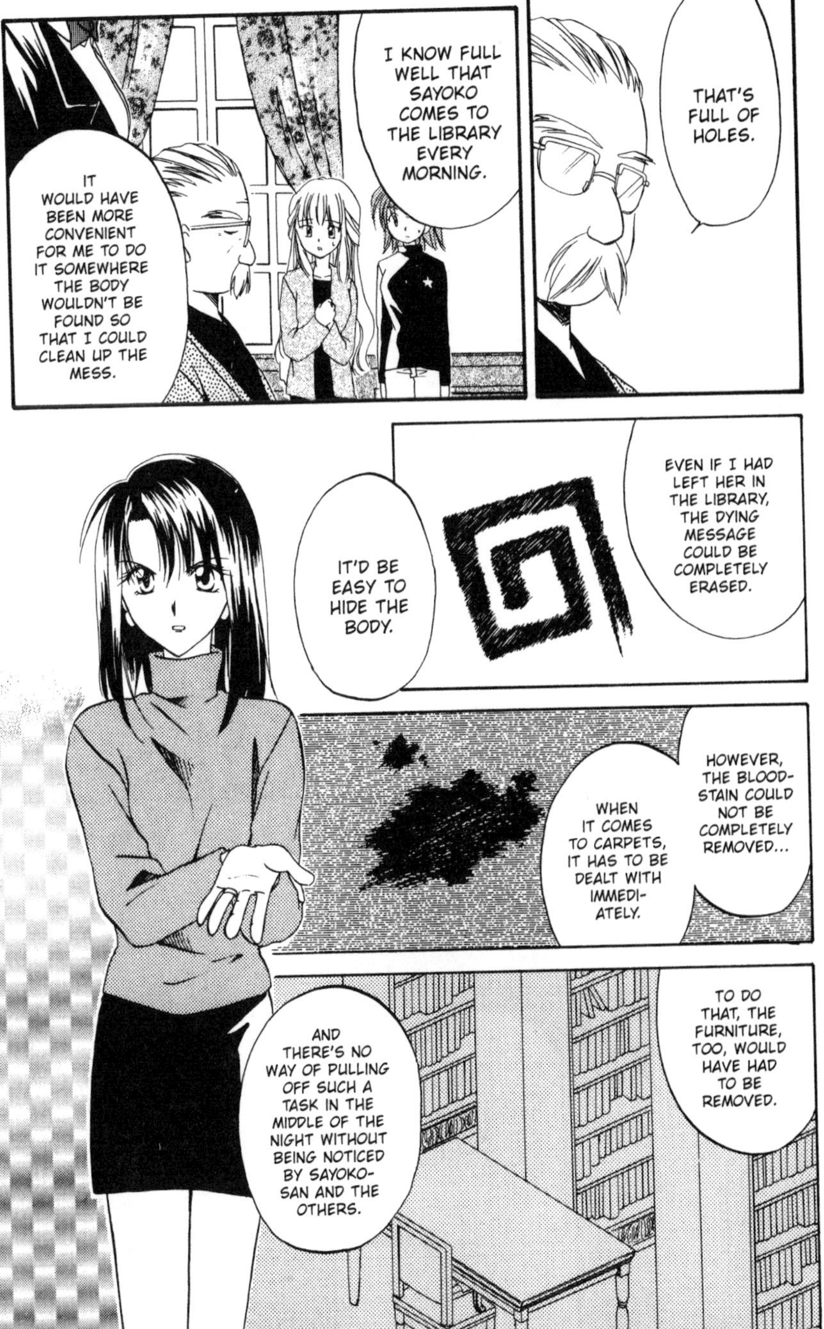
THAT'S FULL OF HOLES.
I KNOW FULL WELL THAT SAYOKO COMES TO THE LIBRARY EVERY MORNING.
IT WOULD HAVE BEEN MORE CONVENIENT FOR ME TO DO IT SOMEWHERE THE BODY WOULDN'T BE FOUND SO THAT I COULD CLEAN UP THE MESS.
EVEN IF I HAD LEFT HER IN THE LIBRARY, THE DYING MESSAGE COULD BE COMPLETELY ERASED.
IT'D BE EASY TO HIDE THE BODY.
HOWEVER, THE BLOOD-STAIN COULD NOT BE COMPLETELY REMOVED...
WHEN IT COMES TO CARPETS, IT HAS TO BE DEALT WITH IMMEDI-ATELY.
TO DO THAT, THE FURNITURE, TOO, WOULD HAVE HAD TO BE REMOVED.
AND THERE'S NO WAY OF PULLING OFF SUCH A TASK IN THE MIDDLE OF THE NIGHT WITHOUT BEING NOTICED BY SAYOKO-SAN AND THE OTHERS.

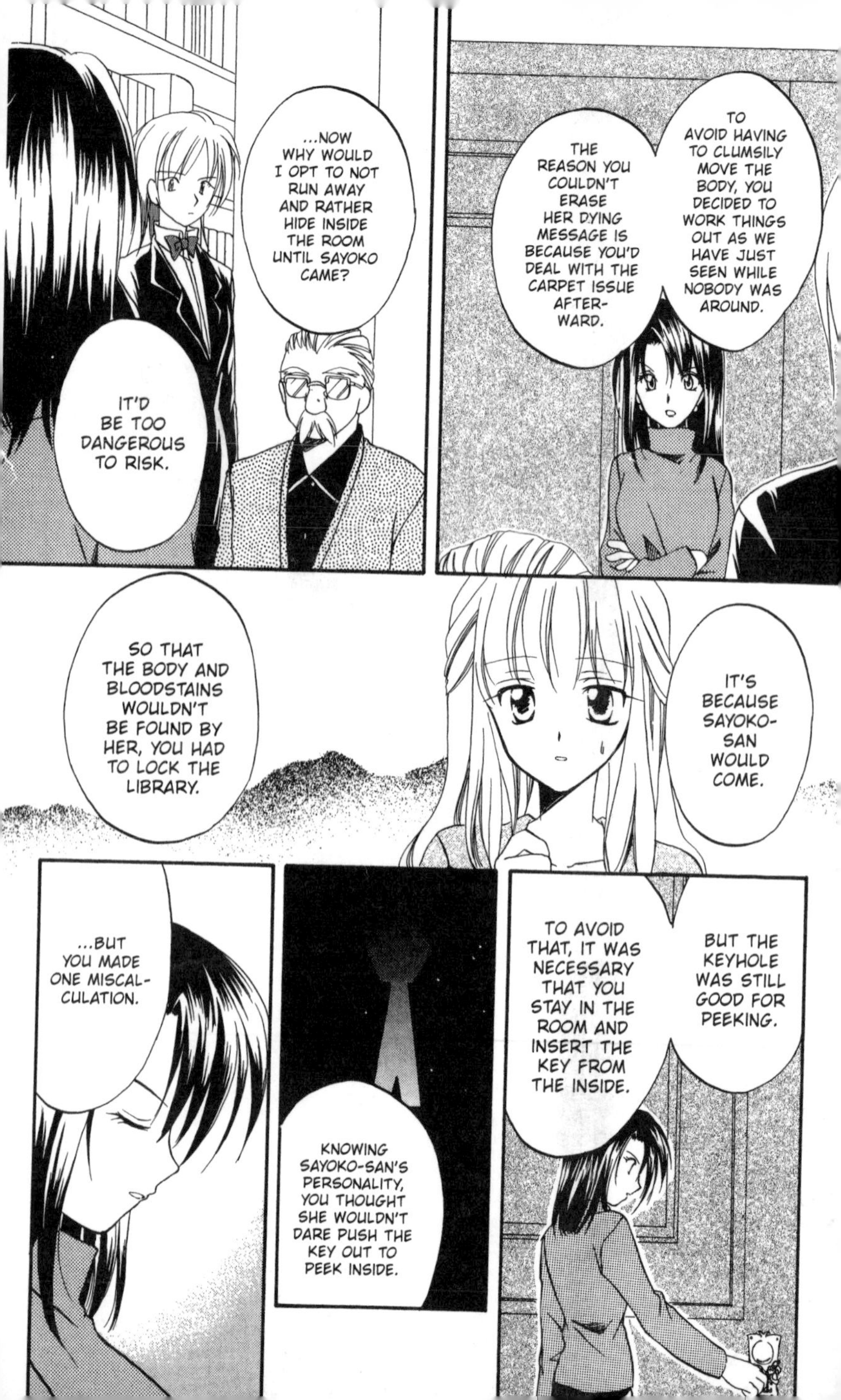
TO AVOID HAVING TO CLUMSILY MOVE THE BODY, YOU DECIDED TO WORK THINGS OUT AS WE HAVE JUST SEEN WHILE NOBODY WAS AROUND.
THE REASON YOU COULDN'T ERASE HER DYING MESSAGE IS BECAUSE YOU'D DEAL WITH THE CARPET ISSUE AFTER-WARD.
...NOW WHY WOULD I OPT TO NOT RUN AWAY AND RATHER HIDE INSIDE THE ROOM UNTIL SAYOKO CAME?
IT'D BE TOO DANGEROUS TO RISK.
IT'S BECAUSE SAYOKO-SAN WOULD COME.
SO THAT THE BODY AND BLOODSTAINS WOULDN'T BE FOUND BY HER, YOU HAD TO LOCK THE LIBRARY.
BUT THE KEYHOLE WAS STILL GOOD FOR PEEKING.
TO AVOID THAT, IT WAS NECESSARY THAT YOU STAY IN THE ROOM AND INSERT THE KEY FROM THE INSIDE.
KNOWING SAYOKO-SAN'S PERSONALITY, YOU THOUGHT SHE WOULDN'T DARE PUSH THE KEY OUT TO PEEK INSIDE.
...BUT YOU MADE ONE MISCAL-CULATION.

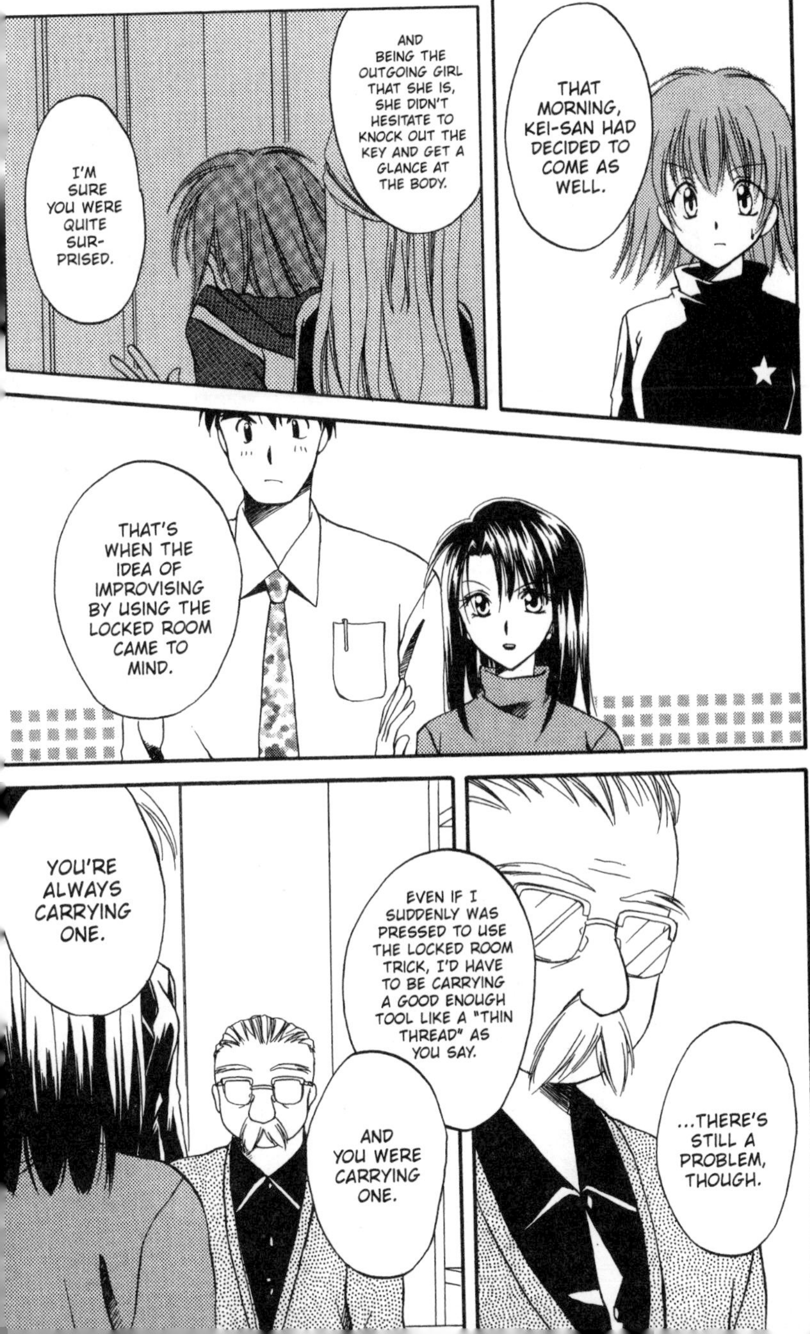
THAT MORNING, KEI-SAN HAD DECIDED TO COME AS WELL.
AND BEING THE OUTGOING GIRL THAT SHE IS, SHE DIDN'T HESITATE TO KNOCK OUT THE KEY AND GET A GLANCE AT THE BODY.
I'M SURE YOU WERE QUITE SUR-PRISED.
THAT'S WHEN THE IDEA OF IMPROVISING BY USING THE LOCKED ROOM CAME TO MIND.
...THERE'S STILL A PROBLEM, THOUGH.
EVEN IF I SUDDENLY WAS PRESSED TO USE THE LOCKED ROOM TRICK, I'D HAVE TO BE CARRYING A GOOD ENOUGH TOOL LIKE A "THIN THREAD" AS YOU SAY.
AND YOU WERE CARRYING ONE.
YOU'RE ALWAYS CARRYING ONE.

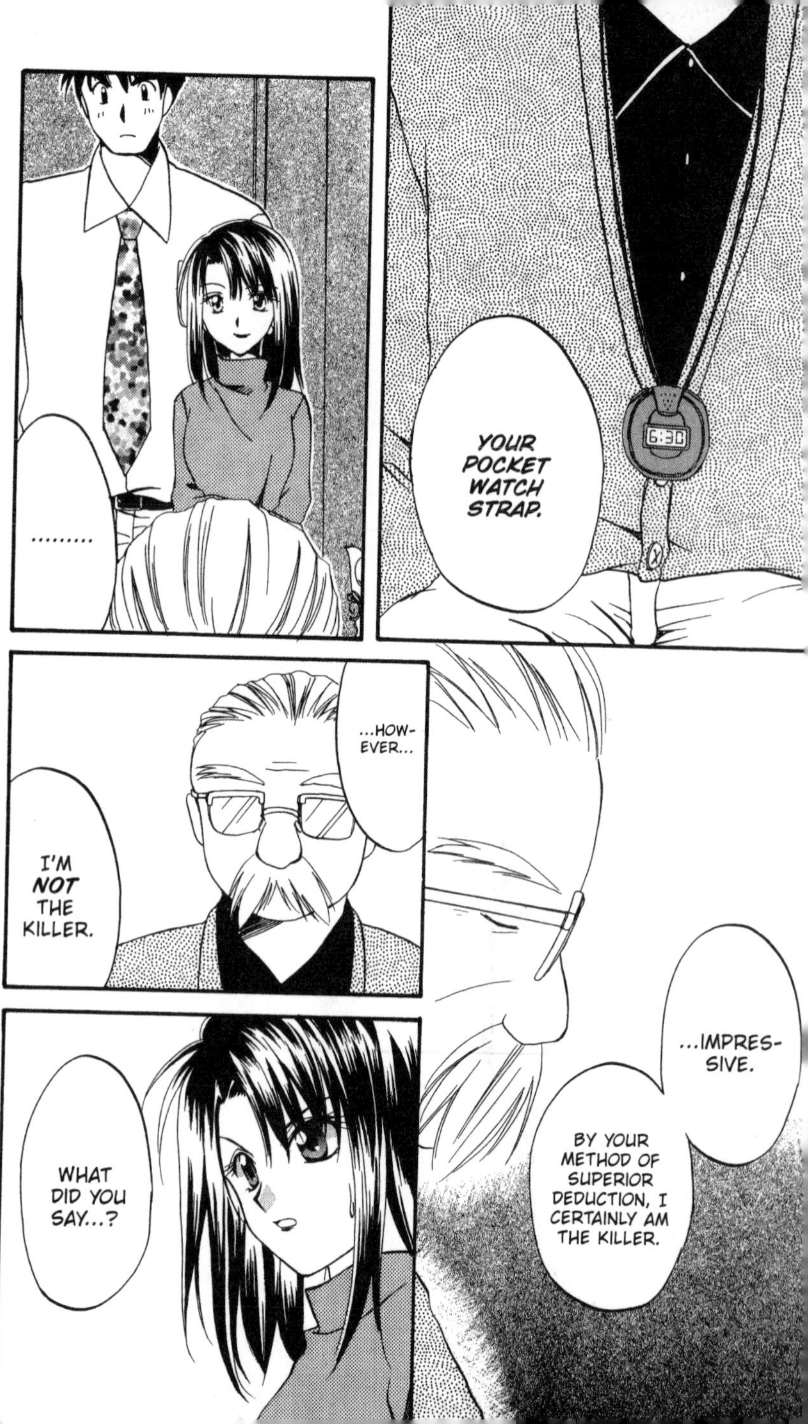
YOUR POCKET WATCH STRAP.
....
...IMPRES-SIVE.
BY YOUR METHOD OF SUPERIOR DEDUCTION, I CERTAINLY AM THE KILLER.
...HOW-EVER...
I'M NOT THE KILLER.
WHAT DID YOU SAY...?

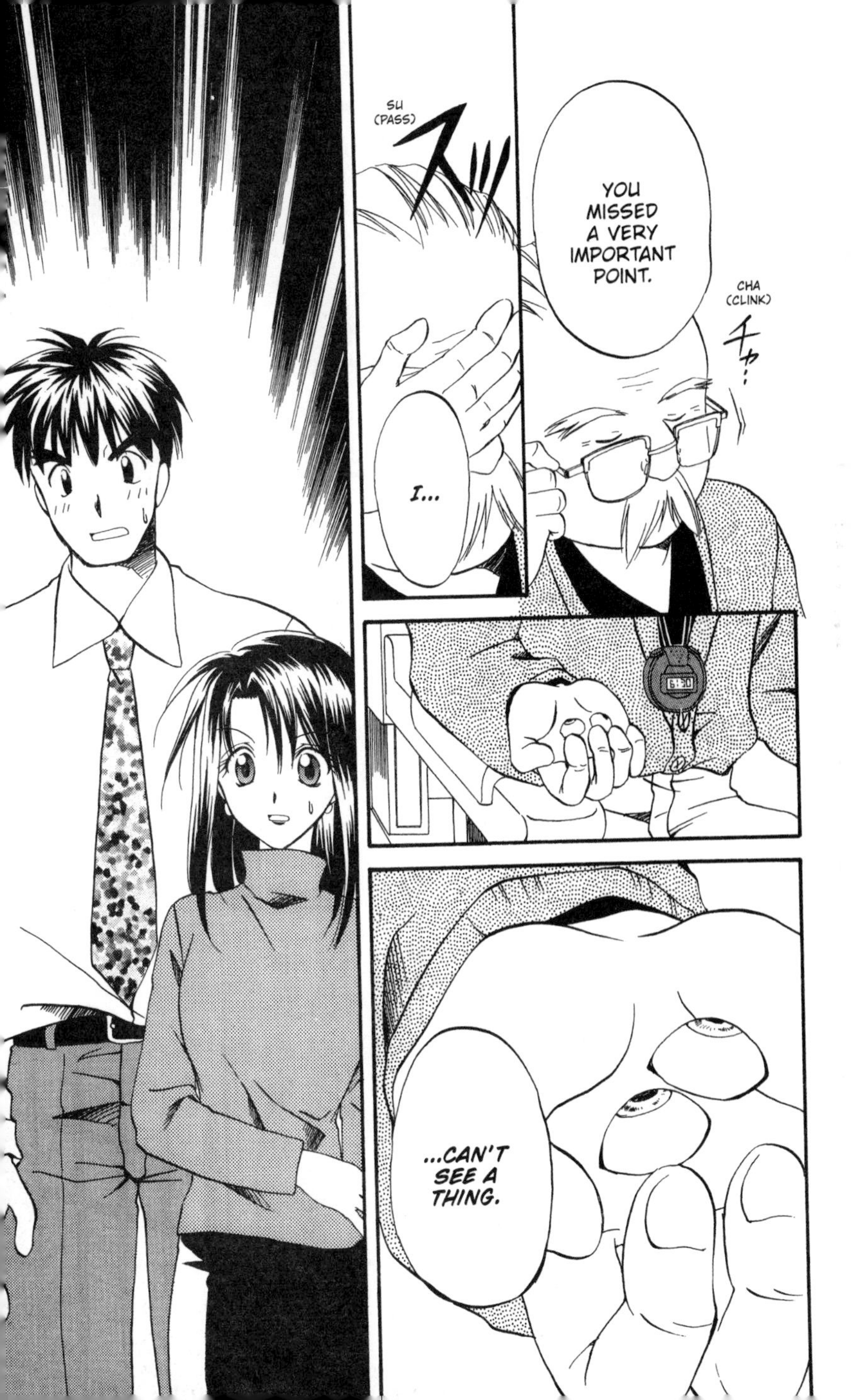
CHA (CLINK)
YOU MISSED A VERY IMPORTANT POINT.
SU (PASS)
I...
...CAN'T SEE A THING.

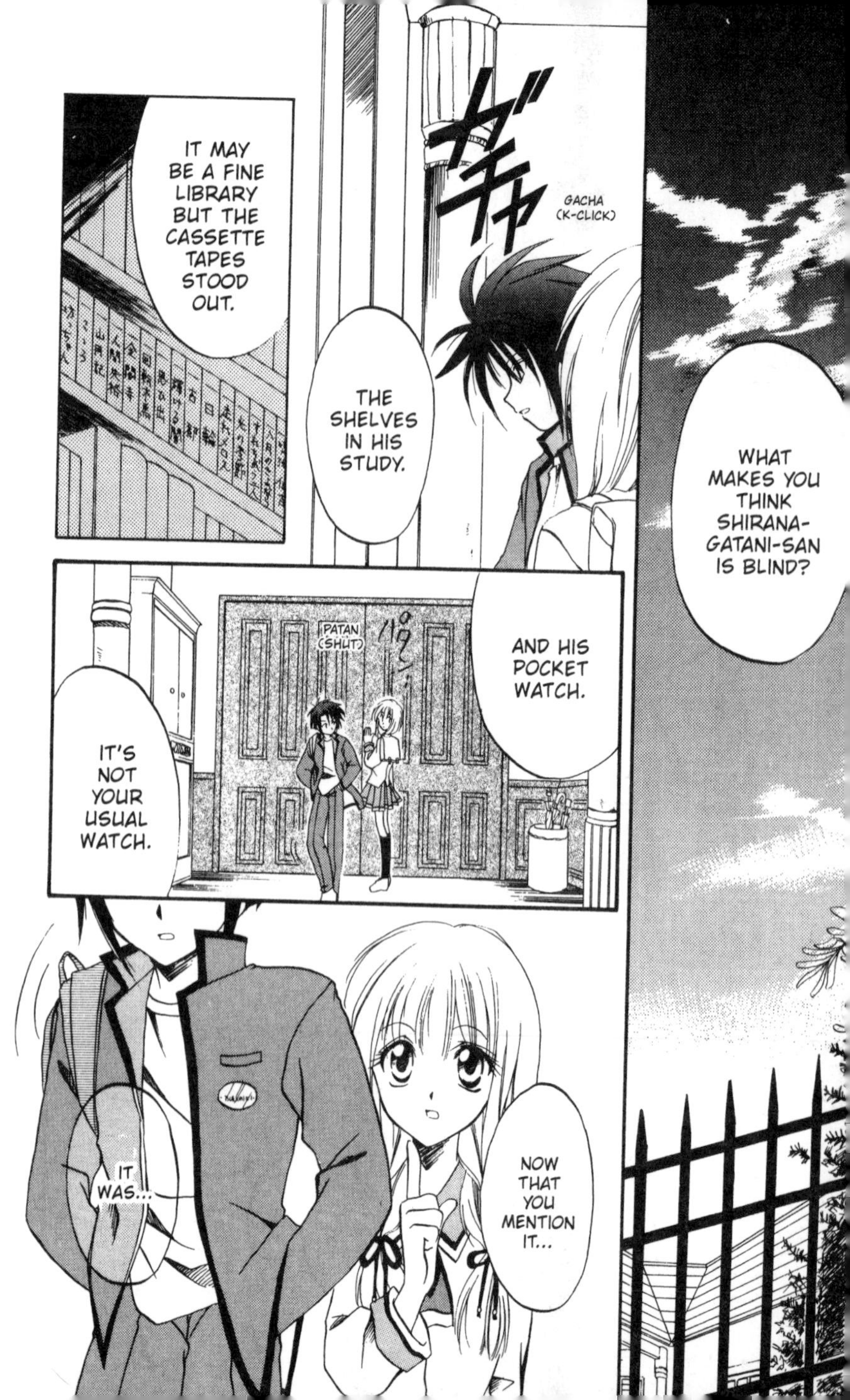

WHAT MAKES YOU THINK SHIRANA-GATANI-SAN IS BLIND?
GACHA (K-CLICK)
THE SHELVES IN HIS STUDY.
IT MAY BE A FINE LIBRARY BUT THE CASSETTE TAPES STOOD OUT.
AND HIS POCKET WATCH.
PATAN (SHUT)
IT'S NOT YOUR USUAL WATCH.
NOW THAT YOU MENTION IT...
IT WAS...

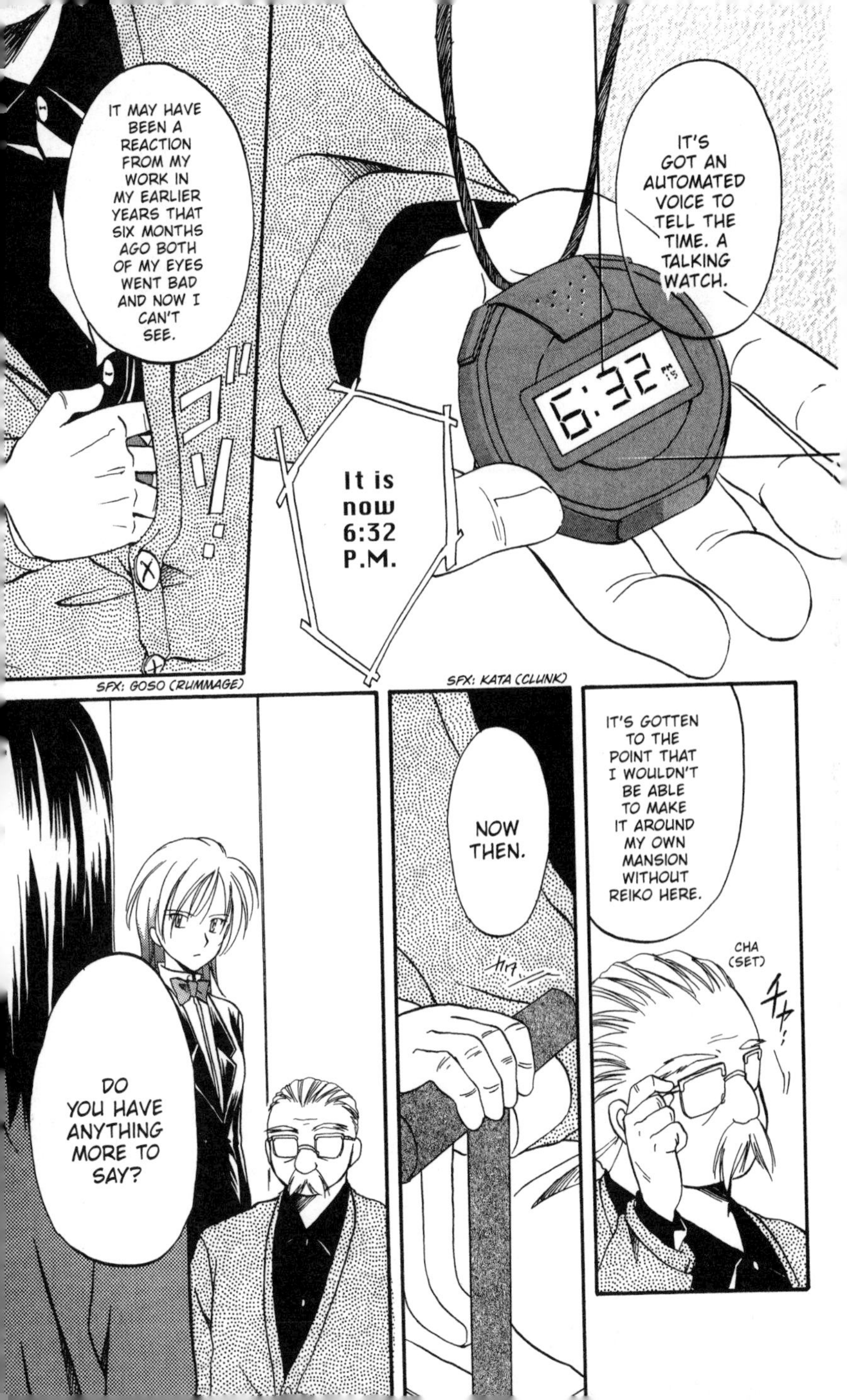
IT'S GOT AN AUTOMATED VOICE TO TELL THE TIME. A TALKING WATCH.
6:32 PM 15
It is now 6:32 P.M.
SFX: KATA (CLUNK)
IT MAY HAVE BEEN A REACTION FROM MY WORK IN MY EARLIER YEARS THAT SIX MONTHS AGO BOTH OF MY EYES WENT BAD AND NOW I CAN'T SEE.
SFX: GOSO (RUMMAGE)
IT'S GOTTEN TO THE POINT THAT I WOULDN'T BE ABLE TO MAKE IT AROUND MY OWN MANSION WITHOUT REIKO HERE.
CHA (SET)
NOW THEN.
DO YOU HAVE ANYTHING MORE TO SAY?

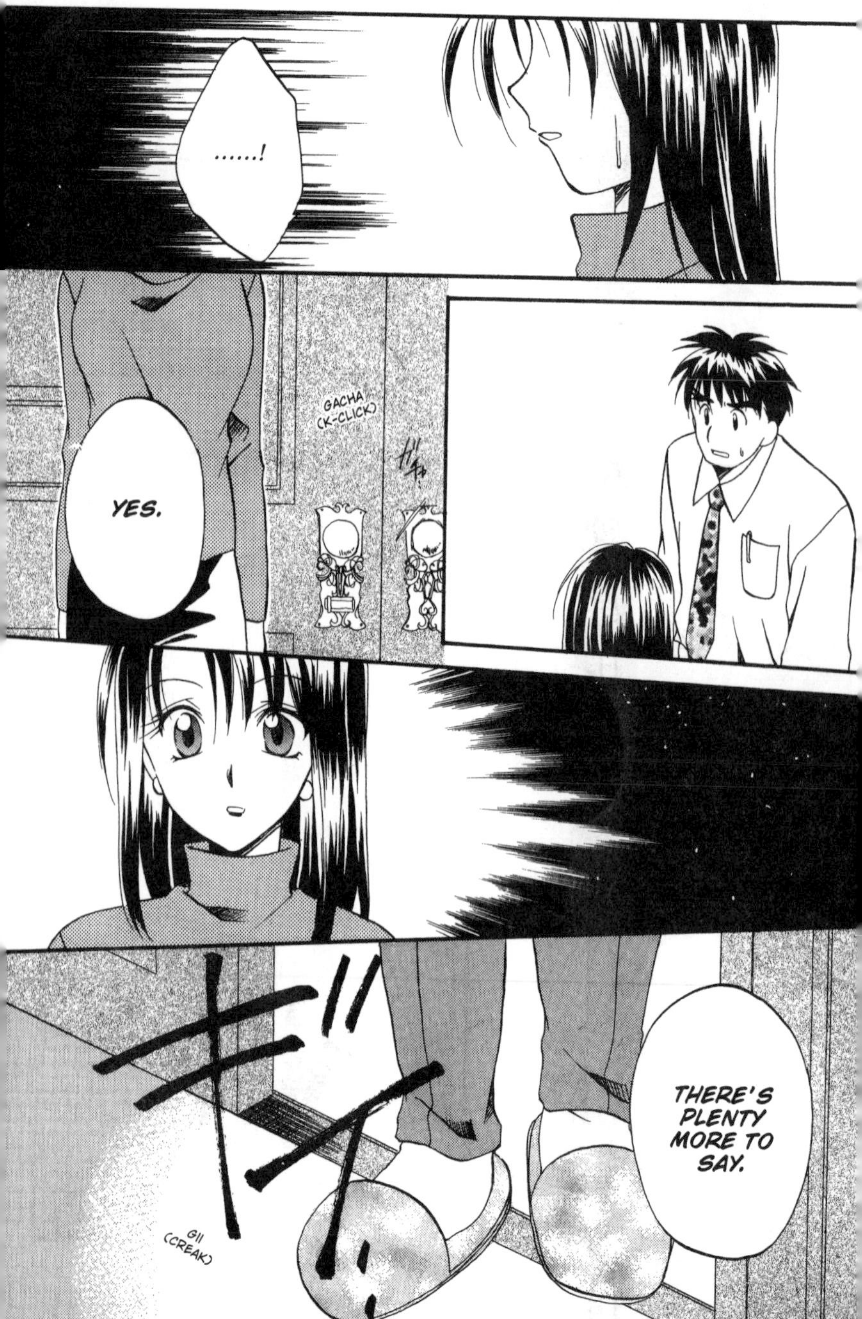
......!
GACHA (K-CLICK)
YES.
THERE'S PLENTY MORE TO SAY.
GII (CREAK)

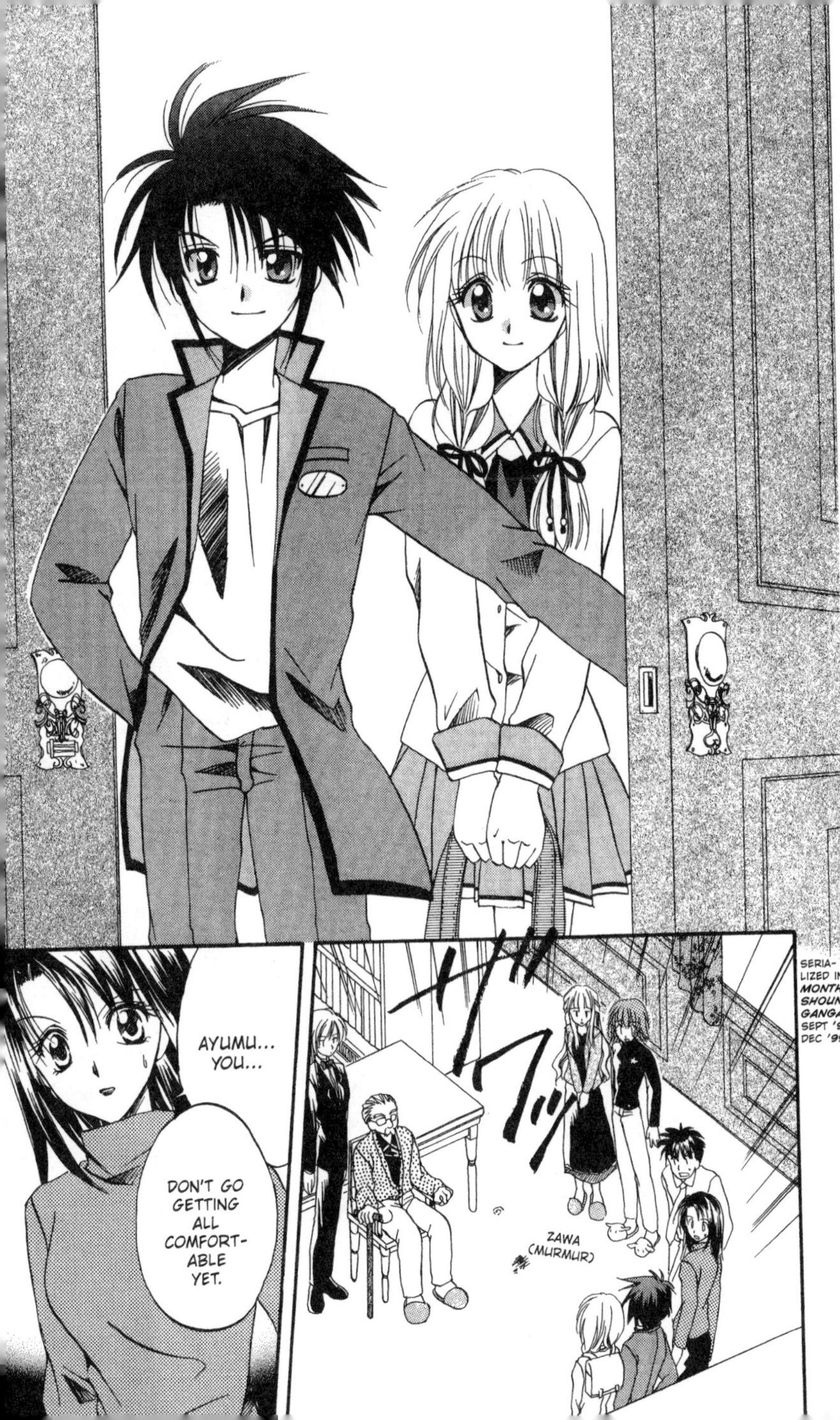
ZAWA
(MURMUR)
AYUMU... YOU...
DON'T GO GETTING ALL COMFORT-ABLE YET.

SERIA-
LIZED IN
MONTHLY
SHOUNE
GANGAN
SEPT '9
DEC '99

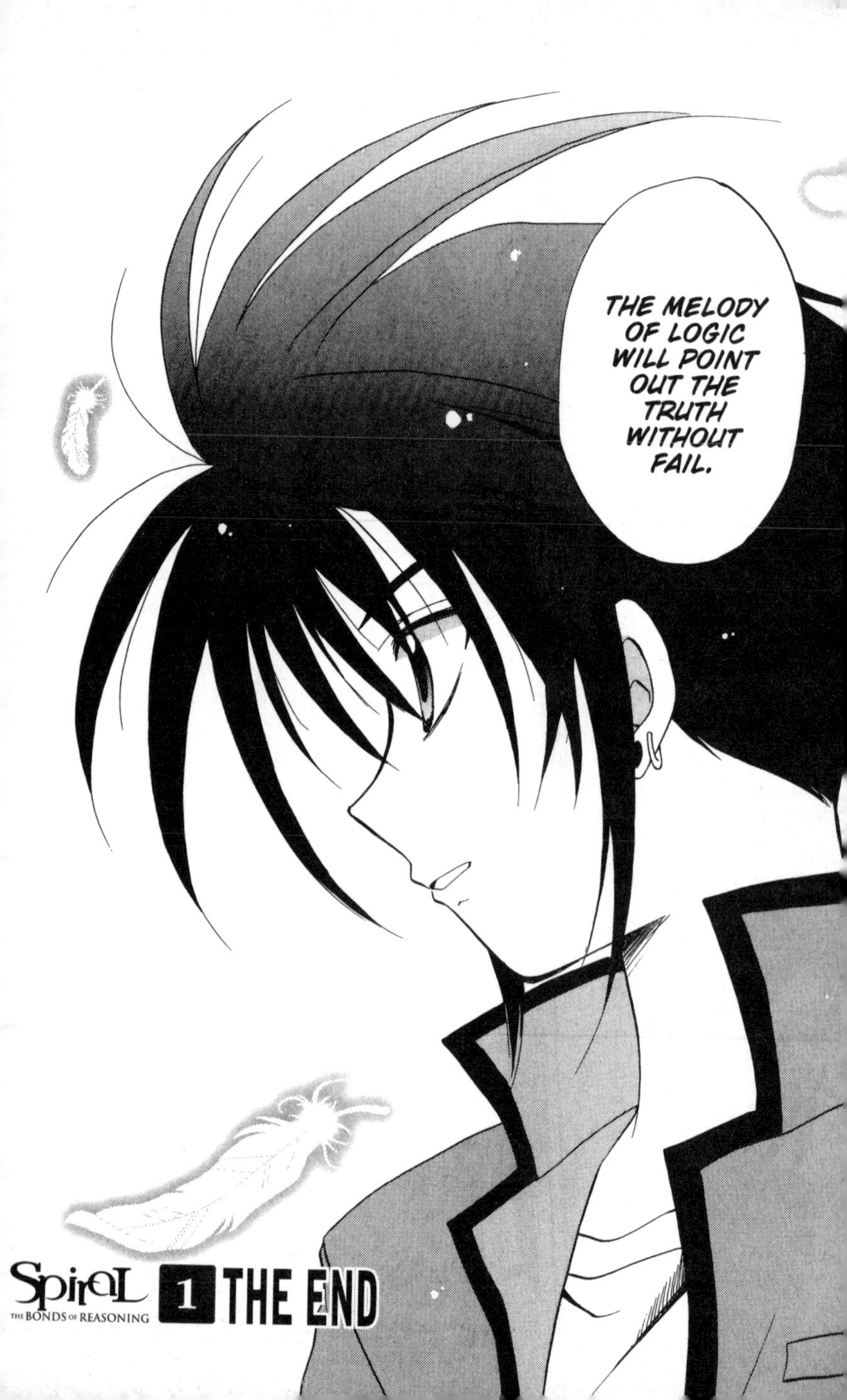
THE MELODY OF LOGIC WILL POINT OUT THE TRUTH WITHOUT FAIL.
Spiral THE BONDS OF REASONING 1 THE END

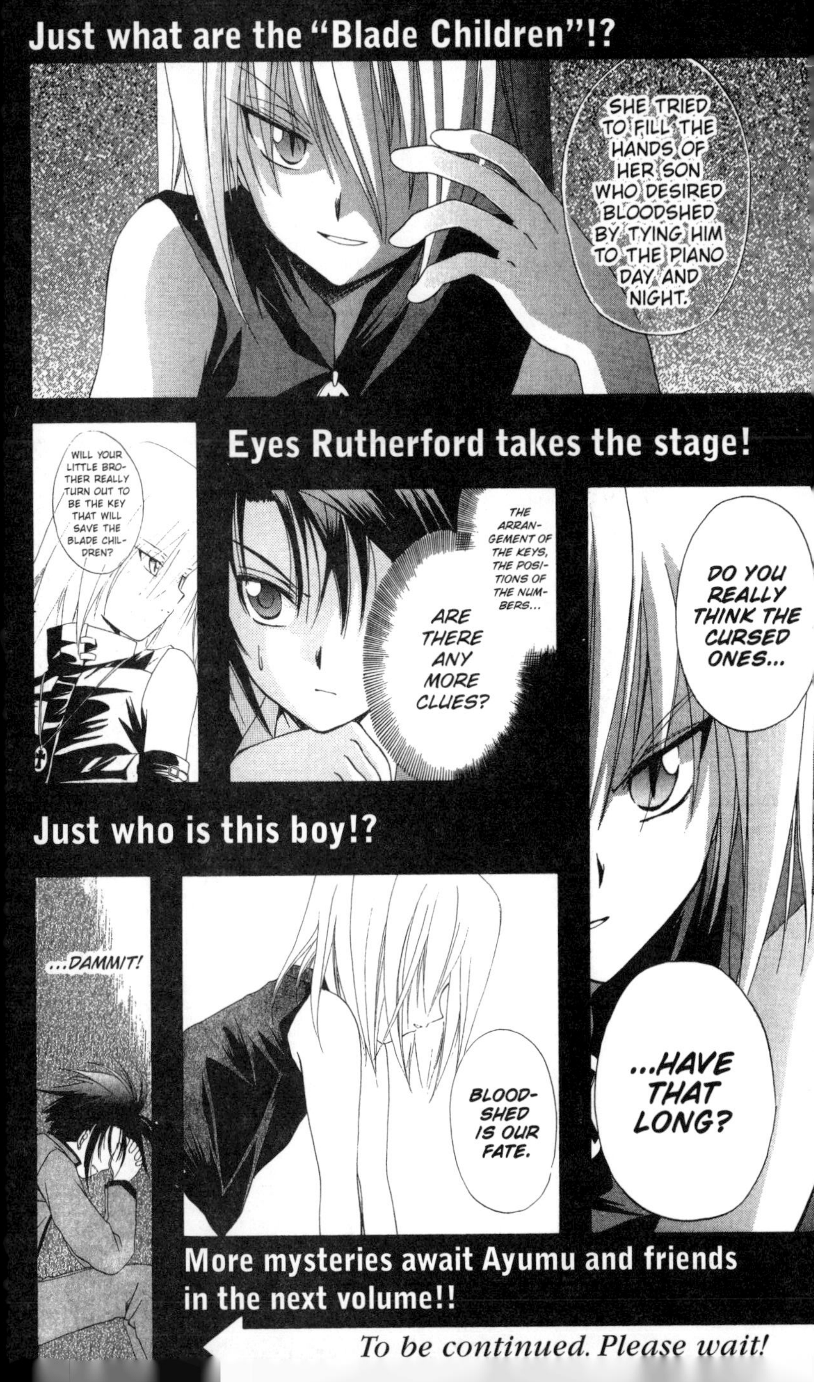
Just what are the "Blade Children"!?
SHE TRIED TO FILL THE HANDS OF HER SON WHO DESIRED BLOODSHED BY TYING HIM TO THE PIANO DAY AND NIGHT.
Eyes Rutherford takes the stage!
DO YOU REALLY THINK THE CURSED ONES...
...HAVE THAT LONG?
THE ARRAN-GEMENT OF THE KEYS, THE POSI-TIONS OF THE NUM-BERS...
ARE THERE ANY MORE CLUES?
WILL YOUR LITTLE BRO-THER REALLY TURN OUT TO BE THE KEY THAT WILL SAVE THE BLADE CHIL-DREN?
Just who is this boy!?
BLOOD-SHED IS OUR FATE.
...DAMMIT!
More mysteries await Ayumu and friends in the next volume!!
To be continued. Please wait!

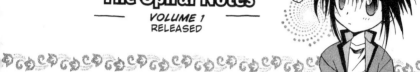

The Spiral Notes

VOLUME 1
RELEASED

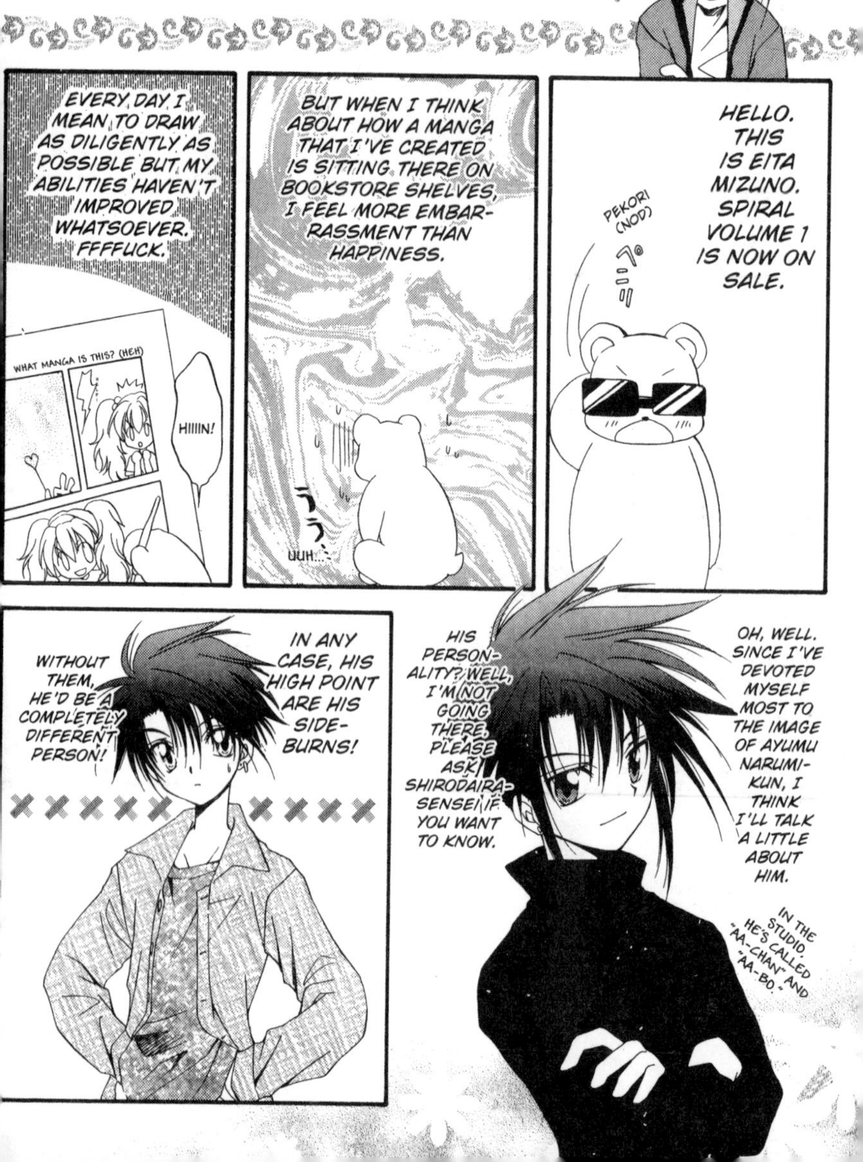

HELLO. THIS IS EITA MIZUNO. SPIRAL VOLUME 1 IS NOW ON SALE.
PEKORI (NOD)
BUT WHEN I THINK ABOUT HOW A MANGA THAT I'VE CREATED IS SITTING THERE ON BOOKSTORE SHELVES, I FEEL MORE EMBARRASSMENT THAN HAPPINESS.
UUH...
EVERY DAY I MEAN TO DRAW AS DILIGENTLY AS POSSIBLE BUT MY ABILITIES HAVEN'T IMPROVED WHATSOEVER. FFFFUCK.
WHAT MANGA IS THIS? (HEH)
HIIIIN!
OH, WELL. SINCE I'VE DEVOTED MYSELF MOST TO THE IMAGE OF AYUMU NARUMI-KUN, I THINK I'LL TALK A LITTLE ABOUT HIM.
HIS PERSONALITY? WELL, I'M NOT GOING THERE. PLEASE ASK SHIRODAIRA-SENSEI IF YOU WANT TO KNOW.
IN THE STUDIO, HE'S CALLED "AA-CHAN" AND "AA-BO."
IN ANY CASE, HIS HIGH POINT ARE HIS SIDEBURNS!
WITHOUT THEM, HE'D BE A COMPLETELY DIFFERENT PERSON!

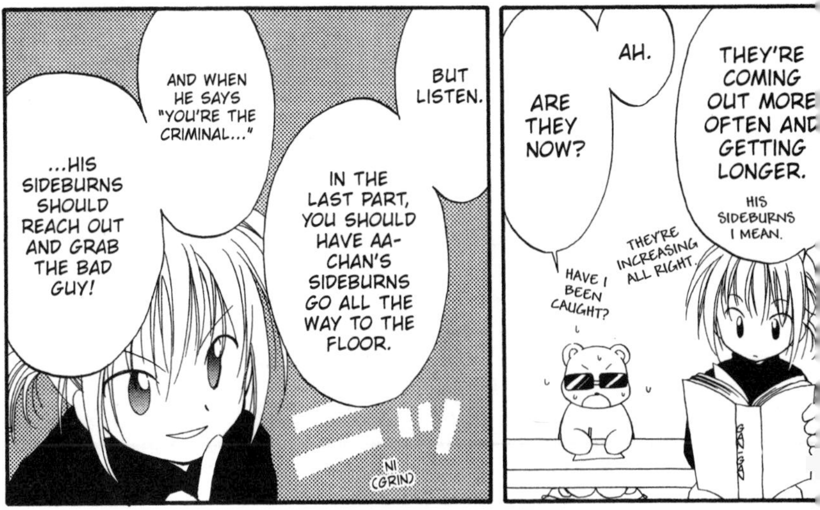
THEY'RE COMING OUT MORE OFTEN AND GETTING LONGER.
HIS SIDEBURNS I MEAN.
AH.
ARE THEY NOW?
THEY'RE INCREASING ALL RIGHT.
HAVE I BEEN CAUGHT?
BUT LISTEN.
IN THE LAST PART, YOU SHOULD HAVE AA-CHAN'S SIDEBURNS GO ALL THE WAY TO THE FLOOR.
AND WHEN HE SAYS "YOU'RE THE CRIMINAL..."
...HIS SIDEBURNS SHOULD REACH OUT AND GRAB THE BAD GUY!
NI (GRIN)

IMAGINING...

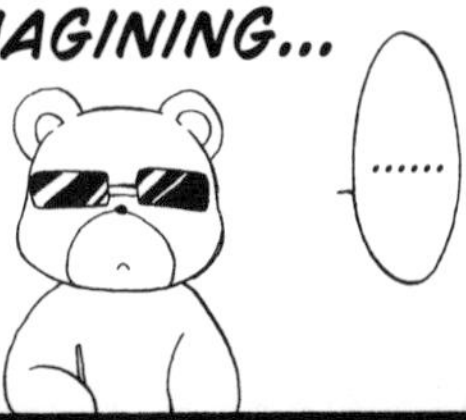
......

I CAN'T EVEN DRAW THAT.

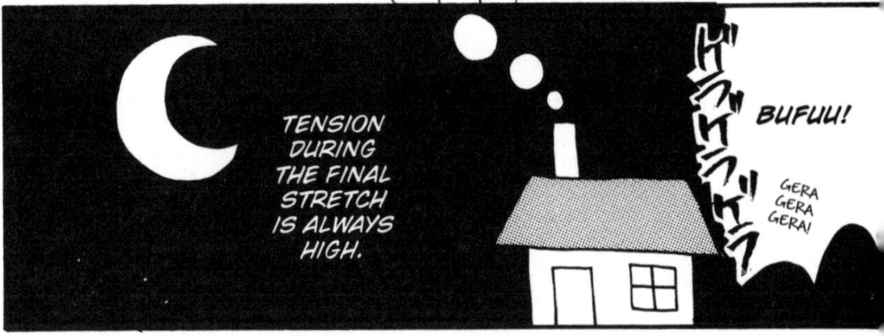
BUFUU!
GERA GERA GERA!
TENSION DURING THE FINAL STRETCH IS ALWAYS HIGH.

AND SO ENDS MY STORY ABOUT SIDE-BURNS.

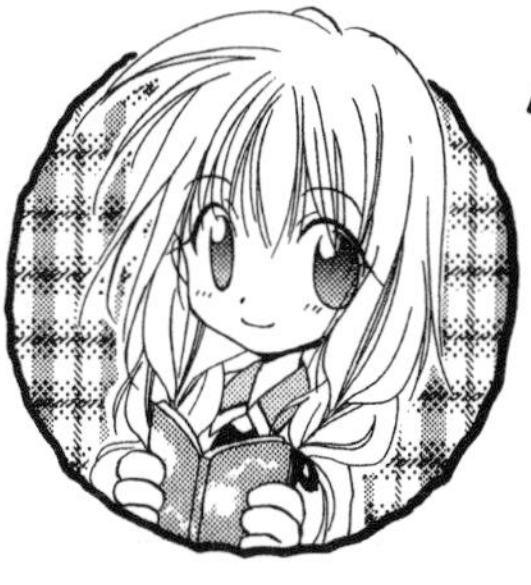

NEXT TIME I'LL TALK ABOUT MORE RELEVANT THINGS... SO I HOPE WE MEET AGAIN!

SPECIAL THANKS!

SUZUCA. U
HIROKO. G
RENYA. N
MIWORA. Y
ENYA. U
MANAMI. N
NARUTO. K
NEGA. H
HARUKA. K
WATARU. Y
NICHIBI. T

AFTERWORD

Hello. This is Kyo Shirodaira. Thank you very much for purchasing this comic.

Looking at the fan letters I've received, I think there may be some confusion. I'm the creator of the ***Spiral*** story, not the one who draws it. I don't do the inking or apply the screentones. I'm just the one who sends Mizuno-san the story in writing and has him draw this cute manga.

Actually, I first made my debut with a novel. It was a long mystery that I wrote called ***A Rose to the Great Detective*** published under the Tsogen Mystery Collection. As for what kind of story it is, it's a sad detective novel about a fear poison called "Children's Hell" and a character called Miyuki Segawa, a great but aloof detective. But depending who you are, you might not be able to stop laughing. Because it's part of a book collection, it's small and cheap. . . and it's not very long. If those of you reading this book picked it up, it'd make me very happy. It's selling so poorly, I could almost laugh. No, but seriously. When I wonder if there are any people out there that would praise me highly for it, people speak ill of me like enemies of my parents. Which type are you? It really is something I worked hard on to make an interesting mystery.

Also, you can see the supplementary novel I wrote for ***Spiral*** on *GanGan*'s website (http://gangan.square-enix.co.jp/spiral/). It's about Ayumu's brother, Kiyotaka Narumi and his detective years. A cute girl enters the scene, too. Since I really put my heart into this piece, those of you have access to the internet, please read it!

As I'm writing, I'm thinking about how I can pull off ***Spiral*** to be a simultaneously manga-esque yet still interesting mystery story. The story in this volume basically followed the pattern of "murder case ‡ reasoning ‡ conclusion" quite faithfully (and I myself have a bit of dissatisfaction about this, believe you me) but, in the next volume, I'm thinking about getting a story with a wider meaning of "reasoning" going.

Well, I'm hoping that we meet again in the next volume!

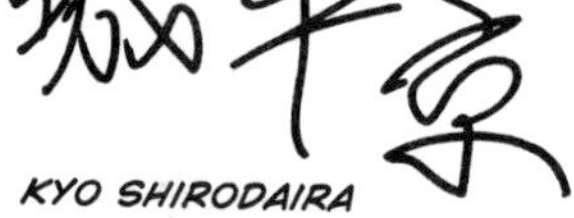

KYO SHIRODAIRA

Spiral 1
THE BONDS OF REASONING
Omake!

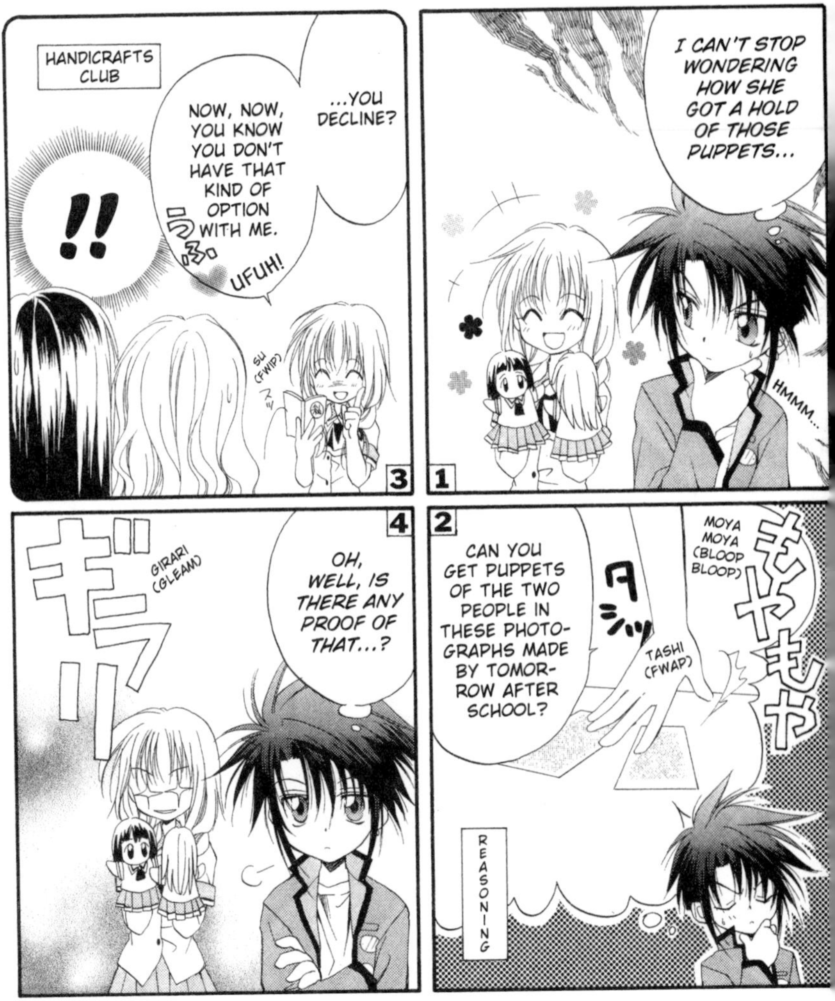

I CAN'T STOP WONDERING HOW SHE GOT A HOLD OF THOSE PUPPETS...
HMMM...
MOYA MOYA (BLOOP BLOOP)
CAN YOU GET PUPPETS OF THE TWO PEOPLE IN THESE PHOTOGRAPHS MADE BY TOMORROW AFTER SCHOOL?
TASHI (FWAP)
REASONING
HANDICRAFTS CLUB
...YOU DECLINE?
!!
NOW, NOW, YOU KNOW YOU DON'T HAVE THAT KIND OF OPTION WITH ME.
UFUH!
SU (FWIP)
OH, WELL, IS THERE ANY PROOF OF THAT...?
GIRARI (GLEAM)

NOTES

p63
The honorific suffix **"sama"** is always used when addressing someone in writing even though it may not be in face-to-face encounters.

p119
"Shinoseiju" means "sacred tree of death." This tree appears later in the volume as the yew tree.

p145
The two characters in the word **raimon** are "lightning" and "figure." It is an architectural design pattern thought to be based on flashes of lightning.

p146
The first character of the mansion-owner **Raizou Shiranagatani**'s name is also that for "lightning."

p186
"In the studio, he's called Aa-chan and Aa-bo."
The "Aa" in these nicknames comes from his first syllable "A-yumu." The suffix of the second nickname—"bo"—means "boy."

SEE YOU IN VOLUME 2!

SPIRAL
The Bonds of Reasoning
by Kyo Shirodaira and Eita Mizuno

Translation: Christine Schilling
Lettering: Marshall Dillon and Terri Delgado

SPIRAL © 2000 KYO SHIRODAIRA, EITA MIZUNO / SQUARE ENIX. All rights reserved. First published in Japan in 2000 by SQUARE ENIX CO., LTD. English translation rights arranged with SQUARE ENIX CO., LTD. and Hachette Book Group USA through Tuttle-Mori Agency, Inc.

Translation © 2007 by SQUARE ENIX CO., LTD.

All rights reserved. Except as permitted under the U.S. Copyright Act of 1976, no part of this publication may be reproduced, distributed, or transmitted in any form or by any means, or stored in a database or retrieval system, without the prior written permission of the publisher.

Yen Press
Hachette Book Group USA
237 Park Avenue, New York, NY 10017

Visit our web site at www.HachetteBookGroupUSA.com and www.YenPress.com.

Yen Press is a division of Hachette Book Group USA, Inc.
The Yen Press name and logo is a trademark of
Hachette Book Group USA, Inc.

First Edition: October 2007

The characters and events in this book are fictitious. Any similarity to real persons, living or dead, is coincidental and not intended by the author.

10 9 8 7 6 5 4 3 2 1

WOR

Printed in the United States of America

WITHDRAWN
No longer the property of the
Boston Public Library.
Sale of this material benefits the Library.